# Between East and West: Israel's foreign policy orientation 1948–1956

Israel's political allegiance to the West is today unquestioned. In the early years after 1948, however, the direction of Israel's foreign policy remained at first uncertain. In this important book Professor Bialer describes the internal debates within the Israeli political parties, and particularly the highly ideological labor movement, on the choices between pro-Soviet, pro-Western or non-aligned foreign policies. Making use of recently declassified documents, the author has carried out extensive research in the State Archives, the Labor Party and in other archives, and his original account is based overwhelmingly on primary sources.

*Between East and West: Israel's foreign policy orientation 1948–1956* examines the ideological components of these debates as well as the more material motivational factors, such as dependence on U.S. aid, trade links with the Soviet bloc, the reliance on Czech arms supplies and the degree of freedom allowed to the Soviet and East European Jewish communities to emigrate to Israel. Professor Bialer concludes that there was no alternative strategy for Israel to adopt; the tilt towards the West was inevitable.

For all students of the history of Israel and contemporary Middle Eastern studies this book will offer an instructive, historic perspective on the crucial policies pursued by current Israeli administrations. It will also provide valuable material for comparative research on the foreign policies and security relationships of small states in the international system immediately after the Second World War.

*Between East and West: Israel's foreign policy orientation 1948–1956*

## LSE MONOGRAPHS IN INTERNATIONAL STUDIES

Published for The Centre for
International Studies, London School of
Economics and Political Science

The Centre for International Studies at the London School of Economics and Political Science was established in 1967. Its aim is to promote research on a multi-disciplinary basis in the general field of international studies.

To this end the Centre offers visiting fellowships, sponsors research projects and seminars and endeavours to secure the publication of manuscripts arising out of them.

*Whilst the Editorial Board accepts responsibility for recommending the inclusion of a volume in the series, the author is alone responsible for views and opinions expressed.*

For a list of titles out of print please see back of book.

# Between East and West:
# Israel's foreign policy
# orientation 1948–1956

**URI BIALER**

*The Hebrew University, Jerusalem*

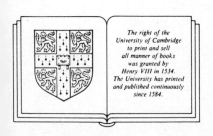

The right of the
University of Cambridge
to print and sell
all manner of books
was granted by
Henry VIII in 1534.
The University has printed
and published continuously
since 1584.

CAMBRIDGE UNIVERSITY PRESS

*Cambridge*
*New York   Port Chester   Melbourne   Sydney*

Published by the Press Syndicate of the University of Cambridge
The Pitt Building, Trumpington Street, Cambridge CB2 1RP
40 West 20th Street, New York, NY 10011, USA
10 Stamford Road, Oakleigh, Melbourne 3166, Australia

First published 1990

Printed in Great Britain
at the University Press, Cambridge

*British Library cataloguing in publication data*
Bialer, Uri
Between East and West: Israel's foreign policy
orientation 1948–1956. – (LSE monographs in
international studies).
1. Israel.   Foreign relations 1947–1982. International
political aspects
I. Title
327.5694

*Library of Congress cataloguing in publication data*
Bialer, Uri
Between East and West: Israel's foreign policy orientation,
1948–1956 / Uri Bialer.
        p.      cm. – (LSE monographs in international studies)
Bibliography.
Includes index.
ISBN 0–521–36249–0
1. Israel – Foreign relations.   I. Title   II. Series.
DS119.6.B53    1989
327.5694 – dc20    89–31510 CIP

ISBN 0 521 36249 0

# CONTENTS

# ACKNOWLEDGMENTS

I am grateful to Professor Michael Brecher who, more than a decade ago, drew my attention and interest to the study of Israel's foreign policy.

I owe gratitude to Mr. Baruch Tor-Raz of the Israeli Labor Party Archive, Mr. Moshe Zemach of the Ahdut Ha'Avoda Archives, Mr. Tuvia Freeling of the Ben Gurion Archive, Mr. Yoram Mayork of the Central Zionist Archives, and Dr. Yehoshua Freundlich and Mr. Gilad Livne of the Israeli State Archives for their valuable help.

For their thoughtful and most useful comments on early drafts of this book I am thankful to Professor Nissim Bar-Ya'acov, Professor Stuart Cohen, Professor Martin Gilbert, Professor Norman Rose, Professor Donald C. Watt and Professor David Vital.

This book could never have been written and completed without several research grants made by the Leonard Davis Institute for International Relations at The Hebrew University and especially the moral support of its past and present directors, Professor Nissan Oren, Professor Dan Horowitz, Professor Yehoshafat Harkabi and Professor Gabriel Sheffer.

The final draft was prepared with the support of grants made by the Eshkol Institute and by the S. A. Schonbrunn Research Endowment Fund at The Hebrew University.

I am obliged to the editors of *The Jerusalem Papers on Peace Problems* and *The Journal of Strategic Studies* for permission to use some material which first appeared in their Occasional Paper and Journal (no. 33 and vol. 8) respectively.

I would like to acknowledge with thanks the help of Mrs. Ruth Rossing and Ms. Ann O'Quigley, whose editorial skills transformed the manuscript into something better, and that of Mrs. Sarah Lemann, who skillfully typed it.

My daughters, Hili, Galia, Maya and Yael displayed good-humoured tolerance towards their father's obsession. Last, but always first, are my deep thanks to my wife Rachel for her endless support through all vicissitudes.

The book is dedicated to the memory of my father, Kalman Bialer, and my father-in-law, Pinchas Warshavsky, who witnessed it all.

# INTRODUCTION

Among the nations of the world Israel is unique. Founded in 1948, it is small in size and population, located in a critical geographic area, and has been, especially prior to the June 1967 War, strategically vulnerable. It is surrounded by hostile neighbors and has lived in a state of continuous siege since the achievement of its independence. Its immediate origins were highlighted by the explicit support of two world bodies, the League of Nations and the United Nations. It enjoys the support of a world-wide constituency haunted by memories of the Second World War which exterminated almost the entire European Jewish community. It was created as a homeland for the Jewish people as a whole, and as a consequence a larger number of persons identifying with the state live outside its borders than within. Finally, it has found itself involved in no less than five wars during its short history. It is these wars and the basic factor underlying them – the conflict with the Arab states – which has drawn a wide range of political and academic attention to the foreign policy of Israel.

Inquisitiveness with regard to one of the principal states in the Middle East notwithstanding, little of scholarly worth has been published on the subject up to the early 1970s. Prominent in its absence until then was an academic analysis of one of the state's significant characteristics – its global foreign policy orientation between East and West. The broad outline of the subject is, however, generally known. Immediately upon achieving independence, the newly born state adopted a clear and unmistakable global policy of non-identification or, put more positively in the government formula of 1949: of "friendship with all freedom loving states and in particular with the United States and the Soviet Union." This is how the first Director General of the Israeli Foreign Ministry described in his memoirs the early days of that conception:[1]

[1] Walter Eytan, *The First Ten Years* (New York, 1958), pp. 138–9.

1

The diplomatic representatives of the United States and the Soviet Union were the first to come to Israel. They arrived within a few days of one another, early in August 1948. In a Tel Aviv packed to the rafters, they found lodging under the same modest roof. The hotel put up two flagstaffs, from which Stars and Stripes and Hammer and Sickle fluttered side by side. Even at that time this was a sufficiently unusual sight to attract press photographers, and for weeks newspapers in every part of the world featured the upper stories of the Gat Rimmon Hotel. The people of Israel saw it as an omen. Israel, beset by Arab armies, could lean on the support of the two mightiest nations on earth. More than this – there was a feeling that Israel had somehow brought East and West together. If they could act in concert, or at least in step, on Israel, why should they not come to agree on other things? The messianism latent in the Jewish soul, stimulated by the miracle of Israel's return, was ready to embrace the entire world. With the fulfillment of biblical prophecy, a new era of peace and good will could be dawning for all men.

This poetic description and its somewhat naive terms should not blur the definitive commitment of the state to that global position during that period. Neither should attention be diverted from the practical reasons for its adoption. Pressing diplomatic, military and demographic circumstances dictated that Israel follow a global policy of "knocking on any door." Indeed such a policy had been considered a *sine qua non* for the attainment of independence. Immediately thereafter, the same circumstances generated a cautious stand of non-identification during the hectic, early period of the cold war.

Gradually, however, this posture started to weaken. Sometime during the first phase of the Korean crisis of 1950 Israel moved towards a *de facto* alignment with the West. In the words of the most prominent analyst of Israel's foreign policy, that policy "was catalyzed by the need for arms and economic aid, rationalized by a perception of renewed Soviet hostility and eased by indifference to the Third World."[2] Concrete identification with the West gradually became more articulate during the 1960s and the 1970s. This was not simply a matter of momentum; it was also a result of the clear and unmistakable Soviet hostility made manifest by Russian support for the Arabs in their political and military conflict with Israel. The 1980s witnessed an intensification of this process. In 1980, Israel and the United States formulated an explicitly anti-Russian "Memorandum of Strategic Understanding." Thereafter (in 1985) Israel sanctioned the siting in its territory of transmitters for the Voice of America; and in 1986 became one of the first states to respond to

---

[2] Michael Brecher, *The Foreign Policy System of Israel* (London, 1972), p. 561.

President Reagan's ambitious Strategic Defense Initiative.[3] No less obtrusive has been the pattern of Israel's voting at the United Nations, where she has become the most consistent supporter of the United States.[4]

The basic dynamics which helped to preserve Israel's non-identification during the first years following independence, on the one hand, and the later pressures to identify and establish strategic contact with the West, on the other, have been recognized and explained by scholars and by ex-practitioners of Israeli foreign policy. The existing literature, however, was written from a perspective which suffers from two drawbacks. First, the phenomenon under discussion is usually – with the exception of Brecher's studies – an isolated, narrow and episodic element in the framework of a wider subject. Secondly, and no doubt related to the above, the entire body of research on Israel's external policy has not been systematically and thoroughly based on the political documentation of that country. As Israel has adopted the thirty-year rule with regard to public access to government documents, it has become possible now for the first time to engage in historical research using the indispensable material in various public and private archives in Israel. The declassification of a vast quantity of such material covering the first three-quarter decade of the state's history now enables scholars to tackle the problem of its foreign policy orientation from new angles and to try to elaborate on it in a way that was impossible prior to the early 1980s.

The present study, which is based on government declassified documents, attempts to grapple with the subject from three little-known perspectives. The first one is the place the issue had in some crucial internal political developments in Israel during the period 1948–53. The historical evidence now open for research shows that the question of the state's foreign policy orientation was not only a pivot for the heated conflict the ruling party Mapai had with the leftist Mapam party, but also played an important role in some internal politics of Ben Gurion's own party. The first two chapters thus focus on the issues of Mapai's international affiliation, the debate within that party on matters of publications concerning the global conflict and the simultaneous discussion on relations with Mapam. All these

---

[3] For perceptive and critical comments on these decisions by a former Director General of the Israeli Foreign Ministry, see Shlomo Avineri, "Speaking for Ourselves" and "Need for Debate over 'Star War,'" in *The Jerusalem Post*, 2.1.1985 and 12.7.1985, respectively.          [4] See Appendix 1.

subjects help to emphasize the little-known ideological inter-party and intra-party political aspects of Israel's foreign policy at that time. The second perspective is Israel's attitudes and policies concerning the Eastern bloc. The existing literature deals almost exclusively with the Soviet perspective of the relations with Israel and neglects the crucial aspect of the Israeli perspective. An analysis of this factor is highly relevant to the understanding of Israel's global stand. Although, as David Vital rightly pointed out, there is "no single decision, not even a small 'cluster' of decisions so crucial in themselves to the total situation as to illuminate it adequately, yet the Soviet factor undoubtedly does impinge directly or indirectly on every major aspect of Israel's external relations."[5] The impact it had on the country's foreign policy is therefore self-explanatory. The six chapters devoted to this facet of Israel's foreign policy concern four major areas of contact between the two sides: Jewish immigration (aliyah); trade and finance; international political cooperation; and the issue of arms. Israel's desires, its little-known financial and political bargaining counters and its hitherto only scatteringly analyzed perceptions of the possible and impossible with regard to the Soviet Union, which are the centers of this part, had direct bearings on the special road it established for itself in the international arena where the two superpowers competed for allies. Finally, although the significance of Israel's decision to support the U.S.A. over Korea in mid-1950 has been well recognized, almost nothing of substance has been written about its wider antecedents and follow-ups. The history of Israel's efforts to establish strategic contacts with the West and especially with the U.S.A. during the first half of the 1950s, which is the subject of the last four chapters, illuminates the parameters of Israel's stand, the changes which took place in it during that period and, most interesting perhaps, the considerations which often militated against the establishment of a formal strategic alliance with the West.

The following study is not only an attempt to fill a significant gap in the historical literature. The two superpowers played and continued to play a role in Israel's external and internal politics. The striking of a balance between the two, although losing much of its significance, still has a certain influence in Jerusalem. Research on the formative period of Israel's foreign policy may therefore suggest an historic perspective for this crucial dimension of the state's

[5] "The Opening of a Field," *Government and Opposition*, 11, 1976, p. 379.

external relations. Furthermore, the study of Israel's foreign policy orientation during the period following independence may also provide material for comparative research of the approach defining foreign policy on global issues as held by small and new states within the international system at the beginning of the cold war.

Several remarks are in order concerning the sources upon which the following account is based. The formal declassification of the Israeli political documents for the period 1948–56 still leaves important gaps. Unlike the British and American cases, the Israeli authorities show a remarkable reluctance to declassify a large number of significant documents. Thus, historians are denied access to the records of the Cabinet, the Knesset (Parliament) Foreign Affairs Committee, the Ministry of Defense and the Army. They have to satisfy their curiosity with the records of the Foreign Ministry and the other ministries, which were eclectically arranged and kept, and sometimes heavily censored at the time of their release. Historical imagination, intuition and guesses are more needed therefore in the Israeli case than in the American and British cases. Private archives, the most important of which is Ben Gurion's, diaries such as Moshe Sharett's and the archives of the political parties are of considerable help, but all apparently leave much for the future. Nevertheless, enough can be traced to draw the general lines of Israel's foreign policy during the first eight years of its history. The definitive study, however, will have to wait for major policy changes concerning the right of the people to know their government's foreign policy secrets, changes which are unlikely to occur for a very long time to come.

## Part I

# THE INTERNAL DIMENSION

Studies of Israel's foreign policy have generally tended to minimize the importance of internal politics as a determinant of that country's external behavior. Implicitly accepting Ranke's dictum concerning the *Primat der Aussenpolitik*, most have proceeded from the basic assumption that external circumstances are primarily responsible for shaping relations among and between states. Whatever the salience of that approach in other cases, it hardly seems appropriate to the present instance. Indeed, a study of recently declassified documents relating to the early years of Israel's statehood suggests quite the opposite. During that period, Israel's foreign policy was to a large extent – certainly larger than has hitherto been acknowledged – determined by the domestic context within which that policy was formulated and instrumentalized.

The following two chapters will attempt to demonstrate why that was so. In so doing, they will also analyze Israel's early external relations from the perspective of the discussions conducted at the time at various forums of Mapai (the acronym of the "Israel Workers' Party").

There are two reasons why these discussions and debates are of crucial importance. One is the overall political hegemony of that party and its leaders, a position which it had already attained within the Jewish community a long time before the establishment of Israel as an independent entity in 1948. After the termination of the Mandate, they continued in that posture. Internal party discussions on various subjects had then decisively influenced the decision-making process of the entire Zionist leadership. Statehood altered the party's hegemony within the country's political system only marginally, and it took some time before a rational apparatus, not directly under Mapai's control, was consolidated into an ultimate, and independent, decision-making body. Meanwhile, however – and certainly for much of the period of this study – national policy remained very much a party matter. This was acknowledged by one member of the party's own Secretariat: "We are responsible for the foreign policy of the state of Israel; the delegates of our movement are those who determined and still determine policy, within the government of Israel as well."[1] This was clearly reflected in the prior political attachment of the senior staff of Israel's Foreign Ministry.

The second reason for the concentration on internal debates within Mapai relates to a matter of style. For various reasons, officials of the Israeli Foreign Ministry rarely engaged in panoramic debates on the present and future of Israel's global foreign policy. Not infrequently, however, internal discussions within Mapai did just that. The records of those debates therefore provide a unique medium, the importance of which can hardly be exaggerated, for understanding the general ideas involved in the formulation of Israel's foreign relations at that time, especially with regard to the issue of the state's global foreign policy orientation.

The papers deposited in the Mapai party's archives, especially when correlated with the extensive newspaper coverage of the same period, facilitate an examination of the manner in which the party – as a body – treated non-alignment. They reveal that the issue had been a matter of intense discussion long before Israel finally made her "Korean decision" in mid-1950. Affecting a wide range of political and ideological subjects, it generated controversies which were often bitter and clearly articulated in terms of internal considerations. Significantly, matters culminated in a series of important *party* decisions before and after July 1950.

The extent to which discussions on non-alignment were affected by ideological considerations of essentially domestic relevance to the Mapai party itself is best illustrated by an analysis of their internal context. Thus perceived, they can be seen to have possessed a dynamic of their own, which was hardly affected by any single external event. It is important to note, for instance, that the contro-

---

[1] Y. Kesseh, "Remarks on the Subject," *Hapo'el Haza'ir*, 16.6.1949 (Hebrew). For a pioneering study on the international orientations of various Jewish political parties in Mandatory Palestine, see S. Sofer, "Political Elites and Foreign Policy Conceptions" (Unpublished Ph.D. thesis, The Hebrew University of Jerusalem, 1982) (Hebrew). See also M. Chizik, "Hashomer Haza'ir's Communism and The Soviet Union 1936–1948" (Unpublished Ph.D. thesis, Tel Aviv University, 1987) (Hebrew) and E. Kafkafi, "Ideological Development in the Kibbutz Me'uchad During the Cold War Period" (Unpublished Ph.D. thesis, Tel Aviv University, 1986) (Hebrew).

versy on this issue which occurred during the early years of statehood had been preceded by a lengthy series of domestic wrangles, which had also centered on the question of "orientation." Commencing during the Mandate period, they had continued into the 1950s. In both eras, the policy advocated by "pro-Soviet" groups within the Jewish community had been challenged by those who were essentially mistrustful of Soviet methods and aims.

Broadly speaking, the history of this dissension can be divided into two distinct phases. The first, which commenced soon after the establishment of Mapai in 1930, was characterized by the fact that alignments were drawn on strict party lines. Mapai was opposed by a coalition of groups organized in Hashomer Haza'ir ("The Young Guard"), Po'alei Zion-Smol ("Zion Workers-Left"), Hatnu'a Le'Ahdut Ha'Avoda ("United Labor Movement") and Mapam ("United Workers' Party"). These parties supported, to a greater or lesser extent, an ideological and foreign policy which looked to "the forces of tomorrow," as the Soviet Union was described in the terminology of the era. Until the establishment of Mapai (in 1930) the ideological basis shared by all leftist parties had stressed the struggle and contrast between world-wide Socialism and capitalism, local solutions being linked to international Socialist progress. This approach gradually gave way to the perception of another dichotomous conflict, that between totalitarian regimes (including the Soviet Union) and liberal polities. Mapai, however, stressed the negative and totalitarian aspects of the Bolshevik Communist road to Socialism, contrasting them with various other liberal options, and warning against "acquiescence" in a Soviet-dominated orientation.[2] Admittedly, some circles within Mapai did oppose this line. Considering it a surrender of Zionist policy to anti-Soviet ideology, they also castigated it as a divisive approach which ignored the potential of international left-wing support. However, this was a minority view which considerably weakened after Siah Bet ("Faction B") seceded from Mapai in 1944.[3] Most of Mapai's leaders were vehemently

[2] Berl Katznelson, "Life Prisoner," in *The Melting Pot* (Tel Aviv, 1941), p. 142 (Hebrew). Berl Katznelson and Moshe Beilinson were most prominent in their sharp and unwavering anti-Communist views in ideological debates during Mapai's early period. On Katznelson, see A. Shapira, *Berl* (Tel Aviv, 1980) (Hebrew). For Beilinson's ideas see his collected writings in B. Katznelson, ed., *World Crisis* (Tel Aviv, 1940); and B. Habas, ed., *The Road to Independence* (Tel Aviv, 1949), (both in Hebrew). See also P. Lavon's remarks in his "In the Web of Socialism and Communism," in *At the Crossroads* (Tel Aviv, 1968) (Hebrew).
[3] See Y. Ishai, *Factionalism in the Labor Movement* (Tel Aviv, 1978) (Hebrew).

opposed to the orientation espoused by the extreme left, headed by
Hashomer Haza'ir. It was their view which Ben Gurion articulated at
the Forty-third Histadrut (Israel's general trade union) Council
meeting at Rehovot in 1941,[4] and at the Fifth Histadrut Convention a
year later. As Israel Kolat defined it, "the difference [was] between
an ideal approach of evaluating reality and future solutions, and
struggling empirical agnosticism, yearning nevertheless to restore an
overall Socialist unity based on moral values."[5]

Until the end of the Second World War, Mapai treated the issue of
an ideological orientation in Zionist external policy as a controversy
between itself and the platform of the extreme left. Prior to 1945, in
fact, the debate was essentially academic. After all, there existed
virtually no contact whatsoever between the Soviet regime and the
Zionist movement, and Britain possessed an exclusive status in
determining Palestinian policy. Thereafter, however, several events
and processes transformed the issue into a matter of practical importance both within the political group responsible for Zionist foreign
policy and within the party from which that group was drawn. One
such process was increasing U.S. involvement in the Palestine problem during and after the Second World War (which served to
emphasize the growing power of the United States in world affairs).
Another was the British Labour government's hardened policy
towards Zionist interests (which on the one hand served to interna-
tionalize the problem and on the other fostered increasing anti-British
feeling within the Zionist leadership). Finally, there were the first
signs of a Russian change of attitude towards Zionist political
aspirations. By 1946, all had combined to form the background for
internal debates which, as far as foreign policy was concerned, were
for the first time in Zionist history concerned with practicalities.[6]

It was this background which stimulated the second internal

[4] See D. Ben Gurion, *Political Debate with Hashomer Haza'ir* (Tel Aviv, 1941) (Hebrew).
[5] I. Kolat, "Eretz Israel Socialism and International Socialism," *Lectures in History* of
the Israeli Historical Society (Jerusalem, 1973), p. 359 (Hebrew). The most important
overall socio-political analysis of the Jewish community in Eretz Israel (Palestine)
during the British Mandate period is D. Horowitz and M. Lissak, *Origins of the Israeli
Polity* (Chicago, 1978).
[6] On the international background to the Palestine problem in this period, see A. Ilan,
*America, Britain and Eretz Israel* (Jerusalem, 1979) (Hebrew); M. Cohen, *Palestine and the
Great Powers 1945–1948* (Princeton, 1982); and A. Nachmani, *Great Power Discord in
Palestine* (London, 1987). On the Zionist leadership's sense of change in the Soviet
position, see an interview with Moshe Sneh, 9.4.1970, Archives of the Institute for
Contemporary Jewry, The Hebrew University of Jerusalem.

debate, which reached its peak in early 1947 with Britain's decision to transfer the Palestine question to the U.N. David Ben Gurion and his supporters regarded the United States as the principal power to whom the Zionists should look for help, Britain being only secondary; other Mapai leaders sought cooperation on the Palestine question between the two powers and refused to recognize Britain's declining value as an axis for political action.[7] That, however, was an essentially sterile controversy. It was shortly superseded by another, which centered on the alignment of the position of the unborn – and later the newborn – state between "the West" (U.S.A.) and "the East" (U.S.S.R.). Essential to an understanding of this second debate is the recognition that it did not reflect disagreement with Israel's official foreign relations formula of non-alignment or neutrality. On the contrary, all of Mapai's factions agreed on the necessity for such a posture. As much became apparent at a Mapai Central Committee meeting held in April 1947,[8] where discussion focused on the possible reformulation of Zionist policy now that the end of exclusive British handling of the Palestine issue was imminent. Pinhas Lubianker (Lavon),[9] who became Israel's Defense Minister in the mid-1950s, expressed in a clear, albeit characteristically extreme, manner the very few options then available to the Jewish community:

Orientation means our readiness to maintain relations with anyone willing to have relations with us, with all those holding the keys of decision. If these be held by England – then it is England; if held by England and America – then England and America; if the keys of decision are held by the U.N. – then there are ten other, smaller countries [and] our orientation should thus lean towards these ten small countries; if to a certain extent they are held by Russia – then Russia too ... Zionist orientation [must be one of] "casting its bread" upon humanity's vicious waters – wherever it reaches, so be it ... No room exists for partisan positions. There is only the wretched position of a dependent nation [which] must follow any power willing to accept it.

[7] See J. Gorni, *Partnership and Struggle* (Tel Aviv, 1976) (Hebrew).
[8] The overall elected body of Mapai is the Convention, convened irregularly and infrequently, as was the smaller organ, the Council. The party's Central Committee was the body that dealt with parallel party problems on a regular basis. The Secretariat stood at the apex of the pyramid and constituted a form of "government"; the Bureau was at the same level and dealt mainly with current administrative-organizational problems. For a detailed discussion, including an analysis of Mapai's institutional and organizational structure, see P. Medding, *Mapai in Israel* (London, 1972). For an analysis of a crucial period in the history of the party, see J. Goldstein, *The Road to Hegemony* (Tel Aviv, 1980) (Hebrew).
[9] For biographical details, see Appendix 2.

Moshe Sharett (soon to be Israel's first Foreign Minister) summed up this position as a policy of "knocking on any door." David Ben Gurion – by far a more influential political figure – treated the matter in much greater detail. For Ben Gurion, the crucial basis for any foreign policy orientation was the fact that the Jews "are the weakest nation on earth, and for the time being – except for certain American circles, and here and there some old friend like Benes – we lack any declared friendship anywhere in the world; and even less do we have secure friendship." The operative conclusion was that "we must take all possible steps to find understanding, if not friendship, anywhere in the world – the first line after England and America being Russia and its satellites." Accordingly, Ben Gurion specifically rejected three of the alternative postures which were currently being proposed as mutually exclusive by different circles within the Jewish community's political elite: the traditional orientation towards Britain, as Zionism's exclusive ally; Anglophobia, which regarded the United States as Britain's antithesis and the source of Zionism's future assistance; and finally the view that, in a world dichotomously divided between Anglo-Saxons and Slavs, the latter constituted Zionism's principal base of support. Ben Gurion's categorical opposition to all of these three alternatives was founded, first, on the very fact that they were so decidedly alternative. He believed, for instance, that a choice between Great Britain and the United States was ideologically and practically impossible. Although Britain and America were no longer "equal countries, as they were at the beginning of the twentieth century . . . they still share common interests sincerely accepted by both. A clearly anti-British policy is hence essentially anti-American as well. As no Zionist policy can exist unless it is supported by the Jewish people, an anti-American policy must be rejected, since half the Jewish people is in America." Just as he rejected the anti-British approach, he also regarded an exclusively British orientation as "a betrayal of our future . . . it means acquiescence . . . This is not a Zionist orientation; it is not justified or well-founded intellectually and academically, nor does it promise us any help in America – on the contrary, accepting England's anti-Zionist policy surely guarantees us an American anti-Zionist policy . . ."

To that consideration must be added Ben Gurion's general perception of the temporary nature of alliances and relationships of hostility throughout history. That, indeed, constituted his second reason for rejecting any exclusive foreign policy orientation. Zionism, he declared, must certainly seek for an understanding with Russia. After all, "this is a great and growing world power, controlling a number of states not hostile to us ... and in it and its satellites lives the second part of the Jewish people." Nevertheless, neither by deed nor "in our hearts and minds" should Zionism declare that between the two global powers presently "fighting for the world's future we will side with the one known as Soviet Russia ... It is not inconceivable that, due to the internal situation in Russia, the requirements of reconstruction may cause great affection between Russia and America, that all [over the] world Communists will sing love songs for Truman (or Vandenberg, if he is president), and that opposition to America may yet become a crime against Communism, just as – at one period in the past – anti-Nazi ideas could not be expressed. We would then have earned us the scorn and hatred of the Anglo-Saxon world, without having gained a thing from the Soviet world." But even if matters did not go that far and great power hostility persisted, Ben Gurion still opposed a one-sided pro-Soviet leaning. Geo-strategic considerations mitigated against such a course: "For at least the next ten years, this region of the world will remain entirely under Anglo-Saxon control ... Even if we did win the friendship of the Soviets and the Slavs, this would not necessarily decide matters if we would thereby engender the outright hostility of the Anglo-Saxon world, because in the near future the latter will still have a decisive influence in this region."

Ben Gurion's advocacy that the Zionist movement keep all its options open, together with the analysis on which it was based, won the unanimous support of the participants in the meeting of Mapai's Central Committee in April 1947. Moreover, that position was consolidated during the subsequent two years. One month after the meeting, the Soviet Union declared its support for the establishment of the Jewish state – an announcement which one of Mapai's leaders later described as "the most revolutionary change in the political status of Zionism and of the Jewish people in the world since the Balfour Declaration."[10] There followed various attempts before May 1948 (especially by the United States) to impede and delay the implementation of the U.N. resolution regarding the establishment of the state. Israel's pressing need for economic, military and political

---

[10] Sharett in the Mapai Council, 18.6.1948, Labor Party Archive (henceforth referred to as LPA).

assistance during and after her War of Independence further enhanced the importance of the strategy advocated by Ben Gurion.

Overall consensus on the principle of non-alignment, however, did not imply agreement regarding its interpretation. Within Mapai debate arose in two related areas, one pertaining to general perspectives on the world and society, the other to specific foreign policy issues. Two differing conceptions concerning the link between party ideology and foreign policy formed the background for this debate. One approach, which regarded the link as essential, was comprehensively expressed by Moshe Sharett:

Some [questions of political regime] may be solved in a negative sense by the adoption of the non-alignment principle: when we ponder the problem of joining a group of nations – the Atlantic Alliance, for example – we say we will not participate, which is a negative answer ... This is clear, but in no way does it resolve the problem or the very serious and profound questions relating to that intangible called "the movement's soul" ... We cannot avoid being a movement, we cannot resolve not to live the life of a movement and live only a national life, since there is a link between the movement and the state; eventually our abstention from movement matters will adversely affect the character of the state, perhaps its very existence.[11]

Pinhas Lavon put forward an entirely different view. He considered the significance of ideology in determining foreign policy "meaningless"; his approach was one of extreme pragmatism. This divergence of views led to a multifaceted debate. In the ideological sphere, it focused on the concrete question of alignment. Did the party, as a Socialist movement, constitute a contender in the international, social and spiritual battle dividing mankind, or was it merely a neutral bystander? Some factions within the party demanded the adoption of a neutral position in the great ideological struggle currently being waged between Bolshevik Communism and democratic Socialism; others emphasized the oppressive character of the Soviet regime, a facet of the case which they considered so overwhelming that it obliged Zionist Socialists to take a stand alongside the members of sister Social Democratic movements elsewhere in the world.

In party discussions on practical foreign policy, two opposing views thus crystallized. One maintained that Israel's neutrality *vis-à-vis* the democratic and Soviet worlds must be absolute; it had to encompass general perspectives on global issues and to influence

[11]  Meeting of the Mapai Secretariat, 18.5.1950, LPA.

economic issues, and even security needs.[12] The second view rejected "neutrality" in all its nuances: it maintained that Israel was part of the "free world," both because of the inherently Jewish nature of the state and because of its social order and moral concepts. Israel's ties with the entire Jewish people thus shifted the center of gravity of her policy "Westward," just as her economic and security interests strengthened her links with the democratic world. Both factions at times used the term "non-alignment." This posture they defined as a condition of independence from the positions of other states and powers (even the most friendly), and as an *a priori* non-commitment to a defined course of action in any given international situation, such as might be taken at the U.N. But having so defined non-alignment, both very often rejected it.

Where they disagreed, fundamentally and most explicitly, was over the matter of what they preferred to term "orientation." Admittedly, a minority in the party posited that a distinction could – and sometimes should – be made between ideological identification and foreign policy alignments. They claimed, for instance, that the struggle against Communism need not automatically generate a total identification with Western policy. But the major positions were more polarized. Briefly summarized, the first advocated political non-alignment based on ideological non-alignment with either the East or the West; the second proposed ideological war against the Soviet Union and complete identification with the West, criticizing – though not always explicitly – the policy of diplomatic non-alignment.

The discussions in Mapai's central bodies to be described below stress the process of gradual change that took place between 1947 and 1953 in the position of the party as a political organization, from a point somewhere in between the two extreme positions to final rejection of the policy of non-alignment.

[12] The emphasis in the term "neutrality" shifted at times; some proponents of this view stressed equal friendship and an equal "link" with the two superpowers. Others emphasized non-alignment and ideological independence – the importance of keeping Israel equidistant from both the Soviet and the "Free" worlds.

# 1 . THE AFFILIATION DILEMMA

The question of membership in the Socialist International had been debated before 1930 by the two parties that subsequently constituted Mapai, Hapo'el Haza'ir and Ahdut Ha'Avoda. The latter emphatically favored that course, which it regarded as a fundamental principle of its platform.[1] Hapo'el Haza'ir, however, found unacceptable the Socialist International's views on class, as well as its Marxist concept of a unity of interests within the world proletariat. Hapo'el Haza'ir did eventually concede and entered the International as part of Mapai after the union of 1930. But the march of events caused the new party and its constituent parts eventually to retract. Even in the 1920s, before most of the European Socialist parties had attained the capacity to form governments, Marxist concepts of a proletarian unity of interests had been subject to severe tests, which had underscored the heterogeneous nature of labor interests in various countries. They were tried even more severely when those parties came to power after the Second World War. One member of Mapai declared that, given current realities, "it was convenient for us not to think about the international Socialist movement, but to concentrate on the Socialist movement in Eretz Israel [Palestine] and its achievements, and from it to gain confidence in total Socialist unification."[2] By the end of the 1940s, matters had become even more complicated. With the foundation of the state, Mapai's earlier ideological problems concerning participating in the International had been compounded by a complex of political questions. These necessitated decisions in an increasingly more fragile and complicated internal and external political context. They also occasioned debates which, more than any other discussions, served to clarify the question of "our place in the

[1] See Y. Gorni, *Ahdut Ha'Avoda 1919–1930* (Tel Aviv, 1973), pp. 117–32 (Hebrew).
[2] Z. Langzam, "Should Eretz Israel Workers Participate in the International?," *Beterem*, 15.12.1947, p. 28 (Hebrew).

world." As such, they gave expression to the range of opinion within the party and the gradual change in Mapai's position.

At the end of November 1947, Mapai's Secretariat[3] debated the party's position *vis-à-vis* an international Socialist convention to be held in Antwerp on the 28th of that month. On the agenda was the renewal of the Socialist International, then a bureau of representatives from various countries with no formal legal basis. Discussions prior to the convention indicated that the delegates of the French and Belgian Socialist parties favored reviving the organization in order to consolidate an international "middle power" between the Soviet Union and the United States, especially in view of the rise of Communism in Western Europe. British and East European delegations objected: the former were reluctant to establish a body that might pass comment on the British Labour Party's foreign policy and behavior towards other countries; the latter were faced with the obvious difficulty of maintaining Social Democratic parties in their own countries. The debate on Mapai's own position on the issue articulated different approaches that were often to be repeated during the next four years when the party debated the problem of its place in the international arena. The first approach favored renewing the International, notwithstanding the knowledge that the convention would not be politically influential; abstention, it argued, was impossible in a world-wide ideological struggle. Melech Neistaat (Noy), a high-ranking official of the Histadrut,[4] for example, contended that "two types of Socialism exist in the world – one which is totalitarian and dictatorial, and another which is democratic; there is nothing in between . . . [Hence] the party must fight for democratic Socialism."

A second approach rejected ties with an organization of Socialist parties, the reason being a sense of alienation and disappoinment with the implementation of Socialism by its Western leaders. This view was expressed by Shmuel Yavnieli, who was actively involved in organizing Jewish immigration:[5] "Something has happened to the Socialist doctrine of the organized worker leading the world, of the worker carrying the ideals of justice, morality and equality. Is the International an alliance of workers' parties conveying the message of world peace and issuing directives to the nations in which they have their support? No, much of the faith shown by various nations

---

[3]  Unless otherwise indicated, the excerpts presented below are from that meeting, held on 21.11.1947, LPA.
[4]  For biographical details, see Appendix 2.          [5]  See Appendix 2.

towards the workers has disappeared, while other nations have never given them their support in the first place . . ." The decisive proof for this thesis as far as Zionist interests were concerned, Yavnieli claimed, was the British case: "With the victory of the Labour Party in England, we thought we were mounting the tide of Socialist victory; but that event brought about a terrible defeat for present-day Socialism . . . Who will now lead this International? The world of labor? Those who betrayed? Whose faith did they justify? Certainly not ours. America still lacks a major workers' party; England leads the movement. Is this the organization which we would appoint to lead the world?"[6]

The third approach to membership in the International denied any relationship between that issue and ideology. As articulated by Pinhas Lavon, this view warned of the danger "that we are adapting our basic positions, our entire outlook, our elementary ideas, to changes in the international power game unrelated to ideology and Socialism." So long as Socialism had been in a position of opposition to existing regimes, it had been a progressive factor in the world; but "today it is in power, in one form or another. Socialism and the International now have no choice but to be tied down to national and international politics." The operative conclusion was, therefore, that "we cannot treat this issue in the abstract, but only through a national Israeli [at the time, 'Palestinian'] perspective . . . we should not be Messiahs of other nations; for a while, we should return Messianism to them." Three circumstances further reinforced this realistic, anti-ideological approach. First, "six to seven hundred thousand Jews live within the sphere of Soviet influence outside the Soviet Union; if they cannot be brought to Israel within the next five to six years, the basic element essential for the establishment of Zionism will have vanished. This is an elementary Histadrut–workers–Socialist–Zionist fact." Secondly, there were the six and a half million Jews living within the sphere of Anglo-Saxon influence. Thirdly, he noted "our economic dependence upon the Anglo-Saxon world [which] will influence our lives for at least one entire generation, or at any rate, for the generation implementing Zionism." Given these circumstances, Zionism "cannot be a pawn in the hands of either East or West; affiliation with either world bloc sentences us to death. No matter how con-

[6] For a historical perspective on the feelings in Mapai regarding ideological cooperation with England, see J. Goldstein, "Anti-English Motives in Mapai during the Thirties," *Me'asef*, 8.5.1976, pp. 122–31 (Hebrew).

venient or inconvenient, good or bad, it may be, history and reality have left us only one course; to exist outside both world blocs as an independent Jewish Socialist factor without pledged allegiance to any power." Specifically, Lavon's faction opposed revival of the Socialist International. This would avoid the accusation that Mapai had lent a political hand to an anti-Soviet act. Moreover, British opposition to the renewal rendered it less difficult to present this recommendation as a neutral approach. After a lengthy debate it was finally decided to abstain. An internal memorandum directed delegates to the Conference "not to interfere as far as possible."[7] This stand changed, as will be shown later, only in 1952.

The proposal to adopt a neutral position was increasingly challenged in discussions on Histadrut participation in the Trade Unions' International. That organization had been revived in 1945 under conditions then quite conducive to its existence: friction between East and West was still dormant, and a framework of cooperation between the two sides still seemed possible. The honeymoon was brief, however, and within a year tensions had generated the onset of the cold war. Both sides to the conflict made increasing use of the trade union movement for the purposes of foreign policy and – at the International – amity was soon replaced by acrimony. At the end of 1948, representatives of the British Trades Union movement demanded that the activities of the body be suspended. It thereafter divided into two factions led, respectively, by the Anglo-Saxons and the Soviet Union. By the middle of 1949, this rift had presented Mapai with a delicate problem of affiliation that emphasized internal political and ideological divisions and was not resolved for almost three years. The issue first arose on 14 May 1949, at the party Secretariat, which had to define its position for the forthcoming Histadrut Convention due to convene ten days later.[8] In anticipation of a debate on the split within the International, the Secretariat adopted what was basically a "neutral" position: the party would recommend that the Histadrut remain part of the original (Communist) Trade Unions' International, but send observers to the minority (Western) conference; it would also call upon all workers of the world to reunite. This decision, which was officially adopted by the Histadrut, was facilitated by the unclear formal situation at the International itself,

[7] 21.11.1947, LPA.
[8] Unless otherwise indicated, the following excerpts are taken from this meeting (LPA), which shed considerable light on Mapai's perspective on the issue.

and by the fact that only some of the Western delegates had left the body. Nevertheless, it was reached only after a stormy debate that underscored divisions on the issue within the party. Some delegates demanded secession from the Trade Unions' International, insisting on clear identification with one of the two sides; others rejected that option but also deplored the final operative recommendation, claiming that it did not clearly express the neutrality it was intended to denote. Yavnieli, furthermore, went on to oppose participation in a "partial" body, which – by virtue of its fragmentation – "ceases to be an International [and] the purpose is lost; the issue and our membership in this International both lose their reality." Most participants in the May 1949 debate, however, did adopt the official recommendation; abstention seemed an attractive and convenient solution to a difficult situation that did not demand an unequivocal decision.

The issue was again raised three months later, on 28 August, at the Mapai Secretariat. These discussions were influenced by two additional developments: the split in the International, which had by then become a *fait accompli*; and the participation by Mapai party delegates in conventions of both factions, at Milan (Communist) and Geneva (Western). Both circumstances rendered a cautious, middle course difficult if not impossible to maintain. As one Mapai delegate, Reuven Burstein (Barkat), later to become Mapai's General Secretary, reported,[9] "both at Geneva and at Milan, middle powers are not recognized," and a neutral position was becoming increasingly uncomfortable. "At Milan, the negative act of not belonging to the new organization being established at Geneva was insufficient," while "Geneva will no longer be content with our leaving the federation." Moreover, as those participating in the debate discovered, the intrusion of the Soviet factor made it very difficult to carry out a simplistic solution of cautious neutrality – leaving the world federation and not joining the Geneva union. Reporting to the Mapai Secretariat, Barkat revealed that the Russians had made it clear that "our leaving [the world federation] would seriously damage our relations with Russia"; in discussions on matters relating to aliyah, in which Russian, Hungarian and Rumanian delegates for the first time took part, there was a readiness to discuss matters

---

[9] See Barkat's report to the Mapai Secretariat, 28.4.1949, LPA. The minutes of that meeting are the source for the following excerpts, unless otherwise indicated. For biographical details on Barkat, see Appendix 2.

"around one table – provided cooperation were shown concerning organizational affiliation."

This background accorded to the Mapai discussions a degree of actuality and urgency previously lacking. Again, rival ideological conceptions and trends argued against each other and against the pragmatists, who eventually dictated the tone of the decisions finally reached. The activist group headed by Eliezer Libenstein (Livneh)[10] demanded an unequivocal decision to leave the Communist organization; the avoidance of any decision, or even the continued participation in both organizations, constituted a grave ideological, political and tactical error. Ideologically, Livneh explained, "our movement's main role is to combat international Communism [which is] our rival and enemy. We belong, as always, to the democratic Socialist group of workers." Later, in an acerbic article in *Hapo'el Haza'ir*,[11] he expanded his position: "Ideologically, the Israeli labor movement is essentially a democratic, Socialist, anti-totalitarian movement. It is inherently opposed to all regimes now existing in the countries ruled by the organizers of the pro-Communist International. It opposes the oppression of spiritual freedom, it rejects single-party regimes, and it is opposed to the process whereby labor unions become police agencies of dictatorships." Politically, this group regarded continued participation in the Communist body as contrary to Israel's general policy and as seriously damaging to its declared policy of neutrality. Moreover, "the two international organizations are faint shadows of international fronts formed by the superpowers, and within these fronts we must, one way or another, reach a turning point. Our fate depends to a greater degree upon the United States than upon the Soviet Union."[12]

Supporters of non-alignment, on the other hand, also marshalled ideological arguments. Arieh Offir, leader of the kibbutz movement,[13] for example, contended that "our movement, in the main, is neither actively anti-Communist nor a Western Social Democratic movement." Matters should remain that way. Meir Grabovsky (Argov), an active member of the Knesset,[14] added a dimension of Jewish historic memory, which itself necessitated isolation from all sides and

[10] See Appendix 2. Livneh was an outstanding and prolific writer and one of the most forceful critics of Communism within Mapai, demanding that the party adopt a clear anti-Communist platform. See, for example, "The Choice," in *The Melting Pot* (Tel Aviv, 1941), p. 87, and his articles in *At the Gate of The Period* (Tel Aviv, 1952) (Hebrew).
[11] "A Gross Error," 6.9.1949 (Hebrew).   [12] *Ibid.*   [13] See Appendix 2.
[14] *Ibid.*

the maintenance of a special identity. "Something astonishing is happening in the West, something that should again surprise Jewish history, and that is the establishment of the German state. This West did not save us from the Holocaust; it was an accessory to the slaughter and burning of millions. Are we going to create an ideological relationship with this West? I cannot agree to it, nor to a relationship with Communism. Our international feelings are identical towards both sides, especially after the events of the last fifteen years." Accordingly, the party should leave both bodies altogether.

Then, there existed a third group. This accepted the ideological premises of both Livneh's active anti-Communism and Argov's "special identity," but rejected their prognoses. Sharett, for example, confirmed his support for the basic premise that "we are anti-Communist in our conception of democracy in general and of democracy in the labor movement in particular," but rejected Livneh's conclusions. He viewed non-alignment as a form of political tactics and as an exigence of reality; the fundamental tendency, which should be hidden until an opportune moment, clearly leaned on one side. "The State Department, and our staunch friends and real democrats in the United States, do not find it that easy to accept our non-alignment. Non-alignment with the West should not be taken lightly ... In any case, one should not believe that our leaning towards the West is unknown." Of cardinal importance, however, was the issue of aliyah:

The sources of aliyah are dwindling, as the great reservoirs in the United States and [Europe] have not as yet been opened. We are left with the North African aliyah; but how large is it? ... This does not mean that there is some panacea for arranging aliyah from Eastern Europe. But I am prepared to continue banging my head against this wall as long as there is a chance of bringing it down. I therefore cannot agree with a political step that relinquishes one side ... We must also explain to the West what keeps us within the International, what our responsibility is, so that there be no mistake about it. We should point out that this is one form of our struggle against Communism, which at this point involves aliyah. Communism prevents us from bringing our people to Israel, and we wish to save them from Communism and help them escape to our country. This dictates certain tactics. Just as many Western countries maintained a dialogue with Stalin during the war, so present conditions force us to sit at one table with Stalin.

Aside from the significance it portended for Eastern bloc Jews, leaving the Communist Trade Unions' International was also viewed as dangerous from a domestic point of view. Lavon, for instance, expressed deep regret for the complication "we ourselves created by deciding to go in both directions instead of avoiding either one – though this was justified ideologically, educationally and politically." Nevertheless, he again rejected the idea of seceding, as this would create the impression that "Mapai is willing to sacrifice Jewish immigration for the sake of leaving the International" – precisely the image often publicly presented by Mapam. Offir feared that Mapam would initiate a split within the Histadrut were Mapai to vote to leave the Communist Trade Unions' International. That would make it impossible for Mapam to join a government coalition. The operative solution proposed by Lavon, and eventually accepted by most of those present at the discussion, called for a bifurcate strategy: to delay the decision on organizational affiliation while immediately negotiating with Eastern bloc delegates on aliyah. Nevertheless, the resolution finally passed stated that "our basic premise is that we shall remain in neither organization."[15] It nicely expressed the growing fear among Mapai's leaders that prolonged participation in the Communist International amounted to "staying on one side of the barricade." It should be noted that passage of this resolution did not halt the sharp debates, expressed also in the party press, between supporters and opponents of the official policy.[16]

Precisely the same debate was resumed five months later. By then, matters had changed. No longer urgent were the three factors which had originally been conducive to a deferred decision – Eastern European aliyah, cooperation with Mapam and the expected political weight of the Histadrut at both the Communist and Western Internationals. In a report to an expanded Mapai Secretariat meeting,[17] which included all members of the Mapai Knesset faction and of the Histadrut Executive Committee, Lavon revealed that "a fraud" had occurred with regard to aliyah. "Purely national considerations, having nothing to do with the International or membership in it, now determined the willingness of the Soviet bloc nations to permit Jewish emigration." During the interim period since the previous debate it had also become clear that no practical chance existed for the construction of a common platform with Mapam in order to form a government coalition.[18] Finally, the polarization between the two

[15] Mapai Secretariat discussions, 28.8.1949, LPA.
[16] See, for example, the series of articles in *Hapo'el Haza'ir*, 3.9.1949 (Hebrew).
[17] Mapai Secretariat discussions, 30.3.1950, LPA.
[18] For details on the negotiations, see the Ahdut Ha'Avoda Archives (henceforth referred to as AHA), Container 8, "Correspondence with Mapai."

Internationals had become an unalterable fact, while the Communist body's "special nature" had become clear in Yugoslavia's removal in the wake of her disagreements with the Soviet Union. Moreover, it had been learned that when the Communist International's executive met in mid-May of 1950, its agenda would include the question of the continued participation of the delegates from Finland, the last non-Communist country other than Israel still a member of the Communist Trade Unions' International.

The problem now faced by party leaders was how to determine the Histadrut's organizational affiliation. This issue necessitated a special meeting of the entire Central Committee of the party.[19] Three alternatives presented themselves: maintaining the status quo; leaving the Communist International and affiliating with the rival Western body; or leaving both organizations. Once again, the respective arguments provide valuable indications of the party's mood on the strategic issue of foreign policy.

Most members supported a resolution to leave the Communist Trade Unions' International, but not all did so for the same reason. A majority stressed the fact that developments within the Communist International categorically negated, as Lavon put it, "the intellectual morality of our movement's educational basis and our position in the world." Sharett was more descriptive, likening the atmosphere of the Communist body to that of a "restricted" hotel in which he had once stayed while in New York: "This was my feeling on the morning I read of Yugoslavia's removal: we are counterfeiting our identity ... this is a forgery our movement cannot morally withstand. We owe it to ourselves ... to our youth and to our good name to leave ... the price is unbearable."[20] Other party leaders emphasized the dangerous domestic political consequences of staying within the Communist body. Yehiel Halperin,[21] at the time one of the party's leading intellectuals, warned: "Let us not be too sure of our friends and supporters either; 'Faction B' [an internal opposition faction which seceded from Mapai in 1944, adopted the name Ahdut Ha'Avoda and merged in 1948 with Hashomer Haza'ir to form

---

[19] See discussions of the Mapai Secretariat, delegates to the Histadrut's Executive Committee and Mapai's Central Committee of 16.4.1950, LPA. Unless otherwise indicated, the following excerpts are from that meeting.
[20] The expulsion of the Yugoslavs increased the fear of a similar act against Israel, which might have been accompanied by anti-Semitic trials.
[21] See Appendix 2. See also n. 34 below.

Mapam] itself did not start out from the point it eventually reached. Hashomer Haza'ir also began as we are now doing: they too believed they could completely distinguish between their own way and relations with some external international proletarian world. I sense confusion about this issue among us too; our youth are asking disturbing questions; what is the difference between a Communist and non-Communist camp, why do we not maintain sufficient respect towards the Communist rulers?" Golda Meyerson (Meir), the first Israeli Minister to Moscow, favored secession as "this very brief and intensive romance is now over, and I believe they have already chosen the Arabs." Herzl Berger, a prominent journalist,[22] expressed a similar view: "In the final analysis . . . this positive Russian approach towards us is only a two-year episode . . . within a thirty-year history. Our role in this part of the world was to expel the British; we have accomplished it and that's that."

Most of those who favored secession from the Communist body opposed joining the Western organization, recommending simultaneous withdrawal from both. Their arguments indicated a current conception of Israeli neutrality in foreign affairs. Many opposed clear affiliation with the West on ideological grounds, pointing out Mapai's attitude towards Communism. Zalman Aharonovitch (Aranne),[23] Mapai's influential Secretary General, claimed that "personally I cannot lend a hand to war and campaign against the Soviet Union." Lavon's view was: "Though we regard ourselves as anti-Communists – or, in any case, we consider our ideas as constituting a conception essentially opposed to the Communist one – we cannot regard active anti-Communism as the sole and decisive element in forging the international labor movement." He maintained that active anti-Communism was the only element uniting the Western International, composed of "various unions, some of which are truly [labor unions] while others are so close to reactionism or semi-Fascism that an analysis based on international labor standards would place them outside an international labor framework." Pinhas Lavon was also one of the few to favor leaving both Internationals because of the international strategic advantages of such a policy. He felt that it "would enhance our strategic position on both sides. What can the East obtain from us in this area? Nothing, since we are in its International; it already has all it can have. But if

[22] See Appendix 2.    [23] *Ibid.*

we are out, then we may join the other International. Our staying within the present International highlights the contrast between us and the West. Our simultaneously leaving [the Communist body] and refraining from joining [the other] encourages Western labor to attempt to bring us closer to it." As expressed by Moshe Sharett, this position was consistent with a policy of non-intervention in the global conflict in any form: "We are not altering our non-aligrment policy; by leaving [the Trade Unions' International] we are only refining it. It is clear that for the time being we cannot enter any other international body, and as with regard to other matters we must remain an isolated nation."

A second group demanded a full strategic turnabout, to be expressed by total affiliation with the Western camp. Underpinning this view were considerations related to Israel's economy and security, as well as reasons related to aliyah and to ideology. As there was no chance of changing the Soviet bloc's position on aid and aliyah, nothing seemed to justify staying in the Communist organization. In this context many recommended leaving the Communist body and joining its rival as "a primary step in changing our whole neutral orientation,"[24] since "we are paying a very high price by not joining the West."[25] On the other hand, a third group favored maintaining the status quo, at least temporarily. There were, it maintained, distinct domestic dangers inherent in making a clear choice. Offir, for example, claimed that "since I believe Mapam and Maki [the Israeli Communist Party] will stay [in the Communist International], I do not wish their membership to be presented as a revolutionary act; I do not want them to exploit it, nor to have them stay within the left and us in the right. We should await the moment that allows us to withdraw for our own reasons – such as refusal on matters of aliyah."[26] Eliezer Galili, another member of the kibbutz movement, thinking along similar lines, urged the delegates to find concrete means to moderate the "inevitable movement Westward" which was caused by "all those external circumstances." He believed a non-alignment policy requires "political claws, even if they are very short ones, in either direction, so that we may preserve a measure of active politics on our part." Thus to sever the connection with the East, a "fictitious" link but nevertheless "the last existing one,"

[24] I. Lam in a Mapai Central Committee discussion, 16.4.1950, LPA.
[25] Y. Kosoy at the same discussion, LPA.
[26] See Central Committee discussion on 30.3.1950, LPA.

would constitute, he believed, "not an enhancement of our political maneuvering ability, but rather its extinction."[27] The aliyah problem was equally prominent in the arguments presented by opponents of secession from the Communist International. Zeev Haring, for example, criticized the "psychological and political passion to remove the chains of neutrality and non-alignment," and favored "putting up a barrier which would be a test of our independent standing."[28] He stressed that aliyah constituted a concrete reason for a decision on the issue: "part of the Jewish people is in the East, whether we stay in the Eastern International or not; what is the Labor movement's right to say 'the road ends,' how can it declare all approaches were blocked, no way or means are open?"[29] Supporters of the status quo also included those who claimed that no single consideration required a concrete decision. Indeed, as all of the arguments raised in the discussion showed, to come down on either side could be dangerous.[30]

This protracted debate was decided in two stages. The first took place in the forum of party representatives in the Knesset and the Executive Committee of the Histadrut. Meeting on 30 March 1950, the Mapai Secretariat decided, by a vote of 16 to 7, to recommend leaving the Communist Trade Unions' International (without joining the Western organization). Two weeks later (on 16 April 1950), following demands for a renewed discussion, the party's Central Committee decided to accept this recommendation, which was subsequently approved as the Histadrut's position on 11 May of that year.

Matters did not, however, end there. The party Secretariat again extensively discussed Mapai's international organizational affiliation one week later, when it debated Mapai's membership in Comisco (the Committee of the International Socialist Conference). These discussions, too, raised the nature, extent and limits of Israel's non-alignment policy. Comisco was formally founded after the Second World War, although it had originated in an international organization of Socialist parties already in existence during the First World War. Mapai had belonged to the body which preceded Comisco in the

---

[27] Central Committee discussion, 16.4.1950, LPA. For biographical note, see Appendix 2.
[28] Central Committee discussion, 30.3.1950, LPA. For biographical note, see Appendix 2.
[29] Central Committee discussion, 16.4.1950, LPA.
[30] See, for example, Sprinzak's speech, *ibid*.

inter-war period, and it entered Comisco passively because it was an extension of the previous organization. For many years Mapai's representative at this organization was Berl Locker,[31] who described it as "a debating club" and "a mutual information body" with no special significance or influence.[32] During the immediate post-war period Comisco included East European parties, but by 1950 it was an exclusively Western, British-dominated organization. Strictly speaking, Mapai's decision to secede from the Communist Trade Unions' International seemed to call for a parallel decision *vis-à-vis* affiliation with a Western international organization. As Sharett saw it, the logic was simple: "From a viewpoint of practical, national convenience it would be better to leave Comisco ... leaving conforms with a more straightforward line, balances our leaving the Trade Unions' International, eases the internal situation ... and does not cause any serious complications for the state." Germany's participation in meetings of the organization also provided "a good excuse for our leaving, since it is beyond debate that the Jewish people have certain feelings towards the Germans and our delegates cannot sit with theirs." However, whereas the debate over the Trade Unions' International had revealed agreement among a clear majority in favor of leaving the Communist group, the debate over Comisco affiliation occasioned a sharp division of opinions.

A large section of the party rejected the simplistic logic outlined by Sharett, stressing the sense of affiliation with a Social Democratic world and the desire to establish a power base for a third force between the Communist and capitalist blocs. Barkat, for example, claimed that "while we are in a difficult conflict with the Communists we occasionally forget that Socialism in the world, especially in countries where it is in power, is involved in a very difficult conflict not only with Communism, but also with Americanism, which is waging war against Socialism. Constant subversion takes place against those Socialist countries; a common world body must be formed, comprising all Socialist parties, which will cooperate to fight Americanism too." Lavon expanded on this topic: "This [Socialist] bloc, which is the weakest in the world, is fighting for its survival between two huge and well-defined entities – the Communist bloc and the bloc of aggressive capitalism in its American form. This is a

---

[31] See Appendix 2.
[32] See his lecture before the party Secretariat on 18.5.1950, LPA. The following excerpts are from that meeting.

rear-defense position and possibly doomed to failure, but we must understand that our future and our ability to live according to our concepts and intentions greatly depend upon the continued existence and activity, or at least maintenance, of this bloc." Others, led by Sharett, saw a different division of the world and a different system of affiliation which also necessitated remaining in this body. "There are two kinds of regimes in the world, not three, with several variants in between. The question of which to choose cannot be answered negatively – by non-alignment . . . we must know which is the camp to which we belong." Whether the division was into two or three blocs, participants in these debates unequivocally defined the pragmatic conception behind the non-alignment policy, a conception which rejected technical balance in organization affiliation. Lavon contended, for example, that "we decided upon a formula called non-alignment, which is neither an ideology nor an abstract position but a posture of convenience. But does this formula express our position in the world – politically and as an Israeli one? Does – and can – a balance exist in our relations with the various parts of the world? In effect, the balance exists only in our minds."

For some delegates the demand to leave the organization did in effect express the desire for balance. One of the participants emphasized Mapai's ideological uniqueness and its detachment from European Socialist parties, especially British Labour: "We are not Social Democrats; we share some of the values of Social Democracy, but not its essence . . . I am not certain whether French Socialists will not one day retreat in the face of Fascists or Communists as easily as they once did; I cannot imagine us doing so . . . The gap between Labour's teachings and its foreign policy is catastrophic, and in this area it is devoid of any moral or ideological foundation. We are an educational movement of a non-imperialistic nation, and we will not consent to the path chosen by Social Democrats, both before they reach power and afterwards."[33] The fact that Israel had itself only recently attained liberation from the bonds of imperialism created a further psychological and ideological barrier to affiliation with an organization led by a colonial power. At Mapai discussions it was proposed that a third bloc of countries be formed, comprising those nations in Asia which were in the process of liberation. Yehiel Halperin, one of the outstanding party writers of the time, presented

[33] I. Cohen, *ibid.*

the argument:[34] "Two blocs exist in the world now, joined by a common purpose: to make the rest of the world believe that nothing else exists. I do not believe this, and I feel that this belief will decrease with time. The two blocs tend to take control of other nations, some of which resent being controlled. For the present, they are weak nations, but their power exists nevertheless. We are such a nation; there is a third factor."

The drawn-out debate, which, as one speaker termed it, was "disproportionate to Comisco's importance," finally ended in a decision to postpone discussion of the issue while suspending participation in Comisco conferences.[35] This decision was in fact balanced against the previous decision on the Trade Unions' International. However, avoidance of a clear stand on secession indicated the direction in which Mapai was moving on non-alignment questions.

Additional organizational decisions were reached more than a year later. Here too the political context was different, and indicative of a further change of atmosphere early in 1952. At the end of April of that year, Mapai's Central Committee was convened to discuss participation in the Socialist International, which had been re-established the previous summer.[36] Mapai, as we have noted, had already decided to suspend its delegates' participation in Comisco, in theory primarily because of non-alignment. Two years later, however, the supporters of Israeli participation held a clear majority. Pinhas Lavon now stood by Sharett, who recommended joining the International while apprehensively watching "the triumphant march of Communism, which has swallowed most of the Asian continent and half of Europe, and which will, ultimately, swallow it all." His abstract diagnosis of global affairs included a special conception of political reality.

There has never been an era, except when the Protestant and Catholic churches politically ruled the world, in which there was so much real, objective internationalism in the lives of nations as there is today. Looking at the two parts of the world ... we see a profound and thorough process of advancing consolidation of nations on either side – due to fear and apprehen-

[34] In addition to scores of articles in *Davar* and *Beterem*, he wrote a book, *Israel and Communism* (Tel Aviv, 1950) (Hebrew) and was one of the founders and leaders of an ideological group within the party's Tel Aviv branch named Hame'orer ("The Waker"), which was critized by the Central Committee in mid-1952. See meeting of the Central Committee, 10.7.1952, LPA.
[35] Conclusions of the Secretariat, 18.5.1950, LPA.
[36] 21.4.1952, LPA. The excerpts below are taken from that meeting.

sion, due to positive intentions, due to mutual suspicion, due to competition for their positions within this consolidation ... Precisely because we do live today in an era of such severe spiritual and political conflict, it is appropriate that the no-man's-land of the world is contracting. Nations are being asked – and justifiably so – which side are you on?

The definitive answer given by Sharett and Lavon to this question was accepted by most of those present. The reason for the change was well explained by Moshe Bitan:[37] "I do not believe that changes have occurred either in our party content or our relation to Communism. It is the matter of Communism which has changed form during the past year and a half. A year ago we were not less anti-Communist than we are today, but some hoped we could maintain our position in a world of conflict and that Communism would not turn militant against us. This was an illusion." Zalman Aranne, who on several previous occasions had attempted to retard the process whereby neutrality was abandoned, was among those who explicitly admitted to disappointment. Some party members continued to oppose joining the International, whether for internal political motives or because they wished to create a bloc of non-aligned countries, especially in Asia; but these were lone voices. In reply to his opponents Sharett responded with a long speech, the content of which suggests the need for a re-examination of his image as a clear and valiant representative of an "Asiatic" line in Israel's foreign policy: "Does our belonging to Asia mean everything? ... Do we throw all we have repeatedly learned into the Mediterranean Sea and then return to the Asiatic origins as they are? Can we compare our link with America to our link with India? ... Of course, it is a great thing for this generation to mend the rifts between us and Asia, but can we present our ties with Asia as a categorical imperative?"

The resolution, adopted by a vote of 37 to 18, called for renewing Mapai's participation in the Socialist International. However, this was not the end of the debate. The issue was passed on to the various party branches for clarification and discussion, and an expanded propaganda campaign was initiated.[38] Only after this stage did the controversy end; on 14 September 1952, at a special session, the Mapai Party Council approved the resolutions with a much more

[37] Moshe Bitan later became a high-ranking official of the Israeli Foreign Ministry.
[38] This campaign is evident in "Our Movement and the Socialist International," in *Information Sheets*, published by the Information Section of Mapai's Central Committee, July 1952, LPA (Hebrew).

significant majority than had been attained at Mapai's Central Committee. Only this concluded the debate on organizational affiliation which had been opened five years earlier.[39]

[39] See the report on the discussion in *Davar*, 15.9.1952. The majority vote was 361 to 32.

# 2. PUBLICISM, INTER-PARTY POLITICS AND NON-ALIGNMENT

Necessarily, Israel's official policy of maintaining friendly relations with the two superpowers required considerable caution in foreign policy activity; it also demanded equal care and consideration in internal public pronouncements. The difficult test for this policy was the treatment of Communism and the Soviet Union by party publicists. Mapai's party line had been strictly observed even prior to statehood. Criticism – some of it sharp – was occasionally voiced in internal debates on orientation issues with Hashomer Haza'ir, "Faction B" and later Mapam. But, in general, party members exercised restraint in oral and written pronouncements affecting the Soviet Union. The motive was essentially pragmatic – the desire to pierce the barrier between the Jewish community in Israel and Russian Jewry, and the fear that adverse comment might be detrimental. Herzl Berger, one of Mapai's ablest writers, aptly expressed this approach at a meeting of the Mapai Secretariat in March 1949: "We have been in an unpleasant situation for years; we have divided the work in the labor movement [referring to Mapai vs. Hashomer Haza'ir] – we know the truth and keep silent, while others know the truth and lie; we hear how they lie while they know the truth, and again we keep silent, because we still hope there is a faint hope to save Jews."[1] This line, prevalent in party publications prior to statehood, was reinforced during the early years of independence because of the official policy of non-alignment. This was not only an "uncomfortable" policy; it also elicited sharp criticism from activist circles within the party, whose members rejected the restrictions imposed by the maintenance of a neutral foreign policy on internal freedom of expression concerning world, social and political issues. Opposition was particularly vehement on what was termed its "discriminatory"

[1] 6.3.1949, LPA.

35

facet: the Soviet Union was assumed to be especially sensitive to written criticism, and therefore far more likely to retaliate than were the Western democracies. This reasoning, some held, was immoral, devoid of truth and potentially damaging. Two circumstances were said to make this so. First, past experience contradicted the assumption that the Soviet Union's stance towards Israel depended on evaluations of Israeli newspaper comment on Russia's own regime; and secondly, the West might conclude from this discriminatory writing that it in fact served Soviet propaganda. Several members of Mapai, led by Eliezer Livneh, campaigned for their position in the monthly *Beterem*, which was not formally owned by the party although most of its writers were party members. They rejected neutrality in the international ideological area, advocating open ideological and political war against Communism.[2] This monthly apart, party publications were quite cautious in matters concerning the Soviet Union until mid-1948. In March of that year the Mapai Secretariat decided to open a daily newspaper, *Hador*, a decision prompted by the difficulty of properly expressing party positions in *Davar*, the official newspaper of the entire Histadrut, especially in view of the circulation of Mapam's new newspaper, *Al Hamishmar*. Livneh was appointed editor of *Hador*, despite his opinions, because of his abilities as a journalist and commentator, and under the assumption that he would toe the prevalent party line.[3] This assumption proved false. Under his editorship, the paper was clearly, albeit not explicitly, anti-Communist, a fact which elicited criticism from members in various party branches[4] and from the party's aliyah emissaries abroad.[5] These reactions prompted an unprecedented series of four marathon debates within Mapai's central organs.[6] The discussions (ostensibly

[2] See, for example, H. Berger, "Is There an Advantage to Hiding the Truth about Russia?" (May 1946); I. Shiz, "Thirteen Questions on the Russian Problem in our Midst" (September 1946); A. Levavi, "Descriptions of Russia and Zionist Realism" (June 1946); E. Livneh, "Hebrew Journalism and its Mission" (December 1947); "Foreign Policy and Freedom of Speech" (December 1948); "Achievement and Duty" (August 1950); and B. Shevivi, "On Silence" (July 1950) (all in Hebrew).
[3] See discussions of the Mapai Secretariat, 3.3.1948, LPA. Sharett and Ben Gurion were on the editorial committee, but their names were not publicized, in accordance with the Secretariat's decision.
[4] On internal criticism within the party, see meeting of the Mapai Secretariat, 30.6.1949, LPA and M. Bar Am's letter to Z. Onn, dated 14.10.1948, Z. Onn files, LPA.
[5] See, for example, M. Agami's report at the Mapai Bureau meeting, 6.3.1949, LPA.
[6] Mapai Bureau, 6.3.1949; Mapai Secretariat, 26, 30.6.1949, and 7.7.1949, LPA.

concerned with the problem of *Hador* but in fact ranging over a variety of international issues) produced unanimity about Livneh's tone. *Hador*, it was agreed, was waging "a continuous war on Communism, whether it needed to or not."[7] But despite the feeling of the majority that the line reflected in the paper was dangerously exaggerated, serious disagreement arose over questions of principle, and particularly over the permissible framework of reference with regard to issues related to the Soviet Union. As Lavon said, "Just as I am unhappy about *Hador* in this area – because it causes damage through its vulgar provocations – so am I unhappy about the insincere neutrality in *Davar*, which lacks all truth."[8] The debate brought into focus questions which had often been voiced but which had hitherto never been answered officially. The range of opinions was wide. Zalman Aranne stated that "if we must wage war, it must be done in both directions";[9] M. Soroka called for the maintenance of a cautious "line of political neutrality";[10] while Berger declared that "we cannot maintain the solution arrived at out of necessity through years of evasion and silence; the dam has burst."[11] Zvi Shiloah noted that "a newspaper is neither Moshe Sharett nor the Foreign Ministry, which must cautiously weigh every word; the paper must openly wage war against international Communism."[12] Disagreement with and opposition to the Communist regime, which was expressed by all speakers, nevertheless did not produce a consensus on publication, a fact that emphasized the disparate conceptions held of the nature and restrictions of the policy of non-alignment. Consequently, the central problem remained: in the framework of the reciprocal relations between ideology and foreign policy, how was it possible to resolve the clear contrast between Mapai's ideological conception of Socialist and Zionist issues, and the Soviet Union's positions? At that forum, only Ben Gurion attempted to confront the complexity of the problem. In a long lecture, later published under a pseudonym in the journal of Mapai's "young generation,"[13] he pointed out that the distinction between relations towards the Soviet Union and relations towards Communism mirrored the difference between moral and political freedom: "There is no absolute political freedom; we are not

---

[7]　Mapai Secretariat, 30.6.1949, LPA.　　　[8]　Bureau meeting, 6.3.1949, LPA.
[9]　Secretariat meeting, 30.6.1949, LPA.
[10]　30.6.1949, LPA. See Appendix 2 for biographical note.
[11]　30.6.1949, LPA.　　　[12]　7.7.1949, LPA. See Appendix 2 for biographical note.
[13]　See B. Ohad's article in *Ashmoret*, 28.7.1949 (Hebrew).

free to do whatever we want ... [This is] not so regarding moral
freedom. Incomplete moral freedom is no freedom at all. Some things,
such as truth, cannot be split in half ... Just as we must avoid giving
the impression that we are Russia's enemies or that we are joining its
enemies, so must we educate [our] workers and youth clearly to reject
Communism." As the speaker must have appreciated, this analysis
still had to grapple with the inherent difficulty of distinguishing
between relating to Communism and relating to Russia, which in fact
prevented a real interim solution: "In reality it is not always easy to
find the borderline at which Communism ends and the Soviet Union
begins its historic existence ... The matter requires acrobatics ..."[14]

The upshot of this series of debates was Livneh's resignation
(notwithstanding Ben Gurion's personal support) and the appointment of a new editorial staff to *Hador*. The resolutions thus
represented a victory for those factions that demanded that militant
anti-Communism not be presented as a central plank in the party
newspaper's propaganda platform.[15] Nevertheless, these discussions
did not end the long process of debates on the question of how to
publicize opinions on ideological issues of international affiliation.
Neither were they conclusive in their vindication of how (and
whether) to draw a line between the various nuances within the
criticism of Communism – on which the party was united – and the
country's foreign policy, which was based on caution and neutrality.
This was a topic which continued to exercise the party leadership,
even though no specific discussions on the issue were held within the
party's central organs. However, from mid-1950, it is possible to
discern a gradual process of decreasing caution in public references to
problems of international affiliation. This is also evident in the party
and Histadrut press and in general discussions on the party platform
and program of action. It became particularly marked after the
decision to support the U.S. position in the Korean crisis was reached
in July 1950.

One of the important internal debates took place in the Mapai
Secretariat in August 1950. It concerned the preparation of the
agenda for the party convention, an event of major internal and
international political significance since it was the first to be held after

[14] Secretariat meeting, 7.7.1949, LPA.
[15] See correspondence between Livneh and Aranne early in November 1949, which
refers to this subject, Z. Onn files, 1949, LPA.

Israel's independence.[16] Discussion focused on the weight to be accorded the relationship towards Communism. Here again opinions diverged. Livneh, as usual, considered the war on Communism a crucial internal and external necessity: "We now have in Israel a mass political organization that is a candidate for [the charge of] treason; today's Mapam is not that of two years ago ... it is now possible to undermine Zionism by undermining the state. We must fight not only the *Yevsektsiya*,[17] but also international Communism, led and supported by the Soviet regime." On the other hand, Aranne refused to accept so militant a platform, declaring that "there are boundaries here which I am unwilling to obliterate." Ben Gurion rejected any boundaries whatsoever. Although he did not seek to turn the convention into a debate on "orientation," he outspokenly attempted to achieve public discussion, and expressed himself unequivocally: "With the exception of the Nazi regime, the world has never known so oppressive a regime of murderers and world arsonists as this one; this is a regime of a Georgian Ivan with new techniques and terminology." None the less, Ben Gurion did not publicly express his opinion at the convention; he retained a certain caution which he was not yet prepared to abandon. The debate, he believed, should be handled internally, against Mapam, and not externally, against the Soviet Union. This caution was indeed evident in his speech at the Mapai Convention one week later. He referred obliquely to the Soviet Union when citing de Tocqueville's book on American democracy and when expounding on the differences between America's culture and regime and those of Russia.[18] Carefully, but clearly, Sharett also presented the direction in which the party and country seemed to be going.

Although the attitudes of two prominent party leaders were thus clear, their opinions were not accepted by another group. Aranne, for example, in rejecting this line claimed that "in certain situations a country fighting for its survival has no choice but to reach serious conclusions; this may be comprehended and justified, but no moral glory should be attached to it."[19] Argov declared his objection to "the

---

[16]  10.8.1950, LPA. The following excerpts are from here.
[17]  The Jewish sections of the Propaganda Department of the Russian Communist Party between 1918 and 1930, which initiated and executed, with the help of government agencies, the liquidation of Jewish cultural and political organizations. See M. Altschuler, *The Beginnings of the Yevsektsiya* (Jerusalem, 1966) (Hebrew).
[18]  16.8.1950, LPA.                           [19]  19.8.1950, LPA.

undertones in the speeches of the two main speakers in this Convention, Ben Gurion and Sharett . . . we will be able to succeed against the Jewish Cominform [the extreme Israeli left] only if we stand firmly on Israeli soil, with no foreign intervention nor any attempt at alignment – be it sympathy only – with any foreign movement."[20] Once again it was feared that the Histadrut would split were the policy of neutrality to be radically changed; once again ideological criticisms were voiced against the Western democracies. Nevertheless, the Convention constituted a watershed with regard to national education and information on questions of international political orientation. At Mapai's Central Committee, convened three weeks after the Convention, Sharett declared that "we are increasingly exposing our true position in world affairs, which is anti-Soviet as a consequence of the fact that our fate is becoming increasingly tied to the West rather than the East."[21] This exposure was nationally expressed that same week when the *Israel Government Yearbook* published an article by Ben Gurion. Entitled "Special Identity and Designation," it employed the historic perspective of the Jewish people's struggle for spiritual and political independence, to stress the danger of identification with "world giants." Furthermore, it also emphasized – virtually unequivocally – the danger of Communism and the Soviet Union.[22] Clearly, at this stage of affairs, the majority within Mapai's leadership was prepared for a much more drastic turnabout than many of the rank and file could accept. This became apparent at a meeting of the Central Committee held on 10 September 1950, when a group of members proposed that global foreign policy issues be discussed in order that wider circles within the party might express an opinion. As Livneh put it: 'I feel that a dangerous disharmony has developed between the party's delegates within the government and the knowledge of the whole movement about the country's direction . . . There exists a dangerous crisis between practical policy and the consciences of many of our members.'[23]

Livneh's analysis was undoubtedly correct. One indication was provided by the Foreign Minister's speech in the Knesset on 31

---

[20] 17.8.1950, LPA.                    [21] 16.9.1950, LPA.

[22] At the Mapai Secretariat meeting of 10 August 1950, Ben Gurion warned that "in two months there will probably be a scandal when the *Government Yearbook* appears including an article on Soviet Russia such as has never been printed anywhere before," LPA. The article may not have been so sharp, but it definitely was unequivocal.

[23] LPA.

January 1951, in which Sharett in effect inaugurated an internal information campaign in this field. In reporting on the subsequent debate, the American Section of the Israeli Foreign Ministry indicated to Israeli emissaries in Washington that "from these speeches ... the general frame of opinion can clearly be discerned. More important, it can be seen that no drastic change has taken place in public opinion concerning foreign policy. If the government thinks of changes in the policy, or of changing the policy, it is clear that a carefully planned public campaign is essential. The public has not [yet] been prepared for changes."[24] A few days later the message was reiterated: "You can see that our public is largely convinced that the government is still committed to non-alignment."[25] It is hardly surprising that Israel's representatives in Washington had found this situation extremely unsatisfactory. A typical reaction was transmitted to the Foreign Ministry early in February 1951: "I told you when I was in Israel," wrote an Israeli diplomat, "that a conspicuous gap has lately developed between our government and the public. Other recent visitors to the country share this view. Much effort needs to be devoted to oral information, lectures, talks with youth ... You should reach Schunat-Hatikvah and Kerem-Hateymanim [poor suburbs in Tel Aviv] and explain to these people in their own primitive language the problem of our foreign policy."[26]

Thus forewarned, Mapai's leadership did indeed respond to this peculiar situation and decided on special efforts in this field. Action was both direct and indirect. On 3 March 1951, the Central Committee and the party's Knesset members convened in secret in order to discuss Israel's non-alignment policy.[27] This discussion was the most extensive, detailed and problematic which had hitherto been held on that issue, and the entire party leadership participated. Its purpose was to clarify for those unfamiliar with the intricacies of foreign policy the meaning of the gradual change, to decide "how far we shall move," and finally, as Aranne put it, "how we should bring this move closer to the people, since most of the Jewish population accepts our foreign policy line, non-alignment, which it sees simply as neutrality. It finds our world non-alignment problems difficult to comprehend."

The decision to support America's policy in the Korean crisis

---

[24] See Ben Horin's letter on 31.1.1951 in Israel's Foreign Ministry files, Israeli State Archives (henceforth referred to as ISA), file 2515/1.
[25] See Bentsur's letter on 4.2.1951, ISA 2460/1.
[26] M. Shalit's letter on 5.2.1951, ISA 2398/3.          [27] LPA.

became an unprecedented public issue, fanned by an intensive propaganda campaign on the part of Mapam and by a stormy public debate in the Knesset and in the press. This interest was provoked not only by attacks from the extreme left, which depicted the decision as marking Israel's complete affiliation with the West; as the debate at the Central Committee showed, it was also generated by a lack of understanding and by disagreement on the nature of the change, if any, within the party. The secret meeting of Mapai leaders was intended to provide answers to these problems, and the very fact that it was convened indicates the internal confusion then current in the areas of propaganda and ideology in Israel's foreign policy.

Moshe Sharett opened the discussion with a long, detailed lecture focusing on Israel's foreign policy *vis-à-vis* the global conflict between the two superpowers. For the first time representatives of the party were explicitly informed that Israel had placed itself clearly and unequivocally in opposition to the Soviet camp. Most of the arguments were familiar; some were not. Given the situation of total ideological war between the superpowers, Sharett explained, Israel was confronted with a "life and death" issue. The decision to align squarely with one camp stemmed from an unequivocal conception: "We do not wish any closed regime to exist in the world; we wish, as a country and as Jews, that such regimes disappear from the face of the earth." Israel's great dependence, as a state, upon civil liberty left no other option:

One could apparently say that the question of which world outlook to support – totalitarian or democratic, Socialist or Bolshevik, or perhaps capitalist – is not a national question for us; this is a social question: the Jewish people could be neutral in this respect. In fact this is not so. The interest of the Jewish people determines our position here. It sets the choice and leaves no room for deliberation, not because democracy is pro-Jewish, not because Communism is anti-Jewish ... but because in a democratic regime there are liberties that enable Jewish self-defense, Jewish self-action, links among various Jewish communities in the world – and this is what we need ... The Jews, as a nation, must therefore oppose Communism and be its mortal enemy; the unity of the Jewish people necessitates abolishing the Communist regime in the world.

Another important consideration was the Communist peril within Israel itself, when "Communism spreads everywhere – among youth, among labor." Even more significant was the increased "need for foreign aid, or crudely – for dollars," necessitated by the influx of immigrants during the early years of the decade. In the reality of the cold war, when "the free world organizes its production, its exports, its arms supplies, and its readiness for loans solely according to one consideration ... Israel had to make a change." Operatively this change meant rejecting declarations of neutrality, both "when there is no chance that either side would see itself bound by Israel's declarations of neutrality ... and [when] such declarations would immediately and practically damage any effort to obtain aid at this time." These declarations, according to Sharett, were also dangerous because of their effect should either side occupy Israel. "Were the West to occupy the country, there would be no danger of its imposing a regime contradictory to the nature of most residents. But such a danger would exist were the Soviet Union to take over – imposing leaders from abroad and, through outside military force, imposing parties and a regime that would make a mockery of everything we cherish." The change from pro-neutrality to its antithesis did not necessitate radical steps: "No conclusions should be drawn from this regarding formal agreements, bases or commitments." Still, those present knew that Sharett's speech perforce implied a turnabout, at least concerning political declarations. This is why his speech gave rise to a lively debate.

Sharett's supporters were numerous: Livneh called for a much more systematic war on Communism than Ben Gurion's "calculated outbursts" against it; Berger emphasized the extent of internal damage involved in maintaining the previous policy; Halperin warned against "being ourselves influenced by our silence and by one-sided propaganda of the other side"; and Shmuel Dayan, founding member of the first kibbutz in Palestine,[28] stressed the military dangers involved in a neutral political position on foreign policy issues. On the other hand, Sharett's militancy was clearly unacceptable to at least half of the participants; they expressed reservations and presented alternatives. Haring, who had on numerous other occasions rejected the party line, warned against a dangerous deviation from the neutral position towards "undeclared alignment." It was his opinion that the party should adhere to a policy of "three negatives": "We will not fight the Soviet Union unless we are attacked by the Soviet Union; if we are forced to fight, it will not be for Western democracy, but for Israel's independence. We will not provide political, economic or military bases, as this would invite invasion and would justify it both in advance and retroactively. And

---

[28] See Appendix 2 for biographical details.

we will not be a party to an ideological crusade against the Soviet Union." Haring found an ally in one of the party's central figures, Zalman Aranne, who completely rejected Sharett's presentation: "The situation does not permit us a choice between black and white." With rare candor he presented his "credo" on the Soviet Union:

I strongly object to the fact that Mapai – after thirty-three years of intricate relations – has adopted as one of its slogans "the Soviet Union is a house of bondage." For all my criticism of that dictatorial regime, I cannot accept this simplistically. I cannot disregard the objective and subjective role the Soviet Union has played in liberating nations under colonial rule, and the fact that economically the Soviet Union and its satellites implement national revolutions; I cannot disregard the fact that were war to break out and the Soviet Union to be dismantled, two things would follow: the annihilation of the three million Jews who live there – and not by Americans – and a dark age such as the world has never before known.

He advised rejecting the acceptance "of extremist slogans" in the internal educational and political area, and perhaps more important, "since we must change our accepted position, I would advise the party and our members who administer foreign policy to apply some brakes, which also have a positive and crucial role."[29] An emphatic reservation also came from Meir Argov, the chairman of the Knesset Foreign and Defense Affairs Committee, who rejected involvement in "a crusade against world Communism" and recommended maintaining "armed neutrality." He felt that adherence to Israel's independent nature was inconsistent with alignment and necessitated standing aside, as a third party, *vis-à-vis* the two world camps. He regarded the threat of conquest or occupation by the West as nationally no less dangerous than the social danger of a Communist takeover – a contention supported by the memory of British Mandate administration in Palestine. And finally, an internal threat: "The conclusion reached by Sharett leaves no doubt of a civil war between two groups of workers. This will not be a war between gangs ... but entire movements. They will come out against us and constitute an armed fifth column, regarding us as Russia's opposition."

The debate did not produce any resolutions, nor was it meant to; however, it emphasized above all an uncomfortable and apprehensive mood within the leadership regarding a drastic change in the position of neutrality or non-alignment which, most speakers felt, was still Israel's required global policy.

[29] For Aranne's views, see also Y. Riftin's report to Mapam's Political Committee on 1.3.1951, AHA.

Astonishment can clearly be discerned in the notes which Sharett wrote while listening to the critical remarks on his pragmatic speech. Those of Mr. Argov, seemed especially annoying. "His [Argov's] problems are how to be loyal, how to prevent civil war, how to defend the state's existence, to ask for or decline to accept [foreign] aid ... [a realistic understanding of the situation] has not been established. No one has criticized 'Operation Matan' [American economic help to Israel]. But what is the significance of this operation? Our importance in the world hangs upon our independence, but this turns on our existence."[30]

It thus became clear that further action was badly needed. Accordingly, the information campaign continued throughout the year. Although Mapai's Central Committee did not directly deal with the matter for some time, the results were apparent as early as the beginning of 1952.

On 3 January of that year Sharett once again attempted to explain the intricacies of Israel's external relations to the Political Committee of his party. He then stressed his conviction that "as a result of the universal ideological struggle, which also affects us and which is a battle for the soul of our youth and the mind of the nation itself, neutrality has become impossible; non-alignment is out of the question." Speaking in his capacity as Minister for Foreign Affairs, he also left no doubt as to his conviction that "our attachment to the U.S.A. is literally a question of life and death for the state of Israel and for its population ... our entire network of connections and communications as well as all our information activities have been directed at one target: to establish a special set of relations with the U.S.A., an atmosphere of trust created by the style of our appearance and the manner of our talks within the U.S. public ... [All are intended to transmit the message] that in case of an international crisis we are with them."[31] In marked contrast to the debate which took place eight months earlier, no critical comments were heard in the discussions which followed the Foreign Minister's speech; the acceptance of his diagnosis and prognosis seemed absolute.

Simultaneously, the internal campaign of explanation and persuasion regarding Israel's foreign policy orientation had proceeded on a parallel track. Indirectly it took the form of an open and sharp

---

[30] See Sharett's undated notes, which most probably referred to that meeting on 3.3.1951, in the Central Zionist Archives (henceforth referred to as CZA), file A245/7011.     [31] LPA.

political struggle, initiated by Mapai against Mapam. Long before the first Knesset elections of early 1949, Mapai had considered Mapam to be a dangerous rival. Were the two camps from which the latter was formed, Hashomer Haza'ir and Ahdut Ha'Avoda, to unite (as they did in 1948), Mapam might even constitute an alternative to the government. This fear was not unfounded; in 1946 the two factions had won almost half the votes for the Histadrut Convention.[32] The elections for the Knesset and for the Seventh Histadrut Convention held in January and May 1949, respectively, showed that Mapam still constituted the second most important political party in Israel.[33] Moreover, the danger from the left was not merely electoral, but also ideological. Addressing Mapai's Political Committee, in September 1951, Ben Gurion claimed that most of Israel's parties had no significance: "I don't regard the General Zionists as a party – they have no ideology and only look out for their own interests at the expense of the country and the public; the same applies to Hapo'el Hamizrahi, except that their interests are religious and spiritual."[34] Mapam was excluded from this category of harmless and innocuous parties. Mapai's leaders were well aware that Mapam was ideologically attractive to at least part of their own electorate. Especially was this so once Mapam could justify its own foreign policy platform on the undeniable and well-recognized grounds of Soviet political support for the creation of a Jewish state.

Ben Gurion, together with some other members of Mapai, regarded Mapam as the ultimate domestic foe and a "fifth column" in the service of the Soviet Union. Accordingly, security investigations were initiated into the reliability of its leaders[35] and the party was ruthlessly attacked on the internal political level. By the end of 1949, this struggle was labeled a war between Socialist Zionism and the *Yevsektsiya*. The nature of the struggle, and the link between it and Israel's problems in international ideological alignment, were elu-

[32] About 43%. See Y. Ishai, "Factionalism in the Labor Movement in Israel" (Unpublished Ph.D. thesis, The Hebrew University of Jerusalem, 1976), p. 350 (Hebrew).

[33] In the elections for the Knesset held on 25 January 1949, Mapai won 46 seats and Mapam 19. In the elections for the Histadrut Convention of 24 May of that year, the figures were 286 and 172. See M. Braslavsky, *The Labor Movement in Eretz Israel* (Tel Aviv, 1962), p. 183 (Hebrew).

[34] 13.9.1951, LPA.

[35] See Y. Karoz, "Mapam's Underground Within the Security Service," *Yediot Ahronot*, 15.12.1978 (Hebrew).

cidated at great length by Ben Gurion at a meeting of the Mapai Secretariat in November 1949:

There is a big difference between Communism and our war against Communism, and the *Yevsektsiya* and our war against it ... The debate between us and Jewish Communists is double-edged. It has a global aspect as a debate between Socialism and Communism, in which we may sometimes reach common ground. Two years ago we met at Lake Success [where the U.N. voted for the partition of Palestine into Jewish and Arab states] and the Communists were in favor of a Jewish state and in favor of partition ... There need be no conflict at every international convention. But this is not the case with the *Yevsektsiya*. This is an internal Jewish debate, in which there can be no agreement ... They hated Zion in our movement even without Communism, just as the *Bund*,[36] which is non-Communist and more anti-Soviet than many among us, hates Zion. Their conception conflicts with ours, and hence there can be no contact, no provisional agreement, between us and the *Yevsektsiya*.[37]

Of the several internal implications of this analysis, the most important was the categorical refusal to consider Mapam as a potential partner in the government's coalition. Foreign policy issues provided one central justification for this attitude. These were bluntly put by Mordechai Namir, one of Mapai's leaders and Israel's second Minister to the Soviet Union, early in June 1949.[38] Because they were so frank, his arguments deserve to be reproduced in full:

I do not understand the soft and apologetic line toward Mapam which I sense from reading our press: I emphasize Mapam because we are creating a disastrous injustice, with far-reaching implications for the objective truth and for the education of our youth, if we differentiate between them and Maki [Israel's Communist Party]. I do not deny that there are theoretical and practical differences in several important areas between them; likewise I do not cast doubt on Mapam's Zionism. But after the creation of the state the former demarcation line dividing ourselves and our internal enemies [Zionism and anti-Zionism] has lost much of its significance. In conditions of a world cut into two blocs, with our state, located as it is at a geopolitical

---

[36] The *Bund* ("General Jewish Workers' Union in Lithuania, Poland and Russia") was a Jewish Socialist party founded in Russia in 1897. It came to be associated with devotion to Yiddish, autonomism and secular Jewish nationalism, envisaging Jewish life as lived out in Eastern Europe. It sharply opposed Zionism and other conceptions of a world-embracing Jewish national identity. See, *inter alia*, E. Mendelsohn, *Class Struggle in the Pale* (Cambridge, 1970); B. K. Johnpoll, *The Politics of Futility* (Ithaca, 1967); and H. J. Tobias, *The Jewish Bund in Russia from its Origins to 1905* (Stanford, 1972).

[37] 10.11.1949, LPA.

[38] The following excerpts are taken from his letter to Friedman on 5.6.1949, ISA 2500/13.

flashpoint desperately striving to hold on to neutrality, foreign policy issues
are, at least for the foreseeable future, real determinants in our inter-party
relations. This is precisely the partition line between ourselves and Mapam
... It is unquestionably in the field of foreign policy that Mapam does not
really differ at all from Maki – both openly preach a unilateral orientation
toward the East. For this reason, and not because they [Mapam] are
excluded from our government, a wretched ideology of two motherlands has
arisen. For one of them [Russia] there is an excuse for everything: dictator-
ship, abolition of civil liberties, expansion, anti-Zionism, anti-Hebraism
(which now includes anti-Yiddishism) to the verge of annihilation of the
character of Russian Jewry. But for the second motherland, the stepmother
[Israel], there is not even a drop of compassion and pity, no matter how
difficult its position may be. We should not be confused and bewildered by the
glory of their kubbitzim and by the heroism of their members on the
battlefield [during the 1948 War]. There is no doubt that their rank and file
are loyal and devoted, but it is not they who determine political policy. That is
the prerogative of the leadership, and they are Communist as far as the basic
principle which decides this issue in this period of mankind is concerned.
Their kibbutzim and whatever they have are directed at one target – the
destruction of the emerging sovereign existence of Israel as an independent
Jewish political unit ... Their participation in government would not at all
improve their behavior. Their ability to harm, well-established while in
opposition, would no doubt only grow were they to be included in our cabinet.

Even those who had not accepted Namir's diagnosis could hardly
minimize the dangerous external import of Mapam's inclusion in the
government. A coalition of that sort would solidify the opinion that
Israel's non-alignment in fact concealed a pro-Soviet orientation.[39]
Nevertheless, it should be noted that several of Mapai's leaders
questioned Ben Gurion's conviction of the necessity for a vicious and
sometimes brutal encounter with Mapam during the first three years
of Israel's independence. Sharett, Aranne, Arieh Offir, and Shaul
Avigur, head of the Mossad Le'Aliyah[40] (to name but the most
prominent), had reservations with regard to the policy initiated by
the Prime Minister; they considered that he had prematurely "closed
the door" to any possibility of political cooperation with that party.[41]
Mapam's internal dynamics, they thought, left some hope that the
party would eventually abandon its extreme line. Accordingly, the
moderate elements within it should be encouraged.

[39] See, for example, Sharett's analysis at the meeting of Mapai's Secretariat on
28.8.1949, LPA.
[40] The office organizing illegal emigration of Jews to Israel (henceforth referred to as
the Mossad).
[41] See Aranne's speech at Mapai's Central Committee meeting of 12.11.1949. Also
Offir's speech before that body on 16.3.1949, LPA.

The significant shadow which explained much of this thinking within Mapai had been the unmistakable danger of civil war. Sharett expressed this fear in September 1949. "I admit that [an attempt to include Mapam in the Government] is a daring move. It is obvious that we have to face the prospect of a civil war ... but at the same time there is a hope of delaying it because history might not repeat itself and events that occurred in other countries might not happen [in Israel]. I say, never abandon hope altogether."[42] Another consideration which often militated against the exclusion of Mapam from the government was the common belief that such an act would create the impression within the Eastern bloc that Israel has definitely aligned herself with the West against the Soviets. Many, therefore, concurred in the formula of a leading Mossad agent, himself a Mapai member, that "even when there is no assurance that the inclusion of Mapam would have improved our relations with Eastern Europe countries their exclusion would definitely damage them."[43]

Ben Gurion rejected this reasoning. From his point of view, the inclusion of Mapam in the government "would weigh heavily upon our foreign policy without any commensurate benefit. Mapam is not [sufficiently] Communist for Russia, they are as much fascists as we are ... it will restrict our actions especially in the economic sphere."[44] The Prime Minister had influential supporters; one of them, Lavon, vehemently opposed any political cooperation with Mapam on grounds of the lack of symmetry in its foreign policy orientation. "In our relations with the U.S.A. we have in that country a fifth column whereas in our relations with the Soviet Union they have a fifth column here."[45]

Mapai's internal debate on this subject had important repercussions with regard to the public campaign of information regarding Israel's external orientation. As long as there seemed to be the slightest hope of moderating Mapam's ideological and political program, Mapai's information campaign lacked much of its force. Ultimately, it was only Mapam's increasing extremism, after May 1950,[46] later publicized, *inter alia*, by the split in the kibbutz move-

---

[42] From his speech at a meeting of Mapai's Secretariat with the party's members of the Knesset on 14 September 1949, LPA. On Mapam's perspective, see Z. Tsur, *Partnership as Opposition: the Partnership of Mapam in the Government 1949–1954* (Efal, 1983) (Hebrew).

[43] Agami's remarks quoted in Barzilai's letter to Sharett, 31.3.1949, ISA 2491/20.

[44] From his speech at a meeting of Mapai's Secretariat on 28.8.1949, LPA.

[45] Protocol of a meeting with Mapam's leaders, 3.11.1949, LPA.

[46] This process found expression in an important doctrinal article by M. Ya'ari

ment, which weakened the hand of Ben Gurion's opponents within Mapai.

Thereafter, the clear-cut debate with Mapam facilitated Mapai's internal information campaign – a strategy recommended by Livneh.[47] Indeed, as of the second half of 1950, the party press – and especially *Davar* – contained numerous articles sharply attacking Mapam and its advocacy of a neutral foreign policy; these reflected various opinions, some expressed more sternly than others, urging a clearer definition of neutrality in foreign policy than merely automatic consensus.[48] Nevertheless, it should be noted that even the process of extremism within Mapam did not immediately permit a full and public exposure of the growing asymmetry between American–Israeli relations on the one hand and Soviet–Israeli relations on the other. That development took another two years. The reason for this caution was the slender hope for improvement in relations with the Soviet Union. Prevalent opinion within Mapai was that clear-cut public declarations on Israel's foreign policy might abort that development altogether. That is why not until the end of 1952 did any Mapai leader of the first rank openly admit the adoption of a militant anti-Communist line.

It is the evidence concerning Russia's hostility towards Israel and Zionism which explains the dramatic metamorphosis in the struggle which Mapai initiated against Mapam and against Communism. Specifically, the Prague Trials of late 1952 constituted a clear and unquestionable external development, depriving Mapam of one of its most effective arguments in the foreign policy sphere and inviting attack and denigration on the domestic front.

published on 1 May of that year. It included the desire that Mapam become a purely Communist party. See Ishai, "Factionalism in the Labor Movement," pp. 362–3. This process became even clearer at the Mapam Convention in Haifa about one year later.
[47] In two articles in *Hapo'el Haza'ir*, "Summary of a Debate" (6.2.1951), and "Explaining the Decision" (27.2.1951) (both in Hebrew), Livneh pointed out the shortcomings of information efforts regarding the foreign policy change.
[48] H. Ya'ari published a series of articles in *Davar*, for example, which purported to debate Israeli policy on Korea with Mapam, but in fact recommended the need for "reassessing positions." See "What the Debate is About" (28.7.1950); "Against the Neutralization Slogan" (23.2.1951); and "Defeatism Instead of Policy" (9.3.1951) (all in Hebrew). This was expressed more clearly in the party newspapers. *Hador*, for instance, published articles by Y. Yagol, who sharply and openly clarified the point: see "Korea – a Second Munich" (16.3.1951); and "In the Face of Impending Disaster" (2.3.1951) (both in Hebrew). *Hapo'el Haza'ir* also expressed this line in articles such as that written by Shmuel Basson, "The Only Choice" (28.11.1950) (Hebrew). Such expressions can hardly be found in party publications before the second half of 1950.

Mapai's public attitude was decided upon at a meeting of its Political Committee at the end of November 1952, soon after the disclosure of the Trials.[49] The discussers were unanimous in proclaiming changes in the form of Mapai's public struggle with Mapam and Communism. All agreed that events in Prague had provided a golden opportunity to attack on two fronts. The first, as Sharett explained, was ideological: "It gives us a good chance to corner Mapam and keep her suffocated ... We are interested in the periphery of Mapam as well ... By reason of lightning tactics we can amplify the shock and the internal dislocation, bringing about far-reaching implications within their movement." The second front was internal; here the campaign was aimed at demolishing all doubts within Mapai itself with regard to the ideological and political dimensions of Israel's foreign policy. To quote Sharett again:

We have not yet made up our minds on this question, which will determine the future of mankind ... It is depressing that several of us still cling to an illusion ... Some [members of Mapai] cannot grow out of the feeling which they experienced in their youth towards the October Revolution. They have been struck with blinding light, which dazzles them even today; they are unable to uproot that spiritual attitude and understand that the light deceived, that it was false. What happened in 1917 is commonly recognized to have been a terrible calamity in Jewish and in general human history ... The Middle Ages are regarded as a dark era in history, its balance sheet was to all intents and purposes negative. This should be History's verdict regarding the October Revolution.

Ben Gurion, for his part, reiterated his adamant refusal to cooperate with Mapam and called for a special effort to "tell the truth." "There are not two Mapams, the bad and the good, there is only one Mapam which supports tyranny ... there has never been such a fraud [as the claim that] Socialism exists in Russia ... That's a deception which we have to uproot from the hearts of our youth [but], first of all from the heart of Argov."

It is therefore hardly surprising that when the Foreign Minister addressed Mapai's lecturers four days later, he stressed that the aim of the campaign was to "free *ourselves* from the complex of inferiority towards those believing in the 'World of Tomorrow' with which we have been infected. If this is the World of Tomorrow – to hell with it!"[50]

---

[49] Excerpts are taken from the protocol of that meeting on 23.11.1952, LPA.
[50] 27.11.1952, CZA A245/36.

The clearest and most important expression of Mapai's new public strategy was formulated in a series of articles by Ben Gurion. Written under the pseudonym "Saba Shel Yariv" – "Yariv's Grandpa" – they appeared in the daily *Davar*, and were subsequently issued as a party propaganda pamphlet entitled "Concerning Hashomer Haza'ir's Communism and Zionism."[51] In those pieces, Israel's Prime Minister gave clear indication, albeit in a context of internal political debate, of a central perception in Israel's current foreign policy orientation. The "Doctors' Trials," which became public early in January 1953, and the breaking of diplomatic relations between Israel and the Soviet Union a couple of weeks later, supplied an appropriate context for the publication of that policy.

Writing several years later, Yitzhak Ben Aharon recalled both the occasion of Mapai's campaign against Mapam, and its results. Frankly admitting the tactical errors committed by himself and his fellow opponents of Ben Gurion, he confessed that:

We made every possible mistake and our shortsightedness enabled our rivals to determine Israel's unilateral alignment with the West and with the cold war against the Soviet Union. Instead of presenting a political and diplomatic platform centered on Israel's neutrality in the inter-bloc conflict and on the cultivation of friendly and decent relations with both the Eastern bloc and [our] friends in the U.S.A., we were swept into an ideological combat in which we placed Socialist Zionism within the spiritual camp headed by Russia, i.e., Stalinist-Communism. As on previous occasions, a faction to the left of the [Israeli] labor movement typically and fanatically crossed the lines and denied Zionism. The sobering came too late, at the time of the Doctors' Trials at the peak of the campaign of annihilation against the Jewish intelligentsia [in Russia], which during the [Second World] War had been permitted to head the Jewish-Anti-Fascist-League ... We became speechless witnesses to a campaign openly carried out with anti-Zionist and anti-Semitic slogans. In these circumstances Ben Gurion managed to defeat even those within his own party who advocated a balanced orientation, and brought about the later split [in the kibbutz movement]. As an orientation, neutrality was thus demolished. Only battered and degenerated political bases had been left on the battlefield. Securing the alliance with the secular and religious right, Ben Gurion laid the foundations for a state and society integrated into the Western capitalist bloc.[52]

In short, Mapai's external struggle against Mapam, which had united the party in the early years of statehood, was invaluable for

---

[51] Tel Aviv, 1953. The articles began to appear in November 1952.
[52] Y. Ben-Aharon, *In the Eye of the Storm* (Tel Aviv, 1972), p. 47 (Hebrew). See Appendix 2 for biographical note.

internally explaining the process of change within Israel's foreign policy, and for easing that process. Unanimity on the importance of the external struggle considerably helped soften the opposition of circles in the party opposed to the pace and nature of change. It also contributed to a stifling of their disagreement.

That the Prague and Doctors' Trials influenced the internal development of Mapam, terminating in its split and thereby generating substantial changes in Israel's political map, has long been recognized.[53] The foregoing analysis has shown that these external events also constituted a watershed in the internal politics of Mapai, particularly in the field of foreign policy. Five years earlier, debates within Mapai had witnessed the crystallization of the concept of non-alignment or neutrality in foreign policy. At the end of 1952, however, the debates on the subject had been transformed into a virtually academic confrontation with Mapam and almost ceased to be the subject of internal contentions. Thereafter, what kept the issue alive in Israel's public and political life was the advocacy of other parties, such as the foreign policy platform of Ahdut Ha'Avoda which, after its split with Mapam, advocated independence or neutrality in contrast with Mapai's "subservience" to the West.[54] Otherwise, however, the political thinking within Mapai, the party that determined Israeli foreign policy until 1977, neglected the issue almost entirely.

[53] See Y. Ishai, "The Vision and its Lesson: The Impact of the Prague Trials on Mapam," *State, Government and International Relations*, 7, Spring 1975, pp. 76–95 (Hebrew).

[54] It was in this guise that the issue of foreign policy orientation continued to have an impact on the question of coalition formation in the government. Nevertheless, as is indicated by a rare item of documentary evidence on negotiations between Mapai and Ahdut Ha'Avoda on that issue in late December 1954, the debate was essentially futile. Ahdut Ha'Avoda's leaders then demanded distinct neutrality in Israel's foreign policy and the freedom of the country from "being harnessed to the Western carriage." But they could provide no answer to the persistent enquiries: "Where do we get planes, oil and equipment? If you know of any source other than the West, let us know," 14.12.1954, Box 5, File "Negotiations with Mapai," AHA.

# Part II

## RED STAR OVER ZION

# 3. "LET MY PEOPLE GO"

Late in April 1953 Moshe Sharett (Israel's Foreign Minister), who was then in Argentina, received the following report from his personal secretary: a week previously a group of fourteen persons had been caught trying illegally to cross the Czechoslovakian border and make aliyah with the help of Mossad agents.[1] While two of the group managed to escape, among the captives was a local employee of the Israeli Legation in Prague and a woman named Biskovska, the daughter-in-law of the Legation's shortwave radio operator, a local Jew. Four days later Biskovska appeared at the Legation and announced that she had been released by the police after promising to work for the Czech secret service. The Israelis decided to permit Biskovska to spend the night in the Legation, which had immediately been placed under open police surveillance. Now, however, she threatened to commit suicide unless offered help and the Israeli Foreign Ministry was requested to grant her temporary asylum in the Legation.

In Israel, the heads of the Foreign Ministry decided that they could not accede to the request. Legally, they pointed out, asylum could not be granted to local citizens against whom criminal prosecution was pending; the Czechs could easily evict the Israelis from the building in which the woman was hiding. In addition, the political and diplomatic repercussions had to be considered. The incident, it was feared, might lead to a break in relations between Israel and Czechoslovakia, especially since several of the Legation's employees were involved. Notwithstanding these arguments, the Director General of the Foreign Ministry decided to consult with the Prime Minister before cabling Prague, "not because he did not want to

---

[1]  The following account is based upon and excerpts are taken from Uri Lubrani's letter of 22.4.1953, ISA 2458/12.

accept responsibility and not because he thought there was any other way out, but because he was certain that the Prime Minister would not forgive himself were such instructions to be issued without his having been given the opportunity personally to weigh the matter." As it happened, Ben Gurion was indeed incapable of accepting the idea of the "poor girl's" delivery, and felt that Israel was morally and publicly obligated to inform the Czechs that "we are not prepared to extradite her nor permit the Czechs to fabricate an appropriate ruse that would end in our having no other choice."

Although it was Independence Day, the Prime Minister decided to convene an extraordinary Cabinet meeting in order to examine the matter, at which the entire Cabinet participated. There it was decided to instruct the Legation in Prague to attempt to persuade the woman to leave of her own free will; should the Czech Foreign Ministry demand extradition, Israel would comply. The cable to Prague stressed that the decision had occasioned deep concern and was based upon the absence of any legal basis for granting the woman asylum. Israel's Minister in Prague was instructed to explain this to the woman and to add that by leaving of her own volition she might improve her situation, since she could tell the authorities that she had remained inside the Legation merely in order to gather information. Consequently the woman, accompanied by the shortwave operator, left the Legation to report to the local police.

I have written to you in detail on this incident [Sharett's secretary concluded his report] not only because of the gravity of the issue itself, but because [it] attests to the deeply rooted moral principles on which the state bases its actions and, in this case, on which its . . . leader also bases his own. Where else in the world would a Prime Minister consider convening his entire Cabinet at the height of national Independence Day celebrations, gathering them from all quarters of the country, cancelling speeches and appearances, upsetting the plans of many people – all in order to clear his conscience of the fate of one Jewish soul? And the Cabinet members, with the exception only of those who are abroad, get into their cars and come.

The episode is presented here in its entirety because it does indeed illustrate the special importance which Israeli policy-makers attached to the issue of aliyah (emigration to Israel) in general and in regard to aliyah from the Eastern bloc in particular. It also illustrates their overwhelming feeling of obligation on the matter. This sense of responsibility found official expression in Israel's Declaration of Independence. As read before the National Council on 14 May 1948 (a few hours before the British Mandate came to an end and the state of Israel was established), that document stated: "The state of Israel shall be open to Jewish immigration and the ingathering of the exiles" and called upon the Jewish people throughout the world to unite around the Yishuv (Jewish community in Israel) through immigration and construction.[2]

Israel's Prime Minister conveyed this responsibility more explicitly and in more detail in April 1949, when addressing Defense and Foreign Ministry officials:

Internal and external policy is always determined by a state's core interest, which may change; and although we are an especially young country, we have experienced change ... Before the state was established, upon its establishment, our core interest was defense ... the question is, what is now the core interest of the state of Israel? It is aliyah ... which can strengthen us considerably, more than anything else ... Perhaps we could capture the Triangle [northwest part of the West Bank], the Golan, the entire Galilee; but such victories could not bolster our security as much as immigration. Doubling and trebling the population [increases] our strength. And ... aliyah saves Jews from the total extinction that might be their fate in the future ... The fate of the state depends on aliyah.[3]

This statement had long been particularly significant with regard to Eastern European Jewry. With the destruction of six million Jews during the Second World War, Jewish refugees in Eastern Europe remained the largest and most promising reservoir of potential aliyah.[4] The need to bring about the aliyah of some 40,000 Czech, 200,000 Hungarian, 350,000 Rumanian, 50,000 Bulgarian and over 230,000 Polish Jews (most of whom were in the U.S.S.R.) became a paramount goal for the leaders of the Yishuv at the end of the Second World War. Especially was this so once it became clear that an "iron curtain" was about to descend upon the countries of Eastern Europe, foreclosing the possibility of Jewish emigration.[5] Legal aliyah was impossible to arrange, both because emigration was forbidden from Eastern European countries and because the British had set severe restrictions on immigration into Palestine. Accordingly, the leaders of the Jewish Agency had concentrated their efforts on the organization

---

[2] D. Ben Gurion, *The Restored State of Israel* (Tel Aviv, 1969), p. 92 (Hebrew).

[3] From a protocol of a meeting on 12.4.1949, ISA 2441/7.

[4] For further details, see L. Dawidowicz, *The War Against the Jews* (Tel Aviv, 1982), pp. 393–424 (Hebrew).

[5] See, for example, a debate in Mapai's Secretariat on 15.5.1945, Ben Gurion Archive (henceforth BGA), and Z. Hadari, *Refugees Defeating a Great Power* (Tel Aviv, 1985), p. 72 (Hebrew).

of "Bricha" – the secret evacuation of Jews from Eastern and Central Europe into Southern and Western Europe and, of course, the organization of illegal aliyah into Palestine.[6] From the end of 1944 until Israel was established in 1948, the Bricha organization managed to move a quarter of a million Jews out of Eastern and Central Europe and into Italy, France and Germany; it also organized the clandestine entry of some 85,000 Jews into Palestine.[7]

Nevertheless, when the state of Israel was established in May 1948 some 2.5 million Jews remained behind the Iron Curtain, 80% of them in the Soviet Union itself. After independence, one of the central goals of Israel's foreign policy was the maintenance of the tie with this portion of the Jewish world, the concern for its existence and, especially, the effort to ensure the possibility of its aliyah. Precisely the same link was equally crucial for the Jews of Eastern Europe. Messages they passed on to Israel frequently stressed that point,[8] and Israeli Foreign Ministry documents indicate, unequivocally, that it formed the crux of Israel's relationship with the Eastern bloc.

If a correct assessment is to be made of the pivotal nature of this facet of early Israeli foreign policy, several questions need to be addressed. The first is essentially statistical; how many Eastern European Jews did in fact emigrate to Israel, whence did they come and when? Secondly, how did the Israelis view the possibility of organizing aliyah, whether on a bilateral level (with each of the countries involved) or with the bloc as a whole (via the U.S.S.R.)? Thirdly, what political, strategic and economic price was Israel willing (and able) to pay in order to ensure aliyah during these years? In sum – how did this consideration affect the assumptions that in the event determined Israel's global orientation?

Since the nature of the relationship between Israel and the Eastern European states differed from one case to another, and since each of these relationships was complex, the following account will briefly review the course of events in each country in turn.[9]

[6] On these important subjects, which have not hitherto been fully covered, see the pioneering studies by Y. Bauer, *Flight and Rescue: Bricha* (New York, 1970); Hadari, *Refugees*; and B. Pinkus, ed., *Eastern-European Jewry from Holocaust to Redemption* (Sde Boker, 1987) (Hebrew).

[7] Bauer, *Flight and Rescue*, p. 320; S. Avigur, "Summarizing Aliyah Activities," in M. Naor, ed., *Aliyah "B"* (Jerusalem, 1982), p. 132 (Hebrew).

[8] A typical example of these messages is given in a letter from the Chief Rabbis of Rumania to the Israeli Foreign Minister early in June 1951 (no exact date is indicated), ISA 2387/15.

[9] The following account is based upon: A despatch from the Israeli Legation in

*Rumania*

Between the end of the Second World War and 1948 some 45,000 Jews went on aliyah from Rumania. Of these, some 15,000 left legally; the remainder by means of the Bricha, mainly through Hungary. As was the case in other Eastern European countries, the comparative ease of this aliyah was associated with the general policy apparently set in Moscow, whose main thrust facilitated aid to the Yishuv in many areas, not the least of which was immigration. As will be seen, Moscow's motivations were strategic. Although virtually no emigration was permitted from Rumania between late 1948 and November 1949, agreement had been reached between Mordechai Namir, representing the Jewish Agency, and the Rumanian Foreign Minister Anna Pauker (herself a Jewess), early in 1948. This allowed for the clandestine emigration and aliyah of some 5,000 Rumanian Jews per month.

Rumanian renunciation of this agreement in mid-1949 was accompanied by the severe imposition of intensive anti-Zionist measures, which included the imprisonment of local Zionist leaders and the destruction of most of the movement's organizational frameworks. In return Israel stepped up her own efforts to bring to fruition the Rumanian promises regarding aliyah. Quite apart from attempting to exert political pressure through meetings between the Israeli Prime Minister and the Rumanian Minister in Israel, protest meetings were called in Israel and elsewhere. Towards the end of 1949, Jews within Rumania itself had begun to demonstrate. In November 1949 the Rumanians seem to have decided to permit mass emigration of Jews; that month 3,200 Jews departed legally, and between November 1949 and April 1952 nearly 90,000 Jews left Rumania for Israel, at monthly rates of between several hundred (in the last months of 1952) and 7,000 (August 1950).

Budapest to the Foreign Ministry on 29.3.1951, ISA 2387/14; Memorandum on relations with the Soviet Union (with no exact date but most probably from April 1953), ISA 2457/14; Data on ties with Hungary (with no exact date but most probably from December 1952), ISA 2457/21; H. Ofek's letter to Y. Raphael on 21.7.1950, CZA s6/5024; Report on immigration from Poland on 10.8.1951, ISA 2502/11; Memorandum from the Eastern Europe Section of the Israeli Foreign Ministry to the British Commonwealth Section on 6.7.1951, ISA 2499/2; Report on immigration from Poland (with no exact date but most probably from early May 1953), ISA 2457/18; Report on immigration from Rumania (with no exact date but most probably from March 1953), ISA 2457/19; H. Kishalis, *History of Bulgaria's Jews* (vol. 4) – *Bulgaria Behind the Iron Curtain 1944–1952* (Tel Aviv, 1969), pp. 235–87 (Hebrew); and Hadari, *Refugees*, pp. 187–94.

The Rumanian approach was, however, erratic. Sometimes passports were issued almost immediately; sometimes applicants were told to reapply six or twelve months later; in some instances passports already issued were confiscated at the point of departure. Early in 1952 the flow of passports slackened considerably, and in April of that year the passport office was closed on the pretext of "total reorganization in the Foreign Ministry." Three months later the office did reopen, but the aliyah permitted was limited and ultimately halted almost entirely early in 1953. From then until mid-1955 only a few Rumanian Jews emigrated to Israel, despite unceasing Israeli efforts (see below) to continue aliyah. It is noteworthy that the overwhelming majority of immigrants during the period of mass immigration consisted of elderly relatives of Jews already living in Israel. In fact, at the height of aliyah, between April 1950 and December 1951, more than half the immigrants were over fifty years old.

*Poland*

Between the end of the Second World and the establishment of Israel, some 12,000 Polish Jews emigrated to Palestine. By the end of 1952, an additional 104,000 Polish Jews had gone on aliyah. Of these, only about one-third entered Israel direct from Poland; most set out from the countries in which they found themselves at the end of the war, principally the displaced persons' camps of Germany and Austria. Between 1948 and 1949 aliyah from Poland was sluggish; the Polish government seems to have come to no definite decision on the issue, and generally permitted the emigration of the elderly and of those who were not affiliated with the Zionist camp in Poland. Israeli representatives inside and outside Poland frequently attempted to persuade the authorities in Warsaw to permit Jewish emigration, and in mid-August 1949 did elicit a formal Polish assurance. The Minister of Public Administration, who was also responsible for issuing passports, then promised that during the following eighteen months, every Jew seeking to do so would be permitted to go on aliyah, provided that he or she renounced Polish citizenship. Massive aliyah from Poland did indeed ensue; but it ended sooner than the Israelis had forecasted. After some 28,000 emigrants had left the country between October 1949 and December 1950, the flow of aliyah was halted and the Polish authorities made it clear that they had no intention of seeing it renewed. Although a trickle of some 2,500 emigrants made their way to Israel during the course of 1951, between then and mid-1955 only several scores of Jews were permitted to leave Poland.

## Hungary

Until the end of 1949 Jewish aliyah from Hungary was illegal. The Mossad did manage to transfer some 30,000 Hungarian Jews to Mandatory Palestine prior to May 1948 and, in similarly clandestine circumstances, another 10,000 during the following eighteen months. Not until October 1949 was an agreement reached with the Hungarian authorities whereby 3,000 Jews would be allowed to leave, to be chosen according to criteria of age (over fifty-five) and family ties (relatives of Hungarian Jews already living in Israel). About 2,000 Jews were to permitted to leave Hungary during 1950, and the remainder, at a much slower pace, over the following two years. Despite Israeli expectations, mass aliyah did not ensue. In fact, between early 1953 and mid-1955, only several hundred Hungarian Jews emigrated to Israel.

## Czechoslovakia and Bulgaria

In these two states the problem of aliyah was solved shortly after the establishment of the state of Israel. The Czech government permitted mass emigration early in 1949 and, in the course of a year, over half of the Jewish population of Czechoslovakia (some 18,000) came to Israel. Of the 16,000 or so Jews who remained in the country, only a few thousand were refused permission to emigrate. Bulgarian aliyah was completed even earlier. In February 1948 representatives of the Mossad reached an agreement with the Bulgarian government and, during the course of the following fifteen months, 35,000 of Bulgaria's Jews came to Israel. The local Jewish community that remained numbered less than 10,000 – 2,000 of whom wished to leave.

## The Soviet Union

Between 1948 and mid-1955, only 131 Jews left the U.S.S.R. for Israel, 9 of them before 1953. To this striking difference between the case of the Soviet Union and that of the Eastern bloc states, must be added the fact that, as will be elaborated later, Israel did not exert large-scale pressure on the Soviets to permit mass Jewish emigration.

Table 1. *Aliyah from the East 1948–55*

| Country of origin | Period | Number of immigrants | Remaining Jews | Official Israeli estimate of Jews wishing to leave (1952) |
|---|---|---|---|---|
| U.S.S.R. | 15.5.48–1.2.53 | 9 | 1,700,000* | ? |
| | 1.8.53–30.6.55 | 122 | | |
| Czechoslovakia | 15.5.48–31.12.49 | 17,804 | | |
| | 1950 | 263 | | |
| | 1951 | 150 | | |
| | 1952–3 | 40 | | |
| | 1955 | 40 | 16,000 | 3,000 |
| Poland | 15.5.48–31.12.49 | 76,132 (including "illegals" and Polish Jews arriving from elsewhere in Europe) | | |
| | 1950 | 25,071 | | |
| | 1951 | 2,529 | | |
| | 1952–3 | 489 | | |
| | 1954–5 | 318 | 45,000 | 15,000 |

| | | | | |
|---|---|---|---|---|
| Hungary | 15.5.48–31.12.49 | 10,307 ("illegal" emigration) | | |
| | 1950 | 2,302 | | |
| | 1951–2 | 1,155 | | |
| | 1953–4 | 278 | 100,000 | |
| | 1955 | 275 | | 60,000 |
| Rumania | 15.5.48–31.12.49 | 31,274 (including "illegals") | | |
| | 1950 | 47,041 | | |
| | 1951 | 40,625 | | |
| | 1952 | 3,712 | | |
| | 1953–5 | 349 | 200,000 | 100,000 |
| Bulgaria | 15.5.48–31.12.49 | 35,089 | | |
| | 1950–3 | 1,962 | | |
| | 1954–5 | 393 | 7,000 | 2,000 |
| Totals | | 297,709 | 2,068,000 | 180,000 (excluding Soviet Jews) |

* No reliable figures exist as to the size of what is called "Soviet Jewry." The number of Jews inscribed as "Jew" in the nationality section of their internal passports is approximately 1,700,000. As many as a million more (which some still consider too conservative an estimate) are inscribed as Russian.

Table 1 provides the basic information on the aliyah of Eastern and Central European Jewry during the first seven years after the establishment of Israel.[10] It clearly illustrates the periodization of aliyah from Eastern Europe. Some 180,000 immigrants from this part of the world came to Israel between its independence and the end of 1949. In 1950, 70,000 Jews emigrated; the next year, 40,000; in 1952, 4,000. From then and until 1956 annual aliyah from the Eastern bloc totaled no more than a few hundred. Quite apart from the perspective provided by internal political documentation, these figures themselves explain the prominence that Jerusalem was obliged to accord during that period to the question of aliyah from Eastern Europe. They also underscored the importance of Israel's political relations with those countries, at least during the first four years after independence, when so many Eastern bloc Jews emigrated.

Even without the insights provided by hitherto classified sources, it is not difficult to appreciate why, even after this mass aliyah came to a halt at the end of 1952, the issue of Jewish emigration from Eastern Europe continued to exercise a hold on the mind of Israeli policy-makers. They realized that there existed a vast reservoir of potential aliyah in the population of about 200,000 Jews left in the Soviet bloc countries – and in Soviet Jewry itself, which numbered some two million. This perception outweighed even the possibly fatalistic realization that continued aliyah from Eastern Europe might have been unlikely. Throughout the period, it remained a cardinal goal that the state of Israel continue to maintain contact with a Jewish population which, at the start of the 1950s, exceeded that of Israel itself. As far as possible, Israel had also to offer Eastern European Jewry assistance.

Although impressive, the statistics are essentially dry. In themselves, they cannot adequately express the complexities of the ongoing Israeli struggle to ensure aliyah during the course of the historical period with which this book is concerned. What they do not reveal are the constant estimations of the likelihood of the success of Israeli initiatives in this field and, above, all, the effect of those evaluations as an influence on the choice of Israeli foreign policy orientation between

[10] The sources for this table are: Material for a meeting of the Defense and Foreign Affairs Committee of the Knesset on 31.12.1950, ISA 2514/8; Debates of the American Section of the World Jewish Congress on 22.2.1950, ISA 2498/5; a despatch from the Eastern Europe Section of the Israeli Foreign Ministry to Michael Arnon on 10.8.1952, *ibid.*; Bentsur's despatch to Arnon on 13.10.1952, ISA 2498/5; and Bentsur's letter to the Foreign Minister on 12.7.1955, ISA 2502/8.

the East and the West. These complex issues are only made explicit in the historical records recently made available in the various archives in Israel. These sources pose the issue of how the state of Israel might have advanced the goal of ensuring mass emigration of Jews from Eastern Europe during that period. This is a central question which has hitherto not been accorded analytical attention; yet its answer encompasses solutions to several other problems. With the opening of the archives, it is now possible to discern several directions and primary techniques in this field during the period between 1948 and the Sinai Campaign.

# 4. THE ALIYAH TIE WITH MOSCOW

In their studies of the period, Sovietologists have long surmised that the U.S.S.R. assisted Jewish emigration from the Eastern bloc after the Second World War in order to achieve her own objectives in Palestine. Prior to November 1947 Soviet support of aliyah was directed primarily towards exerting pressure on the Western powers to find a solution to the problem of Palestine; thus, she encouraged the emigration of Jewish refugees to Western and Southern Europe in order to cause embarrassment to Britain in the Middle East. After the U.N. accepted the Palestine Partition Plan that month, and especially from mid-1948 onward, the Soviets advocated the entry of the largest possible number of Jews in order to ease this first and most critical test of Israel's survival. The U.S.S.R. apparently anticipated the Israeli military victories which would ensure that Britain would not return to the land from which she had been ousted. The most striking example of Soviet activity thus motivated is to be found in the case of Poland: Russia permitted a large number of Polish Jews who had reached the U.S.S.R. during the course of the Second World War to return to Poland, whence their aliyah to Israel was facilitated. Before this process began, in the summer of 1945, some 50,000 Jews still lived in Poland; a year later some 150,000 left the country, for Germany and Austria. In 1947, 90,000 Jews remained in Poland.[1] Thus, of the 250,000 to 300,000 Polish Jews resident in the U.S.S.R at the end of the Second World War, some 200,000 were permitted to return to their homeland (partly for internal Russian reasons too). Most of them subsequently left Poland with the consent and assistance of the Soviet Union, which then directed Polish internal and foreign policy.[2]

---

[1] For statistics see P. Meyer, B. Weinryb, D. Duschinsky and N. Sylvain, *The Jews in the Soviet Satellites* (Syracuse, 1953), pp. 240, 256–7.
[2] On this subject see Y. Ro'i, *Soviet Decision-Making in Practice* (London, 1980), pp. 20–33.

Bricha representatives were not unaware of this aspect of Soviet policy. Indeed, in August 1946 a senior Soviet diplomat in Warsaw informed them that Soviet ambassadors throughout Eastern Europe had received instructions to influence their host governments to permit Bricha activities.[3] These instructions were duly carried out.[4]

Soviet strategic motivations seemed obvious. While Soviet officials did not admit that the U.S.S.R. was actively encouraging Jewish aliyah from Eastern Europe, they did not explicitly deny the fact and were sometimes willing to discuss it, specifically, for instance, with the Mapam party representatives inside and outside Israel.[5] To this must be added two further considerations. First, the paramilitary training received by Jewish immigrants in several of the Eastern European states before they went on aliyah must have been countenanced and endorsed by the Soviets. Secondly, Eastern European leaders informed the Israelis in mid-1948 that the entire bloc had an interest in aiding Israel in this area. Most explicitly was this so in the conversation between Mordechai Namir and Rumanian Foreign Minister Anna Pauker early in 1948, which as will be elaborated later led to the agreement (never effected) permitting the aliyah of thousands of Rumanian Jews.

Israeli leaders were certainly cognizant of the Soviet stance and motivations. For their part, they did their best to convince the Russian representatives whom they met of the indispensability of continued Soviet support. This point was particularly stressed after the end of 1948, when the pro-Israeli atmosphere seemed to change. In November of that year a virulent anti-Zionist campaign was launched in Hungary and Rumania; Bulgaria decided to end all local Zionist activity; and the Poles closed the "Eretz Israel Office" and limited aliyah. In October, Golda Meir, Israel's Minister to Moscow, had met with Molotov and raised the problem of aliyah from Eastern Europe. Reporting to the directorship of the Jewish Agency two months later, she recalled: "We emphasized the importance of the matter from Israel's point of view. We stressed that a government that has given us so much aid in order to found our state, must help us to maintain it, and in this quarter of the world no state can arise whose population is so small."[6] The request had been made at a higher level

[3] See R. Frister *With All His Heart* (Tel Aviv, 1975), pp. 17–23 (Hebrew).
[4] See Z. Hadari, *Refugees Defeating a Great Power* (Tel Aviv, 1985), pp. 169–71, 186–7 for testimonies attesting to this contention.
[5] See Ro'i, *Soviet Decision-Making*, pp. 177–8.
[6] Meeting of the Directorate of the Jewish Agency on 13.12.1948, CZA.

when on 12 December 1948 Moshe Sharett met with Soviet Deputy Foreign Minister, Andrei Vyshinsky, the first Soviet politician of so high a stature to have met with the Israeli Foreign Minister. During the meeting, intended primarily to raise the problem of aliyah from the Soviet bloc countries, the Israeli claim was most clearly and unequivocally clarified:

It is not enough to establish Israel formally [Sharett explained]; it is not enough to defend her successfully – we have a vision of peace with the Arab world around us. We will not attain it tomorrow. But if we do attain it, it will be thanks to our being a power ... not militarily only, though this is very important, but in the sense of many masses of people dwelling in their land, cultivating it and developing it. This requires massive aliyah – otherwise we cannot hold out. If you took a stance in favor of the state of Israel and decided that our issue was a just one – you must draw the obvious conclusions and understand that this state in its present dimensions cannot hold out and you must be interested in this country growing, and first of all in the numerical sense.[7]

To demonstrate the strategic importance of aliyah, Sharett made use of the problem of the future of the Negev (the southern part of the country). This was an area which at the time greatly concerned Israel's leaders and which also generated a great deal of Soviet interest, in view of various attempts to exclude it from Israel's territory:

The Jews have won the campaign for the Israeli Negev and for the time being we have succeeded in this, we ... have eliminated the Bernadotte Plan and have also enjoyed military victory, but can we settle for that? No. We cannot be satisfied with that because these victories alone do not yet ensure our rule in the Negev; so long as the Negev is unpopulated and undeveloped we cannot justify to the world our domination of the Negev, unless we fill it with people and development. Without many people we cannot do this.

The operative demand to the Russians was baldly presented in the summation of that conversation: "If we want to build the state [of Israel] it is vital to make every effort to bring masses of Jews from Eastern Europe."

This argument was repeated during the course of several meetings between Israeli leaders and diplomats and representatives of the U.S.S.R.: by Ben Gurion, who met Yershov, the Russian Minister in Israel, on 28 December 1948;[8] by Sharett to the Soviet envoy, 23 March 1949;[9] by Golda Meir in her meeting with Andrei Vyshinsky

---

[7] ISA 2502/8 from which the following excerpts are taken.
[8] Ben Gurion diary entry for 28.12.1948, BGA.                    [9] ISA 2513/13.

in Moscow, 14 April 1949;[10] and by Sharett in his meeting with Gromyko at the end of that month.[11] The Israeli argument for mass aliyah from Eastern Europe as a direct and natural outcome of the Soviet bloc's basic support for the creation of the state of Israel was also transmitted in many meetings with Eastern European representatives. The Israelis argued that such immigration had special value precisely because it came from the East of Europe. Sharett explained this simply (and in a manner he certainly would not have employed on public occasions in Israel) to Vyshinsky in a long and unanswered monologue in December 1948:

[The problem of aliyah] is not so much a question of quantity as of quality ... Our task in Israel is a pioneering one and we need people who have [already] been forged. We are greatly interested in bringing the Jews of Morocco to Israel and are making great efforts in that regard. But we cannot depend on the Jews of Morocco alone to build Israel, because they are not suitably gifted for it. We do not know what awaits us, what military and political disasters lie ahead. Therefore we need people who will withstand all difficulties and who can bear great suffering. In the past there were the Jews of Russia ... After the condition of Russian Jewry changed in the wake of the Second World War, the Jews of Poland and Rumania filled this role.[12]

Had there been real grounds for the fear that the state of Israel might collapse after 1949 without the continued assistance of the Soviet bloc, especially regarding aliyah, these arguments might have carried some weight. That, however, was not the case; the Israelis knew it, and so, apparently, did the leaders whom they spoke to in the Soviet bloc.[13] The political, demographic and military aid which the states of Eastern Europe provided to Israel was primarily intended to ensure Britain's ejection from Palestine. When this was achieved at the end of 1948, Israel's leaders indeed feared that the "honeymoon" in relations with the Eastern bloc had come to an end.

In any case, soon after independence Israeli policy-makers dis-

[10] ISA 2492/16.
[11] Friedman's despatches to Avriel on 27.4.1949, ISA 2514/11 and to the Israeli Legation in Bucharest on 22.5.1949, ISA 2493/1.
[12] See report of the meeting which took place on 12.12.1948, ISA 2502/8. The same line was taken in a meeting between the Israeli Minister in Rumania and the local Deputy Foreign Minister on 23.9.1949, ISA 2493/12. Sharett expressed a clear conception that was widely accepted within the state's leadership at that time, see T. Segev, *1949: The First Israelis* (Jerusalem, 1984) (Hebrew).
[13] On 16.6.1949 Ben Gurion recorded in his diary a meeting with Israel Barzilai, Israeli Minister in Poland, who informed him about the Polish attitude: "They do not regret their help so far. If Israel had been in danger they would have supported her again," BGA.

covered that the Soviet Union clearly distinguished between support
for the state of Israel and any form of encouragement to the aliyah
movement. Consequently, as early as the end of 1948 there already
existed a general consensus in Israeli government circles that their
efforts to increase aliyah from Eastern Europe should not concentrate
on Russian Jewry. Primary among the causes for this policy (which
has not hitherto been analyzed in detail) was the unequivocal Soviet
reaction to Russian Jewry's own manifestations of support for Israel.
This was in evidence from the moment an accredited Israeli diplomat
reached Moscow during the second half of 1948.[14] The Soviet attitude
was first articulated in a striking article published in *Pravda* on 21
September 1948 by Ilya Ehrenburg, a Soviet Jewish writer and
journalist who decisively rejected Jewish aliyah from the Soviet
Union (and from the other "People's Democracies").[15] It was further
emphasized during the second half of 1948, when Israel submitted
requests for emigration visas for relatives of families residing in Israel;
only four such exit visas were issued by the end of November 1948, to
"Jews of extremely limited labor capabilities."[16] The Israeli leadership reached the operative conclusion effectively to concede the issue
of Russian Jewry, at least temporarily, and to shift the focus of
attention to other countries in the Eastern bloc. On 13 December
1948, at the meeting of the Jewish Agency Executive, Golda Meir,
Israel's first Minister to Moscow, reported that "in discussions we
held in Moscow we tried not to touch on aliyah from Russia [to
forestall] a negative answer; at a meeting with Molotov and his aides
we raised the issue of aliyah ... not necessarily from Russia."[17]
During Sharett's meeting with Vyshinsky a day earlier, at which the
problem of immigration from the Eastern bloc was broached for the
first time at so senior a level and in so formal and candid a manner, the
Israeli Foreign Minister also was careful to explain his desire "to
bring masses of Jews from ... those countries allied with you."[18]
Golda Meir was far more specific at her farewell meeting with
Vyshinsky in mid-April 1949; she approached with a request "on a
special matter [which] does not directly affect your government ... I
refer to the question of the aliyah to Israel of Jews from Rumania and

[14] See A. Levavi's memorandum on 18.11.1948, ISA 2514/15.
[15] See G. Meir's cables to Sharett on 23 and 24.9.1948 in ISA 2325/3–4, Levavi's
memorandum referred to in n. 14 and Friedman's despatch to Sharett on 30.9.1948,
ISA 2507/8.
[16] Levavi's memorandum referred to in n. 14.      [17] CZA.      [18] ISA 2502/8.

Hungary. The Soviet Union has ties of deep friendship with these states and we request your friendly influence in the matter of immigration [from them]."[19]

The policy thus formulated was translated into action between 5 September 1948 and December 1949; in that period the Israeli Legation in Moscow passed on only a handful of requests for exit visas for old people and children (not all of which were granted);[20] during the next three years no Israeli requests were submitted, nor was there any heightened or straightforward activity regarding the general aliyah of Soviet Jewry.[21] Sharett did plan to speak to Vyshinsky regarding Soviet Jewry in December 1949 at the U.N. General Assembly, but the meeting did not take place; in any event, the intention had been not to bring up mass immigration but rather to reach terms regarding contact with Soviet Jewry and, perhaps, the aliyah of Israeli relatives.[22]

Six months later Ben Gurion noted in his diary the continuation of this approach: "I consulted with [Walter] Eytan [Director General of the Israeli Foreign Ministry], Reuven [Shiloah] and Ehud [Avriel] [two senior Israeli diplomats, Shiloah in the U.S., Avriel in Eastern Europe] regarding aliyah from Russia. They oppose raising the matter at this juncture."[23]

In a conversation (whose details remain unknown) between Sharett and the Russian Foreign Minister in November 1950, the Israeli policy was apparently maintained. This seems to have been in response to the Soviet leader's own reaction. "[It was] impossible in any way to interpret it positively as far as chances in the near future are concerned."[24] Not until the following year was the question of aliyah raised candidly and officially by Israel simultaneously in two forms. On 9 December 1951 the Israeli government for the first time approached the Soviet government in writing (in response to a Soviet approach to the Middle East countries, including Israel, not to join

[19] 14.4.1949, ISA 2492/16.
[20] See "A List of Matters Raised with the Soviet Foreign Ministry," ISA 2491/16.
[21] See *inter alia* Friedman's despatch to Avriel on 5.12.1949 in which the former informed the Israeli diplomat that a decision has been made not to raise the problem of aliyah from the Soviet Union in the prospective meeting at the U.N. between Sharett and the Soviet Foreign Minister, ISA 2493/4. See also Ben Gurion's diary entry for 1.6.1950, BGA; Walter's despatch to Avriel on 27.10.1950, ISA 2507/2; and Y. Govrin, "Israeli–Soviet Relations 1953–1967" (Unpublished Ph.D. thesis, The Hebrew University, 1983), pp. 131–59, 186–209 (Hebrew).
[22] Govrin, "Israeli–Soviet Relations."          [23] 1.6.1950, BGA.
[24] Levavi's despatch to Argaman, 15.12.1950, ISA 2397/18.

the Middle East command initiated by the Western powers – see below); Israel requested "that the Jews in the Soviet Union who wish to emigrate be permitted to do so."[25] Two weeks later Sharett raised the issue with the Russian Foreign Minister at a meeting in Paris. There, however, the Russian categorically rejected what he termed the first Israeli demand in "the question of emigration."[26] It is noteworthy that the end of that year witnessed a formal turning point on the issue; but the meaningful change, which found expression in the planning and implementation of a systematic Israeli policy regarding the aliyah of Soviet Jewry, did not occur until mid-1955.[27]

This attitude blatantly contradicted the basic aim of Israel's foreign policy. The contrast was heightened by the existence, as early as the spring of 1949, of severely pessimistic forecasts regarding the future of Soviet Jewry and the possibility of maintaining contact with that community. Thus, at the end of April of that year, the Israeli aliyah officer in Moscow commented on the mass demonstrations held by Moscow's Jews in honor of the Israeli Legation. He also described the fears of the Soviet authorities that "the Soviet Jews [might] fail to retain their civil loyalty in the event of a third world war against the West and especially against America." This might, he forecast, "lead them to decide on the territorial concentration of Soviet Jews via mass transfers to Birobidzhan. This drastic move would divide Soviet Jewry into two separate linguistic and territorial nations."[28]

Notwithstanding these fears, the Israelis backed off temporarily. One reason was their view that pressure would be unproductive, and might even harm Israel in other matters. The political, economic and internal freedom allowed to members of the Israeli Legation in Moscow was severely limited, especially since the Zionist movement possessed no bases in the U.S.S.R. Israeli diplomacy in the Russian capital was thus strictly fettered and left with very little room for maneuver beyond contacts with the Soviet authorities which were coldly official, fragmentary and irregular. The other side of the coin was the evaluation that vigorous Israeli activity on behalf of Russian–Jewish aliyah would foreclose the possibility of aliyah from Eastern European countries where, for various reasons to be dealt with below, conditions seemed to be more propitious.

[25] See ISA 341/58.
[26] See report on the meeting which took place on 22.12.1951, ISA 2594/1.
[27] Govrin, "Israeli–Soviet Relations."          [28] 24.4.1949, ISA 2496/14.

This logic worked, at least during the first four years of Israel's independence.[29] Explicit expression is found in a document written by the Director of the Eastern Europe Section of Israel's Foreign Ministry early in December 1949:

The question is if and when will our representatives be able to raise this issue [aliyah of Russian Jewry] in discussions with Soviet representatives. Two conditions have to be met: One, we have to reach a position in which we, the state of Israel, are not as dependent on the Soviet Union's stance as we are now, that we do not fear that by raising what is for them an internal matter we might ruin relations and forfeit their support for our state; [second] the tense relations between East and West must be relaxed so that the leaders of the U.S.S.R. agree to discuss their citizens with another country and so that they will be able to consider a comprehensive solution regarding mass emigration of their citizens, something that contradicts the entire atmosphere now current in the Soviet Union.[30]

It is this current of thought which explains why the first real Israeli demands for aliyah from the U.S.S.R. were not made until after the doors of Eastern European aliyah had virtually closed at the end of 1951. There is no doubt that this circumstance generated considerable frustration among Israeli policy-makers, as was poetically expressed by Moshe Sharett in a letter to the Israeli Minister in Moscow early in March 1950:

. . . your final report has arrived and unleashed a new torrent of profound fear as to what is happening and what is about to happen to Soviet Jewry. We stand helpless and forlorn before this fate.

As I write we have managed to bring about the deliverance of a Jewry that similarly appeared doomed to total severance from the body of the people and quivered helplessly in the talons of an oppressive regime. I refer to the decision of the Iraqi government to permit the emigration of Jews to Israel. This surprising turn-about was reached thanks to our unceasing efforts. Here, in a land of unenlightened zealotry and ruthless despotism, we succeeded in penetrating into its very bowels, maintaining a living connection and acting . . . In the Soviet Union we can only observe and take note, and this too only fragmentarily and partially.

From time to time the thought recurs of traveling to Moscow to get to the highest rung of the ladder. But serious doubts still mitigate against such moves: will we be allowed to arrive? And if so – will the effort bear any fruit?

[29] See Avidan's despatches to the Foreign Ministry on 20.10.1952, 4.11.1952, ISA 2493/1 and ISA 2503/2 respectively.
[30] See his despatch to Israel's Ministers in Eastern Europe on 4.12.1949, ISA 2492/14. Friedman stressed in his despatch that "I am saying all this in order to make you understand the acute problem even when it is not actual. This is just for your orientation. I warn you and stress that none of this should be known to others."

Or shall we fail and lose? And in the meantime who knows what price we will pay for this daring attempt in other parts of our international arena? Such are the thoughts that must be considered and which forestall the initiative... The tragedy of Soviet Jewry infinitely dejects my spirit and darkens all our skies.[31]

Israel's strategy during the first years of her existence was to solicit Russian support for Jewish aliyah from other Eastern European countries; Sharett feared jeopardizing this support by plunging into the issue of Soviet Jewry. The paradox was cruel: to save less than 200,000 Eastern European Jews, Israel tacitly agreed (at least for the time being) formally to ignore the fate of some two million Soviet Jews.[32] To Israel's advantage, the Soviets did not seem to be put out by what could have represented a dangerous precedent; but there was also a substantial disdavantage: this approach provided the Soviets with a convenient method of formally evading responsibility and influence over aliyah activities in Eastern Europe. Contacts between Israeli and Soviet representatives between 1948 and 1953 yield many examples of this phenomenon.[33]

Israeli Foreign Ministry officials persistently raised the question of Eastern European aliyah with Russian diplomats during this period; but as has been noted, the strategy employed gradually lost its force. Israel thus resorted to a second argument, claiming that her international orientation was not only not antagonistic to Russia but, by virtue of being non-aligned, in fact served Russia's interests. One of the outstanding experts on Eastern Europe and the U.S.S.R. in the Israeli Foreign Ministry, Arieh Levavi, wrote early in 1950:

Let us not delude ourselves that we will succeed in isolating the problem of... Jewish emigration from Rumania and Hungary from the whole of our political and economic relations with the Soviet bloc. Moreover, we cannot even isolate this problem from something as seemingly unrelated as our relations with Trans-Jordan or our voting record ... at the U.N. ... Whenever we can take a line favored by the Soviet bloc, this must be stressed to the Soviet representatives and we must try to link it to Jewish emigration.[34]

This policy too was problematic, as well be shown below, and

[31]  8.3.1950, ISA 2514/1.
[32]  See discussions of the Jewish Agency's Directorate on 10.1.1949, CZA.
[33]  One of the rare occasions when Soviet delegates agreed to talk on the subject occurred during the (Eastern) International Trade Unions' Congress in Milan in July 1949. The reason for this outstanding move by the Soviet appeared to be their willingness to prevent the secession of the Histadrut from that organization. See Friedman's despatch to Avriel on 27.7.1949, ISA 2493/4.
[34]  See Levavi's memorandum on 1.1.1950, ISA 2514/15.

became increasingly dubious as 1950 drew to a close. Israel's weak rhetorical arsenal, however, must not obscure another unequivocal fact – in all her contacts with the U.S.S.R on economic, political and strategic matters during this period, Israel never wavered in her estimation of the importance of the goal of bringing about Eastern European Jewry's aliyah and maintaining contact with Soviet Jewry. Nevertheless, the real struggle for Soviet Jewry's immigration did not begin until 1955.[35]

[35] See Govrin, "Israeli–Soviet Relations," pp. 186–209.

# 5 . THE EASTERN EUROPEAN ARENA

With the visible hardening of the Soviet Union's official stance on aliyah from Russia and Eastern Europe in general, Israel's Foreign Ministry officials realized that Jewish emigration from those regions was impossible without the consent (in one form or another) of the Kremlin. This was especially true as an anti-Zionist line developed throughout the Eastern bloc during the winter of 1948–9, with the completion of the sovietization of those countries which the Red Army had occupied during and after the Second World War. Although the Russians did leave their satellites with some internal room for maneuver, they clearly exercised ultimate control. Accordingly, and as one Jewish Agency leader, Berl Locker, put it in June 1949: "We knew that Soviet Russia was a hard nut to crack but we looked for a way to reach her."[1] Six months later, Arieh Levavi's categorical assessment was that "we must reject any Soviet attempt to claim that the emigration of Jews from Rumania and Hungary is in no way a concern of the Soviet Union."[2]

The success of Israeli aliyah activities in Eastern Europe during the two years after late 1948 seemed to verify several assumptions: that the Soviets had not banned aliyah from those lands outright; that the leaders of those countries were perhaps less rigid regarding aliyah than was the Kremlin itself; that the Eastern bloc possessed no concerted line on the issue; and that the Israeli freedom of maneuver was therefore not as restricted as had initially been thought.[3] Underpinning these assessments were two principal factors; one which will be analyzed below was the economic incentive that Israel could hold out to Eastern bloc countries, and which to a certain degree evoked a response; the second was the political and economic realities of

---

[1] See discussions of the Jewish Agency's Directorate on 27.6.1949, CZA.
[2] 1.1.1950, ISA 2514/15.                                        [3] *Ibid.*

Eastern Europe which made a partial emigration of Jews congruent with the national interests of some of the countries of the region.

## LUBRICATING THE WHEELS OF ALIYAH

In general, the Israeli interest in Eastern European aliyah clashed with the basic aims of the local regimes. The physical closure of the Soviet political system, throughout the bloc, was and remains one of its most salient characteristics. It is therefore no surprise that Israel's representatives were confronted with substantial political difficulties in their negotiations for Jewish emigration from Eastern Europe.[4] However, they did possess the advantage of having gained rich experience in such contacts even before 1948. That experience, which had occasionally been tinged with success, even outside Europe,[5] influenced Israeli activity after independence.

One of the most important tools used by the Israelis had been forged during the course of the three years in which the Mossad had been active in the Eastern bloc after the Second World War. In particular, the organizers of Eastern and Central European aliyah had then learned the uses of bribery, genteelly referred to within the Mossad as "lubricating expenses." These consisted of enormous sums of money which Mossad agents had paid to senior police or military officers, border guards and even politicians, in order that they turn a blind eye to Jewish emigration from their countries. Sometimes the bribes were paid as private transactions. The commander of the Turkish Guard responsible for passage through the Bosporus, for instance, was in December 1947 thus persuaded to permit the passage of two large ships carrying illegal immigrants to Palestine, *Pan York* and *Pan Crescent*. Local consuls in various European cities, among them those of Panama and Honduras, were "lubricated" in exchange for their willingness to ignore forgeries and misleading expropriation of their national flags.[6] In other instances,

---

[4] In his diary (entry for 16.6.1949, BGA) Ben Gurion reported on a talk between the Israeli Minister in Bucharest and the Rumanian Foreign Minister. The latter objected to the demand for aliyah on the grounds that "If we allow Jews out what would the Rumanians say? Why not let them leave? In any case they [the Rumanians] say that we have a Jewish Government." Anna Pauker, the Rumanian Foreign Minister, was born into an orthodox Jewish family.

[5] For one of Israel's significant successes, see U. Bialer, "The Iranian Connection in Israel's Foreign Policy 1948–1951," *Middle East Journal*, 39, 2, 1985, pp. 292–315.

[6] See Z. Hadari, *Refugees Defeating a Great Power* (Tel Aviv, 1985), p. 104.

however, bribes were also paid as part of quasi-official "arrangements" with governments, who – especially in Eastern Europe – were in desperate need of foreign currency after the Second World War.

A revealing and authoritative exposé of this technique was recently published (in Hebrew) by a former Mossad agent, Ze'ev (Vania) Hadari, in *Refugees Defeating a Great Power* (1985):

enormous sums of money would be passed in bags, sometimes even suitcases because of the immense number of bills. Generally the sum to be paid was not cited. The messenger would arrive with the estimated amount of money and secret bargaining would ensue there and then. As is the case in any form of business, the merchant tried for more, the Mossad agent for less. When agreement was reached the payment was made and the deal closed. Mossad officers accepted a verbal report from the messenger. If any change remained it was returned to the Mossad treasurer. The Mossad did not need bureaucratic supervision methods – its trust in people was total. The messengers themselves felt that their controllers believed their words and actions. In retrospect, one smiles at the naiveté of the bold youngster travelling to Istanbul in Turkey carrying a suitcase laden with some $50,000 intended for bribes while at the same time, to save a dollar, sleeping in a dubious hotel that possessed no safe and therefore required him to tie the suitcase to his hand and to his flea-bitten bed.[7]

Rumania witnessed the first successful attempt to use bribery in order to gain governmental consent to large-scale Jewish emigration from Eastern Europe. Beginning in mid-1946, representatives of the Mossad, including Moshe Agami and Shaike Dan, pursued negotiations with Rumanian government representatives. Ultimately, the latter agreed that 50,000 Jews would be allowed to leave on condition that the emigrants give up their property, waive any indemnification and take no money out of the country. In addition, however, the Mossad had to pay what was termed a "poll tax" for each Jew leaving Rumania. Only then did the *Smyrna* (*Max Nordau*) leave Rumania with 1,700 "illegal" immigrants to Palestine on board. Illegal immigration from Rumania reached its peak late in 1947 with the embarkation of the two ships *Pan York* and *Pan Crescent*, carrying over 15,000 Jews between them.

The second instance in which "lubricating funds" were paid to a government was Bulgaria. The affair began with the attempts of Mossad emissaries to gain the consent of the authorities in Sofia for the transit of Jewish emigrants from Rumania to Israel in January

[7] Hadari, *Refugees*, pp. 53–4, on which the following account is based.

1947.[8] That month, at a meeting between Shaike Dan and Yitzhak Frances, a prominent Bulgarian Communist, the Israeli explained how aliyah was likely to bolster the struggle against British imperialism and assist in the establishment of an independent Jewish state. The Bulgarian countered: "In this case the struggle against British imperialism in Palestine, or the possibility of the establishment of a Jewish state, interests me less than the possibility of getting foreign currency for the Bulgarian government." Negotiations were broken off and no results achieved. But in June of that year the Mossad emissary managed to reach agreement with Bulgarian government representatives for the transit of 24,000 Rumanian Jews in return for the payment to Bulgaria in foreign currency of a "poll tax," plus transit expenses, for each Jew. The Bulgarian government charged $50–$60 for each foreign Jew leaving Bulgaria via the port of Burgas.[9]

The Mossad emissaries did not rest on their laurels. As 1947 drew to a close, they tried to come to an agreement with the Bulgarian government for the emigration of Bulgarian Jews as well. Initially, no bargain was struck. In the words of one historian of Bulgarian Jewry, who was himself one of the participants in these attempts: "At first the government refused to grant a general permit for regular aliyah; afterwards a higher sum was demanded for each emigrant. The price seemed exorbitant to the Haganah [Mossad] agent and he rejected the offer."[10] None the less, when the Mossad succeeded in raising a suitable sum, an arrangement was reached, in mid-February 1948, for the payment of $100 for each Jew leaving Bulgaria.[11]

Because the relevant documents in Israel remain classified, it is hard to say exactly how much ransom money of this kind was paid in Rumania and Bulgaria.[12] But at a rough estimate some $5 million seems to have entered the Rumanian and Bulgarian coffers as a result of aliyah transactions. We have no evidence of such arrangements with other countries in Eastern and Central Europe prior to Israel's independence. There is no doubt, however, that in Poland, Czechoslovakia and Hungary, as in Rumania and Bulgaria, personal

---

[8] The following account is based on H. Kishalis, *History of Bulgaria's Jews* (vol. 4) – *Bulgaria Behind the Iron Curtain 1944–1952* (Tel Aviv, 1969), pp. 235–8 (Hebrew).
[9] See Hadari, *Refugees*, p. 104.
[10] Kishalis, *History of Bulgaria's Jews*, 4, p. 238.
[11] *Ibid.* and Hadari, *Refugees*, p. 104.
[12] It should be noted that the subject is still considered sensitive in Israel whose authorities decline to declassify relevant documents.

bribes were handed over, even to persons of high political and professional standing, as a standard part of the Mossad's activities.[13]

This method required a great deal of financing and here, too, the experience acquired during the course of aliyah activities in Eastern Europe prior to May 1948 proved to be useful and significant. The organization of aliyah involved numerous other expenses, notably payment for land and sea transportation and main'enance of the refugees from their departure until their disembarkation in Palestine. Despite efforts to finance these activities independently after the Second World War, the Jewish Agency managed to raise only one-quarter of the tremendous costs involved;[14] the bulk came from the American Jewish organization known as "the Joint" (the American Jewish Joint Distribution Committee). The Joint's support was clandestine, reflecting its ambivalence to Mossad activities: the organization's leaders were sensitive to the preservation of the Joint's posture of legality and to the absence of direct links with the Zionist movement. They also felt uncomfortable about contributing to illegal activities which were directly harmful to Britain, America's ally. Under these circumstances, the Joint's assistance to the Mossad had to be secret; indeed, it was not defined in any official document. Nevertheless, opponents of aliyah were certainly aware of the Joint's role. When British Foreign Minister Ernest Bevin reviewed the Palestinian problem in parliament early in December 1947, he strongly alleged that illegal immigration into Palestine would not be possible were it not financed by the Jews of America through the Joint.[15] Historical evidence now available entirely supports Bevin's claim.

It is hardly surprising that the technique employed before independence was viewed as promising after May 1948 as well. The past success of the *modus operandi*, the complexities of aliyah from the Eastern bloc (which Israel's statehood did not reduce) and the continuity of personnel and of organizations involved all contributed

[13] One of the Mossad's emissaries reported to a research institute in Israel that in the Eastern European country to which he was assigned prior to Israel's independence, he used to pay bribes to high-ranking officials and to transfer the money to their secret bank accounts in Switzerland. In a report to the Israeli Legation in Moscow on 15.5.1949, Friedman wrote that "Bricha" (illegal emigration) from Hungary had reached the number of 2,000 per week and that "The Hungarian authorities do not interfere," ISA 2513/13. It is most probable that in this case, as in many others, the technique of personal "lubrication" had been successfully applied.
[14] The following account is based on Hadari, *Refugees*, pp. 94–105.
[15] See his speech in the House of Commons on 11.12.1947, quoted by Hadari, *Refugees*, p. 103.

to the view that bribery be employed as a legitimate means of promoting Israel's fundamental interest. As much emerged during the winter of 1948–9, when a series of meetings were held between Israel's senior representatives in Eastern Europe (including Golda Meir, Ehud Avriel and Israel Barzilai) and officials of the Foreign Ministry and Jewish Agency in Israel.[16] They culminated in a decision to "travel the road we took in Bulgaria – payment per person." According to Yitzhak Raphael, head of the Jewish Agency's aliyah department, "this method, which succeeded in Bulgaria, will succeed ... in other countries as well because they need foreign currency and another form of help that we can offer. Of course there was no objection [to this suggestion at our discussions]. I gave my opinion to [Moshe Sharett] and he did not oppose our investigating the possibility in each and every country."

Not surprisingly, the Joint was expected to pay for this activity, as it had financed others in the past. As Yitzhak Raphael phrased it, "the money is transferred by the Joint to the state treasury without it reaching the Jews; that is the agreement, otherwise we cannot work." The files of Israel's Foreign Ministry for the first years of statehood prove unequivocally that the end of 1948 and beginning of 1949 witnessed tremendous efforts to apply the Bulgarian model to other Eastern European countries. Success was perhaps not impressive, but aspirations persisted for several years.

The first approach was to Hungary, whose significant potential as a source of immigrants made it a prime target for Israeli aliyah efforts. As early as January 1949 a plan was formulated and presented laconically by the head of the Jewish Agency's aliyah department to his colleagues: "In Hungary it has been agreed with the Joint to raise $2.5 million to bring out 50,000 people."[17] In the expected bargaining the negotiators were instructed "to begin with $25 per head and to bargain ... even if it costs $40–$50 [per person] we will pay." Contacts were to take place in Budapest using Joint officials rather than Israeli representatives – further evidence that from the end of the Second World War the Joint was the major financial source maintaining Hungarian Jewry and its institutions. The local authorities

---

[16] See Y. Raphael's report to the Directorate of the Jewish Agency on 10.1.1949, CZA on which the following account is based.

[17] Meeting of the Jewish Agency's Directorate on 10.1.1949. This forum was informed on 8.4.1949 that the Joint had decided to allocate most of its budget, $40,000,000, to enable the aliyah of 220,000 Jews.

encouraged activities which brought so much foreign currency into
Hungary.[18]

Early in 1949 the Zionist Federation in Hungary was disbanded,
lending greater urgency to aliyah activities. On 6 April of that year,
the Director of the Eastern Europe Section in Israel's Foreign
Ministry reported on talks between Joseph Schwartz, a Joint leader,
and senior officials in the Hungarian Foreign Office in which
attempts were made to "find a solution [to the problem of aliyah] on
the Bulgarian model but at a higher rate."[19] Two weeks later the
Hungarian Interior Minister informed Israel's Consul in Budapest
that his government had taken a decision in principal regarding
aliyah: "at first relatives would be permitted to leave and at a later
stage younger people as well."[20] This announcement accelerated
Israeli efforts. The Joint representative in Hungary made a generous
financial offer to promote the matter, details of which are not known.
Unfortunately, that move was not coordinated with the local Israeli
Consulate, a fact that was to hinder negotiations with the Hungarians
during the coming months. The Director of the Eastern Europe
Section in Israel's Foreign Ministry notified the Israeli Legation in
Rumania: "The opinion here is that Dr. Schwartz exaggerated in his
offer there and that we may be able to reach a more modest sum on
our part. If we are quick to give everything that is demanded we will
become an address for increasing demands [from others] that we will
not always be able to meet. [On the other hand] . . . the very request
for money proves that not only we need something, but that the other
side does too."[21]

Negotiations were protracted and arduous. Israeli diplomats were
in contact with Hungarian authorities but "at the stage where the
offer was translated into figures . . . Schwartz took over."[22] At the end
of May Hungary proposed that 1,000 Jews be permitted to leave in
exchange for $1 million. Israel's Foreign Minister and the Jewish
Agency's directors decided to reject the offer.[23]

Three reasons apparently brought about the Israeli decision. First,
the price seemed too high and the number of Jews too low; secondly,

[18] See a despatch from the Israeli Legation in Budapest to the Foreign Ministry on
29.3.1951, ISA 2387/14.
[19] ISA 2513/1.        [20] ISA 2513/18.        [21] 9.5.1949, ISA 2493/1.
[22] Friedman's despatch to Barzilai on 25.5.1949, ISA 2412/2.
[23] Meeting of the Jewish Agency's Directorate on 12.6.1949, CZA; Friedman's
despatch to Israel's Minister in Prague on 22.5.1949, ISA 2493/4; and the diary of the
Eastern Europe Section in the Israeli Foreign Ministry on 8.6.1949, ISA 2513/18.

the Hungarians demanded an Israeli undertaking not to assist illegal emigration in the future;[24] finally, the sides disputed the composition of the emigrants. The Hungarians agreed to permit only elderly relatives of persons who had left Hungary for Israel long before the proposed agreement. Israeli objections were obvious.[25]

During the course of these negotiations, however, Hungarian agents gave the Israelis to understand that an initial agreement was likely to pave the way for mass emigration at a later time.[26] This prospect undoubtedly tempted Israel to reach an agreement with Hungary, however harsh the terms. In mid-July Avriel protested against the decision to reject the Hungarian offer: "in my opinion [there is no] other way but to purchase souls; we cannot renew negotiations if we create the impression that the agreement between Vas [Hungary's Deputy Foreign Minister] and Schwartz was nullified because of us."[27] Two weeks later the Hungarian government put forward a radically different proposal: 3,000 Jews in return for $1 million.[28] The Israeli government considered $300 per emigrant too high and rejected the offer, also citing the restriction of the emigrants to "elderly persons."[29] This decision was vehemently opposed by a number of aliyah activists, including Avriel, Golda Meir and Yitzhak Raphael. They argued that Israel had to accept the Hungarian offer principally because it represented a precedent: "It is a vital matter that can seal the fate of 160,000 Hungarian Jews."[30] This pressure, together with the fact that the Joint representative had already carried out certain *faits accomplis*, in the negotiations with the Hungarian government, brought about a change in the Israeli position; during the last week of September 1949 Israel decided to accept the Hungarian offer.[31] The Hungarians were to permit the

24 Y. Raphael's report to the Directorate of the Jewish Agency on 12.6.1949, CZA and Avriel's despatch to Sharett on 19.7.1949, ISA 2414/1.
25 Raphael's cable to the Jewish Agency in Jerusalem on 5.8.1949, s6/5024, CZA.
26 See a report to the Israeli Foreign Minister on 29.5.1949, ISA 2513/1 and Avriel's despatch to Sharett on 19.7.1949, ISA 2414/1.
27 The diary of the Eastern Europe Section on 15.7.1949, ISA 2513/18.
28 See B. Locker's report to the Directorate of the Jewish Agency on 7.8.1949, CZA.
29 See Raphael's report to the Directorate of the Jewish Agency on 22.8.1949, CZA. In his cable to Arthur Lurie on 17.8.1949 Sharett wrote that the Israeli decision was a direct result of an assessment that a consent to the Hungarian proposals would "block" further emigration from Eastern Europe and that most of the Jews selected for emigration by the Hungarians would prove a "liability" and not an asset to Israel, ISA 2329/13. 30 ISA 2329/13.
31 The following account is based on Ofek's letter to Raphael on 21.7.1949; Dr. Langens' despatch to the Eretz Israel Office in New York on 4.5.1950, s6/5024, CZA;

aliyah of 3,000 Hungarian Jews, most of whom were the parents of children or the children of parents already in Israel on 1 January 1949, as well as others over the age of fifty-five. In exchange, the Joint was to pay the Hungarian government $1 million, a quarter of which was to cover the costs involved in the actual emigration.

Sharett's instructions to Avriel were guarded. They clearly reveal Israel's hesitation to allow her official seal to appear on this agreement, as well as her reservations regarding the Joint's management of the negotiations: "Only because we have no choice," the Israeli Foreign Minister stated, "and if it is completely clarified that the implementation of the agreement depends on the Legation's signature on a proposed protocol, are you hereby authorized to sign the document. The government shall inform the Joint that henceforth it is to refrain from entering into any binding agreements with Eastern European governments regarding emigration to Israel without the consent of the Israeli government." For their part, the Hungarians were also interested in keeping the agreement as quiet as possible. Early in November 1949, the Israeli Minister in Budapest reported to his Foreign Ministry that he had been warned that the publicity given the agreement in Israel and abroad might cause its cancellation.[32]

Israel hoped that this agreement would be followed by others. In mid-November Shmuel Friedman, Director of the Eastern Europe Section of the Foreign Ministry, informed the Israeli Minister in Moscow of his hope "that after this agreement we will be able to conduct negotiations for a sequel; the positive side of the matter is that at any rate something has moved in Hungary."[33] Two weeks later he reported to Sharett that "the impression from the talks [in Budapest] is that the Hungarians will be ready for another agreement immediately after the aliyah of the 3,000."[34]

The Israeli diplomats were to be disappointed. The "aliyah of the 3,000," as it was termed in internal memoranda, was a lengthy process. One major reason was the Hungarians' intentional creation of delays and complications.[35] Obviously, so long as the aliyah covered by the agreement was not completed, the Hungarians were

Sharett's despatch to Avriel on 26.9.1949, ISA 2502/15; and Ben Gurion's diary, 20.9.1949, BGA.
[32] See Blomberg's despatch to Raphael on 4.11.1949, s6/5024, CZA.
[33] 14.11.1949, ISA 2513/14.
[34] 28.11.1949 ISA 2513/1.
[35] See a report by the Eastern Europe Section in the Israeli Foreign Ministry on 1.9.1950, ISA 2492/14.

unlikely to sign another agreement, despite the hopes that the same techniques could in fact be used again in order to facilitate aliyah.[36] Direct contacts were renewed at the end of 1950, when the bulk of the agreement had been implemented; they bore no fruit.[37] The Hungarians excused their lethargy by accusing Israel of refusing to permit the return to Hungary of those Hungarian immigrants to Israel who now sought to leave.[38]

Nevertheless, the Israeli hope of achieving aliyah through "lubrication" did not waver. During the course of July 1951, Israel's Consul in Budapest, Shmuel Bentsur, met Dr. Charles Jordan, the Joint's agent in Hungary. Jordan indicated that his organization was about to terminate its activities in Hungary, mainly for lack of funds. Bentsur claimed he was "convinced the Hungarians had few sources of hard currency outside the Joint and that if the budget were cut off, ways would be sought in Hungary to cover the deficit, in my opinion even by permitting aliyah."[39] Tentative movements in this direction seem to have been made during the next few months,[40] but they produced no results.

The Hungarian incident is unique; that was the only Eastern European country where open and official use of bribery was successful. No evidence exists to indicate such attempts in Poland or Czechoslovakia. In this sense the Rumanian case belongs to a separate category and deserves treatment in some detail.

Legal emigration from Rumania, it will be recalled, took place between 1946 and 1948 on the basis of an agreement calling for a "poll tax" on each Jew leaving the country. We do not know the entire substance of a second agreement, concluded between the Rumanian government and the Israeli representative, Mordechai Namir, in February 1948. As has already been noted, on behalf of the Rumanian

---

[36] See Walter's despatch to Eliashiv on 17.12.1950, ISA 2492/6. Israeli diplomats realized that a direct "purchase" of aliyah by the Joint had been highly improbable. The reasons seemed to be the lack of funds and most probably the certain publicity which accompanied the "aliyah of the 3,000". See report of a meeting late in November 1950 between Eliashiv and Dr. Schwartz in ISA 2429/6.
[37] See report from the Israeli Legation in Budapest on 7.9.1950, ISA 2502/15; a despatch from the Director of the Eastern Europe Section of the Israeli Foreign Ministry to the Israeli Minister in Belgrade on 26.10.1950, ISA 75/9 and a report from the Israeli Legation in Budapest on 16.2.1951, ISA 2492/12.
[38] See a report of the Eastern Europe Section on 5.11.1950, ISA 2513/1.
[39] See his despatch to Levavi on 18.7.1951, ISA 2387/14.
[40] For hints, see Walter's despatch to Bentsur on 11.7.1951, ISA 2497/6 and also a report to the Knesset's Defense and Foreign Affairs Committee, ISA 2457/21.

government Anna Pauker permitted the emigration of 5,000 Rumanian Jews per month; the emigrants undertook automatically to renounce their Rumanian citizenship and the Israeli authorities accepted responsibility for arranging transport from Rumanian ports. Only 3,600 persons had left under this agreement by the end of that year, at which point legal aliyah was halted.[41] Since the Rumanian authorities had demanded an individual "poll tax" in the agreement that preceded the embarkation of the two large illegal immigrant ships at the end of 1947, it is reasonable to assume that they did not easily relinquish this source of foreign currency when negotiating a second agreement at the beginning of 1948 (although no direct evidence on the matter has been declassified to date in the Israeli State Archives). In the event, the arrangement finally reached in February 1948 apparently did not stipulate payment.[42] From mid-1948 until the Rumanian decision one and one-half years later to permit mass aliyah, the Israelis repeatedly attempted to change the status quo by offering a "poll tax" as the basis for an aliyah agreement. In mid-April 1949 the Israeli Minister to Rumania reported that he had learned from "very reliable" sources that the Rumanian Politburo had decided "positively regarding [Jewish] emigration in exchange for hard cash and the decision has been passed on to Russia for endorsement."[43]

In the light of this information, the Israelis were ready to copy the "political lubrication" model of Budapest on to Bucharest. At the end of May 1949, Friedman wrote to the Israeli Minister in Poland, citing criticism within the Foreign Ministry of the Joint's exaggerated financial offers to Hungary; "we want to begin with lower offers on our part in Rumania."[44] In the same letter he added, "we know that the other side [Rumania] is willing to go this way, but there has been no news since the other side expressed its desire that we send someone in this matter." One reason the Israelis anticipated that "lubrication" would be effective was that an agreement had been reached that month between the Israeli representative in Bucharest and members of the Rumanian government. This had enabled the release of several heads of the local Jewish Funds arrested for monetary and other crimes by the local authorities, in exchange for "an enormous sum"

---

[41] See a report on aliyah from Rumania which was prepared in the Foreign Ministry during May 1953, ISA 2457/19.                    [42] Private sources.

[43] Friedman's cable to Sharett on 18.4.1949, ISA 2329/12.

[44] 25.5.1949, ISA 2412/2 on which the following analysis is based.

transferred by Israeli diplomats.[45] Senior Rumanian sources also hinted that the Rumanians were prepared for a deal. In mid-June of that year, Israel's Minister in Bucharest reported to Ben Gurion that "in Rumania nothing can be done without money – from the bottom to the top. The Party demands money too ... Anna Pauker recommended [Jewish aliyah] on humanitarian grounds for a specified sum."[46] None the less, tentative approaches made from the second half of May by the Israeli diplomat in Rumania and others proved fruitless.[47] The current Israeli assessment was that the financial factor, *inter alia*, could effect a positive Rumanian response. As Berl Locker of the Jewish Agency reported, "[the Rumanians] want money, and lots of it."[48]

Despite disappointment, the local Israeli Legation insisted that "complete distrust of such an arrangement should not be expressed." Thus, during the second half of 1949 contacts between the Rumanians and the local Israeli Legation continued. Moreover, although no official agreement was then reached, internal memoranda prepared in Jerusalem, proposed – and discarded – plans for aliyah against payment.[49] The Rumanian decision to permit large-scale aliyah reached at the end of that year thus came as a surprise, not having been coordinated with Israeli representatives.[50] It seems to have been

---

[45] Friedman's despatch to Namir on 15.5.1949, ISA 2513/13.

[46] Ben Gurion's diary, 16.6.1949, BGA.

[47] In reports which the Israeli Minister in Bucharest submitted to the Foreign Minister in Jerusalem on 7 and 10 June 1949, he disclosed that "in one conversation with the [Rumanian] Prime Minister he proposed a certain arrangement concerning aliyah and gave numbers," ISA 2513/18. See also a despatch from the Israeli Legation in Bucharest to the Eastern Europe Section on 30.5.1949, ISA 2493/12.

[48] See protocol of a meeting of the Jewish Agency's Directorate on 19.6.1949, CZA. The Israeli Minister in Bucharest was at that time of the opinion that the reason for the Rumanian refusal was that his "[Financial] proposal had been too low." See Friedman's despatch to Avriel on 17.7.1949, ISA 2493/4.

[49] See a despatch from the Israeli Minister in Rumania to the Eastern Europe Section on 29.9.1949, ISA 2493/4; a report on a visit by the Rumanian Minister to Israel's Prime Minister on 13.10.1949, ISA 2411/7; and Friedman's despatch to Namir on 14.11.1948, ISA 2513/14. In a conversation with the Rumanian Minister for Labor and Insurance on 5.12.1949 the Israeli Minister in Bucharest proposed "special income" and "extra transportation fees" for a mass aliyah, ISA 491/11.

[50] In early December 1949 Israel suggested to the Rumanian Foreign Minister that an aliyah of 5,000 people would be carried out by Israeli ships and that the sum of $50 per head would be paid to the Rumanian National Travel Organization. See a despatch from the Israeli Minister in Bucharest to the Eastern Europe Section on 8.12.1949, ISA 2493/12. In a working proposal he submitted a day later to Ben Gurion, the Israeli diplomat recommended, *inter alia*, "The preparations of the financial means which would be needed as a reward for the aliyah," BGA.

brought about by internal political considerations, unconnected directly or substantively with the financial incentives Israel had proposed over the preceding two years.[51] These incentives had indeed created an atmosphere more amenable to immigration negotiations during the latter half of 1949, but subsequent assessments in the Israeli Foreign Ministry and Mossad indicated that the Rumanians were motivated by other considerations, and merely exploited Israel's willingness to provide financial indemnification.[52] Recently released Israeli documents do indicate that some arrangements were made, including a special rate (quite separate from "travel expenses") of several dozen dollars paid by Israel to the Rumanian travel agency for each immigrant.[53] When mass aliyah from Rumania ceased early in 1952, Israel does not seem to have offered Rumania direct payment for the release of its Jews. The reasons can be found in later Israeli interpretations of the Rumanian motivation for their late-1949 decision to permit emigration.

TRADE AGREEMENTS

Prior to May 1948, the Mossad's representatives had been able to offer the governments of Eastern Europe little beyond bribery in exchange for aliyah. After that date, matters changed. Admittedly, "lubrication" was still practiced; but during the first five years or so of Israeli independence the prospect of mutual economic ties proved to be a greater inducement. The Israeli aim was threefold. First of all, Israel's economy during that period was very clearly based on the import of industrial and agricultural goods.[54] To a certain extent, trade relations with Eastern Europe had existed even before Israel's

[51] See Avriel's despatch to Sharett on 29.6.1950 and a despatch from the Eastern Europe Section to the Israeli Chargé d'Affaires in Budapest on 5.8.1951, ISA 2502/15.
[52] *Ibid.* See also Aviezer Shlosh's despatch to the Foreign Ministry on 7.2.1950, ISA 2493/1. This impression was confirmed during the author's interviews with Mr. Moshe Avidan (an official of the Eastern Europe Section at that time) on 21.3.1985 and with a former leading Mossad emissary (who dealt directly with this issue) on 19.4.1985.
[53] See n. 49. Early in August the Rumanians had demanded that the "transportation fees" be raised from $55 to $90. It is not clear whether the Israelis concurred. See Eytan's despatch to Walter on 4.8.1950, ISA 2463/14.
[54] The following account is based on B. Meron's memorandum of 13.8.1951, ISA 1664/2; H. Eliasberg's memorandum on "Israel's Commercial Agreements," 19.4.1953, File no. 4519/c/2051, Ministry of Commerce and Industry, Israeli State Archives (henceforth MCI); and on the following two books (in Hebrew), N. Halevy and R. Klinov, *The Economic Development of Israel* (Jerusalem, 1968), and M. Michaeli, *Foreign Trade and Capital Imports in Israel* (Tel Aviv, 1963).

independence. Rumania and Czechoslovakia were Israel's almost exclusive sources of wood; Poland supplied coal for industry; Rumania and Hungary furnished foodstuffs of all sorts; and Czechoslovakia provided various machines and industrial products. The maintenance of these links was not only natural, but also vital, especially in view of the absence after 1948 of relations between Israel and the Arab countries and the geographic proximity of the Eastern bloc to Israel. Eastern European products could not only continue to arrive with relative speed and at comparatively low cost; some of them could also be paid for with Israeli exports (oranges, juices, textiles, false teeth, buttons, razor blades, etc.). Moreover, trade agreements facilitated this traffic.

To keep things in perspective, however, it should be noted that Israeli purchases in Eastern Europe never rose above 10% of her total imports between 1948 and 1955. Indeed, the absence of essential credit facilities in that part of the world generally kept the figure as low as 5%. It is therefore not surprising that Israel's major motivation in developing economic ties with the Soviet bloc was not limited to the narrow economic context. Political considerations were much more important. Israel's purchases from the Eastern bloc outbalanced her sales there; Israel paid for the surplus with foreign currency of which the Eastern bloc was in vital need. This provided Israel with a means of applying pressure for aliyah.

Overriding both of these considerations, however, was a third factor. Abandoned Jewish capital lay frozen in Eastern Europe as a result of large-scale aliyah. Although she gave little publicity to the fact, Israel had a distinct interest in using this Jewish capital to pay for part of her purchases. Her aim was thereby both to save foreign currency and, far more important, preserve the finances and property of hundreds of thousands of Jews which otherwise would have been lost. It was in consideration of this circumstance that, early in 1949, Israeli officials formulated what they termed the policy of "transfer."[55]

The above elements can best be understood if the hitherto totally neglected bilateral commercial relations between Israel and each Eastern European country are analyzed in turn.[56]

[55] See report on the subject on 24.2.1949, ISA 2513/18. See also D. Horowitz's letter to E. Kaplan on 12.4.1949, File no. 5625/c/16/18/4 of the Finance Ministry in the Israeli State Archives (henceforth FM).
[56] It should be noted that only a limited amount of Israeli Foreign Ministry's material on economic relations with the Soviet bloc has been declassified in the Israeli State

*Poland*

Israel began attempts at establishing economic ties with Poland in October 1948, shortly after the arrival of her first Minister to Poland, Israel Barzilai. Writing to Moshe Sharett at the end of March 1949, in the midst of economic negotiations towards a trade agreement, Barzilai stated: "I do not believe, simplistically, that we can buy aliyah with a trade agreement, but the trade agreement is an extremely helpful factor as far as aliyah is concerned – and this is not simply a matter of assessment or guesswork. Decision-makers tell me that they view this not only as an important indicator of relations between [our] countries; but also as the acid test which will directly influence aliyah. This we hear from important people in the state and from our friends there."[57]

Barzilai's assessments were based on information to the effect that the question of large-scale immigration from Poland was to be settled in the first months of 1949, and that the Polish Cabinet was divided on the issue. Beyond creating an atmosphere conducive to talks with the Poles, Israel was interested in coming to an agreement whereby local Jewish capital could be used in order to pay for some of her trade deficit with Poland. Obviously, this was a problematic issue for the Poles.

After three months of negotiations, Israel and Poland signed a trade agreement on 21 May 1949. This stipulated that Israel was to purchase from Poland, by the end of May 1950, goods to the value of over $16 million. Most of the sum was to be spent on products vital to Israel (foodstuffs, iron, wood, pharmaceuticals, piping, etc.); but Polish pressure and threats to break off negotiations led Israel also to purchase goods of which she was in less need (lead, cotton, cloth and clothing totaling $3.75 million). Under the terms of the agreement Israel was to pay for 63% in foreign currency and 20% through Israeli exports to Poland of goods hitherto not purchased by Poland from

Archives. There are apparently two reasons: one is technical and financial and the other involves political considerations with regard to certain transactions with Eastern European countries ("money for Jews"). As a result, the very important files of the Foreign Ministry's Economic Section have not yet been released and shall not be opened in the near future. Nevertheless, it is still possible to deduce the general lines of this aspect of the relations between Israel and the Eastern bloc.

[57] 31.3.1949, ISA 2492/20. The following account is based on the above despatch; on a memorandum on the subject written at the end of January 1950, File no. 5510/c/531/02, Prime Minister's Office, Israeli State Archives (henceforth PM); and on a memorandum of 14.6.1951, MCI 4588/c/51/57/1.

Israel (razor blades, dental drills and scrap iron).[58] The remaining
17% of the transaction was to be financed by the transfer of Jewish
emigrants' funds. The Polish government permitted each emigrant to
take out of the country $150–$200 at the official Polish exchange rate
(i.e., 400 zlotys instead of 1,700–2,000 zlotys at the unofficial rate). In
addition, the Polish Interior Minister expressed his willingness to be
accommodating on two further matters. First, if emigrants were to
deposit the remainder of their cash in zlotys in a closed bank account,
the Polish government would be ready to negotiate the release of those
funds. Secondly, the Polish government was prepared to negotiate
with Israel on Jewish property appropriated in Poland. On the basis
of these two announcements, Israel hoped that trade links would
create an amenable basis for discussing the Jewish funds frozen in
Poland, which at the time totaled some 150 million Polish zlotys –
$375,000. However, even as it stood, the agreement benefited Israel
by allowing her to use some $3 millions worth of local Jewish capital
(a respectable sum at that time) within the framework of the
agreement.

Poland permitted Jewish emigration in significant numbers some
eight weeks after the trade agreement was signed. Israel saw a
connection between the two circumstances, and a memorandum
prepared for Ben Gurion announced: "Time has proven this prognosis [Barzilai's – see above] correct." But the signature of the
agreement did not ensure its full implementation and the Israelis soon
confronted an embarrassing situation. One reason was related to
domestic stringencies within Israel itself. At least some of Israel's
purchases were to be carried out by private Israeli companies; but for
this unusually large sums of money were required. Israel feared that
failure to implement the trade agreement was liable "first and
foremost to harm aliyah." Accordingly, at the end of January 1950,
during a peak in aliyah from Poland, special measures had to be taken
to allocate extraordinary foreign currency funds.[59] In addition,
however, conditions within Poland were not altogether conducive.
Polish Jews were apparently unwilling to deposit their foreign currency (possession of which was illegal) into the special bank accounts
from which Israel was to buy goods; they were "afraid of investiga-

[58] This represented a drastic change from the previous scope of commercial relations
between the two countries. In 1947, for example, trade between the two countries
reached the sum of $760,000 worth of imports and $250,000 worth of exports.
[59] See Meron's letter to Kaplan on 29.1.1950, FM 5316/c/9/4/1.

tions and arrest," the Israeli Legation's advisor in Warsaw reported
at the end of 1950. The Israeli representatives in Poland suggested an
arrangement whereby emigrants could deposit their money in the
Polish National Bank anonymously; but the Polish Treasury rejected
this proposal.[60]

By August 1950, sixteen months after the agreement was signed,
Israel had still managed to meet less than half her dollar commitment
to Poland, the "transfer" amounting to only some $1.5 million.
Austerity in Israel had forced her to forgo non-essential commodities
and had created an acute deficit in foreign currency.[61] Early in
January 1951, the Polish authorities announced that Jews would no
longer be issued with passports: the mass emigration of Polish Jews
was about to end.[62] Nearly 50,000 Jews remained in Poland, one-
third of whom would have emigrated to Israel had the authorities
permitted. This, together with the uncertainty of exactly how intractable the Poles were in their decision, were behind the continued
Israeli attempts to use economic agreements as incentives for permitting increased aliyah from Poland. At the end of January a Polish
trade delegation arrived in Tel Aviv for discussions; for three months,
the Israelis pressed for a second commercial agreement.[63] But, as was
characteristic of all representatives of the Eastern bloc, the Poles
proved to be very hard bargainers. "The typical line of negotiations
taken by this [the Polish] delegation," wrote the Director of the
Economic Section of the Israeli Foreign Ministry early in 1951, "is
inflexibility stemming from the fact that they are bound in the
smallest details to specific instructions from the Center ... This
inflexibility of course leads to extremism even on minor questions and
lends discussion the character of hard bargaining. Sometimes one
cannot help feeling that negotiations are being conducted with a
troupe of puppets animated by some far-off Center."[64]

Israel's major problem during these difficult talks, however, was
that of the "transfer." At the beginning of 1951 the Poles had made it

[60]  See a report on the implementation of the agreement on 13.6.1950, *ibid.*
[61]  See Teslers' letter to Levavi on 11.10.1950, ISA 2514/4 and a report by the
Economic Section of the Israeli Foreign Ministry on the commercial agreements
between Israel and foreign countries on 14.6.1951, MCI 4588/c/51/57/1.
[62]  See Niv's letter to Levavi on 16.1.1951, ISA 2502/11.
[63]  See reports by the Eastern Europe Section on 20.2.1951, ISA 2491/14 and on
13.3.1951, ISA 2513/1.
[64]  See report on the commercial agreement with Poland on 9.4.1951, MCI 4938/c/2/
AA, and a report of the Eastern Europe Section on 20.4.1951, ISA 2492/14 on which the
following account is based.

clear that large-scale emigration was over. During the economic discussions held during the first months of that year the Israelis realized that the Polish decision was final. The Poles refused to discuss the "transfer," claiming that the movement of emigrant funds stipulated in the earlier agreement "had ended together with the cessation of immigration from Poland." They also refused to discuss the fate of Jewish funds in Poland. Israel estimated that some £1 million was involved in these two categories. The first issue, however, was a key one and the Polish refusal to consider it during the economic talks confronted Israel with the risk that discussions might be discontinued entirely. In the event, Israel ceded on this point, primarily because she still hoped that an agreement would open the door to subsequent talks regarding emigrants' funds and aliyah.

The new agreement also increased the ratio of reciprocal trade over foreign currency payments by Israel. Definitely in Israel's interests, the change apparently reflected the shortage of goods currently available in the world market, which made the Poles less anxious for Israel's foreign currency. In addition, and no doubt as a consequence of Israel's disappointment regarding emigrants' funds, she refused to purchase non-essential goods. Eventually an agreement was reached for trade amounting to $5,600,000; 41% was to be paid for in foreign currency and 59% by Israeli exports. This sum and the terms of payment were clearly linked to the cessation of large-scale aliyah from Poland.

Although Poland's position on emigration remained consistent after early 1951, Israel still hoped for a change and her representatives in Poland continued to advocate economic concessions in order to further aliyah.[65] Israel's economic difficulties were, however, now pressing; and, as it became increasingly obvious that Poland was determined not to permit aliyah or the transfer of emigrants' funds, her ability and willingness to take extraordinary steps in this sphere declined. The deterioration of Polish–Israeli relations, as expressed by the expulsion of the Israeli Envoy in December 1951,[66] and the withdrawal of the U.S.S.R.'s minister in February 1953, put a stop to economic relations between Poland and Israel for a long time.[67] Earlier, in the course of 1951, Israel's imports from Poland had

[65] See, for example, Laron's despatch to the Foreign Ministry on 12.5.1952, ISA 2492/2.
[66] See report to Israel's legations abroad on 2.1.1953, ISA 112/18.
[67] See summary of a consultation with the Foreign Minister on 30.8.1953, ISA 2498/5.

reached nearly $2,600,000 and exports to Poland some $170,000. In 1952 imports equaled $2 million and exports only $50,000.[68] At the end of September 1952 Israeli imports from Poland totaled $11,100,000 and exports to Poland reached $3,400,000. The transfer of Jewish capital equaled $1,500,000 and Israeli payments in foreign currency amounted to $6,150,000.[69]

From mid-1953, despite the thaw in relations between Israel and the Soviet bloc, and despite the new trade agreements signed in Warsaw on 15 June 1954, Israel no longer focused on Poland as a target for trade agreements and economic allowances in exchange for aliyah concessions.[70] The scope of trade was not defined in the terms of this agreement; but Israel estimated it would reach $2.5 million on each side.[71] Two years later, a report submitted to the Director General of the Israeli Foreign Ministry outlined the major developments of this period:

An agreement exists and the turn-over shows an increase. Currently, it is some $3 million in each direction . . . They are serious purchasers of tires, citrus fruit and, in the future, of phosphates and chemicals as well. We are interested in buying from them metal products and such agricultural produce as sugar. We sense good intentions on their part but they are not doing all they can to increase reciprocal trade . . . We have asked them to negotiate with us on renewing the agreement in Israel, since previous negotiations were held in Poland. We must remind them of this offer and encourage them to take part in the talks, in which we are very interested, for increasing exports.[72]

As far as Israel was concerned, trade relations between 1951 and 1956 thus became divorced from the aliyah issue.

### Hungary

Israel's first trade agreement with an Eastern European country was signed with Hungary and went into effect in January 1949. Archival material on the agreement is meager: the terms of the agreement

[68] See summaries in ISA 2512/8.
[69] See Bartor's report to the Minister for Industry and Commerce on 6.10.1952, MCI 419/c/2051.
[70] See, for example, Bentsur's despatch to Avner on 24.1.1954, ISA 2503/8.
[71] See a report on Israel's relations with Eastern Europe in 1954 on 15.2.1955, ISA 2511/9.
[72] See a memorandum on 17.5.1956, ISA 2415/33.

stipulated that Israel was to purchase $10 million worth of goods from Hungary and Hungary $2.5 million worth of goods from Israel. Thirty percent of Israel's imports were to be paid for by means of "transfer" and the remainder in foreign currency.[73] In discussions held during September and October 1948, Israel viewed the possibility of an agreement as extremely important, especially since it would call for the availability of "transfer" funds at a figure higher than that agreed upon with any other Eastern European state. This was seen as an obvious potential influence on opening the gates of Hungary to Jewish emigration. Israel therefore undertook to purchase non-essential goods from that country.

The 1949 trade agreement represented an enormous expansion in the scope of reciprocal trade; Hungary's trade with Mandatory Palestine, for example, had amounted to only $500,000 in 1947. The Hungarians were also certainly interested in developing further trade relations, and took the unprecedented step of sending a Commercial Attaché to Israel in mid-February 1949, even before the Hungarian Legation in Tel Aviv had been established.[74] Nevertheless, the terms of the agreement were only partially implemented, mainly because of economic difficulties in both Israel and Hungary. In 1949 Israel purchased less than one-fourth of her commitments ($2,121,000); exported just over one-tenth of the Hungarian commitment ($298,000); and made use of only one-seventh of the anticipated "transfer" funds (some $506,000).[75] Israel's interest in maintaining economic relations, however, was clear even after the agreement expired at the end of 1949; and although at that point an agreement was reached facilitating the legal emigration of 3,000 Jews from Hungary (see above), this figure fell far short of the potential. Israel therefore looked upon renewing the agreement as a worthwhile tactic that could create conditions amenable to further aliyah negotiations

---

[73] See diary of the Eastern Europe Section of the Israeli Foreign Ministry for 3.5.1949, ISA 2513/18; Meron's letter to Kaplan on 29.1.1950, FM 5613/c/9/4/1; and Meron's memorandum of 18.6.1951, MCI 4588/c/51/57/1.

[74] See Friedman's despatch to Namir on 22.2.1949, ISA 2513/13.

[75] See details in ISA 2457/21; there is little doubt that Israel's lack of experience in international commerce accounted for the unrealistic obligations she took upon herself in the agreements with Hungary and with other countries. See, for example, Meron's letter to Kaplan on 29.1.1950, FM 5615/c/9/4/1; and Levy's letter to Kaplan on 1.3.1950, *ibid*. The poor quality of Israel's exports was sometimes another disturbing factor. Thus, for example, a consignment of cocoa from Israel which reached Hungary during 1949 and which should have contained 22% fat had only 16%. See memorandum referred to in n. 76.

and, of course, to the continued removal of Jewish capital from Hungary.

An Israeli delegation was sent to Budapest at the end of the first week of 1950 and for the remainder of the month attempted to negotiate a new trade agreement.[76] The central problem that arose in these discussions was the ratio of "transfer" funds and of foreign currency. From their own sources the Hungarians had learned of the terms of other agreements Israel had signed (e.g., with Poland) and apparently also of the "transfer" then being offered to the Czechs. They claimed that they had been mistaken, late in 1948, when allowing 30% of the agreement to be paid for through "transfer" funds. A second problem was that a considerable portion of the Israeli exports offered during 1949 did not meet Hungarian specifications. Israel was therefore forced to pay in foreign currency for 60% of her purchases in Hungary for the duration of the first agreement instead of the anticipated 45%. This was an important Hungarian bargaining counter in her demand to reduce the quantity of Israeli exports offered her in the second round of talks. In the accord finally signed Israel committed herself to purchase goods to the value of some $4 million. Unlike the first agreement, Israel's list of imports comprised only essential goods. Israel undertook to pay for these imports by means of exports equivalent to 25% of the transaction's value, the "transfer" figure was to be 20% and the remainder in foreign currency.

Both Israel and Hungary attempted to fulfill the terms of the agreement during that year. In August 1950, in meetings between a Hungarian trade delegation and Israeli negotiators held in Israel, the parties reached agreements intended to overcome their difficulties; the Hungarians exhibited greater flexibility in providing essential goods to Israel and evinced some willingness to accept greater percentages of the payment in "transfer" funds and Israeli goods.[77]

In most of the internal debates in Israel regarding Hungarian emigration at the time, there was a general feeling that economic cooperation between the two countries might be a valuable way of

---

[76] The following account is based upon Friedman's circular despatch to the Israeli representatives in Eastern Europe on 14.2.1950, ISA 2491/14; Bartor's despatch to Bentsur on 23.2.1950, ISA 2512/3; Levy's letter to Kaplan on 1.3.1905, FM 5613/c/9/4/1; and a memorandum to members of the Israeli Cabinet on 8.3.1950, PM 5519/27/531/03.

[77] See a circular despatch by the Eastern Europe Section to Israeli legations on 1.9.1950, ISA 2491/24.

softening Hungarian opposition once the "aliyah of the 3,000" was completed. Thus it is not surprising that the economic agreement was renewed for a further year early in 1951.[78] The list of goods and terms of payment remained unchanged; but the future purchases of each side were not predetermined. The main reason for renewal of the agreement seems to have been Israel's inability to carry out the original terms. Thus, for example, in 1950 Israel purchased goods from Hungary on a scale approaching $1,700,000 instead of $4 million as stipulated, and exported some $300,000 worth of goods instead of the $1 million called for. This was considerably less than had been planned, but none the less brought the total Jewish capital saved in Hungary at that time to over $1 million.[79] Neither did this figure encompass all of the Jewish capital transferred from Hungary to Israel via transactions between the two countries. For example, in negotiations prior to the 1950 agreement, the Hungarians were ready to sell Israel goods (mainly foodstuffs) outside the formal accord and were willing to accept payment in local Hungarian currency at the black market rate, paid in part by local Jews who could also pay in dollars. Particulars of this transaction are lacking; but it apparently permitted Israel to transfer between $0.5 and $1 million of Jewish capital.[80]

In the course of the year, however, the Israeli Foreign Ministry concluded that the chances of massive aliyah from Hungary were negligible, notwithstanding the trade agreement. Hints supplied by Hungarian diplomats were unequivocally substantiated at the end of August 1951. Israeli intelligence managed to get hold of a copy of a despatch sent from the Hungarian Foreign Ministry to the Hungarian Economic Attaché in Tel Aviv containing a clear direc- tive: "You mention the fact that the Israelis hinted darkly about linking trade problems with problems of a different nature [aliyah]. This is to instruct you, Comrade Attaché, that if this *in any way* comes up, even by allusion, you are to demur completely without expressing any interest whatsoever. If necessary, and should the Israelis raise a similar problem in the future, you are hereby empowered to cease negotiations." Israeli intelligence also obtained the report of discus-

---

[78] See reports of the Eastern Europe Section on 20.4.1951, and on 27.5.1951, ISA 2513/1.
[79] See a table on the implementation of the commercial agreements with Hungary early in 1953 in ISA 2457/21; and Meron's memorandum referred to in n. 73.
[80] See Wolf's despatch to Palgi on 13.2.1950, MCI 203/c/11/4.

sions between the Hungarian Attaché and the Israeli representatives, compiled early in September 1951. This recounted that: "In the course of the negotiations the certain Israeli issue of which I informed you several times was not mentioned, and it goes without saying that, had they raised this problem in any way, I would have acted in accordance with your instructions."[81] The Israelis, however, did not entirely abandon this tack; in November 1951, for example, Israel tried to sell Hungary industrial diamonds with the hope of thereby facilitating talks on aliyah, despite pessimistic assessments of the effectiveness of such a maneuver.[82]

Israel's trade with Hungary in 1951 was conducted under the terms of the 1950 agreement but at a decreased level. Imports totaled only $700,000 and she exported some $30,000 worth of goods, taking some $100,000 of Jewish capital out of Hungary via "transfer."[83] Trade with Hungary in 1952 amounted to half of the 1951 level.[84] From this point on, Israel's interest in trade relations with Hungary was purely economic; she tended to enter into agreements for the strict exchange of goods without payment in foreign currency, in the mold of the agreements with other countries at that time.[85] By the end of December 1952 sales to Hungary had reached $950,000, imports amounted to $4,800,000; and Israel had paid some $1,400,000 in "transfer" funds and $2,200,000 in hard cash for imports.[86]

The rift between Israel and the Soviet bloc in 1953 brought about the virtual cessation of trade relations with Hungary. When negotiations were resumed in February 1954, Israel's representatives were instructed to consider economic factors only.[87] The Israelis did drop hints about "payment in free currency" in exchange for a renewed agreement on aliyah; but the Hungarians were categorically unreceptive.[88] The accord finally signed at the end of February 1954 was balanced, based on an equal but unspecified quantity of goods to be exchanged between the two countries.[89] That year reciprocal trade

---

[81]  See both documents in ISA 2512/3.
[82]  See Bentsur's despatch to Levavi on 22.11.1951, ISA 2493/8.
[83]  See n. 79.
[84]  *Ibid.* The fact was well appreciated by the Hungarians; see, for example, Avner's despatch to Levavi on 6.6.1953, ISA 2381/21.
[85]  See Bartor's despatch to Avner on 12.10.1953, ISA 2512/7.
[86]  See Bartor's letter to the Minister of Commerce and Industry on 6.10.1952, MCI 4579/c/2051.
[87]  See report of the Israeli Legation in Budapest on 28.2.1954, ISA 2493/11.
[88]  *Ibid.*
[89]  See Nedivi's despatch to Bartor on 8.3.1954, ISA 7/3.

was limited, Israel importing some $120,000 worth of Hungarian goods.[90] This increased in 1955 and 1956, yet remained relatively insignificant ($400,000 each year); it was entirely unrelated to aliyah.[91]

## Rumania

Identical motives governed trade negotiations with Rumania. As in the case of Hungary and Poland, Israel attempted to use economic incentives as a way to take Jewish capital out of Rumania and to influence Rumania's policy on Jewish emigration. Relative success in Hungary prompted the Israelis to approach Rumania as early as January 1949. In a meeting on Jewish emigration then held between Israel's Minister, Reuven Rubin, and Rumanian Foreign Minister Anna Pauker, the former proposed a $10–15 million trade agreement "that would leave Rumania with a considerable and favorable balance of foreign currency."[92] This proposal came after the Israeli Foreign Ministry had concluded that "we should make the effort to develop serious trade relations with Rumania and increase our purchases there even if, in strictly economical terms, it would be better to deal with another country."[93] Israel wanted agreements that would include arrangements for the transfer of Jewish capital, on the Hungarian, Polish and, later, Czech models. The Rumanians proved stubborn on this point, and Rumania's Foreign Minister uttered a phrase that echoed throughout Israeli–Rumanian contacts: "We do not have Jews for export, the Jews are not merchandise."[94] Rumania's stance precluded any trade accord with Israel, on Israeli terms, for several years.[95] Despite Israeli pressure in 1949, Rumania was unwilling to reach an agreement. For her part, Israel seemed hesitant

[90] For statistics, see ISA 491/9.
[91] See Bartor's letter to the Director General of the Israeli Foreign Ministry on 17.5.1956, ISA 2415/33.
[92] See report on the conversation on 21.1.1949, ISA 2449/1.
[93] See Friedman's despatch to Rubin on 8.3.1949, ISA 2493/1.
[94] See Agami's despatch to Friedman on 14.7.1949, ISA 491/11.
[95] See a protocol of the meeting between Israel's Minister in Bucharest and the Rumanian Minister of Commerce on 18.3.1949; Meron's letter to Heyman on 13.8.1951, ISA 1664/2; report on a meeting between Rubin and Tomma on 29.5.1949, ISA 24293/12; a despatch from the Israeli Legation in Bucharest to the Director of the Eastern Europe Section in the Israeli Foreign Ministry on 30.5.1949; and a report on a meeting between the Rumanian Minister in Israel and Ben Gurion on 16.10.1949, ISA 2411/7.

to make large foreign currency payments without the "transfer" being effected, especially in light of Rumania's obdurate position on Jewish emigration. Yet Jerusalem's proposals continued to stream into Bucharest. David Giladi, aliyah officer in Bucharest at the time, stated in discussions with Rumania's Finance Minister in December 1949: "We are ready to do business with you. We have items to sell you, we have beautiful textiles, a well developed pharmaceutical industry and many other products ... We are interested in good business but if [it is] connected to aliyah, we are willing to suffer a [financial] loss."[96] In order to establish some sort of economic ties with Rumania, Israel was willing to forego the formality of trade accords and instead to transact business through private firms; in this framework, during the latter part of 1949, Israel purchased goods worth $1 million from Rumania and exported to her products valued at $350,000.[97] Israel's activities were also directed at ensuring Rumania's economic advantage through special "transit" arrangements.[98]

As already noted, Rumania's decision to permit large-scale Jewish emigration at the end of 1949 came as a surprise. In the absence of any Israeli–Rumanian agreement the latter's motivation remained obscure, and Israel attempted to draw the conclusion that future aliyah from that country could be promoted. Within Israel's Foreign Ministry opinions were divided. Among others, Ehud Avriel and Moshe Agami pointed to economic interests – the trade factor.[99] Early in 1950, however, it was concluded that economics was not the central factor in relations between the countries; this assessment gained popularity as time passed. In a wordy memorandum, rare in the Foreign Ministry documents hitherto declassified, Aviezer Shlush, one of the opponents of the "positivist" view, summarized opinion prevalent early in February 1950: "it seems that trade relations between Israel and Rumania should not be viewed as a decisive factor likely to solve the question of aliyah. True, trade relations bring countries closer, but on condition that there exists a

[96] 16.12.1949, ISA 491/11.

[97] See material prepared for the meeting of the Knesset Defense and Foreign Affairs Committee on 31.1.1950, ISA 2514/8; Sternbach's despatch to Epstein on 15.8.1949, MCI 203/c/11/17; and Agami's despatch to Meron on 18.8.1949, ISA 491/11.

[98] See pp. 116–18.

[99] See, for example, Agami's despatches to Friedman on 14.7.1949, and on 15.9.1949, ISA 491/11; his despatch to Ben Gurion on 9.12.1949, BGA; and Avriel's despatch to Sharett on 20.6.1950, ISA 2503/1.

minimum of mutual understanding and goodwill. Where open enmity exists, trade relations can produce no change. From the Rumanians' point of view, an enemy remains an enemy even if objective conditions force [them to] trade with him, and there is no doubt that they view us as hostile or at least as one of their [enemies'] allies."[100]

Despite the tendency in the Israeli Foreign Ministry to subscribe to this thesis, the government did enter in 1950 into a few special economic transactions with Rumania, primarily in order to pave the way for discussions on aliyah. These were effected as reciprocal trade between the states.[101] In the first such transaction, Israel undertook to purchase various items (corn, frozen meat, wood and food oils) worth some $1 million; she was to pay 50% through exports (medicines, diamonds, citrus fruit and extracts) and 50% in foreign currency. The second transaction was much smaller; Israel purchased some $220,000 worth of Rumanian goods and paid for the entire sum in exports.

During the following years, economic relations between the two countries declined. In 1951 Rumanian exports totaled some $1,840,000; Israeli exports to Rumania were valued at $350,000. A year later trade fell even more, amounting to only $335,000 in imports and $130,000 in exports. The reduction was apparently prompted by the Rumanian assessment of Israel's inability to supply vital goods and, perhaps, by her doubts as to Israel's ability to meet commitments. At any rate, the Israeli unwillingness to make economic sacrifices for the sake of large-scale aliyah (which was on the decline) proved to be the final and decisive factor in determining commercial ties between the countries at the time.[102] Thus, with the cessation of mass aliyah from Rumania early in 1952, there emerged a general consensus among Israeli policy-makers that the disintegration of economic ties between Rumania and Israel bore no influence on Rumanian decisions regarding aliyah.[103] Representative of this con-

[100] 7.2.1950, ISA 2493/1. See also E. Halevy's letter to the Director of the Eastern Europe Section in the Israeli Foreign Ministry on 10.2.1950, ISA 2503/1.
[101] The following account is based on Levy's letter to Kaplan on 1.3.1950, FM 5613/c/9/4/1; a memorandum on Israel's relations with Rumania written in early March 1953, ISA 2457/19; and on a memorandum entitled "The State of Israeli–Rumanian Relations," 16.2.1952, ISA 2509/1.
[102] See Lador's despatch to the Israeli Legation in Bucharest on 26.8.1952, ISA 2512/4.
[103] See, for example, Avidan's despatch to the Foreign Ministry on 29.5.1952, ISA 2493/1.

sensus was the suggestion made by Israel's Chargé d'Affaires in Bucharest in September 1952 regarding Rumanian trade proposals: "[we must first decide] if it is worthwhile *for us* politically or economically to resume negotiations at our initiative ... if it is not worth our while to continue ... first and foremost economically, [then] it is best not to resume contact."[104] These assessments doubtless explain why no trade agreement was signed between the countries in 1952 or 1953, when relations between Israel and all the Eastern European countries reached a nadir.[105]

By then, Israel had herself become disenchanted with the idea that economic incentives might promote aliyah. As the Deputy Director General of Israel's Foreign Ministry wrote to the Israeli Mission in Bucharest at the end of the year: "I do not have a shred of belief that we can make any economic proposal likely to overcome a political veto. Were there no political veto perhaps [the Rumanians] would not be averse to deriving whatever peripheral profit we might offer, [but] in this case our chances are nil because we do not have any proposals of substance."[106] None the less, at the beginning of 1954 talks were held with the Rumanians on the possibility of reaching a trade agreement. These were conceived within the general political framework of relations with the Soviet bloc countries, as crystallized in Israel early in January of that year.[107] True, the declared intention was still "to gain concessions on aliyah on the basis of trade agreements";[108] but few Foreign Ministry officials shared such hopes. Negotiations continued sporadically for about seven months[109] in the course of which the Israeli diplomats were warned against deluding themselves that the commercial negotiations were likely to pave the way to talks on aliyah or family reunions – "past experience in Rumania itself and current experience in Hungary ... should serve to remove all illusions [especially in regard to] Rumania, the most difficult of [Eastern] bloc nations in this regard; even if Hungary had been conciliatory, we could not compare her position to that of Rumania."[110] On 3 August 1954, in Israel, a trade agreement and

[104] See Avidan's despatch to the Economic Section of the Israeli Foreign Ministry on 24.9.1952, ISA 2512/4. Emphasis added.
[105] For statistics, see ISA 2512/8.
[106] See Levavi's despatch on 28.6.1953, ISA 2503/2.
[107] See Bentsur's despatch to Avner on 24.1.1954, ISA 2503/8.    [108] *Ibid.*
[109] See Nedivi's despatches to Argaman on 11.3.1954, ISA 491/9 and on 28.3.1954, ISA 2512/4.
[110] See Shlosh's despatch to Israel's Chargé d'Affaires in Bucharest on 18.5.1954, ISA 2512/4.

schedule of payments was finally signed between the two countries, to the sum of $2.5 million on each side.[111] Details are not available, but it is perfectly clear that the accord was entirely unrelated to aliyah.

A report submitted two years later to the Director General of the Israeli Foreign Ministry surveyed the development of economic ties between the two countries:

Trade has expanded in the course of the last two years, but not sufficiently. The turnover is currently some $4 million per year (import and export together, more or less balanced). A trade agreement exists. Objectively speaking the turnover can be expanded to at least 8–10 million [dollars] per year, if they agree to provide us with oil for industrial uses at reasonable prices, which they promised to do a half-year ago and still haven't done. We buy their wood, various raw materials and agricultural produce and sell them citrus fruit, fruit extracts, bananas, pharmaceuticals, thread and various industrial products. Their approach to trade with us is positive, but they are slow.

The absence of any link between these problems and aliyah was fully appreciated. Indeed, the latter subject was not even mentioned in the report.

## Czechoslovakia

Economic ties between Czechoslovakia and Israel differed from those between Israel and the Eastern European states discussed above. In the first place, a military, political and economic network of relations with Czechoslovakia had existed even before Israel was established, and was strengthened after 14 May 1948. As we shall subsequently note,[112] Israel was a substantial purchaser of Czech armaments. Before independence the Jewish Agency's purchases from Czechoslovakia totaled some $12 million; another $10 million worth of goods was purchased by the end of 1948.[113] According to Ehud Avriel's estimates, Israel was then Czechoslovakia's principal source of foreign currency, contributing 25% of the total of her imported dollars.[114] Even if these estimates were somewhat exaggerated, they expressed the general state of affairs. The Czech economic–political

[111] See report on Rumanian–Israeli relations in 1954 on 1.1.1955, ISA 2507/1 and also Bartor's letter to Eytan on 17.5.1956, ISA 2415/33 which is the source for the following excerpts.
[112] See Chapter 8.
[113] See Peres' letter to Kaplan on 23.12.1948 and the enclosed list of purchases in Czechoslovakia, FM 5625/c/14/18/4.
[114] See his despatches to Kaplan on 24.7.1948 and on 14.8.1948, *ibid.*

interest in this transaction was accordingly clear; Israeli motivations are likewise hardly a mystery. Trade talks between Israel and Czechoslovakia from the end of 1948 were therefore greatly influenced by the positive experience of their earlier commercial ties. Moreover, these had become crystallized during a period when aliyah from Czechoslovakia presented no problems since the Czechs had agreed to a large-scale emigration (some 20,000 persons) at the outset of 1949.[115] Details of the contacts that brought about the Czech decision to permit the massive emigration of its Jews have not been declassified, but it is clear that there was no "lubrication" at the political level. What cannot be discounted, however, is the possible influence on Prague's decision of Israeli purchases in Czechoslovakia and activities in the sphere of "transit" arrangements (see below) during 1948–9.

Commercial negotiations between the two countries were thus clearly affected by Israel's large-scale arms purchases from Czechoslovakia and by the fact that the question of aliyah was more or less settled. The primary Israeli objective in developing trade relations with Czechoslovakia was to reach "transfer" agreements, a goal defined unequivocally by David Horowitz, then one of Israel's senior financial experts. In a letter to Finance Minister Eliezer Kaplan early in April of 1949, he wrote:

The arguments are: that every trade agreement must take into account reparations for nationalized property, transfer of capital of new immigrants [to Israel], etc. ... For these reasons ... we are interested in using the bargaining power which we have by virtue of the fact that our purchases are several times greater than our sales to Czechoslovakia in order to reach such an agreement. As time goes by, it will become progressively harder to reach any sort of satisfactory [arrangement] in the above matters and perhaps [it will] even [be] impossible, since in the meantime the immigration of Czech Jews to Israel will end. Therefore ... it would be vital to try at least to save what we can of Jewish capital and in this way to save Israel foreign currency.[116]

The first economic initiative was, nevertheless, not Israel's. As soon as Israel's governmental offices began to function, the Czechs initiated talks with the clear goal of commencing trade negotiations.[117] In August 1948 Czechoslovakia's Consul General in

[115] See Friedman's despatch to Namir on 20.3.1949, ISA 2513/13.
[116] 12.4.1949, FM 5625/c/16/18/4.
[117] The following account is based on a report on "The negotiations for a commercial agreement between the Czechoslovak Republic and Israel" on 30.3.1950, *ibid.*; the text

Jerusalem contacted various ministries in Israel and submitted a memorandum regarding most-favored-nation status and other questions that had been covered under the trade agreement between Czechoslovakia and the United Kingdom and which, as far as Israel was concerned, had expired with Israel's independence. Also in Israel at that time was Dr. Sommer, one of the directors of the Czechoslovakian National Bank, who delivered the draft of a schedule of payments to the management of the Anglo-Palestine Bank. A few months later talks were held in Prague between the Israeli Minister in Czechoslovakia, Avriel, and the Czech Financial Minister and the Deputy Minister for Overseas Commerce, Dr. Lobel. The talks led Israel to believe that an accord could be reached with Czechoslovakia which would also provide a solution to the "transfer" problem. Accordingly, the Israeli government decided to despatch a trade delegation to Czechoslovakia and negotiations were scheduled to begin in mid-March 1949.

But Israeli hopes for the rapid signature of an agreement on the Hungarian and Polish models were dashed. Negotiations dragged on for an entire year, ending with an agreement only on 20 March 1950. Czech negotiating techniques were partially responsible for the length of the talks; but several central disagreements also existed between the Israeli and Czech delegates.[118] One concerned the scope of the trade agreement and the list of goods. The Czechs insisted that only an Israeli purchase of at least four million Israeli pounds (some $11 million) would make the agreement worth their while. Obviously, the Israeli tendency was to purchase as little as possible; but on the other hand, the more Israel imported, the more feasible were hopes for a substantial "transfer" agreement. Eventually, Israel agreed to import goods worth three million Israeli pounds. The Israelis also decided to make concessions regarding Czech exports, and in many cases agreed to accept goods of which the country had no real need. The "transfer" issue was central from Israel's point of view. For the Czechs this was a difficult question "that they treated with trepidation." Throughout the negotiations they stressed their fear that their

of the agreement in ISA 530/11; Levy's letter to Kaplan on 1.3.1950, MCI 5613/c/9/4/1; and R. Ben Shalom's despatch to the Eastern Europe Section of the Israeli Foreign Ministry on 11.4.1950, ISA 530/1.
[118] The fact that relevant documentation on other agreements between Israel and Eastern European countries on this subject has not been declassified renders a detailed account of the arrangement with Czechoslovakia indicative and essential.

agreement (even in principle) might create a precedent *vis-à-vis* other countries. The Czechs were also aware that the "transfer" agreement with Poland was for a much smaller sum of money than that reached with Hungary. Not surprisingly, Czech pressure to reduce the "transfer" ratio was successful; contrary to their original instructions, the Israeli negotiators ultimately agreed that it cover 17% of the total sum of the agreement. There is no doubt that Israel's concession was dictated, *inter alia*, by her moral obligation to Czechoslovakia for armaments aid. None the less, Israel did not accede to the Czech demand for most-favored-nation status regarding duties and tariffs. After extensive discussions the Czechs accepted the Israeli reservations but clarified that their concession was being made, as the chief Israeli negotiator expressed it, "in order to prove ... their positive approach and their good-will *vis-à-vis* our young and problematic state."

The Czech undertaking to import Israeli goods to the value of one million Israeli pounds (some $3 million) was the largest reached at that time. The "transfer" agreement with Czechoslovakia was also singular, in that the Czechs insisted that the arrangements be stipulated in detail in the formal agreement. Accords with other Soviet bloc countries had been different. They had either left the particulars of the "transfer" clause to special discussions with the national bank of the specific country (often in stages), or had not stipulated the matter in writing at all, leaving it to be independently taken care of by the national bank. The Czech agreement, however, included particulars of the arrangement together with the specific – albeit obvious – demand that silence be maintained. Now that the records have been de-classified, this fact provides historians with the details of the substance of the accords. It also permits the extrapolation of some conclusions regarding the problematics attendant upon the conclusion of the other agreements, about which information is still unavailable.

The Czech "transfer" arrangements applied to specific cases. Included were Jews who had reached Israel after 9 May 1945, and before the conclusion of the agreement, i.e., 20 March 1950, and who, at the time of their emigration from Czechoslovakia, had been Czech citizens; who had resided in Czechoslovakia during the year preceding their emigration and had lived in Israel for at least six months on the date of the request for "transfer"; and who could prove their legal ownership of the relevant property or funds in Czechoslovakia.[119]

Despite the enormous difficulties involved in exploiting the "transfer" agreement, this remained the underlying cause of Israel's interest in a trade agreement with Czechoslovakia. But the gulf between intention and capability was substantial. Israel was pressed to keep to her contractual obligations; her foreign currency reserves were low, and she had committed herself to import Czech goods without any serious regard for domestic market requirements. Consequently, few transactions were actually concluded during the weeks following signature of the agreement,[120] a fact that necessarily influenced Czechoslovakia's import of Israeli goods.[121] Trade between the two countries was limited in 1950 (which was more detrimental to the Czechs than to the Israelis), with Israel importing $186,000 worth of goods, and exporting to the sum of $560,000. Only about $32,000 were transferred from Jewish emigrant funds.[122] Trade dropped even further the next year: Israeli imports totaled some $278,000, Czech imports from Israel came to about $50,000, with $75,000 in "transfer" funds. By the time trade halted completely in 1952, in the wake of the Slansky trial and severe anti-Zionist sentiment in Czechoslovakia, Israel had exported more to Czechoslovakia than Czechoslovakia had to Israel; Israel's foreign currency payments amounted to only one-sixth of Czechoslovakia's anticipated foreign currency income under the 1950 agreement.[123]

By mid-1952 Israeli representatives in Prague viewed trade relations between the countries to be at an end,[124] principally because all Czech commerce with countries outside the Soviet bloc was diminishing. Furthermore, whereas Czechoslovakia exported many vital commodities to Israel, few Israeli products were vital to Czechoslovakia and those that she did wish to acquire were, for political reasons, unavailable. More specific, however, was the effect of the Slansky trial. It was this which clarified to Israeli diplomats that the Czech

---

[119] See Ben Shalom's despatch referred to in n. 117.

[120] See report on "The Implementation of the Commercial agreements" on 13.6.1950, FM 5613/c/9/4/1 and a circular despatch from the Eastern Europe Section of the Israeli Foreign Ministry on 1.9.1950, ISA 2491/14.

[121] See circular despatches of the Eastern Europe Section on 21.21.1950, ISA 2429/14 and on 8.1.1951, ISA 2513/1.

[122] For statistics, see ISA 2457/22.          [123] *Ibid.*

[124] The following account is based on "Report no. 15 (from Prague)" on 15.6.1952, ISA 2494/3.

authorities had come to view the signing of an agreement with Israel as a serious political crime. By the end of November 1952 Israel's Economic Attaché in Prague estimated that Israel's prospects of attaining one of the main goals of the agreement had evaporated: "According to the indictment handed down against Slansky and his partners," he emphasized, "the 17% 'transfer' was considered an integral part of the sale to Israel and thus a condition harmful to Czech interests. It can be assumed that this aspect in fact motivated the Czechs to torpedo the agreement from the outset."[125] The conclusion was obvious:

A new trade agreement and schedule of payments cannot be considered, since any ordinary trade agreement between Czechoslovakia and a non-Communist country would henceforth be considered treason; the chances of Czech agreement to a financial arrangement in general and [one involving] "transfer" in particular are even slimmer ... We can expect increasingly severe directives regarding property of Israeli residents still located in Czechoslovakia ... and expropriation of property of communities heretofore kept in trust by the courts.[126]

The Israeli Foreign Ministry accepted this assessment, and after 1952 made no serious attempts to break the ice in trade relations between the two countries.[127] Even after the general thaw in relations with the Soviet bloc in 1954, Jerusalem insisted that the two Israelis arrested during the Prague trials (Oren and Orenstein), be freed as a precondition to any economic negotiations between the two states.[128] An additional factor hindering resumed relations, as far as Israel was concerned, was the debt of $0.5 million that the Prague authorities had stubbornly refused to repay since 1951. The situation remained static for the next two years and in mid-1956 the Director of the Economic Section in the Foreign Ministry reported to his Director General that "trade to date has been completely paralyzed."[129]

[125] See Y. Gera's despatch to the Economic Section of the Foreign Ministry on 28.11.1952, ISA 2491/12.
[126] *Ibid.*
[127] For statistics, see ISA 491/9.
[128] See Bentsur's despatch to Kedar on 5.8.1954, ISA 2512/5; a report on Czech–Israeli relations on 3.10.1954, ISA 522/4; Nedivi's despatch to Shek on 12.11.1954, ISA 491/9; Nedivi's despatch to Kedar on 29.11.1954, ISA 2512/5; and a report on Czech–Israeli relations for 1954, written probably early in January 1955, ISA 523/3.
[129] Bartor's letter of 17.5.1956, ISA 2415/33.

## Bulgaria

Israel's trade relations with Bulgaria were beset by the same problems that attended those with Czechoslovakia. Since large-scale immigration from Bulgaria had ended at the beginning of 1949, Israel's principal interest in developing trade relations (as in the Czech case) was the "transfer" of Jewish capital. During the second half of 1949 the Bulgarians took the initiative, and pressed for negotiations towards a trade agreement.[130] In the exchange of messages that preceded the talks at the end of January 1950, Israel emphasized that the despatch of her trade delegation to Sofia was conditional; Bulgaria had first to agree in principle to include in any trade agreement a clause regarding the "transfer" of Jewish property and funds in her territory.[131] Since the initiative had come from Bulgaria, the Israelis assumed her willingness to conclude a transaction of the sort that had already been signed with the Poles and the Hungarians, and was currently being considered with Czechoslovakia. But the Israeli negotiators (who reached Sofia at the end of January) were to be disappointed: the Bulgarians refused to agree to a trade accord that would include a "transfer" clause. The Israelis were adamant.

Since Bulgaria rejected Israel's demands for "transfer," the two delegations agreed to try and reach a limited agreement on the basis of full reciprocal trade. Israel was not sanguine about this possibility: after four years of drought, Bulgarian grain, which represented a significant share of Israel's import, was unlikely to be available. Secondly, it transpired that a considerable portion of Israel's export list did not meet Bulgarian requirements. Moreover, since Israel had not previously developed economic relations with Bulgaria and no local Israeli legation existed there,[132] trade was hardly expected to

---

[130] See diary of the Eastern Europe Section of the Israeli Foreign Ministry for 3.5.1949, ISA 2513/18.

[131] The following account is based on a report on 30.1.1950, ISA 2457/20; Bartor's letter to Meron on 31.2.1950, ISA 2457/20; and Levy's letter to Kaplan on 1.3.1950, FM 5613/c/9/4/1.

[132] This was due to the Bulgarian request to Israel not to open a diplomatic legation until the end of the massive aliyah. Thereafter, however, especially in view of Israel's desperate economic situation, the Israelis themselves did not attach "any particular urgency" to the matter. It was only in June 1951 that Israel's Minister in Hungary was nominated as Chargé d'Affaires in Sofia. See Walter's circular despatch on 1.9.1950, ISA 2492/14 and a report by the Eastern Europe Section of the Foreign Ministry on 18.6.1951, ISA 2513/1.

expand. In the course of that year Bulgaria sent a commercial representative to Israel, and a limited reciprocal agreement amounting to $150,000 was signed and effected,[133] followed by an additional agreement, amounting to $250,000,[134] in 1952. By the beginning of 1952 other transactions of this sort, totaling about $400,000, had been carried out. In addition several small Israeli purchases were made in exchange for foreign currency. At the same time, it was arranged that Turkish Jews might purchase goods (chiefly cement) in Bulgaria on Israel's behalf. This enabled them to transfer their capital to Israel, and allowed Israel to import goods for which she did not have to pay in foreign currency.

Trade with Bulgaria remained limited during the next three years, not exceeding $1.5 million annually, mainly because Israel had set the "transfer" precondition on any trade agreement with that country.[135] At the end of December 1954 an agreement of this sort was in fact signed, as well as a schedule of payments, amounting to about $1.5 million on each side.[136] Particulars of this agreement are not available. But in view of Israel's previous vigorous opposition to any agreement that did not include Israeli payment via "transfer," it is not impossible that the Bulgarians acceded to this Israeli demand at the end of 1954.[137] Trade remained constant in 1956 as well.[138]

TRANSIT TRADE

Notwithstanding the objective economic difficulties that prevented the development of large-scale trade between Israel and the Eastern bloc, an additional economic conduit between the two sides was created. The Soviet bloc countries were in need of industrial products and raw materials that they could not obtain in the quantities and quality required – if at all – from Eastern Europe or the Soviet Union. The U.S.A.'s imposition of severe restrictions on trade between her

[133] *Ibid.*
[134] The following account is based on Kalev's despatch to Bentsur on 28.2.1952, ISA 2457/20.
[135] For statistics, see a table prepared on 12.11.1954, ISA 491/9.
[136] See a report on relations between Israel and Eastern European countries on 15.2.1955, ISA 2511/9.
[137] As much is hinted at in a report compiled by the Research Section of the Israeli Foreign Ministry, entitled "Successful Israeli Attempts to Strengthen Israel's Ties with Eastern Europe," 30.3.1955, ISA 2511/9.
[138] See Bartor's letter to the Director General of the Israeli Foreign Ministry on 17.5.1956, ISA 2415/33.

allies and the East had virtually closed the West as far as the Soviet bloc was concerned. One way to get around the virtual blockade was for the Eastern bloc states to purchase such items via "transit" transactions with non-Communist countries. Not subject to strict American supervision, the latter imported the goods from the U.S.A. or from her strategic allies, ostensibly for their own use, and immediately re-exported them to the East. By virtue of her geopolitical position, Israel constituted a potentially ideal "transit" country and soon after her independence, policy-makers in Jerusalem were quick to see the advantages that lay in such transactions. Israel first exploited this potential in the cases of Czechoslovakia and Yugoslavia.

During the first half of 1948, whilst intensive negotiations on the question of the supply of Czech weapons were in progress, Israel found herself confronted with severe funding problems. One possibility, attractive both as a solution to the immediate problem and as a method to gain advantages in other spheres, was to enter into a "transit" transaction. At the beginning of September 1948 Ehud Avriel reported to the Israeli Minister of Finance (Eliezer Kaplan) on the meetings he had held with Jan Sommer, a director of the Czech National Bank, who was in Israel that month for discussions regarding payment for Israeli purchase and other bilateral economic questions. According to Avriel's report, it was then proposed that Israel pay the Czechs by means of:

a three-way agreement between us, Czechoslovakia and countries that will sell to us but not to them. This proposal whetted his [Sommer's] appetite and in my opinion this is the way to reach a trade balance between us and several countries ... For your information, lately we have taken advantage of various connections especially via Dr. Max Kimbe[139] and Robert Abramovici (who is traveling with Sommer) in order to acquire raw materials of various sorts for Czechoslovakia and which are required for industries in [whose products] we are interested. They regard our help as an important service ... Obviously this activity is not being carried out in our name and only under conditions of the strictest secrecy.[140]

Specific information on the development of this connection is not available. But scattered evidence regarding Israeli economic activi-

---

[139] According to Avriel's despatch to Kaplan on 23.8.1948, this gentleman had rendered a considerable help to Israel "not for any reward" and "established our contacts with the [Czech] heavy industry during a much cooler period than now," FM 5625/c/16/18/1.
[140] No exact date is given, September 1948, *ibid.*

ties in Prague, initiated by Avriel, suggests that the possibility was pursued. Early in 1949, for example, the Israeli diplomat investigated ways and means to finance a loan in the United States on behalf of the Czech National Bank.[141] A stop was put to this initiative once fears were aroused that it might jeopardize Israeli interests in the United States.[142] Nevertheless, in his letter to Friedman in mid-March of that year, Avriel endorsed "increasing our economic weight by serving as agent of the type of which we spoke when I was in Israel."[143] Avriel's wife Hana has testified to the author that the question of a three-party transaction figured prominently in the meeting held between Moshe Sharett and the Czechoslovak Foreign Minister during the former's visit to Prague on 19 May 1949.[144] The special nature of this activity and the not inconsiderable risk it involved, in addition to the current Israeli decision not to declassify documentation on the matter, explain why we cannot estimate the dimensions of such activity. Of its existence and importance, however, there can be no doubt.

What is more, the Czech case was not unique. A larger and more structured attempt to arrange for "transit" was carried out in Yugoslavia. To the best of this author's knowledge, only in that instance did the Israelis try to gain specific advantages in terms of aliyah by establishing an organization for transit purposes.

Yugoslavia had always been the location of one of the most important Mossad centers in Eastern Europe. This situation was the result of the special relationship which the Yugoslavs had developed in the course of the Second World War and thereafter with representatives of the Yishuv who had operated in the framework of the British war effort. After the war, it seems to have been buttressed by ideological perceptions. As one of the Mossad emissaries in the Balkans phrased it: "The Yugoslavs saw in the [Mossad] an embodiment of the struggle against imperialism. The Yugoslavs saw the British as imperialists and foes, allies from the time of the war who had returned to their evil ways; moreover, as former partisans, they felt an emotional affinity for the small nation struggling against an enemy that vastly outnumbered and overpowered it."[145]

[141] See Kaplan's cable to Sharett on 14.2.1949, ISA 2329/5.
[142] *Ibid*. See also Avriel's despatch to Sharett on 7.1.1949, ISA 2514/14.
[143] 16.3.1949, ISA 2493/4.
[144] Letter to the author, 26.10.1984. For the visit, which has hitherto escaped the attention of historians, its press coverage notwithstanding, see ISA 2514/11.
[145] See Hadari, *Refugees*, p. 173. For the special relationship, see E. Avriel's *Open the Gates* (Tel Aviv, 1976), pp. 183–92 (Hebrew), and A. Ettinger, *Blind Jump* (Tel Aviv, 1986), pp. 181–203, 273–307 (Hebrew).

Yugoslavia's unique approach doubtless also stemmed from the fact that neither organizationally nor ideologically did it constitute an integral part of the Communist bloc.

Altogether, Mossad agents were appreciative of the immense assistance which Yugoslavia had provided to the representatives of their embryonic state before 1948, willingly and without asking for reimbursement. Accordingly, they could not refuse the Yugoslavs when in mid-1948 they requested assistance in the purchase of industrial products that the latter could not otherwise obtain, e.g., tractors, transformers, heavy trucks, heavy-duty cranes and oil-drilling machinery.[146]

By the standards of the time, the dimensions of the Yugoslav request were enormous. For precisely that reason it generated the idea that Israel might reap political benefit throughout Eastern Europe were she to establish a governmental corporation to deal with such matters. In the summer of 1948 the proposition was discussed by Efraim Ilin, an Israeli businessman living in Milan – who had previously provided the Mossad in Yugoslavia with assistance and who had become a party to putting the idea into effect – and Levi Eshkol, then Director General of the Defense Ministry. After several meetings it was decided to establish an economic corporation whose partners in equal shares would be Efraim Ilin and Avraham Friedman (another Israeli businessman) on the one hand, and the Israeli construction company Solel Boneh, on the other. The partners referred to the corporation as "Hadad" – an acronym of the initials of Hillel Dan and David Ha-Cohen, managers of Solel Boneh who, together with Meir Giron, were principally responsible for instrumentalizing the corporation on that side. According to Ilin the cooperative corporation was never formally established and "every transaction was carried out *ad hoc*." Nevertheless, several transactions were effected on behalf of the Yugoslavs, valued at many hundreds of thousands of dollars. The "Yugoslav connection" paid various political and military dividends (*inter alia*, Yugoslav permission to refuel Spitfire airplanes that Israel had purchased from Czechoslovakia at the end of 1948 and which had to be flown to Israel). Not unnaturally, it also raised hopes that the Hadad corporation's activities could be put to use in Soviet bloc countries, especially in order to soften

---

[146] The following account is based on an interview with a former Mossad emissary who prefers to remain anonymous on 19.4.1984; H. Dan, *Unpaved Road* (Tel Aviv, 1963), p. 271 (Hebrew); and two chapters of Efraim Ilin's draft memoirs. I am grateful to Mr. Ilin for allowing me access to this material.

opposition to widespread legal emigration of Jews. One important instance took place in Rumania.[147]

The Israelis first proposed commercial services of this sort to the Rumanians in October 1948. Then, as at other times, the Israelis did not propose a clear *quid pro quo* – "We will supply you with merchandise and you will supply us with Jews" – as the Rumanians were very sensitive on this point. Israel sought rather to create a more positive atmosphere for talks on aliyah. In mid-March 1949 the Rumanians agreed to enter into transit relations with Israel and at the end of that month, after a series of consultations and deliberations at the highest levels, it was decided in Israel to entrust the operation to the Hadad corporation. Israel did not make her decision lightly. Risk was always implicit in such activities, which in substance were contrary to American policy. Then, too, there were those who cast aspersions on the abilities and motivations of the major functionary in the company, Efraim Ilin. But Avriel, Shaike Dan, Shaul Avigur and Moshe Agami, Israeli's senior Eastern Europe experts, managed to carry the day in the discussions. A meeting was subsequently authorized between Hadad representatives and a Rumanian trade delegation in Prague during the first week of April.

The Rumanians were primarily interested in purchasing piping and oil-drilling machinery, but expressed many doubts regarding Israel's capability to supply the required merchandise. Accordingly, and as a preliminary step to negotiations, a meeting was arranged in Belgium between Rumanian Deputy Minister of Trade Abramovici and Ilin. The time and place of the meeting were deliberately calculated to engender the Rumanian's trust: at the end of June 1949, a ship was docked in the port of Antwerp onto which were to be loaded piping and oil-drilling machinery purchased, legally and illegally, by Hadad in Germany and intended for shipment to Yugoslavia. At the business meeting in Brussels Hadad agents, acting on instructions from Reuven Shiloah, a central figure in the Israeli Foreign Ministry (and against the advice of Mossad activists in Rumania), raised the question of reimbursement – the aliyah of Rumania's Jews. The

[147] The following account is based on sources in preceding note; a protocol of a conversation between Israel's Minister in Bucharest and the Rumanian Minister for Foreign Commerce on 18.3.1949, ISA 491/11; Agami's despatch to Friedman on 9.4.1949, ISA 491/11; Friedman's diary, 13.5.1949, ISA 2513/18; Friedman's despatch to Avriel on 22.5.1949, ISA 2493/4; Agami's despatch to Friedman on 30.5.1949, ISA 2493/12; Agami's despatches to Friedman on 22.6.1949, on 14.7.1949 and on 13.9.1949, and Rubin's despatch to Friedman on 10.8.1949, ISA 491/11.

Rumanian officials responded that they had notified the proper authorities of the demand, and that they were empowered to proceed with commercial discussions. Israeli assessments were therefore optimistic and in this spirit an agreement was initialed by the parties for the supply of merchandise worth about $1 million, the bulk of which consisted of oil-drilling machinery.

There remained one last step. After a few weeks, at the beginning of July, final agreement was reached in a session between Ilin and representatives of the Rumanian national oil company, Rompetrol. Under the terms of the transaction, which was in the range of $750,000, the Hadad corporation undertook to supply 10,000 tons of piping of various sorts, oil-drilling machinery and a few score heavy tractors; the Rumanians would pay in corn. Aliyah was apparently not mentioned in the discussions, and certainly not in the formal agreement, but there were patent expectations on the Israeli side that the transaction would bear fruit in this sphere. Israeli pressure reached a peak in August–September of that year and was articulated at a meeting between the members of the Israeli Legation in Bucharest and the Rumanian Foreign Minister Anna Pauker on 13 September. The Israeli Minister then raised the question of the true reimbursement that Israel expected to receive for the transit deal, underscoring the "efforts made to supply drilling pipes which are, as is well known, strategic materials." "As is [also] known," the Israeli diplomat explained, "purchase and shipment of this sort to Rumania is not easy [and involves] not a few political risks and difficulties."

The Israeli demand was sharply defined: "You must know," the Rumanian leader was told, "that it will be extremely difficult for us to keep [our side] of the agreement if there is no immigration from Rumania, because the government and public opinion [in Israel] will not be able to support our effort."[148] Pauker replied that "she preferred to distinguish between two problems, aliyah as distinct from trade." The Israelis understood the operative meaning of her response: "The Rumanians are not willing to discuss matters . . . in a give-and-take formula." At the same time they had not categorically refused to continue the political–economic relationship. Moshe Agami, the senior Mossad official in Rumania, concluded that while the activities of the Hadad company were not the sole factor affecting

---

[148] From Agami's despatch of 13.9.1949 referred to in n. 147. This is the basis for the following account.

aliyah as far as the Rumanians were concerned, it did exert "considerable influence." Shortly after this meeting large-scale emigration of Rumania's Jews did indeed commence.

Understandably, the Israelis involved viewed this development as a clear case of cause and effect, and still tend to do so today. Efraim Ilin, for example, considers his activity to have been the direct and almost exclusive reason for the Rumanians' positive decision on aliyah. Others have reservations, even while stressing the pivotal role played by the "transit" deal in creating an atmosphere conducive to aliyah discussions. At the time, there were many in the Foreign Ministry who apparently viewed the matter even less heroically.[149] It is striking that the Hadad company failed to follow up its success by making preliminary inquiries into the possibility of another such agreement with Rumania. Indeed, the entire organization was closed down at the end of 1949, after an Israeli assessment of the increasingly risky political effect such activities were liable to bear on U.S.–Israeli relations.[150] Israel did transact one more "transit" deal with Rumania; early in 1950 she sold the Rumanians Argentinian wool in exchange for Rumanian wheat.[151] It is to be noted that the Israelis coupled the "Wool Campaign" with Jewish aliyah in talks with the Rumanian authorities.[152]

Even after the closure of the Hadad company, Israel's ability to serve as a commercial bridge between East and West attracted other Eastern European states, and Israeli policy-makers too. Discussions on trade accords held between Israel and several Eastern European countries illustrate this fact. They also clarify the special interest which the Soviet bloc had in establishing a commercial connection with Israel in order to promote "transit" deals. One indication is provided in the summary of the negotiations preceding the signature of the second trade agreement between Israel and Hungary early in January 1950, written by Moshe Bartor of the Foreign Ministry's Economic Section: "We sensed a strong desire on the part of the Hungarians to reach a trade accord, for two reasons: (a) they see us as one of the few remaining windows to the West and they hope to use us to transfer their surplus products as well as to acquire materials vital to them from the West; (b) they are generally overstocked with

[149] See above, pp. 102–3.
[150] Hints in Avriel's letter to Horowitz on 18.11.1949, FM 5625/c/16/18/1.
[151] Meron's letter to Heyman on 13.8.1951, ISA 1664/2.
[152] Halevy's despatch to Eliashiv on 31.3.1950, ISA 2503/1.

surplus merchandise, especially foodstuffs and light industrial goods, as a result of the disruption in their trade with the West."[153]

In official conversations the Hungarians proposed that "one of the trusted transit dealers" be sent to Budapest in order to endorse transactions outside the framework of the formal trade agreement. Israel, they suggested, would thus supply unprocessed wool from South Africa, leather and several other items which they did not wish to name. Hungarian representatives were willing to receive this merchandise even on account of payments in Israeli currency within the framework of the direct accord. Alternatively, they were prepared to supply other merchandise in exchange, outside the framework of the agreement, which would be sent by transit to Israel.

The trade agreement signed at that time with Hungary, however, makes no mention of any "transit" deals. These required a great deal of time, especially since, after the end of 1949, Israel no longer maintained an economic organization for such matters. But the Israeli export list appended to the agreement does include the very items that the Hungarians sought – leather and wool – which were not then usually produced and exported by Israel. Similarly unstipulated were the dimensions of "transit" trade. But that the Israelis were, nevertheless, willing to keep their promise to the Hungarians is clearly evident from the summary compiled by the chief Israeli negotiator:

There is no doubt that our commercial relations with Hungary can be further expanded, but outside the framework of the agreement. For this I propose that we send, as per the Hungarian request, a representative of one of our commercial concerns to Budapest in order to examine and effect a transit deal ... Encouraging transit deals with Hungary is not only desirable from a purely economic point of view, in that it saves us currency, but also from the point of view of negotiations regarding Jewish aliyah where it is likely to enhance our condition, to the extent that we can become a more attractive factor for the Hungarian economy.

Considering Israel's willingness to assist Hungary in purchasing tractors in previous "transit" deals – and later hints to the effect that such arrangements had in fact been carried out[154] – as well as the

---

[153] See a report dated 13.2.1950, PM 5519/27/531/03 on which the following account is based.

[154] See report by the Eastern Europe Section on 1.9.1950, ISA 2492/14 and some Hungarian diplomatic correspondence which fell into the hands of the Israeli Intelligence in ISA 2512/3.

agreements signed with other Eastern European countries,[155] it is reasonable to assume that "transit" deals between Israel and Hungary took place in 1950–2. Notwithstanding Hungarian reticence, Israel probably also attempted to link these matters to the issue of aliyah. Clearest written evidence is provided in the records of the series of Israeli–Hungarian contacts between July and September 1951 regarding Hungarian purchases of $300,000 worth of diamonds. During the course of the talks, the Hungarians indicated a wish to exploit Israel for the "transit" of additional strategic materials worth some $10 million. The Israeli Chargé d'Affaires in Budapest stressed "the readiness to assist the Hungarians economically in three-way trade if they show willingness to reimburse us in terms of aliyah."[156] How this affair developed is not known, but it is virtually certain that several such transactions were carried out in spite of the Hungarian refusal to recognize a linkage with the aliyah issue.[157]

The Hungarian episode is only one example of Eastern European interest in "transit" deals. Reporting on the second trade accord with Poland, Moshe Bartor wrote in April 1951: "This issue ["transit" deals] was the main reason that the Poles reached a trade agreement with us. We feel that this is also the reason for dispatching the trade delegation to Israel. For they hope that through us they can get hold of embargoed goods such as metals, various chemicals, wool, etc. Their illusion in this regard has at times led them to make far-reaching concessions."[158] Although Israeli negotiators could not commit themselves to meet all the Polish demands, the agreement stipulated the supply of various "transit" goods, including wool and leather, to the value of $2 million. Though the Poles did not agree to the inclusion of a "transfer" clause, the Israeli approach was to provide "transit" goods whose "supply would not entail any political risk" in order to create good-will towards a future "transfer" agreement. As in other instances, hard data on the development of this special type of trade with Poland is not available. But the Hungarian

[155] See Bartor's memorandum on 17.6.1951, ISA 2512/8 and a despatch from the Eastern Europe Section of the Israeli Foreign Ministry to the Israeli Chargé d'Affaires in Budapest on 5.8.1951, ISA 2502/15.
[156] Bentsur's despatch to Levavi on 22.11.1951, ISA 2493/8. See also an unsigned and undated report (probably from November 1951) on the subject, ISA 1664/2.
[157] See n. 154. The Hungarian Economic Attaché received unequivocal orders from Budapest to terminate all discussions if the Israelis try to link transit trade with "certain Israeli subjects [aliyah], for it is unthinkable that the Israelis would interfere under the cover of business with internal affairs of Hungary," ISA 2512/3.
[158] 9.4.1951, MCI 4398/c/2/1/ᴀᴀ.

precedent strongly suggests that "transit" deals with Poland were probably carried out at least until the end of 1951.[159]

That year represented a significant turning-point in this form of commerce between Israel and the Eastern bloc, unrelated to regular trade. During the early fifties the United States intensified its economic cold war with the Eastern bloc, primarily by means of trade restrictions. Initially these applied only in time of war (the Kem Amendment); but regulations were tightened under legislation passed in June 1951, known as the Battle Act.[160] The United States now made the provision of foreign aid strictly conditional on the non-transfer to Soviet bloc countries of American-made war material or other merchandise in any way related to war. Violation of that condition would result in cessation of American aid. These restrictions applied to Israel as well, who (as will be discussed below),[161] was already benefiting from American economic aid.

America's intensified efforts to halt the export of vital commodities to the Eastern bloc undoubtedly created severe problems for Israel's foreign trade.[162] On the other hand, however, by tightening the embargo they also increased Israel's worth as a source of "transit" deals to Eastern Europe. Quite apart from Israel's economic interest in these transactions (not only substantial foreign currency profits but also the supply of vital commodities then hard to come by, such as steel piping and coal), there remained the questions of "transfer" and aliyah. The severity of the American restrictions jeopardized future "transit" deals involving many millions of dollars (often transacted in Trieste, Belgium, Switzerland and even Tangiers). It also threatened to stifle the development of two fledgling Israeli export industries, antibiotics – for which a growing market existed in Eastern Europe – and industrial diamonds. The latter was particularly important. In 1950 Israel exported more than half a million dollars worth of industrial diamonds, most of them to the Soviet bloc; in 1951 this figure had jumped to $3 million and, with a stock of sufficient stones to

[159] See, for example, Y. Golan's despatch to the Economic Section of the Foreign Ministry on 16.9.1951, ISA 2512/5. Mr. Golan was the Israeli Commercial Attaché in Warsaw.
[160] See the document "N.S.C. Determination No. 12: Report by the National Security Council on trade between Israel and the Eastern Bloc in light of Section 1302 of the 3rd Supplement Appropriation Act 1951," 13.9.1951, ISA 3063/13.
[161] See Chapter 10.
[162] The following account is based on Bartor's memorandum on 17.6.1951, ISA 2512/8.

supply Poland, Czechoslovakia, Rumania and Hungary at highly competitive prices, the future looked promising.

As soon as the Battle Act was enacted Israel's Foreign Ministry appreciated that the era of "transit" deals in strategic products was about to come to an end; the draconian American regulations, however, which presented a severe obstacle to the development of direct economic relations with Eastern Europe, especially in the area of industrial diamonds, generated opposition to their automatic acceptance.[163] Israel therefore decided on a dual strategy. She agreed to cease direct and indirect exports of strategic material to Eastern Europe as per the American definitions; at the same time, she approached relevant parties in Washington with a request for appropriate financial compensation, at least in regard to industrial diamonds. Specifically, she asked that American purchasing institutions agree to buy the Israeli stones for sums higher than the world market price. Totally independently of the outcome of this approach, Israel decided to commit herself to uphold the regulations; on 28 January 1952 an undertaking to that effect was submitted to the Department of State in Washington.[164] Available evidence indicates that Israel kept her word. Only one shipment of industrial diamonds was sent to Poland, early in 1952 (and even that due to a bureaucratic error). Israel did not carry out any further "transit" deals affecting strategic material or industrial diamonds to the Soviet bloc.[165] Indeed, in 1952 she even succumbed to American pressure to halt the export of antibiotics to the Eastern bloc, despite the fact that these were not included in the list of banned goods.[166] There is no doubt that the winter of 1951–2 clearly signaled the end of the period during which Israel could expect economic and political dividends from serving as an economic bridge between East and West. No longer in a position to offer Eastern Europe any economic incentive, she was thus deprived of any effective economic weapons in the struggle for aliyah and contact with Jews in the Soviet bloc.

The available archival material suggests that the idea of using "transit" deals to further aliyah from Eastern Europe was discussed only once more, early in 1953. Gershon Avner, head of the Israeli

[163] See Meron's letter to Heyman on 13.8.1951, ISA 1664/2.
[164] See correspondence in *ibid.*
[165] See a cable from the Economic Section of the Foreign Ministry to the Israeli Legation in Prague on 28.10.1951; Bartor's despatch to Levin on 8.10.1951; and Raviv's despatch to the Israeli Embassy in Washington on 6.3.1953, *ibid.*
[166] See correspondence in ISA 1664/2.

Legation in Budapest, had transmitted a proposal to Israel late in
1952 calling for a three-way deal: export of Swedish iron to Hungary
to ensure the aliyah of Hungarian Jews. The Israeli Foreign Ministry,
fearful of the implications of such an act for Israeli–American
relations, rejected the proposal. A year later the plan came up again;
this time it was claimed that the slow delivery of iron from Sweden to
Hungary (unconnected to Israeli activities) was the result, not of
American pressure, but of purely economic factors. At this stage it
was proposed that the Americans be asked to withdraw all possible
objections to speeding up the export of Swedish iron to Hungary; the
Swedes would receive economic compensation from Israel and Hungary would open her gates to Jewish emigration. But, for the same
reasons as before, the Israeli Foreign Ministry again rejected the
idea.[167]

One final element in Israel's economic relations with the Soviet
bloc deserves mention. During the early fifties Israel had helped the
Jews of Eastern Europe, as well as her own national economy, by
removing millions of dollars through "transfer" deals. Considerable
Jewish capital reached Israel by other means too. Israeli legations in
Eastern European countries used to accept foreign currency, jewels
and other valuables and transfer them by diplomatic pouch to Israel.
In return, the Jews were given chits confirming receipt and reclaimed
their possessions upon their aliyah to Israel. This activity remains
classified in the Foreign Ministry Archives, but occasional hints
indicate that its scope was considerable.[168]

[167] See, *inter alia*, Bentsur's despatches to Avner on 11.3.1953 and on 29.3.1953, ISA
2502/15; Avner's despatch to Eytan on 16.10.1953, ISA 2387/14; and Bentsur's
despatches to Avner and to Herlitz on 9.11.1953, ISA 2502/15.
[168] See a report of the Western Europe Section in the Israeli Foreign Ministry on
3.1.1951, ISA 2515/1.

# 6 . TRADE WITH THE SOVIET UNION

An analysis of the economic ties between Israel and the leading state in the Soviet bloc perhaps best illustrates two claims already partially made above. First, that Israeli trade with the Eastern bloc was unequivocally influenced by interests of aliyah. Secondly, the notable absence of references to the aliyah of Russian Jews in Soviet–Israeli relations exerted a negative influence, at least for a certain period, on the development of economic ties between the two countries.

The most prominent feature of economic relations between Israel and the U.S.S.R. between 1949 and the latter half of 1953 is Israel's failure to attempt to expand and develop them. Between 1948 and late 1949 Russia had supplied Israel with merchandise worth some $750,000, most of which was fuel, a product that Israel desperately needed during the critical months of the 1948 War and which was hard to acquire elsewhere.[1] She also sold Israel wheat, when that commodity was similarly hard to come by. However, Israel did not reciprocate with any of the steps taken in Eastern Europe in order to establish an economic relationship via trade agreements. Between mid-1948 and early 1949, the Israeli Economic Attaché in Moscow, Moshe Bejerano, repeatedly requested instructions regarding an agreement of this sort, emphasizing the enormous sales potential for Israeli goods in Russia, as well as the political benefits implicit in such a relationship.[2] Uniformly, responses from Jerusalem stressed Israel's foreign currency problems; these, it was said, imposed "priorities" on the arrangements involved in trade agreements.[3] Additional clarifications emphasized that Israel preferred to sign

---

[1] See Meron's letter to Horowitz on 11.11.1948, ISA 1664/3.
[2] See, *inter alia*, his despatches on 11.10.1948, 20.11.1948, 1.11.1948 and 18.11.1948, *ibid*.
[3] See, for example, Meron's despatch to Bejerano on 27.10.1948 and Dr. H. Grunbaum's despatch to the same man on 16.11.1948, *ibid*.

trade accords with those countries in which "transfer" transactions would provide significant advantages, as was the case elsewhere in Eastern Europe, and in Holland and Argentina. Evident – even if rarely stressed – was the supposition that the "transfer" mechanism stood no chance of success with the Russians, and that there was no real intention to raise the issue of mass aliyah from the Soviet Union at that time. In the instances of Poland and Hungary, purely economic considerations (which might otherwise have mitigated against signature of a trade agreement) were overridden by considerations of aliyah and the preservation of Jewish capital. But they emerged as the determining factor in Israel's approach to the development of trade agreements with the Soviet Union. Broader political considerations, such as the insertion of an economic "tile" in the mosaic of Israel's relations with the U.S.S.R., did not then appear important enough to outweigh economic considerations.

An early example is provided by an incident which occurred in 1949. At the beginning of that year the Israeli Economic Attaché in Moscow, working independently and without proper authorization, signed a transaction whereby the state of Israel would purchase Russian wheat to the value of some £600,000 sterling.[4] Israeli policy at the time called for the cessation of Soviet wheat purchases, mainly because Israel had signed an international wheat agreement permitting her to purchase that commodity more cheaply elsewhere. Bejerano was deeply disappointed by Israel's decision to attempt to cancel the "private deal," and argued that governmental thinking on the matter was politically misguided. "There is no guarantee," he claimed, "that this source of supply ... will respond positively [if we need to use it again] after we cast it aside in so impolitic a manner when we happened to get better terms [in the West.] I am not well versed in our foreign policy and not qualified to interfere in economic assessments but I doubt if the problem of trade with the Soviet Union ... and its economic worth has been sufficiently investigated by the cognoscenti in terms of its ... far-reaching effects. At any rate, I am almost certain that insufficient consideration was given to the external political aspect."

The official Israeli approach was even more prominent regarding the acquisition of commercial credit. In February 1949 Israel had

---

[4] The following account is based on a letter from the Economic Section of the Foreign Ministry to its Director General on 13.3.1949, ISA 2513/13 and on Namir's despatches to Sharett on 2.6.1949, ISA 2513/17 and on 7.6.1949, ISA 2514/15.

received an American loan of $100 million, which was vital for her purchases on the world market. Her acute foreign currency deficit made commercial credit a key economic question. This background explains why, virtually simultaneously, Israel approached the Soviet Union for financial credit.[5] But the two requests were very different. Israel did not seriously expect to elicit a positive Soviet response; she was principally interested in deriving political credit from what in effect was a demonstration of a balanced foreign policy. As much is evident from both the formal approach made by the Israeli Envoy in Moscow in April 1949 and from internal correspondence on the matter. The Israeli Economic Attaché to Moscow in August 1949 informed his superior that, to the best of his knowledge, Russia had never before granted credit; the only exception was a grant to Czechoslovakia designed to facilitate Czech purchase of raw materials from the West in order to fulfill the terms of export transactions to the Soviet Union. The rest of Russia's transactions, according to the Israeli economic expert, were for cash; "but I think we did well in asking for credit from the Soviet Union, even if we get no response, which usually means 'no.' If the answer is 'no' at least it will give as a convenient *excuse* . . . for the fact that trade has decreased as of March 1949 – the absence of foreign currency."[6]

Almost from the moment the request for credit was submitted, Israeli economic activity in Russia did indeed cease until 1950. In his sharp criticism of this policy in February of that year Mordechai Namir, then Israel's Minister in Moscow, pointed out that since the end of 1949 "not a single proposal has come [from Israel] for us to attempt any economic operation . . . an absolute zero in the U.S.S.R. paragraph of our trade balance will not keep us going."[7] The figures substantiate Namir's claim: in 1949 Israeli imports from the Soviet Union totaled some $400,000 and exports some $26,000; the next year imports were reduced to $20,000 worth of goods and Israeli exports to Russia were about one-third of that sum.[8] Economic logic alone

[5] The Israeli requests were made during Golda Meir's last meeting in Moscow with Vyshinsky in April 1949 (see report in ISA 2492/16); in meetings Bejerano had in Moscow in May (*ibid.*); and in a meeting on 17 May between the Director of the Eastern Europe Section of the Foreign Ministry with Mr. Muchin of the Soviet Legation in Tel Aviv, ISA 2507/8.
[6] See his despatch to Meron on 24.8.1949, ISA 1664/3 (emphasis added). On 25.11.1949 Israeli representatives in Washington were informed that the request for credit from the U.S.S.R. was mainly intended to show "good-will," ISA 2517/7.
[7] See his despatch of 3.2.1950, ISA 2512/1.
[8] For statistics, see ISA 2457/14.

determined Israeli actions the following year too. In May of that year Bartor received instructions from the Ministry of Trade and Industry regarding possible food purchases in the Soviet Union: "in the framework of the allocations to the Food Section [it is possible] to buy in Russia if the supply is better or if prices are lower."[9] In response to repeated requests from the Israeli Legation in Moscow for an Israeli economic initiative, the same source noted: "You are of course aware that the Treasury constantly faces a currency deficit; [when the American] grant funds start [to arrive] we will have to use them for urgent purchases in America or countries with whom we have special payment arrangements, and to pay current debts. If sales in Russia can get us free currency we will not be able to keep these sums for later use unless the Treasury expends them immediately for urgent payments."[10]

That remained the situation for several months, despite the fact that, at the end of 1951, Russia and Israel signed an agreement for the supply of 125,000 crates of citrus fruit worth $100,000. In the Foreign Ministry this Soviet step was interpreted as a Soviet regional tactic, prompted by rumors of the establishment of a Mideast Command at American initiative; purchases from Israel were perhaps intended to "reinforce neutrality in the Middle East."[11] Contrary to the opinion of Shmuel Eliashiv, Israel's Minister to Moscow at the time, policy-makers in Israel did not believe that the Russian step was primarily the result of special Israeli initiative; but even Eliashiv was realistic about the political and economic implications of the "orange deal." Writing to the Director General of the Israeli Foreign Ministry in February 1952, he pointed out:

It is hard to describe our pleasure when we see in food shops and on tables and in kiosks in the street the stacks of our oranges, prominent in their shape and color at the end of the gray winter in Moscow, against the background of massive drab goods. Has this influenced our political relations? I don't think there is room for illusions here and we cannot draw analogies with small countries. First of all – we are viewed here as sellers, not buyers; second – what is for us a significant transaction is negligible in terms of the astronomical figures of the local governmental market; third – after all is said and done, we are not selling vital commodities.[12]

[9] M. Peleg's letter of 20.5.1951, ISA 1664/3.
[10] His despatch to Argaman of 10.12.1951, *ibid.*
[11] (Undated) despatch in December 1951 from the Director of the Eastern Europe Section of the Foreign Ministry to Israel's Minister in Moscow, ISA 2381/10.
[12] 3.2.1952, *ibid.*

The scope and form of trade between the two countries changed during the winter of 1953–4. This was not due to any fundamental modification of the Israeli conception of her economic relations with the Soviet Union (which continued to distinguish between economics and politics), but because of Israel's fuel problems. Between 1951 and 1953 Shell Oil and Israel's Delek Company, via British firms, brought crude oil from Kuwait to Haifa for refining.[13] Despite the circuitous route it had to travel (around the Cape of Good Hope), this oil was cheaper than that brought to Israel by South American companies. During the first nine months of 1953, 374,000 tons of crude Kuwaiti oil reached Haifa. In September of that year the British–Iranian Oil Company, one of the two franchise holders of Kuwaiti oil, announced that it could no longer sell to the Delek Company because of Arab League pressure on the Sheikh of Kuwait. Shortly thereafter the same announcement was issued by Shell (whose oil was supplied by the Gulf Company, the second franchise holder of Kuwaiti oil). This meant a 40% loss in Israeli crude oil supplies, which left the country with a severe shortage.[14]

One Israeli decision made in the wake of the oil companies' announcements called for the purchase of a "certain amount" of oil from Russia. Russian oil was seven dollars a ton cheaper than any other and especially attractive in view of the fact that the Soviet government's commercial company had, early in October, approached the Israel Citrus Marketing Board with an offer to buy citrus fruit in exchange for oil, wheat and rye. At the end of 1953 it was estimated that Israel could purchase 150,000 tons of crude oil from Russia, about 15% of Israel's general consumption, and up to 150,000 tons of fuel oil, which represented no less than half of Israel's import requirements. The Israeli decision was unaffected by possible reservations about American political or economic reactions; Israel's need was too desperate for such considerations. In any case, from Israel's point of view, the Americans and British were in fact responsible for her predicament.[15]

This was not the first occasion on which the Russians had offered Israel sale of their oil. In May 1952 the temporary Chargé d'Affaires

---

[13] The following account is based on a memorandum entitled "The Disruption of Oil Consignments from Kuwait," 14.10.1953, ISA 2420/2.

[14] See memorandum entitled "Russian Oil," 14.10.1953, Bartor's report, 13.10.1953, Sharett's letter to Eytan, 14.10.1953, ISA 2420/2; and M. Sharett, *Personal Diary* (Tel Aviv, 1978), vol. 1, pp. 33–4 (Hebrew).

[15] See Sharett, *Personal Diary*, 1, p. 130.

in Israel's Moscow Legation informed the Foreign Ministry that the director of the Russian national oil company had offered to sell Israel "various petroleum products of all types" but this offer did not apparently elicit any response.[16] As is so often the case, documentation is classified; but it is reasonable to assume that, apart from the relatively low quality of Russian oil,[17] a political consideration was involved – the possible implications of such a transaction on the willingness of American and especially British oil companies to supply oil to Israel.

Discussions began in Moscow in December 1953 and in March 1954 an agreement was signed for the supply of 100,000 tons of crude oil and the same amount of fuel oil, totaling some $3 million, half to be paid for by the export of Israeli citrus fruit.[18] Three months later the Israeli Finance Ministry and the Petroleum Administration devised a plan for massive imports: 600,000 tons, worth about $10 million, 45% of Israel's total petroleum consumption.[19] Israeli economic experts considered that purchases of Soviet oil were indeed advantageous. According to Bartor's summary in August 1954:

Obviously a purchase of so large a quantity of oil from the Soviet bloc . . . has political impact. Probably Russia is very interested in such a major inroad into the Israeli oil market as it enhances her position in the Middle East. We may even be able to make economic use of this aspect in negotiations on the price and terms of payment. We should also try to exploit the situation to have our products penetrate the Russian market. [However] there is a certain risk in our dependence for such a large percentage of our oil on a source [U.S.S.R.] which tends to be motivated by variable political considerations . . . On the other hand, it is perhaps . . . politically advantageous for us in that our dependence on the supply of this vital commodity will be divided equally between East and West, which may improve our position somewhat. At any rate, for us the economic consideration of saving significant sums of hard currency is the determining factor and ultimate justification in the face of any counter-claims that may be made.

Apparently, no significant quid pro quo was presented and one of the most interesting and hitherto least known facts in Israeli–Soviet

[16] See Argaman's despatch to Bartor, 29.5.1952, FM 2952/c/138.
[17] See n. 15. It should be noted that the Russians reiterated in June 1953 their offer to sell Israel oil partly in exchange for citrus fruits. Their proposal remained unanswered; and only six months later, as a result of the oil companies' decision, did Israel accept the offer. See FM 2552/c/7138.
[18] See Kosloff's letter to the Minister for Finance, 15.3.1954, ISA 2599/8.
[19] See Bartor's letter to the Foreign Minister on 9.8.1954, ISA 2420/2 on which the following account is based.

Table 2. *Israel's trade with the Soviet Union – oil and fruits (1953–1956)*

Israel's imports from the U.S.S.R.

| Year | Industrial oil (tons) | Crude oil (tons) | Total (tons) | Total ($) | Total Israeli consumption of oil products (tons) |
|------|------------------------|-------------------|---------------|------------|---------------------------------------------------|
| 1954 | 175,000 | 100,000 | 275,000 | 3,650,000 | 1,092,000 |
| 1955 | 285,000 | 156,000 | 450,000 | 6,400,000 | 1,230,000 |
| 1956 | 285,000 | 185,000 | 470,000 | 7,000,000 | 1,350,000 |

Export of citrus fruit and bananas from Israel to the U.S.S.R.

| Year | Value |
|--------|--------------|
| 1953–4 | $2,527,253 |
| 1954–5 | $2,555,773 |
| 1955–6 | $2,102,841 |

relations in the mid-fifties is that the "oil connection" between the two countries grew increasingly close. Table 2 is clearly indicative of this development.[20]

For three years, until oil deliveries from the Soviet Union were halted in the wake of the 1956 Sinai Campaign, Russia supplied Israel with more than 30% of her oil consumption needs, 30–70% of which was paid for through Israeli exports – a boon to Israel's economic balance of payments. For various reasons, however, Israel did not utilize trade with the Soviet Union to make demands for Jewish emigration. During the early fifties, the aliyah of Eastern Europe's Jews played a role in the Israeli decision to refrain from putting such pressure on Russia: once such aliyah ended Israel still maintained her silence lest Russia accuse her of meddling in internal matters. In any case, since there was little official or public awareness in the West, especially in the U.S., of the importance of aliyah from the U.S.S.R. for Israel, the Soviet position seemed quite intractable.[21] Furthermore, although Israel purchased 8–10% of the Soviet Union's exported oil,[22] within the context of the general Russian economy this was not a significant figure. It certainly did not possess the impact attained by Israel's trade with Eastern Europe during the early fifties.

In the end, "situation logic" prevailed; economic relations between the two countries were based on a patent asymmetry beneficial to the Russians. This, of course, goes far towards explaining why the Israelis did not tie aliyah into their trade relations with the U.S.S.R. So too does the current Israeli assessment that the Soviet motives in selling oil to Israel were purely economic.[23] Finally, despite the importance of Russian oil for Israel, Israeli policy-makers felt that her interests could be best served if dependence on the Russians be temporary and limited.

For several reasons, Iran and not Russia was a preferable future source of Israel's fuel supplies.[24] The logic for this view was grounded in economic reality. First of all, gases for fertilizers and chemicals

---

[20] The source for the following account and statistics is Y. Govrin, "Israeli–Soviet Relations 1953–1967" (Unpublished Ph.D. thesis, The Hebrew University, 1983), pp. 111–12.

[21] *Ibid.*, p. 135.          [22] *Ibid.*, p. 112.

[23] See Dr. C. Nawratski's memorandum entitled "Russian Oil and the World Market," 13.11.1953, FM 2952/c/7138.

[24] The following account is based on Kosloff's report to Sapir, 24.11.1954, ISA 2420/2 and on Sharett, *Personal Diary*, 2, p. 391. In his diary, Sharett wrote on 9.3.1954 that according to Israeli oil experts "we have already tested to the utmost Britain's patience

could be extracted from Iranian oil; Russian oil was poor in chemical content. Secondly, even without taking into consideration political factors, Russian delivery was at best uncertain. Russian national consumption at the time was nearly 90% of its production capacity and any increase in consumption could eliminate surplus for export. Iranian potential at the time was fifty times greater than internal consumption and there existed no operational problems in delivering the required amounts. Moreover, in view of the limited quantities which the Russians had at their disposal, and the interest many nations had in exporting to Russia, there was a certain risk that they might be willing to pay more than Israel for oil, if only to maintain exports to Russia. Israeli experts believed that the price of Iranian oil would be linked to the international market and therefore more or less constant and one of the lowest in the world. Thirdly, Israeli interests in Iranian oil were linked to an important strategic objective – breaking the blockade of the Suez Canal. Were this possible, Iranian oil would be many times cheaper than Russian oil. Fourthly, maintaining refineries in Israel for Israeli export via international companies was feasible only if Iranian, not Russian, petroleum were used. Fifthly, it was feared that Western oil companies would react sharply and unfavorably to massive Israeli oil purchases from Russia. The general Israeli approach at the end of 1954 was thus that Russian oil purchases were of limited value. They did provide an immediate solution to the abrupt cessation of Kuwaiti supplies; they also gave Israel a bargaining counter in negotiations with various world suppliers and facilitated Israeli exports. Nevertheless, Israel did not wish to expand her oil purchases from Russia beyond the rate of one-third to one-fourth of her total consumption.

in view of our growing purchases in Russia. The hinted threats of impending abandonment of Israel by the oil companies should be taken seriously. They are already under Arab pressure and our moving in a collision course with them could decide the issue. If they leave the country it would have world-wide disastrous results – discouraging investors, cutting off commercial relations and leading to total economic isolation," *ibid.*

# 7 . POLITICAL COOPERATION

Russia's policy towards Israel between 1948 and the 1956 Sinai Campaign have been skillfully analyzed in two valuable works: Ya'acov Ro'i's *Soviet Decision-Making in Practice – The U.S.S.R. and Israel 1947–1954* (London, 1980) and Arnold Krammer's *The Forgotten Friendship* (Illinois, 1974). Both books have clarified the ergonometrics of the various Soviet moves and the dynamics in the development of Russian policy. The present book aims to broaden the scope of discussion. As a preliminary to that task, I will briefly outline the main points of the development of Soviet political support for Israel in the international arena during this period.[1]

Formal Russian involvement in the Palestinian problem commenced on 27 April 1947, when Great Britain officially requested that the Secretary General of the United Nations place the topic on the agenda of that body. Three weeks later, Gromyko enunciated Russia's official position. Addressing the U.N., he declared that if it were not possible to create a bi-national Arab–Jewish state in Palestine, the Soviet Union would support partition of the country into two independent halves. Primary among Russian interests in this position was the desire to eject Great Britain from the Middle East; potentially, at least, support for a Jewish state assured her of a political presence in the region. Russian policy was confirmed on 11 October 1947, when the U.S.S.R. officially stated that she supported the United Nations Special Committee on Palestine (U.N.S.C.O.P.) Partition Plan and when she voted in favor of partition in the General Assembly on 29 November 1947. Both before and after 15 May 1948 (and especially during the 1948–9 Israeli War of Independence) Russia actively supported the implementation of the U.N. General

---

[1] The following account is based on Ro'i, *Soviet Decision-Making in Practice*, and Krammer, *The Forgotten Friendship*.

Assembly resolution and opposed attempts to change the borders Israel established for herself at the end of the 1948 War. Accordingly, she opposed Bernadotte's mission and his report, and stood firm against the attempt to exclude the Negev from Israel's territory. To that end, she even passed on to Israeli operative intelligence information on Egyptian plans for military actions in the area. It was with these facts in mind that Moshe Sharett reported to the government in October 1948: "the Soviet bloc has stood firmly by our side; in the Security Council the Russians act as if they were our emissaries."[2]

Continued Soviet political support was forthcoming. The U.S.S.R. was one of the first states to recognize Israel; after November 1948, she also consistently supported Israel's candidacy for admission to the U.N. Matters changed, however, once Israel was formally accepted as an equal member in May 1949 and, several months later, after the signature of the armistice accords that officially ended the 1948 War of Independence. Thereafter, a pronounced change could be discerned in Russia's position towards Israel in the U.N. forum. In marked contrast to their attitude between April 1947 and early 1949, in the years to follow up to 1955 the Soviets were distinctly vague and unwilling to be drawn into U.N. discussions on Israel. In principle, they rejected the suitability of that forum for the settlement of the Israeli–Arab conflict, and consistently called for direct discussions between the parties. The Soviet Union clearly supported the Arabs, but only in the global context of the struggle against the "imperialist" powers; her basic support for Israel's right to exist remained unchanged.

In the formulation of her Near East policy, Russia's considerations were thus apparently global and not regional. Support for this contention is provided by Ro'i's detailed analysis of the Russian position on a range of issues arising from the Arab–Israeli conflict – the status of Jerusalem, the delineation of boundaries, the refugees and rights of passage through the Suez Canal. Israel's U.N. representatives were very conscious of the change in the Soviet line, which one of them described at the end of 1952: "It is indeed possible to note that at the present stage [the Russians] are helping the Arabs at the U.N. while not directly harming Israel; however, we should not delude ourselves that this is their final policy."[3] The real change in policy

[2] D. Ben Gurion, *The Restored State of Israel* (Tel Aviv, 1969), p. 302 (Hebrew).
[3] Eban's remarks in a meeting of Israel's delegation to the United Nations on 23.12.1952, ISA 2505/27.

occurred at the end of 1955, with the signature of the Egyptian–Czech arms deal. That event signaled Russia's intensive, physical involvement in the international politics of the region and constituted an open challenge to the Anglo-Saxon world. It also opened a new chapter in Russian policy towards the Arab–Israeli conflict.

A number of crises between the two countries preceded the Czech arms deal, notably the Prague trials and the "Doctors' Trials" of 1952 and 1953 (see below). Severe though they were, those crises did not match that of 1955. Neither can the latter be compared to the unprecedented Soviet Security Council veto early in 1954 which, as will be analyzed later, seemed to be a clear anti-Israel move. Even at the height of her "good" relations with Israel in 1948, Russia had consistently refused to allow cultural, scientific or social ties between citizens of the two countries. Anti-Zionist comment in the Soviet press further indicated that there was to be no "normalization" of relations between the two countries. Israel's aspirations and efforts in this regard, and the proportionate disappointment at their failure, are revealingly described in the autobiography of Israel's second Minister to Moscow, Mordechai Namir (*Mission to Moscow* (Tel Aviv, 1971)).

Although intrinsically important, the known facts do beg some basic questions: what was the Israeli perspective on such moves and on Russian motivations in general? How did Israeli decision-makers assess possibilities for, and limits on, international political cooperation on such issues as Palestine both inside and outside the U.N.? These and other topics can only be treated by an analysis which deliberately looks at matters through the eyes of the Israeli policymakers, a stratum of the case which has hitherto been largely neglected.[4]

Perhaps the most prominent influence on Israeli attitudes towards the Soviet bloc was emotional rather than rational. In many cases, their perceptions of the issues involved were colored by a mixture of feelings, comprising both political hopes and disillusionment. Although this dimension of their attitude is often difficult to analyze, its importance can hardly be exaggerated. It was certainly a unique

[4] Official Israeli documents were still classified when Ro'i and Krammer wrote their books; A. Dagan's *Moscow and Jerusalem* (New York, 1970) similarly makes no explicit use of them. Y. Govrin, "Israeli–Soviet Relations 1953–1967" (Unpublished Ph.D. thesis, The Hebrew University, 1983), is partially based on such documentation; but his use of the available material is fragmented and selective.

factor, and one which was entirely absent from Israel's relations with any other country in the contemporary international system.

Several important circumstances contributed to these feelings. One might be classified as ideological empathy. Although most Mapai leaders had recovered from their initial intoxication with the Russian Revolution long before 1948 (indeed they had become disillusioned with the way in which the Soviet Union put the Socialist ideal into practice), few were able to forget the allure of their erstwhile dream. Moshe Sharett expressed this feeling in a closed lecture delivered to Mapai members at the end of 1952: "A wonderful thing once happened in history, there was a revolution. This revolution portended much, promised much, professed much. It was like that blinding northern light, a sight full of glory and luster, as if from another world, as if the heavens had come down to the earth and lit a flame in our hearts, and yet people are attracted to the brilliance of that light, and just as a spark shines and then disappears and it seems that you can still see it, it has long been extinguished and will not shine again. This ... is what happened here."[5]

Underpinning this ideological link were two other important elements. First, the overwhelming majority of Israel's political elite after independence was of Eastern European or Russian origin. (In a pioneering piece of research on the topic Moshe Lissak states that some 78% of this elite were born in Eastern Europe.)[6] At a bureaucratic level, this vastly improved the potential quality of the state's diplomatic service. Diplomatic positions in Eastern Europe could be easily staffed by persons born in the country to which they were accredited, fluent in its language, and deeply and personally acquainted with its culture. It was also thought to serve a deeper purpose. As much is apparent from the briefing given in August 1951 to the Israeli Envoy in Warsaw. The atmosphere of his talks with his local counterpart, he was instructed, might be "improved" were he to point out that "a high percentage of Israel's residents [were] of Polish origin, and thirty members of the second Knesset had been born in Poland."[7]

The second element was a profound awareness of the tragic course of recent Jewish history in that part of the world. As Shmuel Eliashiv the Israeli Minister to Moscow (who was born in Pinsk) wrote to the

[5] From his speech at a meeting with Mapai's spokesmen, 27.11.1952, CZA A245/36.
[6] M. Lissak, *The Elites of the Jewish Community in Palestine* (Tel Aviv, 1981), p. 45 (Hebrew).    [7] 17.8.1951, ISA 2492/20.

Foreign Ministry in February 1952, "[a gentile] who comes here does not have the special Jewish burden that depresses us here. For him this is a new land he must get to know without the gloom that enwraps us."[8] Israel Barzilai (born in Neszawa, Poland), the first Israeli Minister in that country, expressed the same sentiment, in a touching despatch which he sent to the Foreign Ministry the day after presenting his credentials in Warsaw early in October 1948: "Yesterday we laid wreaths on the grave of the unknown soldier and on the monument to the ghetto uprisings. They played 'Hatikvah' [the Israeli national anthem] and there was an elegant military service. When we reached the ghetto the sky darkened and rain poured down, the heavens cried, the people cried ... You will probably find it strange, this sentimental report from a governmental representative – but please don't forget that we are talking about the Warsaw Ghetto and that our hearts have experienced much."[9]

Notwithstanding the absence of references to the emotional dimension of Israeli–Communist relations in the conventional literature, there seems to be no doubt of its importance. Specifically, it played a significant role in helping to nurture the feeling that a breach had been made in the wall which, for several decades, had separated the millions of Soviet and Eastern European Jews from their brethren throughout the world, Communism from Socialist-Zionism, the U.S.S.R. and Eastern Europe from the land of Israel. The Soviet Union's political and military assistance to the emergent Jewish state during the critical period of her struggle for independence augmented this feeling. So, too, did the major wave of aliyah from Eastern Europe. (It must also be admitted that other contributory influences were the political naiveté of the pre-state Zionist leaders and the fact that they had no direct and unmediated knowledge of the Communist bloc.) Altogether, these factors generated a hope – cautious but nevertheless tangible – that policy-makers stood on the verge of a significant turning-point in the traditional Soviet attitude towards Zionism, and that Israel would perhaps be able to safeguard and broaden its impact.

The hope may not have been great, but as will be analyzed later, the disappointment was monumental. The direct contact Israeli representatives experienced with the realities of Eastern Europe and the U.S.S.R. and with those governments' representatives in Israel,

[8] 3.2.1952, ISA 2381/10.     [9] 2.10.1948, ISA 2492/20.

left behind a depressing personal, emotional layer that was especially important in the formation of a clearly fatalistic political prognosis. A few examples will serve to illustrate this point.

Israel's inexperienced diplomats in the Soviet bloc were perhaps naturally hopeful that their duties would enable them to promote ties between Israel and the countries to which they were accredited. The conclusions they reached soon after arrival, especially in the U.S.S.R., were, however, quite categorical. At the end of February 1949 a member of the Israeli Legation in Moscow summarized six months' experience of contacts with the Russians:

Immediately after arriving we were told, and discovered for ourselves, that social relations with the Russians do not exist at all; this applies to the political, cultural and economic spheres as well. Contact is entirely restricted to business matters ... It is an unalterable rule that we never speak with a Russian except on business (and such conversation is never on a one-to-one basis, there is always a witness present), so that it doesn't matter how carefully you learned Russian – it's not worth the effort since you are not given the chance to practice this difficult and attractive language. Naturally you lose one of the central reasons for your being a diplomat here: getting to know the fascinating Russian people; here you learn the hard way ... only by rough assumptions and their prolonged testing, which is why as a rule only young and very intelligent people are sent here, prepared to stay at least two years, if not three, in Moscow. In less than that very little work can be accomplished here; under these conditions a member of the diplomatic corps is under severe pressure.[10]

Equally candid was the depiction provided the following year by the Chargé d'Affaires in the Israeli Legation in Moscow: "I am not revealing anything new when I say that all the diplomats feel that in fact there is no diplomatic work here in the sense of what is accomplished and customary in other countries. We do not meet with government representatives except on extraordinary occasions and even then you must limit yourself to a particular topic without any possibility of developing a general conversation on a specific political issue."[11] The Israeli Envoy to Moscow wrote in a similar vein to the Foreign Ministry at the end of April 1954; in response to pressure exerted from Israel that he attempt to employ customary diplomatic techniques in Moscow in order to promote Israel's interests:

I must admit that I was somewhat surprised when, in your cables, you assigned me the task of acquiring a commitment from the Soviet Foreign Office to support a special position and then afterwards ... not to be satisfied

[10]  22.2.1949, ISA 2492/16.          [11]  8.1.1951, *ibid.*

with a "vague promise" but to insist on a clear response. It seems to me that six years' experience should be enough for us to know that we don't get any clear answers or commitments here. It is extraordinary when you get a totally negative response, as when Mrs. Golda Meir approached Vyshinsky regarding weapons sales and when I approached Gromyko not long ago regarding aliyah. Even in such cases they do not say "no" outright but let you understand that you have no chance of [getting] a positive answer, as was the case in my conversation with Gromyko in 1949 regarding a loan. At other times you simply do not get a response and your conversations for the most part are monologues, and if the person you are speaking with exchanges opinions with you and makes comments you note it as an extraordinary event ... That is the most depressing thing for the man whom fate has sent to represent his country here.[12]

Under circumstances such as these, it is hardly surprising that customary rules of diplomatic behavior were sometimes cast aside. For example, at the conclusion of a most frustrating interview with a senior official of the Rumanian Foreign Ministry at the end of May 1949, the Israeli Minister could no longer contain himself. Contrary to diplomatic protocol, he shouted, "Maybe you would like to hear more? Do you have any other questions? You always sit there like statues when people talk to you!"[13] The Military Attaché in Russia expressed himself no less sharply in mid-January 1950, noting that "under these conditions ... obviously we cannot even dream of developing friendly ties at all. Of course ... there are formal relations, but these are limited to a visit to General Sarajev when the Attaché arrived in Moscow and greetings on state occasions: the First of May, Air Force Day (one day in September), and 7 November; nothing else ... these are the possibilities for contact with the Soviet army." His prognosis was obvious: "my being here is completely useless, if you ignore the personal pleasure my wife and I feel in the lives we lead here in the resort – although I must admit that even this pleasure is beginning to become dubious after ... nearly three months."[14] Much more serious than the frustration, disappointment and inability to function professionally or socially, were the conclusions that the Moscow Legation staff reached regarding the prime role of creating contact with Soviet Jewry. Ze'ev Argaman wrote in mid-February 1951:

In no way should the terms "the Legation" and "Soviet Jewry" be connected. These are two different worlds who daily grow farther apart and we can see no

---

[12]   25.4.1954, ISA 2492/17.          [13]   29.5.1949, ISA 2493/12.
[14]   Quoted in Namir's despatch to the Foreign Ministry, 15.1.1950, ISA 2495/13.

signs of any hope whatsoever on the horizon for halting this process and changing its direction. I believe that there is no Jewish community so much in need of a functioning Israeli Legation as the Russian, the most unfortunate and depressed of all Israel's diasporas, and there is no Israeli Legation maintaining less contact with the Jews than ours ... Not only is contact with the Legation or its staff dangerous, but there is also the feeling that the very mention of the term "Israeli Legation" or "State of Israel" frightens the local Jews, and very few are brave enough to endanger themselves ... and enter into a conversation with us ... Under such circumstances we cannot speak of relations between the Legation and Soviet Jews – they do not exist at all or, more correctly – the Legation does not exist at all for the Jews of the Soviet Union and it plays no role whatsoever in their condition, not even as a topic for thought.[15]

In view of the coldness, and indeed intractability that characterized the relations between Israeli and Soviet officials during the first years of Israel's independence, we can perhaps understand other incidents. In August 1951, for instance, the Director General of the Foreign Ministry appended the sarcastic label "Are the Russians Like all Human Beings?" to a briefing of Israel's overseas legations, in which he drew their attention to "rumors that Soviet representatives have lately begun to show more warmth in their relations and to be more hospitable than they used to be."[16]

Political and professional frustration were compounded by the inconveniences and petty tribulations which characterized life on the other side of the Iron Curtain – poor mail service (during 1949, for example, the diplomatic courier used to arrive in Moscow only once a month), diplomatic mail that was occasionally opened and to Israeli protest examined by the authorities, lack of telephone contact and surveillance.[17] Even when it was possible to place a telephone call overseas, it was almost always accompanied by "external intervention," as the following episode illustrates: shortly after an Israeli Independence Day celebration in 1949, Shlomo Gal, Second Secretary of the Israeli Legation in Warsaw, placed an urgent call to Paris. When the connection failed to come through he dialed the international telephone exchange operator in Warsaw and asked what was causing the delay. "I'm sorry," she replied, "we have called for our Hebrew interpreter but he has not yet arrived."[18]

[15]   16.2.1951, ISA 2492/16.           [16]  12.8.1951, CZA s41/420.
[17]   See, for example, reports in despatches dated 1.4.1949, ISA 2492/16; 6.4.1949, ISA 2513/13 and 16.2.1952, ISA 2509/1.
[18]   See R. Frister, *With All His Heart* (Tel Aviv, 1975), p. 75 (Hebrew).

Reactions to these working conditions varied. Yosef Avidar, Israel's Ambassador to the Soviet Union in the mid-fifties, used to conduct important meetings in the embassy by having participants pass notes to one another. Several months after his return to Israel he found himself in a government car taking him home to Jerusalem, holding a discussion with his wife on notes he kept passing to her.[19] Others just gave up. Gerson Avner reported in early June 1953 from Sofia that "fatalism exists ... in Eastern Europe regarding security and other arrangements in the legations. We don't bother with locks since they get into everything anyway, we don't keep guards in the legations (at least one) because the authorities know everything anyway."[20] Even though conditions were marginally better in Eastern Europe, the differences were hardly noticeable. Ehud Avriel has described diplomatic activities throughout the "People's Republics" as a personal "battlefield."[21] The reports to Israel on these experiences were extensive but, for obvious reasons, were not made public. Their message was hard to grasp: in the summer of 1950 Arieh Levavi of the Moscow Legation (later Director of the Eastern Europe Section in the Foreign Ministry) gave a series of closed lectures in Israel on life and political activity behind the Iron Curtain confirming these impressions; the typical reaction was shock and calm disbelief – "perhaps you in the Foreign Ministry don't understand properly."[22] More important than this reaction was the fact that these reports and personal experiences, far more than any dry Foreign Ministry briefing, unequivocally dashed unique hopes and aspirations affecting emotions no less than analysis. These diplomats ultimately played a crucial role in creating the fatalism of Israel's operative and political leadership *vis-à-vis* the chances of Israeli political activity in the Soviet bloc.

Political experience, too, contributed to this fatalism, it also converged with the emotional aspects mentioned above (and other factors to be discussed below) to reinforce the assessment of the limited potential inherent in Soviet political support of Israel during the War of Independence and political relations with the entire Soviet bloc thereafter. For most of Israel's political leaders, Soviet support remained enigmatic. This is not to imply that Israeli politicians were under any illusions about the motives underlying Russia's support for

[19] Personal interview, 25.2.1983.
[21] 16.3.1949, ISA 2493/4.

[20] 6.6.1953, ISA 2381/21.
[22] Personal interview, 11.5.1983.

the establishment of a Jewish state. It was clearly designed to eject
Britain from Palestine. But many Israelis did consider the Soviet vote
in the U.N. General Assembly in favor of internationalizing
Jerusalem (December 1949) a dramatic turning-point in the consistent Soviet support of Israel. Israel's Foreign Minister did not
agree with this assessment. However, in a detailed analysis to the
Mapai party he explicitly cautioned against undue optimism:

This [the Russian vote on Jerusalem], not only the decision of 29 November
[which set the principle of internationalizing the Holy City], is because their
guiding line is to get England out of Israel; [that is why] they supported the 29
November decision, not because of our beautiful eyes. Their fundamental
approach has been: England must be removed from Israel. That is all ...
everything stems from this ... in the question of Jerusalem ... every proposal
that does not include internationalization means partition, and the partition
of Jerusalem means England's fortification in the second part [of Israel] and
that must be opposed.[23]

Continued Soviet political support of Israel was an enigma first
and foremost because it deviated so markedly from the unbroken
ideological and political enmity that had characterized Russia's
attitude towards Zionism and the Yishuv for many years. Israel's
leaders were not essentially concerned with an historical analysis of
Russian motives in the past; what troubled them was the future, and
particularly the status of relations between Israel and the U.S.S.R.
once the special Soviet approach to the War of Independence no
longer applied. How far, in other words, would the pendulum of
Soviet relations swing *away* from the direction which it had taken in
1948? In April 1950 the Foreign Minister addressed the members of
his ministerial research section, issuing instructions for intelligence
activities. During the course of his remarks, he revealed several
uncertainties about the Soviet attitude:

What was the Soviet Union thinking of when it decided to support the
establishment of the Jewish state? Was it the dynamic nature of the Yishuv
that they considered? I think that the Soviet Union was ignorant about the
Yishuv ... i.e. that the establishment of the state involved construction and
the immigration of Jews from the Diaspora ... It is very possible that the
Russians did not take into consideration the full significance of their support
for Israel.

[23] Meeting of Mapai's Secretariat with the party's Knesset members, 31.12.1949,
LPA. On the Jerusalem question in Israel's foreign policy in 1949, see U. Bialer, "The
Road to the Capital; The Establishment of Jerusalem as the official seat of the Israeli
government in 1949," *Studies in Zionism*, 5, 2, 1984, pp. 273–96, and M. Brecher,
*Decisions in Israel's Foreign Policy* (London, 1974), pp. 9–53.

To what extent does Soviet denigration of Israel express Russia's attitude to our state and to what extent is it propagated for internal consumption (Russian Jewry)? What does the Soviet Union expect from the state of Israel? What is her policy? We heard one Russian opinion that "we know you aren't Communists but what interests us is that you do not become the vassals of others" . . . Is this in fact the case? or does the Soviet Union wish to establish a "people's government" in Israel?

And above all – the Soviet Union's attitude towards the Arab world. When the Soviet Union decided to disregard the Arab world, she did not do so because she was ignoring this important factor. Now she seems to be awakening in this direction. To keep track of this [process] we must constantly decipher [events].[24]

Internal Israeli Foreign Ministry documents of the period 1949–52 reveal several variants of dismay at the degree to which the Soviet pendulum had indeed swung back. The fatalists and ideologists differed from the pragmatists. Several experts had been very quick to assess that Israel's role in Soviet global calculations had ended with the establishment of the state. Thereafter, they anticipated increasingly drastic retreats from initial Soviet support. Precisely the same ideological and political considerations that had obtained during the "hard-line" period before 1947 could be expected to exert influence, especially against the background of the Soviet Jewish question.

Until at least 1952, however, most of Israel's leadership favored a more cautious and reserved approach. Seeing Russia as monolithic, they sought consistency in the Soviet Union's purposes. The Soviets, they claimed, still wished to decrease Western influence and control in the Middle East; to disrupt Western efforts at military entrenchment; and to attain the "neutralization" of the region. They also believed that the Soviet Union had a clear and unequivocal interest in undermining stability in the area by exacerbating contradictions within each country in the Arab camp and between the Arab and the non-Arab nations in the region, and by a campaign against pan-Islamic movements and regional blocs. Russia's principal tactical policy called for undermining stability in the area, went the argument, in order to prevent an "Anglo–American peace" in the region. To that end, the Soviets could be expected to offer consistent support to de-stabilizing elements in the Middle East and, in the immediate context, the conflict between Jews and Arabs was instrumental. Perhaps even more important as far as Israel is concerned was the

[24] 4.4.1950, ISA 2466/7.

conclusion presented, for example, by a Soviet expert in the Foreign
Ministry early in January 1950:

What, from the Soviet point of view, is the *main* positive basis that justified
their past support of Israel and now justifies its continuation, albeit partially
and with reservations? . . . The only reasonable answer seems to be that the
very existence of Israel in the Middle East is an objective fact that substan-
tially complicates the unification and consolidation of the region under
Western supervision, economically and socially as well as politically and
militarily. It is very possible [that the Soviets believe] that had Israel not been
established, then the Western powers would have succeeded in organizing the
region completely – despite the competition among themselves and despite
the contradictions among the various Arab countries.[25]

The period between early 1949 and late 1952 served as an
important laboratory for testing this thesis. In fact, Israel attempted
to measure the extent of Russian willingness to cooperate politically,
culturally and economically. She presented a protracted sequence of
requests and messages of various levels of importance; the Soviet
response left no room for doubt. For example, out of forty-one
messages and requests from the Israeli Legation in Moscow to the
Russian Foreign Office in 1949 (which included a note of congratula-
tions on the initiation of radio and telegraph ties between Tel Aviv
and Moscow; specific entry visa requests for treatment of a young
man who had lost his eyesight; a request for the curriculum of studies
in the Faculty of Mechanics at Moscow University; applications to visit
a tobacco factory; a forestry expert's request to visit the Soviet Union;
and a request for photocopies of several ancient Hebrew manuscripts), the vast majority elicited no response whatsoever and the few
that did received negative replies. That same year the Legation also
presented fourteen petitions relating to cultural and scientific contacts (such as Russian lexicographic technological sources for the
Hebrew Language Academy and material on Jewish composers in the
Soviet Union). These, too, were uniformly rejected.[26]

Having thus been abruptly cold-shouldered, Israel was understandably reluctant to make similar applications thereafter. The last
attempt to establish any kind of contact with senior Russian leaders
was made at the end of 1951. When Sharett proposed to the Soviet
Foreign Minister that a meeting be arranged with Stalin the offer was
bluntly rejected.[27] Otherwise, however, Israeli comprehension of the

[25] See Levavi's memorandum in ISA 2514/15.
[26] See memoranda on the subject in ISA 2492/16.
[27] See report on Sharett–Vyshinski meeting on 22.12.1951, ISA 2594/1.

severe restrictions on Israeli–Russian contacts was complete. One indication was provided in November 1954, when the Director General of the Israeli Comptroller's Office requested authorization from the Foreign Ministry to meet with the Soviet Economic Attaché in order to discuss the Soviet method of internal controls. A caustic internal memorandum from the Foreign Minister instructed that the Soviet Attaché "was not to be approached, it is foolish naiveté to think that we can present questions such as these to the Soviet Union . . . as if it were an open country like England or Denmark. They will be certain that we are planning to spy on them and it will be very unpleasant."[28]

That memorandum was written well after the critical period in the development of the Israeli perception. The latter had crystallized during the Prague trials at the end of 1952, the "Doctors' Trials" of January 1953 and the rupture of diplomatic relations between Israel and the Soviet Union later that same year. It is impossible to exaggerate the influence of those events on Israeli perceptions and conclusions regarding the degree of Soviet retreat from support of Israel in 1947–8. It was then that the "fatalistic" thesis received influential confirmation, and then too that it played a significant (but hitherto unrecognized) role in shaping Israeli foreign policy.

When news of the Prague trials was made public in November 1952, Israeli Foreign Ministry experts were quick to conclude that they constituted a major turning-point in the Soviet attitude to the state of Israel.[29] At the end of the month, Arieh Levavi reported to the temporary Chargé d'Affaires in Moscow that "the trial is [more than] a watershed in [diplomatic] relations . . . There are insinuations that we have been categorized as one of Stalin's enemy powers. With the trial they seem to be trying to present a demonic trinity to the Communist public: American imperialism, Titoism, Zionism." Levavi added, "there are Catholics in only a few Cominform nations but there are lots of Jews – and almost all the Jews are one people and it is possible that they still preserve some iota of love of Zion or that it may be awakened one day."[30]

The Israeli politicians, at least those in the ruling Mapai party,

[28] 19.11.1954, ISA 2507/8. On Israel's efforts to strengthen her relations with the Soviet bloc from the breaking of diplomatic relations with Russia in 1953 until early 1955, see a report dated 30.3.1955, ISA 2511/9.
[29] For internal debates on the subject, see ISA 43/16.
[30] 25.11.1952, ISA 2492/17.

were even more explicit. In a lengthy and secret discussion on the topic held in the last week of November 1952, almost all the Mapai ministers viewed the trial as Communism's declaration of war on Zionism and Judaism in general.[31] Sharett spoke for many when he said, "for the first time a brutal, poisonous attack has been made on the state of Israel. For the first time since Hitler the Jews as Jews have been placed in the dock in a trial that has reverberated throughout the world." Mordechai Namir expressed concern for the physical fate of the Jews of the Soviet Union: "I see it as a catastrophe that the greatest power in the world has declared war on the people of Israel, on the state of Israel, and holds 2,500,000 Jews as hostages. There is nothing that can exonerate this, it really is the land of unlimited opportunities, as a favorite expression in Russia, even Czarist Russia, has it." And in one of his most castigating pronouncements on Communism and the Soviet Union, Ben Gurion summed up the penetrating diagnosis of the inherent conflict between the Zionist movement and Judaism versus Soviet Communism: "There are 2,500,000 Jews there and they can slaughter them. I am very worried that they will slaughter them."

Nevertheless, the meeting decided to avoid a collision course with the Soviet Union. Instead, it was agreed to undertake a review of the arguments against Communism with the left-wing parties, thereby sharpening the fundamental assessment that had itself been reinforced by the Prague trials as to the essence of Russia's about-face regarding Israel. In a session with Mapai spokesmen, intended to translate the party decisions into the language of action, Sharett said:

We have reached a certain stage in the development of relations for which I am trying to find an analogy in our past, in the experiences we have undergone here in this land, to the situation in which we find ourselves and the shocking experience we are now undergoing ... I will say that this reminds me of Passfield's 1929 "White Paper" and the 1939 Chamberlain–MacDonald "White Paper." There was a chapter, a certain policy, a positive policy; and here it has been overthrown in a few years and we have revolved 180 degrees.[32]

This diagnosis was considerably reinforced early in January 1953 when the "Doctors' Trials" were made public in Moscow. Pinhas Lavon spoke at a Cabinet meeting in mid-January of that year: "The

[31] Excerpts are taken from a protocol of Mapai's Central Committee meeting on 23.11.1952, LPA 26/52.
[32] From his speech at a meeting with Mapai's spokesmen on 27.11.1952, CZA A245/36.

basic point ... is that in a general and uniform political process the [Eastern bloc] countries ... announce that the Jewish nation as a people and the Jews as Jews, together with authorized Jewish organizations, have arranged murders, that this is a nation of well-poisoners sent to destroy the gentiles ... We are confronting a new historical phenomenon, a renewed and more powerful attempt to transmute the view of Jews as saboteurs and as dangerous enemies of the gentiles into policy."[33]

In a letter to Cabinet ministers, Ben Gurion phrased the operative dangers to the Jewish people no less incisively:

The two dangers that the trial exposes ... are most serious. Stalin did not hesitate to kill millions of Russian workers and peasants for the sake of his political plans and for the sake of ... power. He will not hesitate to vilify the Jews of Russia. He will not use Nazi terminology; on the contrary, he will spurn every anti-Semitic and racist term; but in fact he will do what Hitler did, without hesitation or moral restraint.

The second danger – anti-Semitic policies (of course in more convenient terms) in the international arena ... there is no doubt that Stalin is using all his totalitarian methods to wage this war of destruction on the Jews in Russia and the satellite countries of whose loyalty he is uncertain, exploiting hatred of Israel as a tried and true means of gaining allies and supporters, first of all in the Arab and Muslim world and in other lands, even Western ones – these are more than theoretical fears.[34]

The Soviets initiated the rupture of their diplomatic relations with Israel in February 1953, after a bomb had exploded near the Russian Embassy in Israel. Hardly surprisingly, Israeli policy-makers saw the rupture as an effect of what Sharett had defined (in his off-the-record briefing of Israeli journalists) as "developmental logic."[35] His analysis of the deterministic nature of the worsening of Israeli–Soviet relations from the perspective of the mid-fifties is intrinsically enlightening. It also facilitates an understanding of the manner whereby Israeli conception regarding the potential of Israeli–Soviet political ties became confirmed before (and especially after) early 1953.

The victory of the "fatalistic" thesis thus seemed complete, and

[33] From the minutes of the Cabinet meeting on 18.1.1953, ISA 2410/19.

[34] 14.1.1953, ISA 2411/21. These fears were apparently well founded. See M. Agursky, "The Abortive Soviet Plot to Persecute Jews in 1953 and Its Political Background – Tentative Explanation," *Proceedings of the Ninth World Congress of Jewish Studies* (Jerusalem, 1986), Division B, vol. 3, pp. 197–204.

[35] Excerpts are taken from a press conference at the Foreign Minister's Office in Tel Aviv on 12.2.1953, ISA 2457/14.

had significant implications for Israel's approach to relations with the U.S.S.R. from early 1953 until the publication of the Czech–Egyptian arms deal in 1955. Perhaps the most important (and interesting) implication was the emergence of the notion that the resumption of relations could come about only at Russian initiative; Israel had to avoid any conscious attempt in that direction. It was also expected that the break could not be healed for some time, if at all. In March 1953 the Israeli Foreign Minister briefed Israeli missions abroad on how to explain the rupture in relations. His exposition adopted an attacking tone which reflected prevalent opinions amongst the country's leadership:

We must refute three assumptions: first, that the break represents a holocaust for Israel. Second, that it makes for helpless dependence on America without any counter-support. And third, that it serves to aggrandize the Arabs. The argument – the U.S.S.R. has always been hostile to Zionism. The about-face in 1947 resulted from spite ... not from love of us but from hatred of the English. The retreat in the positive approach to the Jewish state started shortly after its independence, when the Soviet Union saw:

a.   That Israel was clearly tilting to the West;
b.   That the Soviet Jews were attached to Israel.

The circle has closed and the U.S.S.R. has returned to the position she held before our independence. In the historical balance we have lost nothing in regard to the Soviet Union ... We must not appear ... beaten and in retreat but stand firm and fight fire with fire.[36]

The last four words in the briefing are especially significant. In late February/early March 1953 the Israeli government decided to formally open an unprecedented international campaign against the anti-Semitism of the entire Eastern bloc. The Israeli mission to the U.N. was instructed to raise the subject before the international body – in fact, to "fight fire with fire."[37]

Stalin's death at the beginning of March and the subsequent relaxation of attacks on the Jews in the Soviet Union, as well as the retraction of some of the indictments in the "Doctors' Trials," blunted Israel's political edge at the U.N. But those events did not affect two additional developments. First, the break in relations helped eliminate lingering objections within the Israeli leadership to

[36]   See ISA 2415/33 and ISA 2410/19 for the briefing on 9.3.1953.
[37]   See ISA 2415/33 and ISA 2511/9. See also G. Meir's remarks in a meeting of the Jewish Agency's Directorate in New York on 17.4.1953, AHA, Container 11, "Mapam After the Split."

the abandonment of non-alignment in Israel's foreign policy;[38] secondly, and despite a softening in Soviet policy, Israel reaffirmed her basic tendency not to press for renewed diplomatic relations with the U.S.S.R. Sharett was adament: "appeasement of the U.S.S.R. will to a certain extent be viewed as locking the door after the horse has bolted."[39]

As is known, in the summer of that year, Israel did respond to Russian overtures that relations be resumed. But that was largely because Sharett was misled about Soviet moves by a member of the Israeli Legation in Bulgaria, Ben Zion Razin. Only when Sharett was convinced, by this report, that the Russians were indeed making a formal approach did he agree to raise the matter in Cabinet. Ultimately contact was authorized and the foundations thus laid for renewed political relations.[40]

Not only substantively was the resumption of relations important. Significant preconditions had accompanied the process.[41] During the laborious negotiations leading to the renewal of formal political contact, the Russians demanded as a *sine qua non* that Israel undertake not to associate herself with any anti-Soviet political and strategic international arrangement. A number of Israel's previous decisions (see below) precluded her compliance, but she did instead agree to a formula which forbad her to "*participate* in any *pact* which had aggressive aims towards the Soviet Union." The significant gap between the two formulas mirrored the path which Israel was

[38] It should be noted that Israel's diplomatic representatives abroad were instructed on 6.3.1953: "For Stalin's death flags should not be lowered. Signatures should not be placed in the [special] book [of condolences] in Russia's embassies. No other formal participation in the mourning should take place" (a circular cable from Eytan), ISA 43/15. At least one Israeli diplomat criticized this policy and advocated "special treatment for Stalin ... a Marshal of the Russian army who defeated Hitler and saved the remnants of European Jewry. One should perhaps have remembered Russia's early favors in helping the establishment of Israel," Amir's letter to Najar, 8.3.1953, ISA 2537/19.
[39] The Prime Minister and some of the Cabinet did not accept the view that Stalin's death had led to a change in the Soviet line. See Levavi's memorandum on 4.5.1953 and correspondence in ISA 2511/9.
[40] See cabled correspondence in ISA 2507/5; Avner's despatch to Sharett on 27.11.1953, ISA 2446/15; B. Razin, "I Conducted the Negotiations for the Resumption of Diplomatic Relations with the U.S.S.R.," *Maariv*, 10.3.1972 (Hebrew); M. Sharett, *Personal Diary* (Tel Aviv, 1978), p. 78, and Razin's private letter to Sharett on 10.1.1954, ISA 2446/15. In this letter Razin admitted his failure and had given a different version of the story he published eighteen years later.
[41] The following account is based upon and excerpts are taken from ISA 2507/5 and Sharett, *Personal Diary*, pp. 851–2.

attempting to follow in the field of global foreign policy orientation. The mend of the rift did result in some positive political developments, notably the reciprocal up-grading in the rank of Israeli missions in the Soviet Union and Eastern Europe, and of Soviet missions to Israel.[42] But nothing occurred to change the perceptions ingrained during the course of the events of late 1952 and early 1953. Shortly after relations were renewed, for example, Sharett asked the Director of the Foreign Ministry's Research Section to explain the entire affair. He particularly wanted to know "why the Soviet Union was so interested in renewing relations and what was the meaning of this sudden love for Israel since then?"[43] Russia's first use of her veto against Israel in the Security Council a few months later constituted fuel for the old fire. As Sharett candidly confided in his diary early in the last week of January 1954:

Vyshinsky cast a veto on the proposal of the Big Three [U.S., Britain, France] and the extensive and grueling argument ended in nought. A Russian veto in the Security Council, wielded for the first time in a matter affecting us, is a clear trend against us and in favor of an Arab state! My own immediate reaction was depression. This is bad in two senses. The U.S.S.R. is redefining its power in support of an Arab front against us, and the U.S. will be forced to draw negative conclusions about us and to increase its competition with the Soviets to gain Arab friendship.

Only after a telephone conversation with Walter [Eytan] in Tel Aviv did I begin to see the other side of the coin. First of all, the formula proposed by the [Big Three] contained serious defects – it was tabled in order to appease the Arabs and avoid a Soviet veto. This attempt failed, but in the meantime the formula has become far worse as far as we are concerned and it were best if it were not adopted ... Secondly, since the entire argument began as the result of Syria's complaint against us, the fact that matters ended in a draw in some respects represents a rejection of Syria's complaint. Admittedly, the U.S.S.R. had not at all planned to get us out of trouble, even less to bring about a Syrian defeat, and the fact that these are the results of the veto does not actually in any way lessen the serious nature of her more malignant aims. But in the meantime we must, for external purposes, for propaganda and to create an atmosphere, hail the results and engrave them on the public's consciousness.[44]

Russia again exercised her Security Council veto at the end of March 1954 against New Zealand's proposal regarding freedom of the seas.[45] This, together with her previous actions, explains why

---

[42] See a memorandum on "Israel's relations with Eastern European countries in 1954," 15.2.1955, ISA 2511/9.
[43] His notes on 13.8.1953, ISA 2410/18.
[44] 23.1.1954, Sharett, *Personal Diary*, pp. 317–18.        [45] *Ibid.*, p. 421.

Israel tended to play down the Soviet rapprochement. The Director of the Foreign Ministry's Information Section wrote to the Israeli Embassy in London in August of that year, expressing dissatisfaction with an *Observer* article underscoring the change.

The facts are facts and cannot be denied or refuted, but it is another question entirely whether or not we should make conspicuous the improvement in our relations with the Soviet Union and the People's Democracies. I am completely opposed and am glad that almost all members of the office share that opinion. We are of course pleased that relations have improved and if this means that the belt has been somewhat loosened, as in the case of freeing Prisoners of Zion in Rumania, all the better. *But none of us is fooling himself that salvation will come from this part of the world or that in the near future any revolutionary achievements will result from our contacts with it.* And thus the question poses itself: by stressing partial successes in this arena how would we affect our standing in the general front? From this perspective it is clear that there exists no analogy between us and the Arab countries. When a rumor is heard of a risk of pro-Soviet tendencies in Arab countries, the West responds by increasing its desire to buy unification of the Arab world and any Arab hint of possible betrayal increases their worth in Western eyes. It is not so with us. Any Israeli hint of a pro-Soviet tendency serves as a pretext to abandon us. Thus we must be careful in publications such as these, and we must be reserved about descriptions of the development of our relations with the Soviet Union and her allies [limiting them] to a straightforward factual account without stressing anything at all.[46]

The Czech–Egyptian arms deal about a year later came as a dramatic surprise to Israel's leaders, as Sharett's diary indicates.[47] But in no way did it dash any positive Israeli hopes regarding Russia.[48]

Considering how rapidly the "fatalistic" diagnosis of Soviet intentions crystallized, it is not surprising that a concurrent conception came to the fore regarding the possibility of Israeli political activity to preserve or strengthen Russian support of Israel. Here too a clear distinction can be drawn between two periods: 1948 to early 1953, and from 1953 until 1956. As was the case in other matters, the first period was characterized by cautious optimism and conscious attempts at political activity to promote Israel's goals. This optimism, and these attempts, disappeared almost entirely at the beginning of 1953.

[46]  16.8.1954, ISA 43/15, emphasis added.
[47]  Sharett, *Personal Diary*, pp. 1214, 1215, 1176–7.
[48]  See Sharett's analysis in his diary on 18.8.1955 following the expulsion of Israeli diplomats from Moscow on the same day, *ibid.*, pp. 1138–9.

It would be difficult to blame the Israeli government for excessive optimism in its assessments of the chances of political activity. Israel had asked much of the Soviet bloc and, at least for the first three years of her existence, had enjoyed enormous political support, as well as crucial armaments aid and hoped for large-scale aliyah from Eastern Europe. During 1947–8 the only important strategic advantage which Israel could have provided the Soviets was that her struggle for political independence brought about Britain's removal from Palestine. After the end of 1948 a different set of questions confronted Israeli leaders: what exactly did the U.S.S.R. expect from Israel in the international arena? what were the demands and expectations whose fulfillment would enable the policy begun in 1947 to continue? Even before these questions were posed Israeli representatives began to learn about the Soviet Union's desiderata.

Late in July 1947 Eliyahu Elath of the Jewish Agency's U.N. mission (later Israel's Ambassador to the United States) met with Mikhail Vasilov, First Secretary of the Soviet Embassy in the United States. The Russian made it clear that the Soviet government "is completely aware that the social and economic structure of the Yishuv is capitalistic and that the [Jewish] experiments in the area of collectivism have no relation to Marxist interpretation. [The Russian government] believes none the less that a democratic, progressive and peaceful community is being built which can curb the anti-Soviet intrigues that are so easy to initiate among Arab reactionary groups."[49] One year later Abba Eban summarized a discussion with Yacov Malik, the Soviet U.N. representative: the Russians do not oppose "the clear Israeli interest in improving relations with the West – they have no hope that Israel will become a Soviet bloc satellite."[50]

Contrary to Eban's assessment, the Foreign Ministry soon learned that the nature and scope of Israel's ties with the West, and in particular the United States, did indeed fall within the realm of Soviet interests and concerns. In his first formal meeting with the Russian Deputy Foreign Minister after Israel's independence, Sharett took pains to clarify Israel's acute need for financial assistance from any possible source and first and foremost from the Jews of America.[51] Vyshinsky responded that Israeli links with American Jewry "portend danger," inasmuch as "when they help you they help out of

[49] 31.7.1947, ISA 364/11.        [50] 12.8.1948, ISA 2384/21.
[51] The excerpts are taken from the protocol of the meeting which took place in Paris on 12.12.1948, ISA 2502/8.

Jewish national [feeling] yet they do not cease to be citizens of the United States and they are liable wittingly or unwittingly to serve as tools of American policy." When Sharett explained that "if there are such dangers they must once and for all be combated" and that "we are building the state of Israel to be free and not subservient," the Russian enthused, "That's it! That's it!"

Numerous Soviet communiqués of this period insisted that American material assistance to Israel not be accompanied by political conditions which might transform Israel into a *de facto* American satellite and an anti-Soviet presence in the Middle East. Several avenues of communication were employed to relay the message. In one instance, the Israeli cousin of a high-ranking member of the Soviet Communist Party, himself close to the Chairman of the Anti-Soviet Counter-Intelligence Section of the Israeli Intelligence Service, was used as a direct channel to Ben Gurion. The message he carried hinted that Israel's policy was likely to influence adversely aliyah from Eastern Europe.[52] In general, however, the Soviets did not require recourse to such devious means; they usually presented their demands openly, in contacts at various political levels. At a meeting held early in February 1949 with Elath, then Israel's Ambassador to the U.S.A., the Russian Ambassador to Washington explained that his country had no intention of forcing Israel into her own bloc; he was aware that "the great majority of Israelis" were not Communists. The Soviet Union's only interest was that Israel remain completely independent, without any foreign influence or domination. He added that Israel's continued independence ensured Russia's friendly relations.[53] Precisely what was required was explicitly defined for the first time in a conversation between Yacov Malik and Abba Eban and Gideon Raphael (a senior Israeli diplomat) some two weeks later. The Russian claimed that his country "has no interest in penetrating the Middle East since they have more than enough commitments in Asia." Therefore their goal was to keep the Middle East "an independent and neutral area."[54] Israel was thus expected to follow a foreign policy of neutrality in the East–West conflict.

Representatives of the Soviet bloc conveyed the same message. At the end of January 1949, the Hungarian Interior Minister pointed out

---

[52] Private sources. On this incident, see Ben Gurion's diary entries for 20.1.1948, 4.3.1948, 21.12.1948 and 3.7.1949, BGA.
[53] See his cable on 10.2.1949, ISA 2308/2.
[54] See Eban's cable on 22.2.1949, ISA 2329/5.

to Ehud Avriel that his government would demand guarantees that Hungarian aliyah would "never serve as a tool in the anti-democratic war."[55] In late March of that year the Czech Ambassador in Washington warned Elath that Soviet–Israeli relations would deteriorate "unavoidably if [Israel] fell an ally under American patronage."[56] The Rumanian Prime Minister intimated as much to the Israeli Envoy in Bucharest six weeks later.[57] Israeli representatives in Eastern Europe and the U.S.S.R. were persistently exposed to intimations of this expectation. It is therefore hardly surprising that the demand to exhibit an "independent line" in foreign policy became an almost permanent feature of their communiqués to Israel. In mid-March 1949 Avriel demanded a Foreign Ministry decision on the possibility of Sharett's visit to the Soviet Union and "diplomatic activity calculated to avoid ... unnecessary activity liable to create the impression that we are about to join the Western bloc."[58] Two weeks later the Israeli Envoy in Poland requested that his Foreign Minister demonstrate appropriate flexibility towards the Soviet bloc's expectations regarding "the processes related to fostering the internal image of our state and its foreign policy." He specifically warned against making too much of the American loan that Israel had received at the beginning of that year; against visits by Israeli officials to the United States; against the disposition towards – and rumors of the establishment of – a Middle East Command organized by the West, and "rumors about discrimination against the Israeli Communist Party."[59] In early April of that year, in light of the fact that "for many objective reasons – the tie with American Jewry, the U.J.A., etc. – a considerable portion of our activities are centered in that part of the world,"[60] Avriel recommended "several demonstrative activities ... to disperse the misleading impression [in the Soviet bloc] regarding our neutrality."

[55] See Avriel's despatch to Sharett, 18.2.1949, ISA 2492/22.
[56] From Elath's cable to Sharett, 29.3.1949, ISA 2308/2. The same refrain can be found in the conversation the Russian Deputy Foreign Minister had with Israel's Minister in Moscow on 15.5.1949. See Friedman's despatch to Sharett, 29.5.1949, ISA 2513/1.
[57] See the minutes of the meeting on 14.3.1949, ISA 2513/1. The Russians had checked closely every item of evidence indicating Israel's affiliation with the West. Thus the Russian Minister in Washington pressed Eban early in August 1949 on the subjects of Israel's connections with the Standard Oil Company and with Ford Motors; see Eban's cable to Sharett on 1.8.1949, ISA 2329/7.
[58] 16.3.1949, ISA 2493/4.
[59] 31.3.1949, ISA 2492/20.          [60] See his despatch on 9.4.1949, ISA 491/11.

Israel's representatives in the Eastern bloc also exploited every opportunity to press that pro-Soviet steps be pursued, despite doubts as to their efficacy. Early in August 1949, for example, Avriel criticized Israel's failure to send a delegation to the Democratic Youth Festival in Hungary. "We have," he claimed, "thereby missed many opportunities to make new political ties and to state our case before the representatives of several nations under favorable conditions." On the same occasion he warned against the "harmful" reactions in the Israeli press to the trial of the leaders of the Zionist organizations in Hungary: "policy should not be conducted on the basis of sentiment and so long as we have not abandoned hope of gaining something through negotiations, we should not fire our cannons, especially since we have none."[61]

Israel's diplomats in the Eastern bloc were indeed deeply conscious of their lack of political weapons, which was felt to be rooted in the general Soviet attitude towards Israeli overtures.[62] They considered, however, that such weakness served only to underscore the necessity of not spurning any overture or demonstrative action, even if it did not possess real content. The Israeli Minister in Moscow presented this argument to the Israeli Foreign Minister early in January 1950. Strenuously objecting to the request from the Israeli Military Attaché in the U.S.S.R. to be relieved of his duties (for "lack of purpose") he argued:[63]

I disagree with the fundamental assessment made by Barnea [the Military Attaché] that there is no point today in maintaining a military attaché from a military–professional point of view and in terms of learning something ... here. This is not new and we were well aware of this here and in Israel ... long before the appointment. And if it was none the less decided to staff the position here, I believe it was for two reasons: (a) so that we do not leave the entire East without a single military attaché at a time when in the United States we have added one or two majors, and in view of the misrepresentations regarding our army structure in accordance with the American system, technical assistance from "American generals" etc.; (b) so that we can prevent the ... impression that we are already "disappointed" in this regard – when there is nothing to be lost if the "Westerners" secretly suspect ... that our military attaché is "running around" here because the Russians and Israelis have an interest in this ... In my opinion the above arguments, and in particular the first, are still valid ... today ... Who knows if we will enjoy "a good life" with the Eastern bloc in the near future. There seems to be

---

[61]  See his despatch on 6.8.1949, ISA 2492/22.
[62]  See Namir's despatch to Sharett on 22.10.1949, ISA 2513/17.
[63]  The excerpts are taken from Namir's despatch on 25.1.1950, ISA 2495/13.

no basis for over-optimism. But we must not, *on our initiative, without external coercion*, take even the slightest step to hasten such processes. How do we know that today's "cold war" is eternal? . . . In the meantime our policies must be to hang on to whatever "friendly relations" we have with the East, even if we presume that they are only superficial.

Israel's envoys in the Eastern bloc were well aware of their country's increasing tilt towards the West as of mid-1949; they constituted a pressure group within the Israeli foreign-policy-making establishment trying as best they could to indicate the dangers inherent in political activity liable to be interpreted in the East as anti-Soviet. In August 1950 the Director of the Foreign Ministry's Eastern Europe Section objected to both the signing of the Israeli– American Treaty of Friendship[64] and to the recommendation put forward by the Israeli Embassy in Washington that Israel join an American aid plan. Such steps, he argued, would create "further difficulties in maintaining a non-alignment policy and are liable definitively to determine the Eastern bloc's relations towards us."[65] Several important Israeli decisions (see below) on orientation, as well as the Soviet bloc's relations with Israel after the end of 1950 blunted the edge of those arguments. Hence, although they were voiced in 1951 too,[66] by the end of that year their influence on decision-making regarding Israel's international orientation had markedly decreased. They then became no more than *post facto* critical analyses, or subdued expressions of hope that further Israeli changes could be avoided. Thus, for example, in criticizing Israeli general voting at the U.N. at the end of 1951, the Israeli Minister in Moscow wrote: "I do not know if we acted as we did after internal wrangling and finally deciding that this was the only way we could act, or if we were subject to unilateral pressure [and] did not attempt to oppose it."[67] The Israeli Chargé d'Affaires in Budapest ended his letter on the last day of 1951 by expressing the hope that Israel would manage to maintain contact with the West in accordance with a formula of "facts and not pacts."[68] Gershon Avner, in charge of the Israeli Legation in Hungary and Bulgaria, was unusually severe; his communiqués during

---

[64]  See Eliashiv's letter to Sharett on 10.8.1950, ISA 2414/26.

[65]  See his letter to Sharett on 15.8.1950, *ibid*.

[66]  See, for example, Eliashiv's despatch to Sharett on 12.1.1951 in which he warned against the carelessness of Israel's publicity concerning General Dayan's trip to Turkey, ISA 2408/9.

[67]  Eliashiv's despatch to Sharett, 1.2.1952, ISA 2507/9.

[68]  From Bentsur's despatch to Levavi on 31.12.1951, ISA 2503/23.

1953 are remarkable for their depth of analysis no less than for the uniqueness of their thesis.[69] His central argument is best expressed in a letter which he sent to Israel during the course of the political maneuvers that led to the renewal of relations between Israel and the Soviet Union.

It is patently obvious to me that in major matters we have no chance whatsoever of changing our policy in international relations. The supremacy of relations with the United States and American Jewry is obviously an essential reality for Israel and cannot be questioned.

But there are also "less major matters" and nuances in political behavior, and my opinion is that in order to create the possibility and chance of action for the benefit of East European Jewry, we must try to establish a framework of [mutual] interests with the East *to the extent possible* and within the ambience of relations with the United States; we must be diligent in this regard ... In the past we did not seriously try to act in less major matters, and minor matters so that perhaps despite everything our account may be in credit. I say "perhaps despite everything" – obviously there is no assurance that such efforts will produce results in terms of Jewry.

But political activity is comprised to a certain extent of "casting one's bread upon the water." In regard to the U.S., do we act *only if we have assurances* of definite results? No. We perform many minor deeds ... in order to compound them into a larger account and *in the hope* that this account will pay off. At any rate – if we do not try – then it is *obvious from the outset* that we will not succeed in anything. So too in regard to the Soviet Union; we must not abandon hope beforehand and say that we will not do anything because it will not lead to aliyah anyway. If we wish to relieve our conscience [regarding East European Jewry] we must do all that is possible – on the chance that it will be useful. And even if there is no *a priori* prospect of success, it will at least maintain the basis of our claims.

At the time this was an unorthodox opinion in the Israeli Foreign Ministry. The views thus expressed by Israeli diplomats had no impact whatsoever on the alternative Eastern European "professional chorus" which, by early 1952, had definitively reached contrary conclusions. These were summarized by Arieh Levavi the Director of the Eastern Europe Section, who at the end of February 1952 sent a memorandum to the Foreign Minister:

So long as Israel is outside the Soviet bloc and so long as sympathy for Israel exists among the Jews of the Soviet Union, these ... will remain, within the framework of existing world circumstances, causes for suspicion in the Politburo! We thus cannot presume that the fluctuations of Israeli foreign policy exert an important influence on the unique policy of the Politburo ...

[69] The following account is based upon and excerpts are taken from Avners' despatch to Levavi on 6.6.1953, ISA 2381/21; italics added.

So long as we are not part of ... the Cominform we will not, under present global circumstances and Cominform policies, achieve popularity in the Soviet Union. No country will ... The choice is only between more and much harsher criticism, or less ... The major factors affecting the fate of Soviet Jewry are: the development of the international situation and the development of the Soviet Union's own domestic situation; changes in Israel's foreign policy are likely to be only very secondary factors.[70]

The thesis was presented even more sharply at a closed conference of Israeli diplomats held in Zurich one year later: "It is a mistake to think that for the sake of the occasional bow [in the political field] it is possible to achieve anything serious with them [the Soviets]."[71] In 1952 this was still a matter for debate; by 1954, however, the "fatalistic" assessment had become part of the ministerial consensus. In the words of one of the Eastern European experts in the Foreign Ministry: "Without going into particulars of Soviet policy in the Middle East and its relationship to the Arab countries on the one hand and to Israel on the other, it can be said that in general our own policy seems to have no influence on that policy, or in other words, unless a fundamental change occurs in Israel's foreign policy we cannot employ conventional diplomatic means in order to change the political line determined in Moscow *vis-à-vis* the Middle East."[72] As will be analyzed below, evolving Israeli strategic concepts with regard to the West rendered a transformation of that sort quite unthinkable.

It would be incorrect to deduce from the above analysis that after 1948 Israel's leaders adopted a strategy of political "non-action" *vis-à-vis* the U.S.S.R.; on the contrary, for the first time they initiated several moves which were designed to show the Kremlin and the Soviet bloc that Israel's foreign policy was independent and that she was not deterministically bound to Western interests. Their purpose was to demonstrate that within the framework of international configurations Israel and the U.S.S.R. might often find themselves on the same side of the political fence. These actions were undertaken notwithstanding the constraining effect of Israel's great dependence on the West, which demanded extreme care in her international behavior at the height of the cold war, and despite the caution necessitated by her sparse resources and relatively limited global interests.

[70] Levavi's memorandum addressed to Sharett on 25.2.1952, ISA 2507/2.
[71] Quoted in Avner's despatch to Levavi on 6.6.1953, ISA 2381/21.
[72] From Shlosh's letter to Levavi on 3.5.1954, ISA 2507/3.

Israeli political activities concentrated on two main areas: first, her votes and postures at the U.N.; secondly, her approach towards the establishment of military–strategic alliances in the Middle East and her decisions regarding her own participation. These two foci of action, the second of which will be examined in later sections of this book, did not become apparent until mid-1949, once Israel had become a member of the U.N. Well before then, however, Israeli diplomats and leaders had taken pains to exploit every possible occasion in order to emphasize that Israel's international orientation would be independent and not subservient to the West. Sharett made a declaration on these lines to Vyshinsky when the two met in December 1948.[73] At the end of January 1949 the Russian Minister in Tel Aviv was informed that no political conditions were attached to the American loan which had recently been authorized.[74] Three weeks later the Israeli Ambassador in Washington explained to the Russian Ambassador to the U.S. that Israel was firmly set "on protecting her [political] independence and safeguarding friendly relations with the Soviet Union."[75]

At the end of February the Soviet representative at the U.N. was assured that Israel had no intentions of requesting aid from the Marshall Plan; because "she was not a backward area" neither would she request aid in the framework of a program proposed by the American President. She preferred instead the assistance offered by the U.N. agencies.[76] Four weeks later the Czech Minister in Israel, who had designated the visits of the Israeli Prime Minister and President to America as signs of their "subservience" to the West, received a detailed answer from the Director of the Israeli Foreign Ministry's Eastern Europe Section: "Our people approach the Jews of America and not just 'America.' Can you blame us for seeking out our brothers at this difficult time? . . . We are not prepared to deviate at all from the path of neutrality that we have declared, not even in exchange for material benefits. The condition of the Jewish people in the Diaspora does not permit the state of Israel to affiliate itself in any way with either side because this might create a division between Israel and a large portion of our people and is liable to affect that same

[73] See the protocol of the meeting on 12.12.1948, ISA 2502/8.
[74] Friedman's despatch to Meyerson, 26.1.1949, ISA 2513/13.
[75] From Elath's cable to Sharett, 10.2.1949, ISA 2308/2. The content of the conversation was passed on to the Rumanian Prime Minister by the Israeli Minister in Bucharest on 14.3.1949, ISA 2513/1.
[76] Eban's cable to Sharett, 22.2.1949, ISA 2329/5.

portion fatally."[77] Two days later Sharett, then in Washington, declared that the government of Israel had no plans to join the Nato Alliance.[78] In mid-April Golda Meir laid particular stress on this aspect of Israeli policy in her farewell meeting with the Soviet Foreign Minister in Moscow:

It is unnecessary to explain how many strong bonds tie us to the Jews of America. We are most interested in their welfare and in cordial relations with their government. This too is a fundamental feature of our foreign policy; but no matter how imbued we are with the desire to create strong ties with American Jewry, we will not agree to any external involvement in our internal affairs and will preserve our independence and neutrality untouched. We are realistic enough to know our true position and we are not doctrinaire. But there are fundamental principles that we will not breach.[79]

Israel also tried to convey this message by a variety of symbolic state visits to Eastern Europe and by inviting Soviet politicians to visit Israel.[80] Thus, Sharett paid a formal visit to Prague on 19 May 1949, during which he met with Foreign Minister Clementis;[81] and at the end of the first week of June of that year Israeli Chief of Staff Yigael Yadin also visited the Czech capital.[82] The idea that Sharett should travel to Moscow arose early in March of that year. The Israeli Legation in Moscow opposed the visit unless "we have assurances that he will not return empty-handed ... [the visit] is possible only after we have a positive answer in principle in order to complete the matter – as a final friendly act."[83] Sharett did, nevertheless, put the proposal to Russia's Envoy in Israel at the end of that month, but elicited no response and not until December 1951 was the topic discussed again in meetings between representatives of the two states.[84] In mid-June, "in view of the large number of high-ranking

[77] See report on the meeting which took place on 28.3.1949, ISA 2513/1.
[78] See Barzilai's despatch to Sharett, 31.3.1949, ISA 2492/20.
[79] For the protocol of the meeting, 14.4.1949, see ISA 2492/16.
[80] See Avriel's despatch to Friedman (with no exact date), most probably from early April 1949, ISA 2493/12.
[81] See press release of the same day in ISA 2514/11; Diary of the Eastern Europe Section of the Foreign Ministry on 13 and 18.5.1949, ISA 2513/18; Friedman's despatch to Avriel on 22.5.1949, ISA 2493/4; and Friedman's letter to Kol on 23.5.1949, CZA s41/410. A study of the declassified documents deposited in the Israeli State Archives revealed no details whatsoever on the content of Sharett's meetings in Prague. Hana Avriel, the wife of the Israeli Minister in Czechoslovakia, claimed that Sharett discussed the "training of Israeli pilots and transit sales of Czech locomotives which Israel helped to sell to France," letter to the author, 26.10.1984.
[82] *Ha'aretz*, 5.6.1949.
[83] Friedman's despatch to Avriel, 15.3.1949, ISA 2493/4.
[84] See protocol of the meeting on 23.3.1949, ISA 2513/13. At his meeting with

Americans and Englishmen visiting our country lately," Sharett
(with the apparent approval of Ben Gurion) raised the idea of inviting
"a [senior] Soviet personality for a friendly visit"; he specifically had
in mind Soviet Deputy Foreign Minister Gromyko "because of his
great popularity in Israel, because of his ties with Israel and his
position both in [his] government and at the U.N. as the head of the
Soviet delegation."[85] Sharett informed the Israeli representative to
the United Nations that the invitation was intended "to show the
United States that we are not totally in their pocket"; on the other
hand, were the invitation to be rejected "it would blunt their [the
Soviets'] contentions that Israel was tied to the United States ... and
was leaving the Russians out in the cold."[86] The invitation was duly
transmitted to the Russians at the end of that month but politely
refused; the excuse was that, in general, "they do not make political
visits unless it is for the practical purposes of signing treaties."[87]

Membership of the U.N. in May 1949 afforded Israel several
opportunities to demonstrate her political line of "non-alignment" or,
more precisely and as it was then officially phrased, "maintaining
friendly relations with the two blocs."[88] The rationale for this policy
was obvious to Israeli policy-makers.[89] First, it was a necessary, if not
always sufficient, condition for sustaining aliyah from the Soviet bloc.
Secondly, the U.N. provided a forum where Israel might demonstrate
occasional political support for the Soviet bloc. Thirdly, it was widely
felt (at least until 1950) that the open articulation of this policy in the
international arena might, under certain circumstances, encourage
the West to pay more attention to Israeli interests in the Middle East.
Finally, there was the "worst case" thesis; were there to be a world
war, and the Russian army to conquer all or part of the Middle East,
the policy might have earned Israel some sort of consideration.

Nevertheless, non-alignment at the U.N. was problematical,

Vyshinski on 22.12.1951 Sharett remarked that "we would very much like to meet
Stalin and talk with him on this (Russian Jewry) problem and on our attitude." The
reply was distinctly cool: "Stalin understands that well," ISA 2594/1.
[85] See Friedman's despatch to Namir, 13.6.1949, ISA 2513/4 and Ben Gurion's diary,
entry for 22.6.1949, BGA.
[86] See Sharett's cable to Eban on 23.6.1949, ISA 2329/12. Sharett indicated four days
later in a despatch to Namir that if Gromyko declined to accept the invitation, "we
would probably have to agree to a visit by some other personality," 27.6.1949, ISA
2513/15.
[87] See Namir's despatch to Sharett, 12.7.1949, ISA 2513/17.
[88] See Sharett's speech at the Mapai Central Committee meeting on 3.3.1951, LPA.
[89] The following account is based on Levavi's memorandum "World Policy and
Israel," 6.6.1949, ISA 2514/15.

especially in view of the East–West antagonisms prevalent at this stage of the cold war. Israel was already economically dependent on the West, with whom her political ties were also increasing. Besides, and as a senior Foreign Ministry official put it: "foreign policy is not a series of arithmetical calculations based on various numerical parts of a fundamental algebraic equation. Only concrete, complex and specific considerations in each case bridges the gulf between the realm of foundation laying and particular decisions demanded of national leaders." Considerations such as these influenced several foreign policy decisions from the end of 1949, and thereby helped to determine the pattern of Israeli voting behavior in international forums. It is to that pattern that attention must now be turned.

The general international posture which Israel adopted towards the U.S.S.R. at that time was defined by Sharett. Israel, he judged, must calculate what was in "her direct interest" and "refrain from condemning them [the Russians]."[90] For example, on the Korean question the majority in the General Assembly favored the appointment of an international committee to supervise the area, the condemnation of North Korea and the recognition of South Korea. Only the Soviet Union voted against that motion, and Israel was one of the few nations to abstain. Responding to an American reprimand, Israel explained that the majority vote was aimed directly against the U.S.S.R. and that in the absence of an agreement "the supervisory apparatus was useless anyway."

On the issue of China two motions were proposed. The first called for all member states to uphold the principles of the U.N. Charter in their relations with China and to honor her territorial integrity and independence. Israel was one of the five abstainers on this motion, which was endorsed by the political committee by a majority of 44 to 5. Her representative absented himself from the vote in the General Assembly, where roughly the same ratio prevailed. In principle, Israel refused to vote on any motion which specifically condemned the Soviet Union for her intervention in the Chinese Revolution of 1949, itself the result of "internal agitation" in China. On human rights issues, and on a proposal calling for international supervision of atomic power, Israel refrained from supporting the West. Finally,

[90] The following account is based upon Sharett's diary, from which excerpts are also taken (with no precise date, but most probably from late 1949 or early 1950), CZA A245/15 and a memorandum on "Israel's votes at the U.N. Fourth Session," 2.1.1950, ISA 2514/1.

Israel demonstratively adopted a policy of non-alignment in the voting on the issue of Greece. Two motions were proposed to the United Nations: one "Western," the other "Eastern." The first extended the mandate of the Balkan Commission (U.N.S.C.O.B.) and directed Albania and Bulgaria to cease their interference in Greece's affairs; it also called for an embargo on arms sales to those countries until it was clear that they had ceased their assistance to the guerrillas in Greece. The Political Committee voted 38 to 6 in favor of this proposal, with 2 abstentions; in the General Assembly the proposal was passed by a majority of 50 to 6, with 2 absentions. Significantly, in both votes Israel was one of the abstainers (the other was India), despite a policy decision to try not to be "isolated [in U.N. voting] with the Russians."[91]

One issue on which Israel did not stand alone was the election of Czechoslovakia to the Security Council late in 1949, in preference to Yugoslavia. Sharett justified the Israeli vote as a means of permitting the major blocs to determine their respective representation in the Council. But Israel's U.N. delegate criticized that argument as intrinsically dangerous on two counts:

a.   We must not support Yugoslavia's candidacy for any council or commit-tee so long as the conflict between her and the Cominform nations persists. It is clear that such a policy is unhealthy from the point of view of justice and law; it is also liable to spoil our relations with friendly nations. Moreover, a posture like that is liable to brand Israel as a supporter of the Cominform against Yugoslavia, since we are also giving Yugoslavia the choice (so far as it depends on our vote) of returning to the Cominform – or cancellation of equal rights as an Eastern European state.
b.   This principle endows the Arab states with the authority to exclude us from all international institutions which are based on the principle of regional representation. For we cannot deprive the Middle East bloc of a right which is granted to the Eastern European bloc.[92]

The Foreign Minister's reply typifies the "political acrobatics" involved in Israel's policy at the U.N.:

I admit that it would have been better had I stated a reservation, to the effect that we were not ready to attribute acceptance of the principle of regional representation to the majority of countries in the area in each and every case. I have no doubt that in this particular case we followed the majority and that this argument was just and thus my contentions were correct. The only other [available] argument could not have been used: that Czechoslovakia had

[91]   See Eytan's cable to Eban, 5.10.1949, ISA 2329/14.
[92]   From Eban's despatch to Sharett, 19.1.1950, ISA 2505/28.

aided us more than Yugoslavia and therefore we chose to vote in favor of the former. We could not countenance such an argument. There is no need for me to stress that we could not possibly explain our vote as a fulfillment of Soviet wishes.[93]

Acrobatics notwithstanding, Israel's U.N. voting at the end of 1949 did earn her Soviet appreciation. In a conversation with Gideon Raphael of Israel's delegation, Tsarapkin (his Soviet counterpart), protested against Israel's clear inclination at the Assembly "towards the United States." But when pressed to gauge whether Israel was not the most independent of the Middle Eastern states he replied, "after consideration and with great hesitation – more or less."[94] Yacov Malik, the Soviet representative to the U.N., was much more frank: he admitted to Abba Eban that the Russians "appreciated" many of Israel's votes in the United Nations;[95] in a conversation held four months later he also concurred with the Israeli diplomat's declaration that there existed an "important identity and similarity between India's approach to the international situation and that of Israel."[96] Israel continued her efforts in the next General Assembly, at the end of 1950. In July of that year, as will be elaborated later, she did support America's position in an important resolution on the Korean crisis; that, however, was a singular aberration. Generally, she continued to implement her earlier policy. Summing up Israel's voting and her position on global questions in October 1950, the former Director of the Eastern Europe Section of the Israeli Foreign Ministry concluded: "[We] elicit attention and congratulation ... from all sides. Other countries, unquestionably obliged to toe the American line, are pleased that at least somebody else, if not they themselves, expresses himself freely. The Eastern bloc ... distinguishes [us] from the other countries and is aware of our effort to ensure that the U.S.S.R. [be taken into account] and that ... she not be isolated while the entire U.N. acts against her. The Americans are perhaps somewhat angry at us for daring [to make] our amendments but this is not articulated and, as I said, our amendments are taken into consideration."[97]

An examination of Israel's voting pattern and positions at the

[93]  From Sharett's despatch to Eban on 27.1.1950, *ibid*. See also Eliashiv's despatch to the Israeli Minister in Belgrade, 25.10.1949, ISA 2493/6.
[94]  See Raphael's despatch to Sharett, 13.12.1949, ISA 2513/14.
[95]  See Eban's cable to Eytan, 8.12.1949, ISA 2329/17.
[96]  20.4.1950, ISA 2512/23.
[97]  Eliashiv's despatch to Levavi, 18.10.1950, ISA 2493/4.

U.N. in 1950 substantiates that claim. With the highly significant exception of her support for the American proposal on Korea in July, Israel's voting behavior was generally independent.[98] On the question of Germany, for example (not a direct issue in U.N. discussions), Israel expressed opposition to the rearmament of the defeated foe. Diverging from the American position, she took every opportunity afforded by the U.N. forum to warn against Germany's resurgence. Regarding China, her policy was equally independent of that adopted by the United States. Israel was one of the first non-Communist countries to extend *de jure* recognition to Mao's People's Republic. Contrary to the American position, she supported Communist China's representation in the U.N. and voted in favor of the Indian proposal on this issue at the Fifth Session of the General Assembly. Sharett expressed his position unequivocally in his speech to the General Assembly, as did Abba Eban in discussions on the Secretary General's peace plan and on Chinese intervention in the Korean War. Israel also opposed the American position when voting not to cancel the diplomatic boycott of Spain. Other expressions of Israel's independence include the elections to the Economic and Social Council (where she supported Poland who defeated the American candidate by one vote); her support for the Soviet proposal regarding admission of new members (recommending that the Security Council re-examine the applications of thirteen candidates); and her election to the U.N. Commission of Peace Observers as a non-aligned nation.

Perhaps most significant of all, however, was Israel's behavior on the question of Korea. Sharett introduced an independent Israeli program at the U.N. Political Committee on 13 December 1950 and Abba Eban expanded on the proposal in his speech of 5 January 1951. The Israeli program formed the basis of the five principles accepted by the first Commission as the foundation for the peaceful settlement of the Korean crisis. Moreover, Israeli activity prepared the ground for the inclusion of the questions of Formosa and of Chinese representation in the U.N. as topics for discussion in the Far East Commission. Her demand that a cease-fire precede any negotiations, including those in the Commission, was accepted as a fundamental principle and at later stages received the official backing of Communist China. All of these steps were directly at variance with the approach favored by the United States, who sought to delay conclu-

[98] The following account is based upon Raphael's despatches to the Foreign Minister and to the Israeli Embassy in Washington on 12.3.1951, and 19.2.1951, ISA 2384/21.

sions of the issue. Despite American attempts to shift Israel's position, she continued to work towards a solution by peaceful means. This, it must be noted, occurred at a time when many public media circles in the U.S., and Congress itself, demanded that the U.N. be increasingly belligerent.

Circumstances such as these largely explain Sharett's mood of self-congratulation. Summing up the delegation's activities at the end of the 1950 session, he claimed that "the atmosphere between us and the Eastern bloc is better than it has been lately. Proof is provided by the Soviet press reaction to our delegation's appearance. This reaction is unusual in every respect and even bears signs of a certain admiration."[99] Whether or not this was in fact the Soviet view is difficult to determine. Some of the reports which reached Israel from behind the Iron Curtain conveyed a different impression. In early November 1950, the Polish Foreign Minister told the Israeli Envoy to Warsaw that "although Israel voted with the Eastern bloc on the question of the People's Republic of China and the Franco question, 'in fundamental matters,' on questions that ultimately determine the fate of the world [such as] (a) the peace proposal ... [and] (b) Korea, Israel is to be found with the United States and in the camp that is not noted for its concern for world peace."[100] Namir reported at the same time that "from a short exchange with [several Russian functionaries] there seems to be no doubt that they view Israel as a bourgeois state slipping unrestrainedly into Western arms."[101]

Whatever the Soviet understanding, Israel's voting patterns at the U.N. during the following year did not exhibit the same degree of adherence to "balance," a phenomenon to which the Foreign Ministry's Eastern Europe Section was most sensitive. Early in 1952, Shmuel Eliashiv the former director of that section, who was then Minister to Moscow, was stingingly critical of Israeli votes in the General Assembly at the end of 1951:

in one of my letters to the Foreign Ministry early in the session I wrote, "to the extent that I follow our votes at the U.N. Assembly, we retain our independence and no reasonable man can say that we are anyone's satellites." Regretfully, I cannot repeat those words now. A discernible move away from non-alignment has taken place, although we still claim to follow

[99] See Walter's despatch to Avriel, 27.10.1950, ISA 2507/2.
[100] Despatch dated 9.11.1950, ISA 2492/20.
[101] Despatch from the Israeli Minister in Moscow to the Foreign Ministry on 19.11.1950, ISA 2492/16.

that course. I cannot judge if there was any other recourse. I fully appreciate the concerns that exert pressure on us and I know from my experience at Lake Success all the weight of that pressure. But this ... leads us to follow the path of least resistance ... I am sorry that the delegation [to the U.N.] did not [unlike the previous year] include a man living under similar pressure from the opposite side [Eastern Europe] in order that he might try to convey his feelings to the other members of the delegation as well.[102]

Eliashiv's letter reflected reality. As much is suggested by the fact that the Foreign Minister did not bother to reply to so unusually critical a despatch. Moreover, in his memorandum to the Foreign Minister, Eliashiv's replacement, Levavi, did not cite a single instance of contrary Israeli behavior or voting at the U.N. Assembly during 1951.[103] No less indicative was a frank discussion held a few weeks earlier between the Israeli and Soviet Foreign Ministers, in which the latter was particularly critical and severely rebuked Israel, citing examples of Israeli behavior in the U.N. that showed her support of "the Soviet Union's enemies all along the line."[104] Sharett, in reply, could cite only one example of an independent Israeli vote, her support of Belorussia's election to the Security Council "which brought us into conflict with the U.S."

Israel's voting behavior at the U.N. did change in the year after this conversation; but it did not revert to the pattern of 1949–50. An internal background survey prior to the U.N. General Assembly on general political questions late in September 1951 stressed the principle of continuing the Israeli policy of the previous year. "Taking into account relations with the West," Israel was to support the U.S. on several central issues on the agenda, (e.g. "peace-keeping measures").[105] The Prague trials and "Doctors' Trials" of 1952 and 1953, the severence of its diplomatic relations with the U.S.S.R. at the beginning of 1953, the anti-Russian campaign Israel had planned for the U.N. in March/April of that year – all clearly indicated that Israel would pay even less attention to "independent" voting in the U.N. Early in June the Israeli Envoy in Hungary recommended trying to

[102] Eliashiv's despatch to Sharett, 1.2.1952, ISA 2507/2.
[103] See Levavi's memorandum, 25.2.1952, *ibid.*
[104] The following excerpts are taken from the protocol of the conversion on 22.12.1951, ISA 2594/1.
[105] See memorandum dated 25.9.1952, ISA 2505/27 and another dated 24.8.1954, ISA 2404/13. It should be noted that a memorandum, prepared late in 1953 by the Eastern Europe Section of the Israeli Foreign Ministry, which dealt with Israel's pro-Soviet voting at the U.N. from 1949 did not cite any such votes after 1949–50. See the undated report in ISA 2457/14 and Appendix 3.

create suitable conditions for a rapprochement with the Soviet Union, once the two countries had completed the process of renewing diplomatic relations. One of his requests was that at the U.N., where "we vote with the U.S. sometimes against our consciences ... shall there arise a minor matter on which, as far as the U.S. is concerned, it will not hurt us to abstain or to vote with the Russians – it is worth doing so even if we are not 100% in agreement with the Russians. We have to 'pay' for Eastern European Jewry!"[106] The Director of the Eastern Europe Section was opposed to this approach, apparently in keeping with the prevailing attitude in Jerusalem: "I put some value on our appearances in the U.N., but I do not tend to exaggerate: (a) it is hard to compete ... with such famously enlightened nations as Afghanistan, Saudi Arabia, etc.; (b) it is hard to point to any effect of our anti-American line on matters such as Communist China, etc.; (c) experience and analysis both suggest a complete distinction in Soviet political planning between regular U.N. problems and one such as the emigration of Eastern European Jewry. We cannot draw analogies between the United States and the Soviet Union in this respect."[107] As Appendix 3 indicates, Israel's voting in the General Assembly in the following two or three years was definitely affected by the consistent tilt to the West.

An interesting example is provided by the Bulgarian and Hungarian applications for admission to the U.N. in September 1954. Both countries asked Israel to support their requests[108] and Israel tended towards a favorable response, despite Hungary's refusal to cooperate on aliyah. She ultimately decided to support both applications, and to draw the attention of the Hungarian government to the fact that "regrettably, we have not lately noticed a tendency on the part of the Hungarian government to permit emigration to Israel ... Our hope is that the Hungarian government will find a way to permit the aliyah of those of her Jewish citizens who desire to settle in Israel. In our belief that Hungary will justify our hopes, we shall vote in favor of the resolution recommending her acceptance as a member of the U.N." Rumania's simultaneous application for U.N. membership afforded more scope for maneuver, particularly since she had not

[106] Avner's despatch to Levavi, 6.6.1953, ISA 2381/21.
[107] His despatch to Avner, 23.6.1953, ISA 2511/9.
[108] The following account is based upon correspondence on the subject in September/October 1954, ISA 2404/14, ISA 2508/13 and also on *Yearbook of the U.N.*, 1955, pp. 22–7.

requested Israel's support. After internal Foreign Ministry consultations during September 1954, the following conclusion was reached: were the U.N. to adopt a general resolution regarding new members, Israel would support Rumania's application while expressing reservations relating to problems of aliyah and Prisoners of Zion in that country. Were voting to be on a country-by-country basis, however, Israel would abstain. Ultimately the U.N. passed a resolution in 1955 that absolved Israel of making the second choice. But her earlier readiness not to support the admission of an Eastern European country to the U.N. is a clear indication of her movement away from the voting patterns established in 1948–50.

During Israel's "non-alignment" period, she made no attempt to demand a direct *quid pro quo* for her votes at the U.N. from the Soviet Union. One possible reason was her perception of her meager political arsenal. Moreover, she seemed to have attained her principal objectives in the Eastern bloc (notably, the emigration of Jews) without resorting to this sort of "deal." As Arieh Levavi put it at an Israeli diplomatic conference held early in 1953: "Aliyah from Rumania continued even after we were no longer 'non-aligned.' "[109] From Israel's point of view this situation changed for the worse after 1952. In her behavior at the U.N. she did not appear so willing to maintain an independent policy in the global dispute between the two superpowers. Of greater importance was the fact that by then mass aliyah from Eastern Europe had ended. However, precisely because of these circumstances, the idea of a political bargain was raised at the beginning of 1953. Conceived by the Israeli Minister to Hungary, it called for an attempt to convince the U.S. and Britain to agree that all states of the Soviet bloc be accepted into the U.N. in exchange for aliyah from those countries.[110] As the Israeli diplomat, Gershon Avner, put it:

It is very important for the U.S.S.R. to get her satellites accepted into the U.N. Maybe she is willing to give something in exchange, especially as we are not talking about aliyah from the Soviet Union. On the other hand, it will not hurt the West if the satellites join the U.N. provided that, at the same time, pro-Western countries such as Jordan, Ireland, Japan, Austria, etc. are accepted as well. The balance of power will not alter to America's detriment. True, the Americans oppose this because the satellite nations have broken the peace agreements, but at the last Assembly the English and French thought it

---

[109]  Avner's despatch to Levavi, 6.6.1953, ISA 2381/21.
[110]  See correspondence in ISA 3043/3.

advisable to bring into the U.N. all the countries desiring admission, with the exception of Communist China and Spain. I suspect that it will be hard for us to get this from the Americans and English, but under present circumstances we must grasp unusual ideas too, routine will not save the Jews of Eastern Europe.[111]

Reactions were cool at the Foreign Ministry in Israel and at Israel's delegation to the U.N. Both were pessimistic about chances of the Eastern bloc agreeing to an "exchange" and of garnering American support for the plan. As Gideon Raphael wrote in response to Avner's proposition: "You seem to suggest matchmaking without being able to get the permission of the couple's parents, whom your plan requires to provide the dowry; the wedding must not take place against their wishes."[112]

This view was further strengthened by meetings with Soviet delegates, where questions of Israeli behavior in the international arena were raised. Early in January 1952 the Israeli Chargé d'Affaires in Budapest argued that "the Eastern European governments, with whose positions I am well acquainted, i.e., Hungary, Rumania and Czechoslovakia, are convinced that the state of Israel has long ceased to be a neutral base. We stress our non-alignment and justify our policies in each and every question in light of the needs and interests of Israel. But they consider these explanations a ruse to hide our real intention of joining the West."[113] On several occasions Israeli representatives received the impression that things were not all that bad.[114] However, once relations with the Soviet Union had been severed early in 1953, they were made unequivocally aware of the Soviet diagnosis and prognosis. This could only reinforce Israel's new political line at the U.N.

A detailed and frank analysis of the Soviet approach to Israel, and an unusually personal one, was provided by the Hungarian Envoy in

[111] Avner's despatch to Raphael, 2.3.1953, *ibid.*
[112] Raphael's despatch to Avner, 19.3.1953, ISA 2398/5.
[113] Bentsur's despatch to Levavi, 2.1.1952, ISA 2492/22.
[114] One of these occasions occurred in a meeting between Israel's Ambassador in London and Mr. Gromyko. Sharett shared Elath's conclusions from his talk with the Soviet diplomat and drew his attention to the fact that "despite our 'Western' development they are sure for some reaosns that we are independent and that we are not hostile to them. They think that they can learn something from us and that we are reliable. This special attitude characterized [Jacob] Malik's talks with Abba [Eban] and Gideon [Raphael] ... at certain times the Soviet Ambassador in Turkey revealed the same attitude to Elias [Sasson]. I regard these relations as a certain asset which we would do well to cultivate, of course *up to a certain point*," Sharett's despatch to Elath, 22.10.1952, ISA 43/15, emphasis added.

Sofia, who was very close to the Communist leadership in Budapest. In a rare instance of Eastern European candor, he described to the Israeli Minister in Sofia the prism through which members of the Soviet bloc viewed Israel at the beginning of 1953:

You ... have interests and you are the judges of what is good for your own interests. Apparently your interests dictate that you be close to the West, to England, to the U.S.; you have enemies, the Arabs, new immigrants, financial needs – these are your considerations. We think these [policies] ... will result in your state's subservience and ruin, but you should not complain if we draw our own conclusions from this calculation – you are firmly set in the camp hostile to us, our philosophy, our concepts, our type of regime. Our entire policy is built on the assumption that one day the hostile camp will attack us in order to destroy our government. You are in that camp; and seek to function in a regional defense command that is no more than part of the American program for the day they attack us.

You always say you wish to be friendly towards the U.S.S.R. and towards us. You say this very often. Let us be frank; this is a diplomatic phrase that you employ so that immediately thereafter you can use it as a base from which to demand the emigration of our Jewish citizens ... You are not friends at all, only speak of friendship in order to establish your demands on this matter.

You know that we are seriously interested in trade with the entire world, including the ideologically hostile world. If trade and the exchange of goods exists, then a mutual interest is created. When we see that some country is making efforts to do something for us, then a calculation of interest is created. And you base all relations with us on your demand [for emigration], which is in any case hard to meet, and in the field of commerce you show no interest at all. Again the account of interests works against you. After all this, explain one consideration on our part that makes it worthwhile to meet your demand.

This does not mean that there cannot be normal diplomatic relations. They can exist and I am sure that they will. Relations such as with Belgium or Italy, but not like those with Switzerland or Finland or the Lebanon.[115]

Another instructive example of this trend of thought was provided by the statement made by the advisor to the Soviet Embassy in London, in a conversation with Gershon Avner in mid-August 1954. The Israeli diplomat had remarked that in view of Israel's weakness and Soviet unwillingness to provide assistance, Israel had "no chance of alternative support in the event of frontal conflict with the U.S." In response, the Russian argued that "it is possible that the state of Israel's policy is dictated by reality ... at any rate the U.S.S.R. has reached the conclusion that Israel is in fact so involved in the policy of the West and her desire to maneuver towards the West is so great,

---

[115] Avner's despatch to the Foreign Ministry, 6.6.1953, ISA 2381/21.

that she will sooner or later be forced to join the anti-Soviet military preparations; thus there is no point in the Soviet Union providing her with special assistance, political or otherwise."[116]

Thus, the "fatalistic" Israeli conception regarding international political activity at the U.N. *vis-à-vis* the U.S.S.R. mirrored a similar conception on Moscow's part. At least partially, the dynamics of Israeli foreign policy-making in this area can be described as a "self-fulfilling prophecy." The complementary aspect of this fatalism becomes further apparent in an analysis of the evolution of Israel's strategic contacts with the West.

[116] Avner's despatch to the Foreign Ministry, 18.8.1954, ISA 2509/9.

# 8. THE MILITARY DIMENSION

Israel was created in the midst of war. Jewish national aspirations for political independence, reinforced after the Second World War, met with increasing opposition from the Arab states and from the Arab population. As early as December 1946, Ben Gurion warned the Political Committee of the Zionist Congress: "The major problem is defense. Until recently it was only a question of defending ourselves against the Palestinian Arabs who occasionally attacked Jewish settlements. But now we confront a totally new situation. Israel is surrounded by independent Arab states ... which have ... the capacity to acquire arms ... While the ... Palestinian Arabs do not endanger the Jewish community, we now face the prospect of the Arab states sending their armies to attack us ... We are facing a threat to our very existence."[1]

This danger became more concrete late in 1947 when the U.N. General Assembly adopted the plan to partition Palestine. The prospect of total war created severe problems for the Jewish leadership in Palestine, prominent among which was the acquisition of arms. Military equipment was unavailable, the British government maintained a tight control over the possession of weapons in Palestine while extending financial and military support to two of the Arab states on the future Jewish state's borders, Egypt and Jordan. Furthermore, at the end of 1947, the U.N. imposed an embargo on the sale of arms to Palestine. Against this background, it is hardly surprising that in September 1947 Ben Gurion considered the acquisition of military material to be of "prime importance."[2] Such was the background to the Czech–Israeli connection.

Contacts commenced in July 1947[3] when Moshe Sneh, Director of

---

[1] D. Ben Gurion, *In the Battle*, 5 (Tel Aviv, 1958), pp. 135–7 (Hebrew).
[2] M. Mardor, *Secret Mission* (Tel Aviv, 1958), p. 181 (Hebrew).
[3] The following account is based on *ibid.*; B. Dinur, ed., *History of the Haganah* (Tel Aviv,

173

the European Section of the Jewish Agency, discussed the procurement of weapons with Czech Deputy Foreign Minister Vladimir Clementis. During the next nine months intensive efforts to that end were made by some of Israel's best agents – Otto Felix, Meir Mardor, Shaul Avigur and Ehud Avriel. The first result was obtained in January 1948 when a contract was signed with the Skoda factory specifying shipment to the Yishuv of 4,500 Mauser rifles, 200 MG-34 machine guns and 5,040,000 rounds of ammunition, at a cost of $750,000. For obvious reasons the identity of the buyers was concealed, the Israeli agents signing as representatives of Ethiopia. Other transactions with Czechoslovakia added to the Israeli arsenal, which by the termination of the British Mandate in mid-May 1948 included more than 5,000 medium machine guns, 54 million rounds of ammunition and 25 Messerschmitt planes. The estimated value of these purchases was $12,280,000 – more than 60% of Israel's total arms purchases in Europe, which was the major source of her military supplies.

While the Israeli motives behind the purchases are self-explanatory, Czech interests seem to have been more complicated. Avriel realized that the Czechs had a clear economic incentive for selling arms; he reported to the Israeli Finance Minister in mid-1948 that the arms deal provided Czechoslovakia with 25% of her dollar reserves.[4] Avriel's figure cannot be corroborated, but there is little doubt that the Czechoslovak government was in need of foreign currency. However, that was not necessarily the sole motive. A substantial portion of the negotiations, at least up to the actual conclusion of the first agreement, was conducted prior to the Czechoslovakian Communist coup in February 1948, at a time when two veteran non-Communist friends of the Zionist cause, Eduard Benes and Jan Masaryk, still served as Czechoslovak President and Foreign Minister respectively. Nevertheless, the country had to all intents and purposes been a full member of the Soviet bloc for several months before the coup. A decision on arms sales must therefore have required Soviet approval and have served Soviet strategic interests in the Middle East.

1972), 3, pp. 1526–39 (Hebrew); Y. Ro'i, *Soviet Decision-Making in Practice* (London, 1980), pp. 149–61; A. Krammer, *The Forgotten Friendship* (Illinois, 1974), pp. 54–101; and Y. Greenberg, "Financing the War of Independence," *Studies in Zionism*, 9, 1, 1988, pp. 63–80.
[4] See his despatch of 24.7.1948, FM 5624/c/16/18/1.

Moreover, after Israel's declaration of independence, the volume of her transactions with Czechoslovakia grew considerably. Additional Messerschmitts were purchased on 20 May 1948. Three days later Avigur informed Ben Gurion that Avriel was negotiating for the purchase of "planes, tanks and heavy guns, and that a credit of $5 million for six months and an immediate payment of $1 million was set by the Czech Cabinet."[5] The following week Ben Gurion recorded in his diary that Israel was "about to buy [from Czechoslovakia] 30 more Messerschmitts, 20 Spitfires and 9 Mosquitos. They are willing to sell us 30 sixteen-ton tanks and another 30 at the end of June, together with 20 nine-ton tanks."[6] Several of the proposed transactions were not ultimately effected. Nevertheless, by the standards of the time the sums involved were large and must have placed a severe strain on Israeli finances. Their strict payment demands notwithstanding, the Czechs were helpful in this respect too. On 30 May 1948 Ben Gurion was informed by Avriel that "we finalized the arrangement with the Czech National Bank for six months' credit of $12 million ... We are to pay the bank two million upon signature. Once purchases reach $8 million, we are to pay them another $1 million."[7] In fact Israel managed to use up only 75% of that credit during the second half of 1948, when she purchased arms from Czechoslovakia to the value of $9 million.[8] The Czechs also helped to train Israeli soldiers in operating the equipment. Furthermore, whereas some of the arms reached Israel by sea (a train hauled them to several ports in Yugoslavia whence they were shipped to Israel), the majority was flown in, mainly from a small airfield in Zatec.

But at the end of 1948, the Israeli–Czech connection appeared to have come to an end. In October of that year Ben Gurion wrote that "because of Arab pressure, the Czechs have stopped selling us planes and other weapons."[9] According to Dr. Michael Stepanek, then Press Aide to the Czech Defense Minister Ludvik Svoboda, instructions were issued in December to halt the shipment of military spare parts to Israel; later that month a group of Israeli pilots was forced to interrupt training in Czechoslovakia and to return home.[10]

On the basis of this evidence, virtually all students of the subject have assumed that the military connection was thereby broken; this

[5] D. Ben Gurion, *The Restored State of Israel* (Tel Aviv, 1969), p. 129 (Hebrew).
[6] *Ibid.*, p. 132.
[7] Ben Gurion's diary, BGA.    [8] See file referred to in n. 4.
[9] Ben Gurion's diary, BGA.    [10] Ro'i, *Soviet Decision-Making*, p. 159.

certainly seems to conform to, and to confirm, the generally accepted
thesis that Russia's support for Israel was fundamentally a function of
the Soviet desire to eject the British from Palestine. Israel's military
successes, which seemed to guarantee her status as an independent
state, had ostensibly secured the Russian objective by the end of 1948.
The termination of Czech arms sales to Israel has therefore been
endowed with the status of a turning-point in Soviet support for
Israel. Documents recently de-classified in Israel necessitate a
revision of that view. Although entire volumes of secret material for
the period are still closed to public inspection (cross-references from
other files have also generally been censored) the available evidence is
remarkable. It proves conclusively that Czechoslovakia continued to
sell vast quantities of military equipment, including heavy weapons,
to Israel long after 1948. This circumstance will undoubtedly generate new interpretations of Israeli–Soviet relations during the late
1940s and early 1950s. As a preliminary to that analysis, the following
pages will cite the evidence, most of which is cryptic and laconic, in
some detail.

Ben Gurion's diary entry for 22 October 1948 mentions an
extremely large arms deal with Czechoslovakia: "The fifty Spitters
have been purchased; however, there are some difficulties in getting
them out. We might have them early in 1949."[11] Avriel's report to the
Foreign Ministry early in 1949 clarifies the identity of the above
plane: "Over the past weeks we have flown a couple of Spitfires from
here."[12] That period witnessed an intensification of Israeli purchases.
On 14 January Dr. Asher Citron of the Israeli Defense Ministry
traveled to Prague in order to establish what was to become Israel's
only full-scale and active arms-purchasing ("Rechesh") mission in
the Eastern bloc.[13] At the same time Avriel reported that the Czechs
"offered to build a munitions factory [in Israel], a suggestion which
has been passed on to the Defense Ministry. I regard this plan to be of
outstanding importance for its military-economic prospects and for
our relations with the Czechs."[14] In the absence of other evidence, it
must be assumed that the plan was scrapped. But the same can hardly
be said of other weapons which Israel continued to receive from

[11] Ben Gurion's diary, BGA.        [12] 2.2.1949, ISA 2514/4.
[13] See cable from Mossad headquarters in Israel to its European headquarters,
14.1.1949, in the Haganah Archive, file 699/14. See also cables referring to Israeli
activities in Czechoslovakia early in 1949, *ibid.*, files 700–701/14.
[14] 7.1.1949, ISA 2514/4.

Czechoslovakia in the last week of January 1949. Following a meeting with the Czech Foreign Minister, Avriel reported that the Czechs are "willing to provide us with heavy guns but they cannot supply us with tanks ... Dr. Citron has already begun to deal with this."[15] The diary of the Israeli Chargé d'Affaires in Prague for the last weeks of August 1949 refers to "negotiations with the manager of the Skoda factory about equipment ordered by the Defense Ministry for our ballistic laboratory";[16] it also mentions a discussion with the director of Zbrojovka, another Czech arms factory, "on our future purchase of light weapons. We are cabling the Defense Ministry to check the arrival time of its purchasing mission."[17] Another entry, dated three weeks later, refers to a discussion with Dr. Benda of the Czech Foreign Ministry "on the inclusion of our arms acquisition within the general commercial transaction."[18]

Since Czechoslovakia possesses no independent outlet to the sea, the arms had to be transported across the borders of other countries. Remarkably, and contrary to their behavior two years earlier, the Poles agreed to allow the passage of at least some of the shipment. Early in June 1950 Israel's Consul in Warsaw reported on talks with Polish officials who had emphasized that "even today arms are being sent from the East [to Israel]. It was only a few days ago that you asked us for passage permits for the weapons from the East [Czechoslovakia] and we agreed."[19] Israeli diplomats and military representatives in the United States were aware of the connection with Prague which, for obvious political and military reasons, gave rise to considerable antagonism. Thus in mid-June 1950 Israel's current President, Chaim Herzog, then Israeli Military Attaché in Washington, pointed out to his superiors that "it seems politically inadvisable, when concentrating our efforts on obtaining arms in the U.S., to enter into negotiations with Czechoslovakia for weapons."[20] He could hardly have been referring to marginal transactions.

Ben Gurion's diary is a unique source for details about the scope of the planned Israeli acquisitions from Czechoslovakia for 1950: "2,500 machine guns, 250 recoiless rifles, 5,000 semi-automatic rifles, 40,000 rifles, 40,000 rifle bolts, 20 million rounds, total – $6,204,500"[21] – no less than one-quarter of the predicted total cost of Israeli arms imports at the time.[22] The flow of arms continued throughout 1950

[15] 23.1.1949, *ibid.*   [16] 22.8.1949, ISA 2414/1.   [17] 23.8.1949, *ibid.*
[18] 12.9.1949, ISA 2494/13.   [19] ISA 2492/20.   [20] ISA 2461/9.
[21] 25.6.1950, BGA.   [22] *Ibid.*

and included more than light weapons. Early in January 1951 the Israeli purchasing mission in Prague reported to Jerusalem that the "consignment of planes is now at Gdynia [in Poland] and are dismantled in eleven of the thirty cases."[23] There can thus be no doubt that Israel maintained military connections with Czechoslovakia for almost three years after the relationship was assumed to have ended.

The arms shipments were accompanied by a tight web of personal and professional contacts entirely absent from Israel's relations with other Eastern European countries. Clearly, the foundations for this network had been laid during the hectic months of early and mid-1948. Czech assistance had then extended far beyond the conventional implementation of arms deals; it included, for example, security cooperation against hostile intelligence services (mainly the British and Americans).[24] A prominent instance of such contact, which persisted well beyond 1948, was the visit already mentioned of Israel's Chief of Staff, General Yigael Yadin, to Prague in the first week of June 1949.[25] The trip included visits to Brno and Pilzen and the review of Czech military exercises, as well as talks on arms procurements.[26] In his despatch to the Foreign Ministry in Tel Aviv in March 1950, Yadin noted that the Czechs had even consented to send experts to Israel in order to help local technicians handle newly acquired weapons.[27] There is no evidence to suggest that they did in fact arrive, but Israeli military officials certainly went to Prague for purposes other than arms procurement: Captain Moshe Zohar, then in charge of physical training in the Israeli Army, was there at the end of August 1949 and met with Czech officers "and others in the same field."[28] According to Rafael Ben-Shalom, then Israeli Chargé d'Affaires in Prague, these activities were organized by the "very large procurements section in the Israeli Consulate," which was in effect a branch of the Defense Ministry.[29]

It is difficult to pinpoint exactly when these relations were terminated; a reasonable assumption is the departure early in 1951 of Dr. Citron, who coordinated all Israeli defense contacts in Prague and

[23]  Despatch from U. Doron of 11.1.1951, ISA 530/10.
[24]  See unsigned despatch to Avriel of 17.5.1951, *ibid*.
[25]  See *Ha'aretz* on 5.6.1949.
[26]  Communication to the author, 9.6.1983.
[27]  Yadin's letter to Sharett, 24.3.1950, ISA 2411/20.
[28]  See Ben Shalom's report, ISA 2414/1.
[29]  Letter to the author, 29.5.1983.

who took with him all the files dealing with arms acquisitions.[30] His recall must have been prompted by Czechoslovakia's refusal to satisfy Israel's request for additional arms, a decision which Foreign Minister Villiem Siroki relayed to Israeli Minister Dr. Shmuel Eliashiv early in February 1951.[31]

If no Soviet involvement had taken place, the significance of Czech aid to Israel after the 1948 War may not be so great. But it is inconceivable that such large quantities of arms left Czechoslovakia without Soviet knowledge and approval; after all, the U.S.S.R. maintained tight control over that country in the wake of the arrests and executions of "treacherous" political and military leaders which followed the coup of February 1948. Moreover, it is also inconceivable that the activities of the Israeli arms-purchasing mission in Prague would have escaped the attention of Soviet intelligence. There are thus grounds for assuming that Soviet proxy military aid to Israel, in the form of Czech armaments, continued for longer than would have been necessary had Russia merely wished to ensure the establishment of a Jewish state.[32] While our thesis must remain speculative, the information now available suggests that the Soviet attitude towards Israel changed only when Israel publicly supported the American position on Korea late in 1950, and when signs of her growing reliance on the U.S. became unmistakable. In other words, Soviet aid was related to Israel's foreign policy orientation to a greater degree than has hitherto been assumed; the U.S.S.R. may have rewarded Israel for her non-alignment in 1949–50 by approving the Czech arms deal; she may have withdrawn that support once Israel altered her global foreign policy orientation.

There is no doubt that the temporal boundaries of the Czech arms deal influenced internal discussions in Israel on global foreign policy orientation during a period which can hardly be described as episodic.[33] Moreover, the procurement of Czech arms clearly had a decisive effect on Israel's military achievements; more precisely, it enabled her to avoid serious defeats during the critical opening stages of the 1948 War. Needless to say, the Czechs were hardly philanthropists. They demanded that all payments be in American dollars; they enforced a strict schedule of payments; the deals enabled them to

---

[30]  See Doron's despatch of 7.5.1951, ISA 2501/5.     [31]  ISA 2492/22.
[32]  See Ro'i, *Soviet Decision-Making*, pp. 339–96.
[33]  See U. Bialer, *Our Place in the World, Mapai and Israel's Foreign Policy Orientation, 1947–1952*, Jerusalem Papers on Peace Problems, 33 (Jerusalem, 1981).

dispose of obsolete weapons; and the sales were for a fixed period of time. But all this does not detract from the benefits which Israel reaped. Czech military assistance became the obvious, tangible and unquestionable symbol of Soviet aid to the creation of the state of Israel, a point Soviet and Eastern European officials repeatedly emphasized when Israel complained about the negative response to other requests, especially in regard to aliyah. In this case, military support also supplied precious ammunition to the Israeli left-wing opposition, which had persistently attacked the Israeli government's "subservience" to the West.

Officially, however, the internal reaction of the Israeli authorities was to play down the military aid within the broad perspective of Soviet–Israeli relations. As early as 18 July 1950 Ben Gurion sent a letter to *Davar*, the influential daily newspaper of the Histadrut. This letter expressed what later became the unequivocal historical judgment on the Czech transaction, and conventional opinion in Israel for years to come:

We are used to the fact that the Mapam newspaper and the Communist press knowingly falsify facts for Communist propaganda, but it is annoying when this occurs in the Histadrut's daily. On Tuesday, someone signing himself H.Y. wrote on the American arms embargo to Israel, which he contrasted with the supply of weapons by the Eastern bloc. Is *Davar* not aware: (a) that the U.S.S.R. imposed and maintains an embargo on arms to Israel which is no less efficient than that of the West? And from that country not a single round of ammunition has been received? (b) that the Soviet Union bans Jewish aliyah to Israel, something not forbidden by any other country, Eastern or Western? (c) that it was not the "Soviet bloc" but only Czechoslovakia that sold arms to Israel? (d) that Czechoslovakia sold arms to the Arabs as well? (e) that arms shipments were received from the West as well, weapons without which we could not have withstood the Arab attack? Isn't it too early to change the history of our period of liberation for the sake of Communist propaganda?[34]

Not all Ben Gurion's facts were accurate. The Czechs needed, and received, the Kremlin's blessings for their military dealings with Israel during and after the War of Independence; Ben Gurion's insinuation to the contrary is significant in its minimalization of the historical implications. But far more important than what he said is what he omitted to say: the Czech weapons had virtually saved the country. A year later Moshe Sharett, urging the government to pay its financial debt for the Czech weapons, wrote that without them "we

[34] BGA.

would have stood on the edge of a deep abyss."[35] Only two decades after the fact did Ben Gurion allow himself publicly to admit this fact to an Israeli journalist: "They saved the country, I have no doubt of that. The Czech arms deal was the greatest help we then had, it saved us and without it I very much doubt if we could have survived the first month." In the same interview he stressed that military relations between the two countries "had halted when the war was over. We had sufficient arms then and everything ended."[36]

The true facts about the duration of these relations, and especially their critical impact on the fate of the newly born Jewish state, have long been kept vague. The authoritative *Israel, Army and Defense: A Dictionary*, for example, refers to the Czech arms deal only in the context of certain 1948 operations. It contains not one word on the sequel to that period under the general heading "arms acquisition."[37]

Official reticence on the matter, both contemporary and subsequent, might be attributed to three plausible sources. One concerns internal political considerations; Israel's government was under domestic fire from the left during the first years of statehood. By minimizing the significance of the "Czech Connection," it may have hoped to complement its defensive posture, especially with regard to the fierce clash between Mapai and Mapam. A second consideration was external. Publicity for the 1949–51 Czech–Israeli contacts might have jeopardized America's readiness to provide much-needed economic assistance, especially during that period of intensive cold war. Finally, psychological reactions may have played a role. As anti-Zionism became increasingly vocal in Czechoslovakia, reaching a crescendo in the 1952 Prague trials, it might have been awkward for Israel to admit the extent to which she had previously been dependent on Czech aid. After late 1955, when Czechoslovakia became the major source of arms to Egypt, the memory of her former assistance to Israel must certainly have rankled. As Israel herself moved steadily closer to the West, her leaders probably thought it best to draw a veil over the entire episode.

Interestingly enough, once massive Czech arms supplies did begin

[35] 29.8.1951, ISA 2501/5.
[36] Z. Shiff, "Stalin Gave Orders to Provide Israel with Arms," *Ha'aretz*, 3.5.1968 (Hebrew).
[37] Z. Shiff and E. Haber, eds., *Israel, Army and Defense: A Dictionary* (Tel Aviv, 1976) (Hebrew). The new Hebrew Military Encyclopedia, *Zahal Becheilo*, refers to the Czech arms deal only cryptically, and even then conclusively places the connection in the context of the 1948 War.

to stream into Egypt in 1955, they immediately became a cause of domestic Israeli disagreements over foreign policy. Word of the Egyptian–Czech arms deal reached the Israeli government early in September 1955; on the 12th of that month Israeli Ambassador Yosef Avidar asked the Chairman of the Middle East Department in the Soviet Foreign Ministry for verification. The Russian denied the existence of the deal,[38] but two weeks later it was made public. Even before the scope of the arms deal – enormous by contemporary standards – was fully exposed, Israel's leadership grasped its dire significance for the security of their country. The transaction seemed immediately to impinge on several aspects of foreign and security policy. By 1955 Israel had a greater interest in preventing the Arab states from acquiring arms than in arming herself, primarily because her preoccupation with the absorption of massive waves of immigration was deflecting much of the budget away from the military. Besides, Israeli military leadership was firmly convinced of its military superiority (even though, for obvious reasons, they had carefully projected an image of inferiority to the external world). As Moshe Dayan bluntly informed several Israeli ambassadors only four months before the Czech–Egyptian arms deal was publicized: "We have no need of a security agreement with the United States; on the contrary, it would be an impediment. Arab potential will not present a danger for the next eight to ten years, even if they receive military assistance from the West; we will retain the advantage because we are vastly superior to them in terms of modern weaponry control."[39] That perception explains why, for some time, Israel had been advocating an embargo on arms sales to the Middle East, or at least their stringent supervision.

When the size of the Czech–Egyptian deal became known, however, Israel found herself in serious jeopardy for the first time since the 1948 War. By its very existence, the transaction had broken through the barrier of Western supervision, flimsy though it was, that had largely prevented massive Arab purchases of arms. The U.S.S.R. had not signed the Tripartite Agreement of 1950; she could thus sell arms at will and ignore the important principle of balance that, at least theoretically, had shaped American, British and French policies regarding arms exports to the Middle East. In addition, the arms deal

[38]  ISA 2410/18. See also M. Dayan, *Story of My Life* (Tel Aviv, 1976), p. 153 (Hebrew).
[39]  M. Sharett, *Personal Diary* (Tel Aviv, 1978), p. 1021 (Hebrew).

threatened to generate international competition for Arab support; Israel would be bound to suffer, since that rivalry would emphasize the geostrategic inferiority of her position. A few days after the arms deal was made public Sharett, then Prime Minister, confided the shock of the announcement to his diary:

For some time I have been hiding the deep embarrassment I myself feel at not seeing my way clear in this difficult situation ... resulting from the Soviet incursion into the Middle East, a political as well as military incursion, boding countless dangers. I am at a loss and feel that I am not holding the wheel firmly and not taking an active initiative. I merely listen first to this suggestion, then to that, in effect behaving like Kutuzov retreating from Napoleon as Tolstoy describes it; this feeling lowers me in my own estimation and leaves me restless.[40]

Sharett's diagnosis, which was shared by many, was one-dimensional; the prognosis, however, was not. Four different ideas were discussed in meetings of the Cabinet, the Foreign Ministry and the Mapai Central Committee; by the standards of the time, two were orthodox and two were revolutionary. The most prominent proposal called for Israel to increase her efforts to acquire heavy weapons (specifically artillery, tanks and airplanes) from the West and particularly from the United States; only thus could she meet the challenge of war in circumstances reasonably close to a balance of power. This was a conventional viewpoint. So too was a second idea, which reiterated the need for a defense agreement with the United States to complement, not replace, Western arms. Of the less orthodox propositions, one was formulated in a cable from the heads of the Israeli Embassy in Washington only a few days after receipt of news of the Czech arms sale. It advised that should the first two ideas prove impractical, the military option had to be considered: "[we] have reached the conclusion that [Israel] cannot depend on receiving weapons and reaching a guarantee which would parallel the Soviet weapons that Egypt is about to receive; but preparations must be made for a preventive war initiated by us to smash the ... Egyptian army before it becomes stronger ... thus defeating Nasser and his gang."[41] There remained a fourth, and final, alternative. Israel's extraordinary situation in 1955, it was argued, called for an extraordinary political response. Since she could not acquire arms and/or a defense agreement with the West, and since a preventive war was problematical, Israel had to make overtures to the East. Specifically,

---

[40] *Ibid.*, pp. 1206–7.          [41] 12.10.1955, *ibid.*, p. 1207.

she had to attempt to procure weapons from the Soviet Union itself. It was around this issue that the controversy on "orientation" principally raged.

Israel had hitherto enjoyed no success whatsoever in attempting to obtain arms directly from the U.S.S.R. In 1948 the Israeli Mission in Moscow did receive hints that the U.S.S.R. would be willing to consider a request for weapons; but when a list of required equipment was submitted, it was turned down point blank. Reminders on the matter, presented in 1949, met with no response.[42] For some five years thereafter the Foreign Ministry did not seriously consider repeating the request. In the absence of documentation, the reasons for this position must remain a matter of conjecture; however, several assumptions do appear reasonable. Since 1948 the Soviets had not once evinced the slightest willingness to provide military assistance. Besides, Israel considered her demand for Jewish emigration from the Soviet bloc to be far more critical. Indeed, she may have been hesitant to submit requests on so sensitive an issue as armaments, especially since her own need of weapons had apparently diminished. Overriding all of these considerations, however, was perhaps the prevailing conception of Israel's appropriate foreign policy "orientation." An approach to the U.S.S.R. for arms, it seems to have been felt, might jeopardize Israel's chances of attaining a goal which had become fundamental since 1951 – the creation of a military-economic-strategic connection with the West, in particular with the United States. That the possibility of acquiring Russian arms was not raised for six years is thus a clear commentary on the military-strategic dimension of the tie with the Soviet bloc in Israel's global policy. Only at the end of 1955, when Israel found herself in serious trouble, was the situation transformed.

The seeds of the idea that Israel approach Russia had been sown a year earlier under circumstances that seem to have been a rehearsal, albeit in a less severe form, of the situation which was to develop in 1955. Publication of the American–Iraqi arms deal in 1954 represented a considerable threat to Israel, not least because of the U.S.'s intractable refusal to compensate her with new weapons' shipments. On 6 September 1954 the issue was raised in the Political Committee of the Mapai party where the claim was put forward that external circumstances dictated revolutionary foreign policy measures. Two

[42] See correspondence in ISA 2384/15, ISA 2479/8 and Ro'i, *Soviet Decision-Making*.

participants in the debate advocated an approach to the Soviet Union with a formal request for military aid. One, Chaim Ben-Asher, expressed himself as follows:

I do not like a world of priests nor a world of sinners. I know between Hitler and Stalin – whom I consider the greater inquisitor – we chose Stalin ... And in security matters we have the same rights. Judah Maccabi made a treaty with worshippers of Jupiter but that saved the Hasmonean state for 200 years ... So long as the Red Army stays on the other side of the Caucasus the danger to Israel's sovereignty from there is less than war with the Arabs; war with the Arabs is serious ... Between Russia and the Arabs we will choose those who will help us. Israel is not a permanent [satellite of] the United States.[43]

Most of the Mapai leadership rejected this approach. Prime Minister Sharett explained why, presenting arguments, which were indicative of the concept prevailing at the end of 1954. Retrospectively, his case shows the essential change that occurred the following year:

Let us assume that a new incursion of the Arab states into Israel takes place and let us assume that America again abandons us as she did in 1947–48 ... and let us assume that under those circumstances there is the chance of getting military assistance from Russia. Would not every Israeli patriot turn the world upside down in order to realize that possibility? The question is: Are we in such a situation?

According to Sharett if all hope was not lost, however, an approach to the Soviet Union would be fraught with unbearable dangers. Israel would then discover that:

our cause is lost in America, it is over and done with, no one will support you, you will be considered a contaminant, everyone will wash their hands of you and you will be left out in the cold. You can say that America is not important, but if you say that by this means you will gain America's heart you say the opposite of the precise truth ... Do you think that America will be frightened if you start moving towards friendship with Russia? The State Department will bless you for it, you will make their work easier, the "Council of Judaism," Dorothy Thompson and all that group will be happy to be able to substantiate their claims that the Chairman of the Knesset Foreign Affairs and Security Committee had said that we must try for greater friendship with the U.S.S.R. For them, this will be manna from heaven.

The Czech–Egyptian arms deal considerably worsened Israel's international and security situation. Accordingly, the idea of a strategic overture to the U.S.S.R. did not seem as fantastic or as

[43] 6.9.1954, LPA which is the source for the following excerpts.

strategically illogical as it had appeared to be in 1954. In the second week of October 1955, Sharett himself estimated that "our public will soon begin to advocate two extreme opinions – a request for aid from the Soviet Union [or] a preventive war against Egypt."[44] This forecast was born out at a meeting of Mapai's Political Committee two days later. Protagonists of the unorthodox view now included several party leaders of the first rank, prominent among whom was Pinhas Lavon, until a few months earlier Minister of Defense. He sharply criticized any public rejection of the possibility that Israel might approach Russia and receive arms from her:

It seems to me politically unwise in this situation for the Foreign Ministry and the government of Israel to take a dogmatic stand that such a possibility is out of the question. We will shoot only with American rifles. If they do not give them to us, we will recite the Kaddish [the prayer for the dead] ... it will not hurt at all if [members of the Knesset] on this point make less considered statements. It is not necessary to issue stupid announcements to the effect that we will go over to the Eastern bloc or that we will become tied to the Soviet Union, but we must state simply the supposition that has been our fundamental political guideline all along: that the interest of ... national existence is the supreme interest and if some paths are closed to us we will take others.[45]

Supporting this thesis, Mordechai Namir pointed out that the risks of such a step were not so very great:

We must not say that we are tied only to one side, policy is not mathematics and diplomacy is not built on the foundations of iron laws, and you do not know what irrational factor is influencing American public affairs ... We must use various and sundry means to attempt to climb the steep wall known as the political East as well, because of the simple rule of politics that nothing remains constant in policy and that something constant today will change tomorrow.[46]

Controversy in this internal forum undoubtedly influenced the Foreign Minister's statement in the Knesset two days later. There he deliberately declared that Israel would request weapons from any source, an announcement which made the headlines of *Davar*.[47] Although his speech did not constitute a practical approach to the Soviet Union for weapons, the idea of requesting military Soviet assistance did not stop at the stage of political action. Its foremost and

[44] Sharett, *Personal Diary*, p. 1214.
[45] Protocol of Mapai's Political Committee, 16.10.1955, LPA.
[46] *Ibid.*
[47] See Sharett's comments on 19.10.1955 in *Personal Diary*, p. 1231.

unequivocal purpose was to enlist the Kremlin's support for the cancellation of the Czech arms sale to Egypt, distant though that prospect was. Sharett did raise the issue in his meeting with Molotov in Geneva on 31 October 1955 but to no avail.[48] Moreover, although he did not raise the matter, he was most attentive to the possibility that an offer of Soviet arms might be forthcoming. That is why he felt it necessary later to confide to his diary: "He did not offer us armaments, not even by the slightest hint." The meeting itself was often noisy – in Sharett's words "the controversy, more correctly the quarrel, was always hot." Nevertheless, from Israel's perspective it did contain one bright spot. Molotov stressed that "if a small country sees itself endangered, a great power is obliged to pay attention to it and I am again willing to examine the question."

This remark, together with the acerbity of the conversation, apparently persuaded Sharett to approach the Russian Foreign Minister directly and in writing. In a message sent a few hours after the conclusion of the meeting Sharett requested that "Israel's security needs be taken into consideration." The Russian Foreign Minister's reply arrived within two days, a speed whose significance was not lost on the Foreign Ministry. The response did not refute Molotov's earlier statement, but it did shift the focus to the need to work towards peace and made no mention of the possibility of Russian military assistance. It is indicative of the gravity of Israel's defense situation as 1955 drew to an end, that even these inconclusive contacts did not bury the idea that she might approach the Soviet Union for military aid.

At this stage the issue became an important element in the creation of a movement within the Foreign Ministry towards a radical revision of Soviet–Israeli relations. Leading the advocates of this school was the Israeli Ambassador to the Soviet Union, Yosef Avidar. It was his fundamental contention that the situation justified a concentrated effort at finding a different way of reaching the Russians. This he felt might be achieved were Israel to try and establish a balance in her approach to the inter-power conflict; specifically she had to rethink her willingness and desire to interpolate herself into the framework of a Western strategic treaty. "We can truthfully say," Avidar argued, "that we ourselves helped create this opinion [Russian disappointment in Israel]; the latest and perhaps most convincing proof is our

---

[48] *Ibid.*, pp. 1272–5, which is the source for the following excerpts.

begging at the doors of the State Department for a defense agreement. No propaganda will convince the Soviet Union that a defense agreement with the United States [will be authorized] without it openly or tacitly obliging [us] to grant [America] bases, and that such an agreement is not directed against the Soviet Union.''[49]

In view of the strategic danger presented by the Czech deal, the Foreign Ministry did accept, at least in principle, the logic of the need for some reassessment of Israel's global policy. The reply to Avidar expressed some willingness to undertake such a reassessment, and a significant degree of concurrence with his thesis.

It is definitely obvious that the Soviet Union today holds out various incentives, suiting their respective needs, to neutral countries or countries which can be influenced to become neutral ... like Sweden. Nehru was offered steel, not being interested in arms, and Nasser, who was not interested in steel mills, was offered weapons. So long as the Soviet Union believes that we are an American satellite we cannot assume that she will offer us anything. If we forgo the idea of a defense treaty with the United States, or if we at least stop talking about it, the Soviet Union may offer us something as well in order to convert us to permanent neutrality. We are liable then to be in the awkward position of not knowing if it is better to accept the offer or reject it, unless, of course, we are offered Jews.

The feeling that a new relationship with the U.S.S.R. was perhaps possible did not only stem from the problems caused by the Czech deal, and from disappointment in the American and British reactions to it. It was also the result of signs from the Eastern bloc that lent some credence to the cautious optimism regarding the possible success of such a new direction. A survey carried out by the Foreign Ministry's Research Section in mid-December 1955 indicated several significant signals. One concerned the Soviet attitude to the work which Israel was currently conducting for the use of the waters of the Jordan River. In 1954 the U.S.S.R. had vetoed the Western proposal on the issue in the Security Council, a vote which the Israelis had at the time interpreted as a significant turning-point in the Soviet attitude to the Arab–Israeli conflict. Early in 1954, however, the Russians were careful to clarify to Israel that they had acted entirely with the aim of harming the interests of the Western powers, not those of Israel. The second signal concerned arms. During the last months of 1955 the

[49] See Argaman's despatch to the Foreign Ministry, 9.12.1955, ISA 244/1 and correspondence in ISA 2410/18 which are the sources for the following analysis and excerpts.

Israeli Foreign Ministry received reports from various sources
(Western and Eastern) that the Eastern European bloc of nations
might respond favorably to an approach that they sell arms to Israel
on the same terms as to the Arabs. Foreign Ministry officials were
aware that Soviet denials referred specifically to arms sales from the
U.S.S.R., not from other People's Democracies. Moreover, on one
occasion a Soviet ambassador explicitly informed an Israeli diplomat
that should Israel request arms "she will get it." Thirdly, and
especially important to the Foreign Ministry, was the fact that on
several occasions as 1955 drew to a close, Soviet representatives
hinted at the possibility of a departure from their traditionally
intractable ban on Jewish emigration. Thus, in a discussion between
Ze'ev Argaman, in charge of the Israeli Embassy in Bucharest, and
the Economic Advisor in the Soviet Embassy in Bucharest on 19 July
1955, the Russian said that were Israel to show any sign of political
non-dependence on the U.S., the Soviet Union might change its
stance regarding Soviet Jewry and the Jews of the People's Democracies. On 22 September of that year, in the presence of bystanders, the
Soviet Ambassador to Hungary announced to the same Israeli
representative that "the Soviet Union would not be harmed if it
permitted those of its Jewish citizens who wished to leave for Israel to
do so ... those applying would receive exit visas." When Argaman
commented that to date no such visas had been issued, the Russian
replied, "that was in the past, let them try now."

There is no way of knowing what lay behind these Soviet moves;
they may merely have been part of a disinformation campaign
intended to soften the blow of the Czech deal for Israel. What is
certain is that they raised hopes in Jerusalem. The Foreign Ministry
was even prepared to overlook such clear expressions of hostility to
Israel as Khrushchev's speech to the Central Committee of the Soviet
Communist Party at the end of December 1955, in which he attacked
Israel viciously.[50] Instead, Israeli leaders considered that new political activity *vis-à-vis* the Russians might be useful. They were particularly keen on an approach for armaments,[51] an issue which occupied
them during the first months of 1956.

Initial consultations were held in the first week of 1956. Despite his
personal misgivings, on 20 January Sharett apparently decided to

[50] Sharett, *Personal Diary*, pp. 1319–20.
[51] See Kidron's cable to the Foreign Ministry on 20.1.1956, ISA 2410/18.

examine the possibility practically, and requested the opinion of the Israeli Ambassador to the United States.[52] The following day a meeting of Mapai Cabinet ministers was held. Ben Gurion, then Prime Minister, surprisingly lent his support to an approach to the Russians, but Sharett's hesitations apparently prevented a decision from being reached. His doubts increased the following day when he was informed that "in Washington they were aghast at the idea of an [Israeli] approach to Russia [for arms]." One week later Abba Eban, Israel's Ambassador in Washington, cabled a stern caution against such an approach.[53]

Israel's persistently unstable political and military situation during the subsequent weeks and months kept alive the possibility of an Israeli request for Soviet arms. For her part, the Soviet Union did not make any move which might have categorically militated against such a request. Meeting with Soviet Foreign Minister Molotov on 1 February, the Israeli Ambassador to Moscow pointed out the dangers to peace inherent in current Soviet policy in the Middle East. Molotov's response, although sharp, did none the less hold out a few incentives:

For our part we are interested in strong ties of friendship, it depends on you. Take Finland – why can she maintain excellent relations with us from which she benefits? ... We have a history of three wars with Finland and nevertheless now maintain excellent relations with her. We make no territorial demands on Israel. If you were not yoked to the anti-Soviet "wagon," which in no way benefits your population, relations between us would definitely prosper. There is no doubt that it is to your advantage, it is worth it for your government, take it into consideration.[54]

These remarks, together with the American refusal to countenance a change in their own position regarding military support for Israel, explain Israeli hesitations. As Sharett recorded in his diary on 14 February 1956:

I went to Jerusalem and throughout the journey I was again prey to the uncertainties and doubts that eat away at me lately all the time – am I doing the right thing by delaying an approach to the East for armaments? What is the correct line we should follow? B-G [Ben Gurion] once stated definitively that we must approach [the Soviets] immediately. I cannot consider such a hasty step so long as we have not lost hope in the United States ... Now in effect the decision not to make the approach has been taken, but I have lost my self-confidence and I re-examine my position and am not always ... convinced of its justice. The last time the question arose in the Knesset

[52]  Sharett, *Personal Diary*, p. 1336.    [53]  *Ibid.*, p. 1337.    [54]  ISA 2410/18.

Foreign Affairs and Security Committee I think I made an impression on Mapam and Ahdut Ha'Avoda ... when I argued (a) that we can only pay for Soviet arms with dollars [which we obtain] from American Jews; they would be repelled by Israel and the U.J.A. [United Jewish Appeal] if they knew what their money was intended for, unless they could be convinced that we had exhausted all possibilities with their government [and that our requests] were to no avail; (b) that such possibilities had in fact not been exhausted; at any rate we could not prove to the public that they had been exhausted; (c) that there is no guarantee of a Soviet response – on the contrary, they may back off and reveal our failure to the Arabs in order to strengthen their ties even more and to make us look bad in the United States. None the less, I myself remained troubled and confused.[55]

Ben Gurion was not the only person to press Sharett on the issue; so did his own staff at the Foreign Ministry itself. During the course of an extended meeting on the subject on 15 February, chaired by Sharett, Avidar took the lead in advocating reorientation: "Of course I do not consider the possibility of Soviet orientation, but between the present situation and Soviet orientation there exist several grada-tions. In our relations with the Soviet Union, we are not restricted to just two possibilities ... there are other examples, Finland, Afghanistan, Sweden, Burma, or even Norway."[56] Five modes of action were advocated: first, to modify Israel's anti-Soviet image; secondly, to shift the Israeli position on the defense agreement with the U.S. ("I do not at all believe we will achieve it ... it may be worthwhile to make our friends heat the issue up a bit and in this way sell it [even though] we do not have it"); thirdly, forcefully to oppose the Baghdad Pact; fourthly, to submit a request for weapons "after preparation of the proper atmosphere"; and finally, "a more flexible stance in the U.N." "I do no know whether or not we will receive the arms if we make the request," Avidar frankly admitted. "I do not know if we will get arms from the United States, [nor do I know] if it will necessarily harm us in the United States. I think not, and it may even help us if we can use it properly. At any rate ... we must try."

The subsequent discussion revealed a difference of opinion within the Foreign Ministry. Amongst the objections cited were the need to justify a Russian approach to American Jewry and to the American administration whose money would ultimately finance the weapons. Besides, there was always the suspicion that the Russians would not respond to an Israeli request. This consultation did not end in

---

[55] Sharett, *Personal Diary*, p. 1348.          [56] ISA 2410/18.

operative conclusions; it certainly did not change Sharett's negative outlook. Indeed, this was confirmed when he later heard for the first time about the mass executions of Soviet Jewish writers and artists which took place at the end of 1952. He wrote in his diary: "in the midst of it all I thought, suppose we had decided on certain steps towards 'closer' relations and in the meantime the horrible news of the murdered writers was made known – how would we implement that plan in the face of the angry outrage that would ensue? Who knows what [other] surprises of this sort await us in the coming days?"[57]

For their own reasons, Soviet messages to Israel indeed seemed to hold out the hope of a positive response to an arms request, were one submitted. One day after the first Foreign Ministry consultation, Israel Barzilai, then Israel's Minister of Health, reported to the Foreign Minister on a long meeting he had held with Abramov, the Russian Ambassador in Tel Aviv. "Several times Abramov had stressed that we had not approached them with a request for arms."[58]

Some days later a second Foreign Ministry consultation was held. Sharett expressed his opposition to the option – "unless worse comes to worst";[59] in any other case, the fear of adverse American reactions were overriding: "[the Americans will say] is Israel also playing a game with us? We will teach her a lesson. They will not get economic aid from Russia ... Egypt will continue to exist even without the Aswan Dam [but] without economic assistance Israel will cease to exist."[60]

This meeting, together with another held on 12 March, produced no concrete results. Effectively, albeit temporarily, a decision had thus been made not to put forward a formal request for Russian military aid.[61] Any lingering hopes that this option might still be viable were dashed on 24 May 1956, when Abramov met Meir Argov, Chairman of the Knesset Foreign Affairs and Security Committee.[62] At the conclusion of a penetrating discussion, the Israeli attempted to push the Soviet Ambassador to the wall: "The question is how to make sure we will not be attacked. Are you ready to sell us 100 MiGs or similar weapons so that we can restore the balance of power, for this is the only thing that can prevent attacks. What conditions do you demand from us? No defense treaty with America – I undertake this. Neutrality – I undertake this. Political independence – I undertake

[57]  Sharett, *Personal Diary*, p. 1351.      [58]  *Ibid.*, p. 1358.      [59]  ISA 2410/18.
[60]  *Ibid.*       [61]  Sharett, *Personal Diary*, p. 1372.      [62]  ISA 2410/18, 2410/20.

this. After . . . all this are you ready to give us weapons?" Abramov's evasive reply left little doubt as to the complete absence of real Soviet readiness to respond positively to Israel's requests.

Brief though the entire episode was, the consideration of military procurements in the U.S.S.R. nevertheless constitutes a significant chapter in the history of Israel's global foreign policy during the first eight years of her existence. In the event, increasingly large quantities of French arms began to reach Israel after mid-1956. Consequently, "the worst case" did not materialize. Israel's leaders did not ultimately find themselves with their backs to the wall militarily as a result of the Czech–Egyptian arms deal, and were therefore not forced to cross the Rubicon by formally submitting a request to the Soviets for military assistance. What deserves to be noted, however, is that the idea of approaching the Soviets for military aid was not rejected out of hand, the issue was discussed seriously by policy-makers in Israel for an extended period, and ultimately there was even a probe in that direction. In retrospect, those months of debate seem to have been the last occasion when there was still a possibility that Israel might strike a balance, however fragile and tactical, between East and West in her foreign policy. The grave security and political situation of late 1955/early 1956 was fertile ground for perhaps the last shades of such thinking among Israeli policy-makers. If only for that reason, the episode is thus endowed with a historic value and significance which has hitherto not been acknowledged.

Part III

---

# THE WESTERN CONNECTION

# 9. THE MILITARY AND ECONOMIC DIMENSIONS

---

Writing in 1972, Michael Brecher presented the following analysis of Israel's relations with the Great Powers:

Israel has never been formally aligned. She is, in fact, one of the few states which do not belong to a pact, bloc alliance, or regional organization ... Israel is excluded from the non-aligned group at the U.N. and elsewhere; at the same time she is denied membership in any Western alliance.

It has not always been so. From 1948 to 1950 Israel followed the path of non-identification ... Thereafter, she moved towards a *de facto* alignment with the West: that shift was catalyzed by the need for arms and economic aid, rationalized by a perception of a renewed Soviet hostility, and eased by indifference to the Third World.[1]

The following chapters will examine the specifics of that process. Their purpose is to analyze the web of economic, political and military-strategic circumstances which generated an Israeli perception that the survival of the Jewish state depended on the Western bloc and, in particular, on the United States. Israeli documents demonstrate that those circumstances exerted a persistent influence on domestic deliberations with regard to Israel's international orientation and eventually persuaded her leaders to abandon their declared policy of "non-identification." Instead of seeking to maintain correct – but unbinding – relations with both protagonists in the cold war, they felt constrained to take sides in that conflict. Whatever the costs, they concluded, Israel had to work relentlessly towards an alliance with the Western bloc, and first and foremost with its leader the United States.

THE ECONOMIC DIMENSION

Throughout the first years of her independence, Israel's foreign policy was formulated against a backdrop of chronic economic stress.

[1] Michael Brecher, *The Foreign Policy System of Israel* (London, 1972), p. 561.

Table 3. *Population growth in Israel (1948–1955)*

|  | 1948 | 1949 | 1950 | 1951 | 1952 | 1953 | 1954 | 1955 |
|---|---|---|---|---|---|---|---|---|
| Total Jewish population (thousands) | 758.7 | 1,013.9 | 1,203.0 | 1,404.9 | 1,450.2 | 1,483.6 | 1,526.0 | 1,590.5 |
| Total non-Jewish population | 156.0 | 160.0 | 167.1 | 173.4 | 179.3 | 185.8 | 191.8 | 198.6 |
| Total immigration Israel | 101.834 | 239.954 | 170.597 | 172.245 | 24.610 | 11.575 | 18.491 | 37.528 |
| Percentage growth in total population compared with previous year | — | 28.3 | 16.7 | 15.2 | 3.3 | 2.4 | 2.9 | 4.2 |

Primary among the causes for that situation was the phenomenon of massive immigration. This was not an entirely new experience in the history of the country. Rapid population growth, a phenomenon in which both Arab and Jewish immigration had played an important role, had also been a characteristic feature of the Mandate period. Between 1919 and 1947 the overall population of Palestine had grown by 3.8% per annum; that of its Jewish community by 8.3% per annum. With independence, however, the rates of demographic expansion – and particularly of immigration – became markedly more intense.[2] Principally as the result of the arrival of some 600,000 new immigrants between 1948 and 1955, the Jewish population of Israel doubled during the seven-year period (see Table 3). Equally dramatic were changes in its composition.[3]

In 1949 the proportion of new immigrants to every thousand residents was 226, in 1950 it was 154, even in 1952 it was 132 – figures which are far higher than those ever recorded in any other country of immigration. (The singularity of the Israeli case is emphasized by some comparisons: in 1845, when immigration into the United States reached its peak, the proportion of new arrivals to every thousand existing residents was 16.1; in Canada and Argentina in 1913, it was 38.4 and 38.3, respectively.) The absorption of such a large influx of population in so short a period of time necessarily entailed enormous expenses, particularly since most of the new arrivals were economically destitute and many of them were also physically handicapped. Some of the costs were direct and necessitated immediate financial outlays; they included the provision of transport for the immigrants from their countries of origin and the construction of transit camps where they received initial food, medical care and other basic necessities. Indirect costs, too, were massive. Unemployment, for instance, ran at a particularly high rate (reaching some 14% of the total population in 1949). This could be reduced – and was reduced – by the initiation of a heavy program of public building and works. But that program could itself only be financed by printing large quantities of paper money, which in turn generated enormous inflationary pressures. What is more, the absorption of immigration was not

[2] See A. Huvna, "Manpower in Israel" (The Falk Institute, Jerusalem, 1961) (Hebrew).
[3] See N. Halevy and R. Klinov, *The Economic Development of Israel* (Jerusalem, 1968), p. 40, and D. Patinkin, *The First Decade* (Jerusalem, 1960), p. 20. These books are the sources of the following analysis unless otherwise indicated.

Israel's only economic burden during that period. She had simultaneously to cope with the heavy burdens which resulted from both the War of Independence and the perennial security problems by which that conflict was followed. These necessitated the establishment and maintenance of a relatively large army and mandated that provisions be made for a run of unusually high defense budgets.

Independence also brought about economic dislocation of another kind. After 1948, the country was precluded from trading with her neighbors in the Middle East and was thus cut off from the region which had provided Palestine with 15% of her imports during the 1930s and over 50% during the Second World War.[4] Particularly difficult were the novel difficulties and expenses involved in the import of oil.[5] Thus deprived of a vital source of energy, and without a developed industrial infrastructure of her own, Israel accumulated an enormous annual trade deficit.[6] The percentage of the import surplus out of the total resources with which the state could meet its various needs was, on average, 20% during three-quarters of the state's first decade. Israel's trade deficit stood at $220 million in 1949, reached $362 million two years later, and did not drop below $240 million until 1956. During the first ten years of Israel's existence it accumulated to the sum total of $3,295 million. Not even the amazing growth in Israel's G.N.P. (which averaged 10% per annum during that period) could compensate for this loss. It had to be financed by means of capital imports. These amounted to about 68% of the total imports to the country during the period under review, one of the highest percentages in the world during the years following the Second World War, and much higher than had been experienced in Palestine during the Mandate period (which itself was not low and stood at 25% of the total imports of products and services to the country).

In view of Israel's clear dependence on external sources of finance, their origin is of intrinsic significance. Table 4 gives an initial idea of what they were. In at least one important respect, these figures are deceptive. They indicate that the United States government financed only 13% of Israel's imported capital during the period under review. In fact, the indirect American contribution was much greater. No less

---

[4] See M. Michaeli, *Foreign Trade and Capital Imports in Israel* (Tel Aviv, 1963), p. 17.
[5] See a report by the Petroleum Section of the Israeli Finance Ministry on April 1954, ISA 418/15.
[6] See Michaeli, *Foreign Trade*, which is the basis for the following analysis unless otherwise indicated.

Table 4. *Imported capital to Israel: 1949–1959 (in millions of dollars)*

| | | |
|---|---:|---:|
| Total capital imports (= import surplus of products and services) of which: | | 3,295 |
| (a) *Transfer payments (net)* | | |
| 1. Gifts and capital transfers by immigrants | 309 | |
| 2. Personal compensation payments from Germany | 232 | |
| 3. Reparations from Germany | 491 | |
| 4. United States government aid | 454 | |
| 5. Transfers from the Joint Israel Appeal and other institutions | 881 | |
| Total (a) | 2,367 | |
| (b) *Capital movements (net)* | | |
| 6. Independence and Development loans | 359 | |
| 7. Loans from the Export–Import Bank | 98 | |
| 8. Other long- and medium-term loans | 71 | |
| 9. Other investments from abroad | 229 | |
| 10. Use of foreign currency reserves | −17 | |
| Total (b) | 740 | |
| Total (a) + (b) | 3,107 | |
| Errors and omissions | 188 | 3,295 |

than $750 of the $800 million transferred to Israel in the period under discussion by the United Jewish Appeal came from United States Jewry, a flow which was doubtless facilitated (as it still is) by favorable U.S. tax regulations. Moreover, the overwhelming majority of the $395 million which Israel obtained from the Independence and Development loans came from the Jews of the United States. The loan from the American Export–Import Bank was conditional upon the authorization of the U.S. government and it can be presumed that most of the sum of close to $230 million listed as "other investments from abroad" also stemmed from that source. If these amounts are compounded, it appears that about 55% of capital imported by Israel in the first decade of her existence stemmed directly from the United States and depended to one extent or another on the decisions of that country.[7]

[7] For the same perspective, though based on different numerical sources, see M. Avidan, *Principal Aspects of Israel–U.S.A. Relations in the 1950s* (Jerusalem, 1982), pp. 93–5 (Hebrew).

This data not only indicates the scope of the most important source of capital imports into Israel during these years. It also identifies the Great Power with which Israel, if for no other than economic reasons, had to develop special political ties and bonds.

### THE MILITARY DIMENSION

Contrary to the expectations harbored by some Israeli leaders, the War of Independence resulted in a series of armistice agreements. It did not lead to formal peace agreements between Israel and her Arab neighbors. That peace accords could still be attained – albeit only after supreme efforts – still remained a persistent aspiration. But that hope could not, of itself, obscure the supreme political significance of the absence of its immediate realization. Israel's isolation in the Middle East remained her most important disadvantage.[8] The psychological effect of this situation was evident even in the very earliest stages of Israel's political history. Characteristic, therefore, were the words of Sharett, the Foreign Minister of the time, who addressed the Mapai Knesset faction at the end of July 1949, shortly after the conclusion of the last armistice agreement:

We are living today in a state of malignant isolation in the Middle East. We possess no transport links with the neighboring countries; they do not recognize our existence. We can hold out in this situation if this is to be our fate, but ... we cannot ignore the burden which isolation places upon our state.[9]

The influence of this situation was not limited to the area of pure sentiment. It necessitated the maintenance of a military framework which would ensure the future existence of the Jewish state. This burden was particularly difficult to bear. To some extent Israel was able to offset her demographic inferiority *vis-à-vis* the Arab states, by adopting – and streamlining – a reserve system. The provision of arms for the defense forces presented much greater problems – particularly of an economic nature. Financial hardships compelled the government drastically to cut all its expenses, the defense budget included. Nevertheless, figures relating to Israel's defense expenditure during this period reveal that it remained extremely high. In 1950 the defense budget amounted to 31.3 million Israeli pounds ($87.6 million), in

[8] For the history of the armistice agreements between Israel and the Arab States, see Y. Rosenthal, ed., *Documents on the Foreign Policy of Israel*, vol. 3 (Jerusalem, 1983) (Hebrew).
[9] 28.7.1949, File no. 11/2/1/, LPA.

1951 – 54.1 million Israeli pounds ($151.5 million), a year later 75.5 million Israeli pounds ($75.5 million) and in 1953, 82 million Israeli pounds ($63.8 million).[10] If this sum is divided by the number of the members of the armed forces, it produces an average figure of about $600 per year for every man and woman. As such, it provides an eloquent illustration of the relative poverty of the Israeli Defense Force (I.D.F.). On the other hand, if the financial outlays on defense are measured against the urgent economic needs of other sectors of national life, it can be seen that the military budget constituted an average annual investment of 6%–8% of the state's G.N.P. between 1948 and 1955. It thus created an extremely heavy burden.

A rare summary of Israeli arms procurement, compiled at the end of 1951, which appears in Ben Gurion's diary and is here published for the first time, explains and illustrates part of the dynamic of the accumulation of Israeli power during the stages of this period (Table 5).[11]

As has been seen, a significant quantity of these arms originated in the Eastern bloc. However, important though that source of supply was (especially in 1948), the weapons thus received did not exceed a quarter of the total in 1950 and mainly consisted then of light arms. Moreover, by the beginning of 1951 military imports from the Eastern bloc had ceased altogether. By that time, Israel's military arsenal had become completely dependent on Western sources of supply. Only in the West, similarly, could she obtain the facilities necessary for the training of the officer corps for her young army. Merely to state these facts is to underscore the extent to which – within a very brief period after independence – Israel's national existence had become tied to the Western half of the emerging bi-polar world.

Israel was not only interested in acquiring arms for herself; equally important (sometimes even more so) was the prevention of military supplies to her Arab neighbors. For the past three decades, the West – and particularly Great Britain – had been the main supplier of such equipment to the Arab states of the region.[12] There seemed every

[10] The following analysis is based, unless otherwise indicated, on E. Luttwak and D. Horowitz, *The Israeli Army* (London, 1975), and N. Safran, *From War to War* (New York, 1969).

[11] Ben Gurion's diary, 13.1.1952, BGA. For the early history of Israel's arms purchases in America, see D. Almog, *Weapons Acquisition in the United States 1945–1949* (Tel Aviv, 1987) (Hebrew).

[12] On this issue, see J. C. Hurewitz, *Middle-East Politics, the Military Dimension* (Boulder, 1982).

Table 5. *Israel's arms procurement (1948–1952)*

| | Procurement prior to 15.5.1948 | Procurement prior to 1.3.1949 | Procurement prior to 31.12.1951 | Total 1.1.1952 |
|---|---|---|---|---|
| Planes | 20 | 184 | 216 | 420 |
| Naval vessels | — | 39 | 46 | 85 |
| Tanks | — | 40 | 21 | 61 |
| Half-tracks | 52 | 67 | 102 | 221 |
| Armored vehicles | — | — | 19 | 19 |
| Cannons | 26 | 390 | 591 | 1,007 |
| Heavy mortars | — | 24 | — | 24 |
| Torpedo | — | — | 23 | 23 |
| Heavy machine guns | 1 | 157 | 403 | 561 |
| Medium machine guns | , 54 | 1,363 | 11 | 1,428 |
| Automatic rifles | 464 | 5,575 | — | 6,039 |
| Rifles | 6,240 | 46,151 | 5,135 | 57,526 |
| Sub-automatic rifles | 417 | 106 | 7 | 530 |
| Pistols | 500 | 1,255 | 3,453 | 5,208 |

possibility that this tradition would be intensified after the establishment of the state of Israel, especially in view of the delicacy of Britain's relations with Egypt and Iraq. Indeed, the British then seemed to have a particular interest in making massive political use of arms exports to these states.[13] An opportunity for her to do so emerged midway through 1949, with the lifting of the embargo of arms supplies to the region, originally imposed by the U.N. As Jerusalem saw it, this situation was particularly dangerous; it threatened to generate an arms race in which Israel would be placed at a decided disadvantage, both because of her acute economic difficulties and because of the American refusal to supply large quantities of high-grade military equipment to the region. Consequently, her leaders felt that they had to work towards an international agreement which might induce the British (especially) to keep their flow of arms to the region to a level which Israel considered acceptable.[14] To that end, too, it was little use to look to Moscow. Israeli attention had to be focused on Washington, London and Paris.

In some respects, a deviation from Israel's policy of "non-identification" was thus a foregone conclusion. Bluntly put, from the very

[13] Roger Louis, *The British Empire in the Middle East* (Oxford, 1984).
[14] The subject still waits for its historian. Yet, see P. Jabber, *Not by War Alone* (Berkeley, 1981), and S. Spiegels' excellent *The Other Arab–Israeli Conflict* (Chicago, 1985). For American–Israeli relations, see N. Safran, *Israel the Embattled Ally* (Cambridge, 1978).

earliest stages of her existence Israel had little choice but to develop a network of links with the Western bloc in general and the United States in particular. However, since research on this topic has hitherto been slight (and has made no use whatsoever of the recently de-classified Israeli sources), there exists a need to examine the manner in which the web of various political, economic, strategic and international considerations fell into place in the arguments over Israel's relations with the West. Accordingly, the following pages will attempt to trace the central Israeli decisions on questions of political identification and strategic links with the Western bloc and with its leadership in particular.

# 10 . FROM NEUTRALITY TO THE SEARCH FOR A LINK

Evidence recently made available in Israel reveals that the possibility of a change in Israel's foreign policy orientation was not discussed at an administrative-political level until the end of 1949. Before then, Israel's basic policy had never been debated at any senior forum. "Non-identification," as it was sometimes termed, had been accepted as a fundamental – and publicly declared – fact of Israeli life. There existed a number of clear reasons why this should have been so. One was Israel's sense of responsibility for the fate and welfare of the entire Jewish people, which was dispersed throughout both major international blocs.[1] Secondly, neither could Israelis ignore the historic fact that their state had been established with the agreement and support of both the superpowers. Israel owed them a certain debt of gratitude and was interested in maintaining good relations with both in order to surmount the difficulties involved in the defense of her independence.[2] The third motive was a sincere concern for peace in the world and the wish to refrain from encouraging inter-power rivalry or intensifying it by identifying with one side or the other.

Equally compelling, although accorded very little publicity at the time, were domestic considerations. Specifically, the desire to keep peace within the ranks of the labor movement in Israel, constituted a fourth reason for Israel's "non-identification." At a time when the political affiliations of numerous new immigrants was still undefined, this consideration was particularly weighty. Indeed, the entire fabric of the Labor Party's culture seemed to be threatened by the possibility of extremist attacks from both left and right. Against this background,

[1] See Sharett's detailed lecture to Mapai's Central Committee on 3.3.1951, LPA. The official terminology was not "neutrality" nor "non-identification" but "keeping friendly relations with both superpowers," *ibid*. For reasons of reading convenience, however, this book employs various terms.
[2] See debate in Mapai Secretariat, 5.4.1948, LPA.

"non-identification" was viewed as being instrumental to the securing of an important internal goal of Israel's policy-makers. Any intensification of the argument over its merits, it was feared, might lead to an irrevocable rift between Mapai and Mapam, which would result in the dismantling of the Histadrut. One particularly grave diagnosis was provided by David Horowitz, a leading economic expert (later to become Governor of the Bank of Israel) during a marathon debate on Israel's foreign policy in April 1949:

We face a danger of epidemics, a danger of famine, the people in the camps and the conquered areas are a second people, a rebellious people which regards us as a plutarchy. This situation is liable to explode. This situation is excellent material for Herut [a right-wing party] and the Communists, this is dynamite...[3]

Finally, there was the immensely important factor of self-perception. Central to the Israelis' own image of their role was the concept of "a people that shall dwell alone," a people with its own morality and responsibility, which aspired to liberate itself from all outside bonds so as to select its own path in accordance with its own ideas, principles and viewpoints. Thus analyzed, non-identification reflected a positive consideration quite divorced from the alignment of domestic political forces, and was the result of a pragmatic assessment of the international political constellation of the period which had produced the rift between the two blocs: in the classic metaphor employed by Israel's Foreign Minister, it constituted "an attempt to navigate safely between Scylla and Charybdis."[4]

As has already been noted, "non-identification" demanded extreme caution. Initially, therefore, Israel refrained from outright expressions of support for the positions of either of the two big powers over international issues. The constraints within which Israel's foreign policy acted until the second half of 1949 precluded significant challenges to this basic line. Indeed, until May 1949 Israel found herself in a relatively convenient situation; until then she had no need to formulate her policy and reveal her hand on political votes within the United Nations Organization. Only thereafter was she faced with

[3] See a protocol of a meeting on 12.4.1949, ISA 2441/7.
[4] See n. 1. For a very detailed and early exposition of Israel's line, see Ben Gurion's speech to lecturers of his party, 7.11.1948, The Eliezer Kaplan Collection, ISA. See also Sharett's private notes of mid-1949 (no exact date cited), CZA A/245/70 2, his detailed letter to Israel's Minister in London, 11.9.1949, ISA 2408/9 and his comparison between Israel's and India's neutrality in a meeting at the Foreign Ministry, 26.10.1949, *ibid.*

the challenge of translating the general policy of non-identification into operative terms, or at least into terms of significant symbolic acts within that organization. Perhaps still more important was the fact that not until the end of 1949 did the U.N. lift its embargo on arms exports to the Middle East. Only then did the question of arms become a serious political problem with inescapable implications for Israel's international political orientation.

To say that is not to imply that the problematics inherent in non-identification were not previously apparent to Israel's leaders. But during the first eighteen months of the state's existence (at least) their policy did not seem to run the risk of bringing about Israel's political isolation from America. Neither did non-identification appear to be an inducement to the United States to reach any operative anti-Israeli conclusions and cut off economic aid. This impression was based on contacts which took place between Israeli representatives and American diplomats and politicians, as well as on a reading of the current political map in America. Admittedly, Israeli representatives in the U.S.A. did occasionally report American fears that Israeli policy concealed a pro-Soviet orientation. During the course of the War of Independence, and particularly towards the end of 1948, for instance, Israel's leaders had to withstand some American pressure that they loosen their arms-procurement ties with Czechoslovakia.[5] They were also aware of American concern with the position of Mapam, and of the Israeli left in general. Indeed, in December 1948 Samuel Klaus, a special research advisor in the American State Department, was instructed to examine whether Israel was "a red state" or, to be more precise, to examine Israel's political tendencies in both domestic and foreign affairs in view of the influence of the Soviet Union and of the extreme left in the country as well as the internal economic implications of the Socialist approach of the Mapai heads of the state.[6] In neither case, however, were relations seriously endangered. Indeed, after a visit of only two months, Klaus was able to report that all American fears were groundless. His conclusions, which were made known to the Israeli authorities, can be summed up in the phrase: "there is no immediate Soviet danger."[7] As regards

<hr/>

[5] See Heyd's cable to Sharett, 12.9.1948, ISA 2308/2 (reporting complaints by the President and Secretary of State), and Sharett's cable to Eytan, 14.11.1948, ISA 2341/1 (on his conversation with the U.S. Ambassador in Israel). See also a report of the same day to the Israeli delegation at the U.N., ISA 131/18.

[6] Ben Gurion's diary, 25.11.1948, BGA.

[7] See Herlitz's cable to Elath, 20.1.1949, ISA 2308/2.

foreign policy, he wrote that despite the existence of certain elements within Israeli society who were interested in prodding the state in the direction of a pro-Soviet orientation, "the Israeli Government's declared policy of neutrality is shared by the majority of the non-doctrinaire public."[8]

Whatever the weight actually attached to Klaus' conclusions in Washington, in Jerusalem they certainly contributed to a feeling that American fears of a "leftward" direction in Israeli foreign policy had been dispelled. Especially noted, for instance, were the remarks made by the deputy Secretary of State to the Director General of the Israeli Foreign Ministry at the beginning of January 1949. He was, he said, more fearful, "of the Arabs falling under Soviet influence than of Israel doing so"; Israel, after all, "has promised to remain neutral," and had proven that she could do so.[9] Domestic developments seemed to confirm that analysis. Elections to the Knesset at the end of January 1949 resulted in a clear-cut victory for Mapai and the relative defeat of Mapam. Analysis suggests that one factor contributing to that outcome was the public perception that there appeared to be no reason for American pressure on Israel to change her formal line in the area of global policy and that consequently there was no danger to the continuation of American aid. In fact, at the beginning of January 1949, Israeli diplomats were informed that the State Deparment had authorized Israel's request for a loan of $100 million.[10] The matter did give rise to a political storm within Israel; Mapam's leadership attacked Ben Gurion for agreeing to what they termed (quite unjustifiably) "terms of enslavement" to the United States.[11] But this seemed a relatively minor price to pay. In general, American behavior towards Israel (and especially American aid to Israel) induced amongst the Israeli leadership the comfortable feeling that the United States would not adopt a policy of "whoever's not with us is against us."[12] "Non-identification" was therefore not seriously put to the test during this period.

Confidence that this situation might persist began to dissipate in August 1949, when the Soviet possession of nuclear weapons was

---

[8]  See Meron's memorandum, 31.3.1949, ISA 2416/26.
[9]  See Eytan's cable to Elath, 11.1.1949, ISA 2308/1.
[10]  See a memorandum on Israeli–U.S.A. relations in ISA 2479/9.
[11]  See M. Sharett, "The Balance Sheet," *Hador*, 4.3.1949 (Hebrew); on the terms of the loan, see Elath's cable to Kaplan, 19.3.1949, ISA 2308/2.
[12]  See Ben Gurion's diary, 1.7.1949, BGA and Elath's letter to Sharett, 30.8.1949, ISA 2479/8.

made public. Reports which reached Israel following this news made it perfectly clear that American policy with regard to "non-aligned" states was about to undergo a change and that there would be unavoidable implications as far as Israel was concerned. Israel's senior representatives in Washington accordingly sent the following warning to the Foreign Minister:

Our neutrality will be more difficult [to maintain] especially if an agreement is reached here with Nehru. We must anticipate pressure from the U.S.A. to make us join the regional defensive scheme ... [We] believe [that] the U.S.A. [will] follow more closely than ever our attitudes and voting at the [United Nations] General Assembly. These will have a direct bearing on determining their views regarding the extent of our neutrality and their practical conclusions on relations with Israel and our request for arms and military training.[13]

Significantly, no operative recommendations accompanied these assessments, or any others. Indeed, members of the staff of Israel's Embassy in Washington themselves counseled moderation. They seriously doubted whether the American State Department was experiencing any "more serious concern as to the direction our policy is taking than exists for example as regards India's policy." They also questioned the supposition that the United States was indeed interested in contracting new strategic and economic obligations in order to establish a friendly bloc of nations in the Middle East."[14] Altogether, indeed, there seemed to be no call for a radical change in Israel's global policy. Hence, when negotiations ensued for the formation of a new coalition government in Israel, Mapai's leaders were able to assure Mapam that they would not tie the country to the West and that "we have no intention of joining the Marshall Plan ... this question is not on the state of Israel's agenda."[15]

Nevertheless, it was impossible to ignore altogether the fluidity inherent in the situation. Accordingly, it was decided to keep a close watch on political developments in the United States whilst at the same time adopting various means in order to clarify to the Ameri-

[13] 14.10.1949, ISA 2408/9.
[14] See Elath's cable to Sharett, 27.1.1950, ISA 2308/16. The cable was considered important enough to justify circulation among members of the Israeli Cabinet, see CZA s41/419/1.
[15] See file "Correspondence with Mapai," Container 8, AHA, Sharett's notes in CZA A/245/70/2 and a detailed analysis of the issue of Mapam's inclusion in the government during the 1950s in Z. Tsur, *Partnership as Opposition: the Partnership of Mapam in the Government 1949–1954* (Efal, 1983) (Hebrew).

cans the essence of the Israeli policy of "non-identification." It was thus that Ben Gurion told the American Ambassador in Tel Aviv that the Vatican's fears regarding Israel's Communist tendencies were groundless and that "Rome will be Communist before Jerusalem."[16] He also despatched a special emissary to the United States, one of whose functions was to disseminate appropriate information, especially amongst American–Jewish leaders.[17] Sharett, too, played a role in this campaign. A considerable part of the message which he sent to the American Secretary of State via the U.S. Supreme Court Justice, Felix Frankfurter, was devoted to an explanation of Israel's foreign policy:

For obvious reasons Israel is unable to give the government of the United States concrete guarantees, such as the grant of bases etc. On the other hand the very existence of American Jewry constitutes both a moral and a material guarantee which might certainly satisfy the United States government. Israel will never be able to sever its ties with the five million Jews living in America today. On the contrary: it is compelled to strive with all its might for the strengthening and broadening of these ties.[18]

A few weeks later Ben Gurion went a step further. In conversation with an American-Jewish leader then visiting Israel, he outlined three clusters of considerations which necessitated the continuation of the policy of "non-identification." These, indeed, were so important that they outweighed the influence of the anti-Communist atmosphere in Washington and the distress possibly caused to American Jewry by Washington's dissatisfaction with Israel's global foreign policy.[19] His first concern (which continued to trouble him for several years) was the obscurity which surrounded America's military plans in the event of a war in the Middle East: "Will America fight for the Near East or will it abandon it to its own fate? In any event America will not send a large military force here just to defend us."[20] Secondly, he referred to the question of immigration (which was, of course, also an abiding concern). "I do not know if and when war will break out. Meanwhile what is important to us is what happens in the coming years. Our security is entirely dependent on immigration. Rumania is closed, but

---

[16]  5.12.1949, *Foreign Relations of the United States* (hereafter *FRUS*), 6, 1949, pp. 1521–2.
[17]  See his letter to Elath, 30.11.1949, BGA.
[18]  15.12.1949, ISA 2416/26.
[19]  The following excerpts are taken, unless otherwise indicated, from Ben Gurion's diary, 20.1.1950, BGA.
[20]  On this point, see also a report on a meeting held late in 1949 at the Israeli Embassy in Washington, ISA 316/41.

we cannot give up so easily on hundreds of thousands of Jews. There is still immigration from Poland, Czechoslovakia, Bulgaria. If there is any chance of bringing Jews from the East and especially from Rumania – we must not abandon them." Finally, there was the issue of relations with Britain. This was a consideration which Ben Gurion often revealed to Jewish confidants, but rarely mentioned to foreign diplomats. Any change in Israel's policy of refusing to enter into an alliance with the West had to take into account the crucial fact that Britain had still the most prominent influence on the formulation of the West's Middle East policy. Ben Gurion, like many of his contemporaries in Israel, was distinctly reluctant to associate Israel with Britain's regional policy:

At a time when as far as America is concerned the main thing is Russia, England has other considerations: Arabs, Sudan, Suez, competition with France, competition with America itself in the Middle East. And if America should be pro-Israel, I do not know whether England for her own reasons will not exploit the sort of hostile policy she is carrying out [now], whether she will not arm the Arabs and prevent them from coming to terms with us.

At the time, a continuation of Israel's original policy of "non-identification" seemed not only desirable, but also feasible. That was certainly Sharett's view. Addressing the top echelons of the Foreign Ministry at the end of January 1950, he declared his aim to be "without for the moment changing the definition of our international policy, to bring the government of the United States to closer cooperation and to the understanding that in our democratic approach we are situated in the Western camp."[21] But this was soon to appear impossible. During the course of their information campaign in the United States, it became clear to the Israeli diplomats on the spot that the situation in America had rapidly changed. In meetings with politicians and public officials, they found growing evidence of pressure for the administration to step up its demands on those nations which had not identified themselves with the U.S.A. in the global struggle. Thus, for example, at the end of March, Senator Lehman, one of Israel's most prominent supporters on Capitol Hill, told Eliahu Elath, the Israeli Ambassador, that after meeting with several senators he had come to the conclusion that Israel's situation was "grave and dangerous. Confusion exists among an overwhelming majority regarding Israel's position [in] interna-

[21] See protocol of a meeting held on 31.1.1950, and Eytan's circular despatch on 26.2.1950, ISA 2479/8.

tional affairs. Many [Senators] suspect [Israel's] pro-Russian orientation and [in a barely veiled reference to Israel's economic interests] consider it a poor bargain for the U.S.A. to support us."[22] Other members of the American administration were even more forthright. At a meeting held ten days earlier, the heads of the Armament Branch in the American State Department pointed out to representatives of the Israeli Arms Purchase Mission in the U.S.A. that "the critical test [for arms supply to Israel] is the political test"; they anticipated that Israel "be neutral in the direction of the United States."[23]

With such information to hand, it is hardly surprising that the Embassy in Washington advocated a deviation from the policy of non-identification. Elath put the case to Sharett at the beginning of April 1950:

I am fully aware [of] our tremendous internal and external difficulties in deciding on clear-cut policy and I support wholeheartedly your general line in dealing with the enormous problems in our foreign relations. I do not hereby advocate sudden and drastic change [in] our foreign policy, believing Russia's growing unfriendliness [toward] Israel's democracy [will] steadily resolve some internal as well as external problems of our political orientation and diplomacy. [I] suggest that while continuing to fight with determination in [the] U.S.A. as well as in [the] countries of the Soviet bloc for the best we can achieve in the [present] circumstances we have to evaluate realistically opportunities and limitations alike under our present policy of neutrality and make decisions on specific occasions motivated by our urgent vital interests and not by static concepts which may paralyze our very struggle for progress and survival.[24]

The substance of Elath's message thereafter became a standard refrain in subsequent despatches from the Israeli Embassy in Washington. That is not, however, the only reason why his telegram deserves to be considered a landmark in the internal Israeli debate over orientation. Even more significant were his recommendations that the government of Israel invite a visit by the American Deputy Chief of Staff and agree to transfer military information to the American authorities. These were radical departures from accepted policy. When the arms embargo on the Middle East expired at the end of 1949, Israel had applied for military aid from the West and especially from the United States. But she had, nevertheless,

[22] 23.3.1950, ISA 2308/17.     [23] 12.3.1950, ISA 2478/4.
[24] 8.4.1950, ISA 2308/7. This source is the basis for the following analysis. See also Elath's cable on 11.4.1950 and a report on 14.4.1950 by the Israeli Military Attaché in Washington on his meeting with his counterpart in Tel Aviv in ISA 2308/81.

attempted to retain a certain freedom of maneuver. Fearful of
intelligence leaks, the Israeli defense establishment had opposed any
kind of American supervision over arms supply and had even objected to complying with a standard American demand that states
receiving military aid reveal information on the size of their military
forces. The policy of non-identification had similarly mitigated
against inviting senior American army officials to Israel in the context
of the arms requests. These arguments did not evaporate during the
two weeks which followed Elath's telegram.[25] But they no longer
seemed quite so convincing. Israeli diplomats in Washington now
stressed the degree to which American foreign policy was determined
by security and strategic considerations; the cold war, they pointed
out, was the prism through which the United States evaluated
requests for aid by various states. Both considerations necessitated a
shift in Israeli policy. At the end of April Elath warned that by
pursuing a "monistic and rigid" line in the interpretation of her non-
identification policy, Israel would forfeit the chance of a grant of
American aid, particularly in the military area.[26]

Israel's friends within American Jewry were also unhappy with the
policy of non-identification. Not surprisingly, they placed particular
emphasis on the economic question. Oscar Gass and David Ginsburg
(who were among the most important of Israel's allies in Washington
at the time) stressed this aspect of the situation to the Israeli
leadership at a series of meetings which took place in April in Israel.[27]
A report of the conversations was sent to the Israeli diplomats in the
American capital:

We exploited the visit of Oscar Gass and David Ginsburg for another basic
analysis of Israeli–American relations, whose starting point was Oscar's
question, "how to keep on milking the cow when we are not prepared and not
able to give her anything." According to them we have so far received from
the U.S.A. more than a small and relatively unimportant state deserves, by
means of both the loan, diplomatic aid and in other ways. However, our
situation demands further aid from the U.S.A., at a time when we have
nothing to give the U.S.A. and nothing to promise the U.S.A. According to
them there is nothing wrong with our being neutral, in other words with the

[25]  See cable to Elath, 24.4.1950, ISA 2308/13.
[26]  See his cable on 27.4.1950, ISA 2308/17. On the same day Keren reported that his
meetings at the Pentagon led him to the conclusion that "the main stumbling block for
our arms request [is] the Joint Chief of Staff who [is] uncertain [about] our attitude [in
a] third world war," ISA 2329/8.
[27]  See Herlitz's despatch to the Israeli Embassy in Washington, 15.5.1950, ISA
2479/8.

fact that we do not identify ourselves publicly and fully with the West. They repeated ... that the Americans are not interested in a military or political pact between us and them. On the other hand we have not succeeded in explaining to the world in general and to the Americans in particular that despite the fact that we are a neutral country we constitute and aspire to constitute a democracy based on Western ideas and that from a "philosophi-cal-moral" point of view we are against the Communist world viewpoint. They await such a declaration, or more correctly, such declarations, by the state of Israel and her leaders.

A more forceful version of precisely the same criticism was relayed directly to Ben Gurion by Eliezer Libenstein, the Prime Minister's personal Envoy to the United States. At the end of the last week of April 1950, Libenstein had met with the Coordinator of the Joint Committee of the American State Department, the Pentagon and the Intelligence Headquarters. The American had made it quite clear that were Israel to announce that: "it would defend the country against an external [i.e. Soviet] attack there would be a basic change in the approach toward our arms requests. They [the Americans] will examine our requests for armament from the viewpoint of overall defensive needs." At the moment, however, he very much doubted whether Israel could obtain "arms by means of negotiations with the State Department while the talks are being held in an atmosphere of total Israeli neutrality." In sum, Libenstein concluded: "The general problem of our place in the disposition of forces and world relations is becoming more acute. Israel's position in 1950 cannot be exactly what it was in 1948. It must move Westwards."[28]

Apparently as a result of these appraisals, Israeli policy did change. But the movement was relatively moderate. As has been noted, in April the institutions of Mapai (undoubtedly influenced by pressure from the Embassy in Washington) recommended that the Histadrut leave the Communist International.[29] Israel and the United States also concluded a Trade and Friendship Agreement, which had no special political significance and which dealt mainly with mercantile trade.[30] These were hardly significant departures from the policy of non-identification. For one thing, the Histadrut did not take a simultaneous decision to join the Western International; secondly, the Friendship Agreement was hedged with attendant

[28] See his letter to Ben Gurion, 1.5.1950, ISA 376/9.
[29] See Chapter 1 and cabled correspondence in file 2324/8, "Daat's" letter to "Gera," 3.5.1950, ISA 3063/10 and especially Herlitz's despatch referred to in n. 27.
[30] See correspondence in ISA 64/5 and Herlitz's despatch referred to in n. 27.

conditions. These were described by the Director of the Eastern
Europe Section in the Israeli Foreign Ministry to members of the
Israeli Legation in Moscow at the end of April: "We have agreed that
we should not refrain from signing the agreement, but efforts should
be made to sign a similar agreement with some other country with
which we have business, especially in the field of transportation, such
as Italy or Holland ... so as to take the sting out of the matter."[31]
Nevertheless, these moves – small though they were – did reflect the
general view, accepted within Israel as a future guideline, that the
political situation in the United States necessitated an increase in the
Israeli information effort with regard to her global orientation. They
also induced an acceptance of the guideline laid down by the Israeli
Ambassador to the United States:

If and when pressed by [the] U.S.A. government for concessions as conditions [for] their acceding [to] our demands we [would] judge each case [on
its] own merit, evaluating [the] pros and cons in light [of] our vital urgent
needs and not by [a] rigid concept of neutrality [which] is relative anyway.[32]

It was one thing to agree, in principle, to the notion of flexibility
and the need for occasional deviations from the policy of "non-
identification." It was quite another to translate that principle into
practice. If anything, Israel's leaders seemed intent on persevering
with their original strategy with what amounted to gritty determination. As much was illustrated in May 1950, when they were called
upon to respond to the declaration of policy on the Middle East then
issued by the United States, France and Britain. Known as the
Tripartite Declaration, this document created a formal equality
between the rights of Israel and the Arab states to buy arms, and also
provided some sort of guarantee of their borders and of the armistice
agreements between them. The Israeli Embassy in Washington
regarded this declaration as an impressive achievement for Israel,
particularly since it seemed to extend formal Western protection over
the state.[33] That, however, was precisely the aspect of the Declaration
which Jerusalem found objectionable. The official Israeli view was
outlined by the Director General of the Foreign Ministry at a briefing
which he gave to Israeli diplomats abroad:

[31] 24.4.1950, ISA 2500/13. Ten days previously the Israeli Embassy in Washington
had been instructed to blur as much as possible the fact that the accord was termed
"Friendship Agreement." See Keren's despatch to Eytan, 31.5.1950, ISA 2960/5.
[32] 5.5.1950, two days later Sharett confirmed this line, ISA 2308/18.
[33] See Keren's despatch to the Foreign Ministry, 29.5.1950, ISA 2461/9.

The Declaration is of course purely Western in nature and this is reflected by the fact that it mentions the role of the states of the Middle East in the defense of the entire region. We responded to this by emphasizing our standing policy for the advancement of peace among all peoples ... they [the three powers] will easily be able to refuse us special grades of arms such as jets on the grounds that these are needed only for the overall defense of the region, something to which we are unable to commit ourselves.[34]

Ben Gurion confirmed this view in a detailed if more cautious manner, in his announcement the following day to the Knesset. In his diary, he expressed his rejection of the Declaration even more categorically: "Israel's worst enemy could have signed this Declaration. It legitimizes unlimited arms supplies to the Arab states without [mentioning an] obligation to Israel."[35]

Israel's diplomats in the American capital protested. Reiterating arguments which they had been making since the end of 1949, they advised that caution (which they sometimes castigated as "mathematical neutrality") was self-defeating. If anything, more publicity had to be given to the increasingly perceptible disparity in Israel's relations with the Eastern and Western blocs. In the words used by Moshe Keren, the Embassy's counselor, to the Director General of the Foreign Ministry:

There exists a contradiction between our declared policy and our actions. There is no comparison between our links with the East and our links with the West. On the one hand we repeatedly make the claim that we stand neutral between the sides; on the other hand we repeatedly demand all sorts of assistance and aid from only one of them. Politicians here have taken good note of this contradiction. But I sometimes wonder whether we sufficiently take this into account. In fact we are totally dependent on the aid of the United States.[36]

Other diplomats even questioned the relevance of the domestic Israeli consideration, an aspect of the situation which Sharett himself tended to emphasize. As Abba Eban put it:

it follows that artificial activities ... such as a fake application to the Soviet Union [for a financial loan] are aimed not at maintaining our relations with

---

[34] Quoted in Arieh Oron's letter to Leo Cohen, 29.5.1950, ISA 2403/18.
[35] BGA. See also the formula in ISA 2449/1. Sharett cabled Eytan a day later revealing his idea that Israel's "major" and "primary" concern was her own defense, which "is more urgent than 'defense of the area as a whole,'" 31.5.1950, ISA 2403/9. On the Tripartite Declaration, see S. Slonim, "Origins of the 1950 Tripartite Declaration on the Middle East," *Middle Eastern Studies* 23, 2, 1987, pp. 135–49.
[36] 31.5.1950, ISA 2460/5.

this power, but rather at appeasing a certain party in Israel which demands of us a degree of pro-Sovietness that even the government of the Soviet Union does not demand. We should put an end to this harmful process, which endangers our vital interests for irrelevant political reasons.[37]

Internal criticism of such force and persistence could not be ignored. Consequently, early in June 1950, Israel's political leaders decided to convene a meeting of the diplomatic corps in order "to re-examine the diplomatic line and to see whether our policy should be adhered to or changed."[38] The eruption of the Korean crisis in the last week of that month forced them to come to a decision even earlier. Indeed, to some extent that external event acted as a catalyst for domestic processes and internal forces which had already generated intense argument over Israel's foreign policy orientation.

Once they had appraised the overall Korean picture, Israel's representatives in Washington were particularly quick to make it grist to their mill. In fact, they immediately understood that the Far Eastern crisis had created a unique opportunity for the implemen-tation of the course of action which they had been recommending for months. They put their case, it must be noted, even before any pressure had been exerted on Israel by the United States to denounce the invasion by North Korea of the South and to express support for the American position in the U.N. over the Korean crisis. As early as 29 June 1950, Moshe Keren despatched an urgent telegram to Israel:

It is probable [that] we cannot avoid for length of time [making] our stand [on] Korea known to [the] U.S. [government] and [the] United Nations ... [the] United States [is] extremely sensitive [about] this affair [and] might see our reaction [as a] test case [for] our real attitude [towards] world conflict ... here [is] perhaps [a] unique opportunity through identification [with the] U.N. [to] support by implication the U.S.A. .... [I] am convinced [that] we would improve perhaps decisively [the] general climate [of] our relations [with] U.S.A. without [at the same time] deviating [from] our line [of] fidelity [to the] U.N.[39]

Very shortly thereafter, the United States did indeed exert moder-ate pressure on Israel to issue a public clarification of her position. Keren who, in the absence of the Ambassador, found himself at the center of the affair, considered his prophecies to have been fulfilled. He now warned that: "Silence [is] dangerous especially [in] view [of

---

[37]  12.6.1950, ISA 64/5.
[38]  Eban's talk at a meeting with Israeli diplomatic corps in Washington, 14.6.1950, ISA 89/1.                    [39]  29.6.1950, ISA 2308/18.

the] forthcoming negotiations [concerning military] training, loan, oil and old arms issues." He even requested formal permission to make a clear statement to the effect that Israel's position was "pro-Western."[40] Reacting to this cable, the Foreign Ministry's legal advisor added a further consideration. His memorandum did acknowledge that: "The U.S.A. has succeeded in converting the United Nations Organization into a kind of glorified Atlantic Pact." But it balanced this danger against the possible regional advantages which Israel might be able to reap from encouraging active U.N. involvement in international crises:

Success in the present endeavor will create a precedent for direct United Nations actions of which small and weak states may ultimately be the principal beneficiaries ... there seems ... to be every reason for suggesting that quite apart from any legal and moral obligations which might be incumbent upon Israel, there is goodly measure of self-interest to justify taking the risks which are undoubtedly involved in accepting the Security Council resolutions and acting upon them.[41]

Formally, the government of Israel did not come to decision on the Korean question until 2 July. Only then did an extraordinary Cabinet meeting unanimously adopt a resolution which supported the American position. In fact, however, Israeli moves in that direction had not awaited that meeting. Three days previously, the policy of non-identification had already been undermined. Sharett then instructed the Israeli delegation to the U.N. to emphasize in political discussions in New York that: "Israel's general attitude is support [for the] U.N. in fulfillment of her obligations under [its] Charter, particularly Article 25. Israel [is] also mindful [of] being surrounded by past potential enemies against whom [it] may need U.N. support."[42]

Events during the next seventy-two hours, when the tone of the cables emanating from the Embassy in Washington became even more strident, merely confirmed that Israel had recognized the extent to which her previous policy was becoming untenable. Embassy staff passed on a series of messages from Truman's Aide For Relations

[40] Officials of the State Department defined late in June Israel's attitude on this issue as "regrettable," see Keren's cable, 30.6.1950, *ibid.*
[41] See a memorandum by the Foreign Ministry's Legal Advisor, 30.6.1950, ISA 2489/9.
[42] *Ibid.* On the same day Arthur Lurie of the Israeli Legation at the U.N. cabled that "our failure to take a stand is becoming incomprehensible in light of our efforts to obtain effective U.N. action when we were ourselves victims of aggression in the past and possibly again in the future," ISA 2329/9.

with Jews and Other Minority Groups which stressed "disappointment" and "anger" over Israel's silence on the issue.[43] Indeed, on the
very day that the Cabinet was to meet, the Head of the Israeli
Economic Delegation in Washington reported to the Minister of
Finance in Israel that the American State Department had suddenly
frozen the loan previously obtained for the development of
Jerusalem's water supply system and sewage treatment. For him, at
least, the message was unmistakable: "[The United] State's action
[concerning] Jerusalem may reflect their reaction, though still only
on low level, to Israeli silence and neutrality in face [of the] aggression
against South Korea, more probably it is certainly [a] political
reaction to Israeli neutrality and stand aloofishness [sic] regarding
the U.S.A."[44]

The fact that the Israeli government thought it necessary to
convene an extraordinary Cabinet meeting in order to debate policy
on the Korean question was an acknowledgment of the special
significance of the decision then reached.[45] Nevertheless, the landmark status of the decision itself was later played down. To the
representatives of the Soviet Union both in Israel and throughout the
world, it was presented as an indication of Israel's support for the
U.N. and not as a sign that she had explicitly taken sides in the inter-
power conflict.[46] This attitude was not entirely camouflage. In
retrospect, Israel's Korean decision does appear to have marked an
important stage in the shift of Israel's international orientation. *At the
time*, however, it was not regarded by the country's leadership as a
significant reversal of their previous policy.[47] Rather, they tended to
view it a necessary act, important but singular, implemented within a
reality of conflicting compulsions, yet not heralding any dramatic
turnabout.[48] As much is illustrated by the lengthy debates at senior
levels which took place during the third week of July.

On 17 July 1950 the first general meeting of Israel's diplomatic

[43]  See Gass' cable, 30.6.1950, ISA 2308/18. See also Keren's and Lurie's cables to
Sharett, 1.7.1950, ISA 2329/9. For pressures from other directions, see "Gera"'s cable,
27.7.1950, ISA 2308/9.
[44]  30.6.1950, ISA 2329/4.
[45]  See Sharett's despatch to Lurie, 6.7.1950, ISA 2329/4. On that decision, see M.
Brecher, *Decisions in Israel's Foreign Policy* (London, 1974), pp. 111–72, and his *Israel, the
Korean War and China* (Jerusalem, 1974).
[46]  See Sharett's instructions to the Israeli embassies in Washington, Ankara, Paris and
Rome on 3.7.1950, ISA 2344/3.
[47]  See Sharett's cable to Keren, 2.7.1950, ISA 2308/13.
[48]  See, for example, Raphael's letter to Eban, 12.7.1950, ISA 2384/21.

corps was held at the Israeli Foreign Ministry. Amongst the participants was the Prime Minister, Ben Gurion. The first and most important topic to be discussed was Israel's global orientation, or, as it was defined at the meeting: "Israel between East and West."[49] The subject gave rise to a lengthy debate, during the course of which two central theses of foreign policy orientation were presented and examined. The first called for moderate revisions in non-identification. The second emphasized the paramount need to preserve that policy. Not surprisingly, the strongest advocates of the first thesis were the "American Branch" of the Israeli Foreign Ministry: The United States Section in the Ministry and Abba Eban as Israel's senior diplomatic representative in the American capital. Their detailed memorandum, distributed to participants at the meeting, contained one central motif: "the network of our relations with the United States constitutes the most important of all Israel's external relations." Jerusalem was massively dependent on Washington, indeed had been so ever since (at the latest) the beginning of 1950. Three central parameters of Israeli foreign policy provided ample illustration. One was the political arena. "Could we," asked the memorandum, "ever be able without the initiative and support of the Americans ... to reach any sort of peace agreement with our neighbors?" Those present at the meeting should remember Israel's short, but extremely significant, experience of American "carrot and stick" diplomacy:

We have had the experience on a number of occasions of asking for the aid of the United States in our political activities. Some of the issues were vital, such as when we recommended that the United States exert pressure on the Arab rulers and especially upon the ruler of Transjordan to make peace with us, and when we asked for help over the departure and airlifting of Jews from Iraq. Other issues were less vital: our application to the United States to put pressure on Iran to recognize us and our request with regard to the prevention of infiltration. We have even experienced examples of American intervention and American pressure in matters between ourselves and our neighbors, over borders, the refugees and Jerusalem.

Much more crucial, indeed a matter of sheer survival, was the economic aspect of the Israeli–American relationship. In presenting the facts of this case (and the memorandum was the first to collate them for the entire Israeli diplomatic corps), particular stress was placed on "the time factor [which] in this area, unlike the political

---

[49] The following account is based upon material in ISA 2384/15, 2479/8.

area, deepens this dependency." It was significant enough that in 1949 Israel's imports from the U.S.A. constituted 30% of her total, and that in the first four months of 1950 that figure had climbed to 40%. What also had to be recognized was Israel's acute dependency on America for everything connected with capital imports. According to Israeli estimates the state would need 110 million Israeli pounds in foreign currency, "just in order to supply the most vital needs," and no less than 60% of this sum would have to come from the United States. Moreover, the needs were hardly likely to diminish. Present incomes, the memorandum pointed out, "will indeed cover the current needs but will not allow us to carry out development plans, to pay debts, to procure arms, to carry out projects on a daring scale in order to solve the problem of the 'ingathering of exiles,' will not leave any reserves and will not allow us to stockpile for a crisis."

To this had to be added the military dimension. At the time, this was a subsidiary consideration – indeed, it remained so until 1968. But it was not entirely insignificant. As the memorandum pointed out, the United States had already authorized the sale of a number of items. With the exception of France, it was also the only country to have agreed to train Israeli military personnel (half-way through 1950 their number had already exceeded 100). In addition, "there is an extremely high percentage of American Jews among the experts and professionals already serving in the I.D.F. and among those who have been invited to come."

There remained, finally – and perhaps most significantly – the argument based on America's regional perception of the entire Middle East:

The declared policy of the United States with regard to this region aspires to "stability and peace" ... [But] As long as there is no peace between Israel and the Arab states we constitute a disruptive factor in [its] execution ... Their complex about a "disunited region" is liable to lead to lack of American support for us, since any support for us will be interpreted as anti-Arab. We need, therefore, to consider the fact that there is a known fear that the United States will follow Britain and attach more importance to seven Arab States than to one little Israel: and this danger will grow should cooperation between Britain and the United States increase.

In sum, there existed a dangerous asymmetry in the balance sheet of relations between the two states: "What we enjoy from the United States is quite disproportionate to the size of our state and its actual importance at a time when we can apparently offer [her] nothing and at a time when the general enthusiasm which we witnessed following the declaration of statehood and during the War of Independence is continually decreasing."

Notwithstanding the force of its own arguments, the memorandum prepared by the "American school" within the Israeli decision-making elite did not advocate a complete break with the non-identification policy. For one thing: "We have never been asked to join the Marshall Plan or regional pacts." Secondly, and as Eban put it: "Even if we identify ourselves with the West, we won't get a lot." What the situation required was a movement away from "mechanical balancing" and towards "the proliferation of practical points of contact between ourselves and the U.S.A. particularly in areas where our final goals are identical [stability in the region, democratic regimes etc.]."

The case thus presented did seem to make some impression on Sharett. It did not, however, carry the day. A spirited defense of the old policy was put forward by all of the Eastern Europe experts in the ministry. Shmuel Eliashiv, Israel Barzilai, Mordechai Namir and Ehud Avriel stressed the contrary force of arguments based on considerations of immigration and the need to preserve the links with Eastern European Jewry. Three additional ministry experts – Ya'akov Shimoni, Marcus Fisher and Avraham Katznelson – also insisted that a cautious strategy was still valid. An analysis of the debate shows that most participants advised the maintenance of the policy to which Israel had adhered since her establishment. Admittedly, no binding conclusions were reached. But neither was any official approval given to the demand that Israeli policy accord doctrinal expression to the objective reality which, in Sharett's words, had thrown the country "into the arms of the West." Equally significant is the fact that the protagonists made no substantive reference to the Israeli decisions on Korea taken some two weeks previously. These were viewed, in the words of the Foreign Minister, as "practical" rather than "decisions of principle" and as special rather than indicative, and certainly not as harbingers of a strategic change in Israeli foreign policy orientation.

Nevertheless, from a number of standpoints the meeting did constitute a significant milestone along the path of Israeli withdrawal from non-identification. It was, apparently, the first occasion on which the demand for a change of direction had been presented at so senior a forum. It thus set a precedent. Indeed, from this point in time onwards, it is possible to identify clear shifts in Israel's global foreign policy in the direction of the recommendations made by the Israeli Embassy in Washington. Eventually, indeed, Israel did adopt the very demand which proponents of the Embassy viewpoint had presented at the Jerusalem meeting: a political strategy which stressed the creation of a *de facto* link with the West in preference to a binding agreement.

Three other circumstances contributed to this development. One was the simultaneous series of internal meetings on Israel's economy and the problems associated with immigration and absorption. These fixed an absorption target of between 600,000 and a million new immigrants within a period of about three years, at an overall cost of a billion and a half dollars. Particularly relevant to the present discussion was the estimate that some two-thirds of the enormous sums thus required were supposed to come from the United States (half a billion from the U.S. government and half a billion from the American Jewish community).[50] The second circumstance was more personal, and can be traced back to Ben Gurion himself. One should be aware of the fact that his anti-Communist views had been sharp and unequivocal for many years prior to Israel's statehood.[51] Still, he was prepared, even for a specified period of time, to establish a non-aligned Israeli foreign policy in light of the country's need for material aid from any source – utilitarian non-alignment, not ideological neutrality. As he explained to Mapam's leaders in a closed discussion in late 1949, he "will refuse to give up his soul, but will give up his pants for absorption of immigration."[52] Ben Gurion's conception of the policy of non-alignment was well known to Mapam's leaders. It was precisely to them that he divulged his feelings, which were quite indicative of the direction he gave Israeli policy. Long before the Korean decision, Ben Aharon reported to his fellows of the kibbutz movement that in a meeting with Ben Gurion the latter had claimed neutrality "is a trick, a Communist political maneuver; the term 'neutrality' applies only in wartime, in an international context." His

[50] See Keren's despatch to the Foreign Ministry, 17.8.1950, ISA 2460/9 and the protocol of a meeting of Israel's U.N. delegation, 18.8.1950, ISA 89/1. According to these decisions a consultation with American Jewish leaders took place in Israel early in September 1950, see the announcement of the Prime Minister's spokesman on 27.8.1950, PM 5536/5734 and protocol of the meeting in ISA 2420/12.
[51] See S. Sandler, "Ben-Gurion's Attitude Towards the Soviet Union," *Jewish Journal of Sociology*, 21, 2, 1979, pp. 145–60.
[52] Mapam's Political Committee, protocol of a meeting, 10.11.1949, AHA.

colleague, Bar Yehuda, told that forum that Ben Gurion unequivocally stated that: "He is unwilling to be neutral; he regards the Soviet
Union as the number one enemy of Zionism and the entire world. He
is prepared to accept only one thing – that there be no anti-neutrality
expressions."[53] Since access to Israeli Cabinet protocols is still
barred, it is difficult to establish Ben Gurion's position at the time of
the debates which led to the decision on the Korean crisis. During the
meeting of the diplomatic corps in the middle of July he did not
publicly divulge his views and merely made some general comments
which did not commit him on either an operative or a doctrinal level.
However, he does then seem to have reached some resolute operative
decisions on the problem of Israel's international orientation. At the
beginning of the last week in July the American Ambassador was
summoned to Ben Gurion and informed of the Israeli intention: "To
build with American arms [an] effective Israeli army of 250,000 men,
able and anxious [to] aid [the] United States, [the] United Kingdom
and Turkey to resist Russian aggression."[54] When the Ambassador
asked how the Israeli left viewed the subject, Ben Gurion told him (in
confidence) that: "The Israeli people would support the crushing in
any form [of] Communist collaboration in [the] event of [a] world
conflict ... [a] pre-equipped and enlarged Israeli army would
guarantee Israeli unity in support of [the] West." Furthermore, Ben
Gurion promised that: "If Russia attacked Israel's strategic airfields,
Israel's new army could and would hold out until the United States'
and the United Kingdom's forces could arrive." As the American
Ambassador pointed out: "The Prime Minister could not have been
more explicit in [his] willingness [to] commit Israel unreservedly to
[the] West."

In more ways than one, Ben Gurion seems to have been jumping
the gun. The Americans had never asked Israel for military
assistance; had they done so, the matter would probably have caused
much more internal debate than the Prime Minister was willing to
admit. (Particularly significant, in this context, is the message relayed
to a State Department official only one month later by Teddy Kollek,
the Israeli Prime Minister's trusted confidant in the Washington
Embassy – "Prime Minister's ideas were definitely not those of the

[53] Protocol of a meeting, 9.2.1950, AHA.
[54] The following excerpts are taken from *FRUS*, 5, 1950, pp. 960–1. See also M. Gazit,
"Ben Gurion's Efforts to Create Military Ties with the U.S.A.," *Gesher*, 32, 1986/7, pp.
57–63 (Hebrew).

Israeli government and would not be supported in Israel at the present time.")[55] Nevertheless, that some demonstrable changes in Israel's policy were called for was becoming increasingly evident as a result of alterations in the political atmosphere within the United States. This, in fact, constituted the third of the circumstances which brought about such changes. As a result of the Korean conflict, all important U.S. decisions were becoming influenced by the pervading context of the cold war. Israel's repesentatives in the U.S.A. immediately experienced this development and, together with representatives of American Jewry, transmitted their feelings on the matter to Israel's leadership throughout July and August.

Avraham Harman, the Israeli Consul in New York, was perhaps the first person to communicate this message. Since he and Sharett were close friends, his letter carried particular weight. Writing at the end of July, he argued that the government's decision on Korea had been unavoidable; any other would have been "disastrous."[56] Furthermore, the changed internal atmosphere within the United States made it imperative that the Korean decision open the way for a radical change in Israeli policy:

It is clear that [Israel's decision on Korea] is only a first step. The government's decision has an inner logic of its own, which will compel it to go further as the situation develops ... our policy of non-identification was one which we were able to pursue only as long as the conflict remained in the "cold war" stage. The real question as I see it is not whom or what we shall choose but when. And the question of time may be fateful. The American scene has been transformed in the past few weeks. Although the attack on South Korea was a very different thing from Pearl Harbor, the effect on the country has in many ways been the same. In this state of affairs the American government is looking urgently for world support – a dramatic change from its position in the two world wars when by way of contrast this country was as it were "on the outside looking in." And as time passes, more and more the position will be taken that "who is not for us is against us." As for the flow of American aid abroad, the primary and determining factor in every case will be the extent to which the country concerned can be counted on for help.

A day later, Mosheh Keren developed the same diagnosis but covered the prognosis more extensively. Also addressing Sharett, he stated his conviction that:

[The reorientation in Israel's foreign policy] is not a question of a single demonstrative step, but of an overall political style expressed through our responses to international crises if and when they arise. It seems to me that

[55]  *FRUS*, 5, 1950, p. 986.
[56]  The following excerpts are taken from his letter on 27.7.1950, ISA 2489/9.

this situation is likely to make it easier to determine our line since it does not make a basic change in our policy necessary; but on the other hand it is clear that we do not have much more time to lose. The day is coming when we will be compelled to demand further aid on a very large scale from the U.S.A. in order to prevent a most grave crisis in our country and perhaps famine and total paralysis. If we combine such a request with political declarations which can be interpreted as an abandonment of our non-identification, this will give the impression that we are ready to sell our ideological independence for a mess of pottage. We have to create a basis for such a step in advance and not in a one-time way but rather as a permanent policy.[57]

Precisely the same message was transmitted to the highest channels in Israel by the leaders of American Jewry, among whom were some of Israel's most enthusiastic supporters. One example is provided by the letter which David Ginsburg addressed to the President of the state of Israel in the first week of August:

In a cold blooded way it is ... necessary to consider whether Israel could, in a sense, blackmail the Western allies in the same way that Turkey and Spain did during the last war ... I don't think this will be possible partly because Israel is likely to be deprived of any true freedom of choice by allied military action and partly because Israel is not big enough or important enough to play the role. I say this with the full awareness that there are a good many Jews in the United States who together exercise considerable political influence. But in time of war they will act, I think, without regard to the possibly conflicting needs and interests of Israel. Indeed, American Jews (like English Jews) will be the first patriots – the first to lean over backwards and to withdraw support from Israel even before such action may be called for by events.
    If this analysis is correct, if the government of Israel has the capacity and the civic courage to counsel ... the people of Israel wisely and to persuade them that neutrality is as irrelevant to security in the modern world as medieval armor to rocket warfare, then and only then can further steps be taken in relation to the United States which may have some true bearing on Israel's economic and military security.[58]

These arguments undoubtedly provided an impetus to the decisions confirmed by the government of Israel at the beginning of August. They did not, however, guarantee the success of a new Israeli policy. (As Keren himself put it: "We should under no circumstances believe that some demonstrative declaration of adherence to the West could be used as a magic wand to open the coffers of the U.S. Treasury.")[59] Neither did they altogether obviate the fact that some

---

[57] 28.7.1950, ISA 2414/26.     [58] 2.8.1950, ISA 2423/12.
[59] See Keren's despatches to the Foreign Ministry, 17.8.1950 and 24.8.1950, ISA 2460/9.

contradictions in Israel's goals were inevitable. Israel did adopt a strategy of active rapprochement with the United States on global issues. Nevertheless, Sharett defined three explicit reservations to the Israeli delegation to the U.N. in the middle of September: "a. Matters of direct concern to us, such as the matter of the Arab League. b. Not to widen the rift between us and the Soviet Union – it is clear that the steps we took over Korea were the cause of the rift between us . . . c. The preservation of independence in Israel's policy."[60]

The principal difficulty was to effect a rapprochement with America on global issues without arousing Soviet antagonism. The operative solution to this problem, which was apparently formulated during the summer of 1950 and which characterized Israeli policy on these issues for a lengthy period thereafter, was tripartite. First, there was to be no public expression, whether by means of votes in the U.N. or open declarations, of doctrinal changes in the non-identification policy; secondly, Israel was simultaneously to stress her ideological proximity to the West's democratic and liberal ideas; thirdly, she was quietly and very discreetly, to attempt to forge some sort of strategic link with the U.S.A.

Of these three elements the last was undoubtedly the most radical. It resulted from a deeply embedded Israeli conviction that the chances of obtaining vital economic aid from the U.S.A. stood in direct proportion to the extent to which Israel was prepared to make an obligation "towards the concept of a political and military alliance with the United States."[61] As a concrete expression of the degree to which Israel had abandoned her policy of "non-identification," however, efforts to try and establish a military link with the U.S.A. is misleading. During the second half of 1950, Israel's foreign policy did not give the impression that it had irrevocably moved into a new era. Rather, it became essentially dual in thrust. One aspect of her behavior becomes evident when a study is made of the pattern of Israel's votes at the U.N. during that period. On such issues as Spain's entry into the organization, the problem of China, the human rights question and above all the problem of how to solve the Korean crisis, Israel voted against the American line. She thus expressed a

[60] 18.9.1950, ISA 89/1.
[61] See Elan's cable to Sharett, 25.8.1950, ISA 2308/18, Lurie and Raphael's cable to Sharett, 2.8.1950, ISA 2329/9 and especially Eytan's cable to Elath, 9.10.1950, BGA. On the Israeli decision to change its line, see also Eliashiv's despatch to the Eastern Europe Section in the Foreign Ministry, 12.10.1950, ISA 75/9.

desire to develop her own policy on various international issues, without being constrained by the need to tread warily with regard to the global conflict.[62] On the other hand, far from the spotlight of the U.N., Israel initiated an entirely different series of actions. These did signify an incremental change in her strategy. They also constituted clear articulations of Ben Gurion's message: "Though in peace we try [to] maintain political independence in [the] event of war we [will] stand [one] hundred percent with [the] West."[63]

The United States was not the only target of those signals. Beginning early in 1950, Israel also made a serious effort to obtain arms from Britain and by the autumn of that year was attempting to buttress her efforts in this direction with arguments which stressed her clear pro-Western global orientation. Half-way through September, for example, Eliahu Elath, by now the Israeli Ambassador in London, attempted to show the British Deputy Foreign Minister that the provision of arms to Israel would serve parallel British interests. Israel, he argued, "was the only democratic country in the Middle East ... During the war she had demonstrated her ability to fight and would do so again and can therefore play her part perhaps not in halting Russian expansionism but in delaying it. Winston Churchill's latest volume showed how the campaign in Greece and Crete had delayed the attack on Russia; Israel might play a similar role."[64] That Israel might fulfill an important function in any future Western military deployment in the Middle East was also an argument put to British officials by the Israeli Chief of Staff (who explicitly asked for "closer relations with Britain especially on defense matters") and by Reuven Barkat, the General Secretary of the Histadrut (who blandly

---

[62] See circular despatch by the director of the International Organizations Section of the Israeli Foreign Ministry, 5.9.1950, ISA 2476/7; Raphael's letter to Eban on the same day, ISA 341/13; the cabled correspondence with the Israeli Embassy in Washington in September/December 1950, ISA 2308/19; protocol of a meeting held on 10.9.1950 at the Foreign Ministry, ISA 2404/9; letter from the International Organizations Section at the Foreign Ministry to Sharett, 15.9.1950, ISA 89/18; protocols of the meetings of Israel's legation to the U.N. during September and October 1950, ISA 89/1; Sharett's despatch to Eytan, 11.10.1950, ISA 89/8; Bentsur's letter to Eytan, 13.10.1950, ISA 2476/7; and a protocol of Sharett's talk to the directors of his Ministry, 26.10.1950, ISA 2409/8.

[63] From his cable to Elath, 9.10.1950, BGA.

[64] The conversation took place on 15.9.1950, British Foreign Office Documents, London [hereafter PRO] File fo371/82529, er1054/47. See reports on other meetings on 22.9.1950 and on 14.11.1950 in which the same motive appeared, PRO fo371/82529, er1059/49, er1054/55.

stated that "Israel was now aligned with the West in all but the provision of bases").[65]

Possible arms procurements from the United States could be approached somewhat differently, principally because Israel was already assured of the supply of some heavy military equipment from France.[66] Indeed, the basic argument employed in order to effect the gradual change in Israeli policy towards Washington stressed economic motives. In Eban's formulation (drafted in August 1950), Israel might hope to maximize her economic opportunities by stressing her willingness to take part in economic frameworks of American strategic planning in the Middle East.[67] Chronologically, her first opportunity to implement this policy occurred in connection with the United States Technical Assistance Plan (known as the Point Four Program). The declared goal of that program (whose budget, in 1950 was $35 million) was the provision of technical assistance to weak states all over the world. This aid was more limited than the direct welfare provided through the Marshall Plan and was not made explicitly dependent on any political conditions. Nevertheless, the relevant Act did contain a clause empowering the President of the United States to cease technical aid to states whose policy was liable to injure American interests. Moreover, even though the President himself emphasized the humanitarian aspect of the scheme, it clearly constituted an integral part of the entire network of propaganda, economic and military activities with which the United States was attempting to contain Communism world-wide. For that reason (and because Israel had tentatively been allocated the tiny sum of only $200,000) Jerusalem was initially reluctant to request assistance within that framework. Once strategic considerations were taken into account, however, they seemed to tip the scales. At the end of November, accordingly, Israel formally presented an application to participate in the Point Four Program.[68]

Far more significant an expression of the new Israeli policy was the plan later referred to as "Operation Stockpile." The basic idea was to persuade the American Administration to stockpile vital strategic

[65] See reports dated 14.10.1950, PRO fo371/82578, p. 63, and 19.12.1950, PRO fo371/82529, er1054/62, 1054 respectively.
[66] See Herzog's letter to Eban, 21.11.1950, ISA 338/23.
[67] See Eban's cable, 30.8.1950, ISA 2308/18.
[68] See M. Shalit's and V. Salkind's letter to Eban, 2.11.1950, ISA 376/38; and protocols of the meetings of Israeli diplomatic representatives in Washington, 28.11.1950, 4.12.1950, ISA 342/26.

supplies in Israel. Although these would remain the property of the United States, their possible significance to Israel could be enormous. Israel could, for instance, ask to purchase some of the products, mainly food and oil. This would not only enable her to bypass the need for Congressional authorization for such commodities, her own quantities of which were often exiguous. In the event that the country's economic links were cut in a war or an international emergency, she could also use the stores to replenish her own severely depleted supplies. Above all, of course, the mere existence of American emergency stocks on Israeli soil would symbolize Israel's place within the Western strategic ambit and improve the chances of obtaining more extensive aid. Altogether, in fact, "Operation Stockpile" possessed several implications which were not strictly economic. Accordingly, it spawned several ancillary schemes. One was to persuade the Americans to make use of the fledgling Israeli military industry for the purpose of possible production for the N.A.T.O. states (which would necessitate the transfer of the required raw materials from the United States to Israel). Another was to request permission to standardize Israel's light arms with those of the United States. In concrete terms this meant the exchange of no less than 150,000 I.D.F. rifles for American counterparts.[69]

The line of argument used to support all these plans expressed a clear strategic conception. In the last week of December 1950, Israeli representatives spent several days attempting to get the message across to the American Secretary of Defense. Ultimately, it was left to Sharett to sum up the position: "On the understanding that the Middle East is a vital area, Israel is anxious to be in a position to contribute as effectively as possible to the security of the region."[70] For their part, the Americans seemed impressed. Summarizing a range of contacts, Acheson informed the U.S. Embassy in Tel Aviv that:

[The] Israelis have said they now convinced fallaciousness [of] their policy [of] "non-identification" and that they know that [the] only hope [for] their

[69] On these issues see, *inter alia*, Fisher's despatch to Avner, 12.10.1950, ISA 2530/4; Eban's despatch to Sharett, 8.12.1950, ISA 3063/13; Herzog's despatch to the Israeli Military Intelligence, 11.12.1950, ISA 2587/7; Herzog's despatch to Salmon, 15.12.1950, ISA 338/23; Keren's despatch to the Foreign Ministry, 18.12.1950, ISA 2475/1; Sharett's letter to Kaplan, 20.12.1950, ISA 342/34; Kollek's letters to Elath, 22.12.1950, ISA 2587/7 and to Ben Gurion, 22.10.1950, ISA 342/19; Sharett's memorandum addressed to George Marshall, 23.12.1950, ISA 2456/6; and *FRUS*, 5, 1950, pp. 1052–3, 1077–83, 1086.

[70] See Sharett's memorandum to Marshall referred to in n. 69.

survival lies with the West. They desire that Israel be taken soonest into consideration in Western plans for N[ear] E[ast] defense and also that Israel begin at once to make contribution within [the] framework [of] these plans.[71]

Equally telling was the American Ambassador's own evaluation. Israel's recent steps, he reported, reflected

[the] degree to which Israeli leadership is now prepared to translate its Western orientation into tangible foreign political commitments. Offer is culmination of gradual change in foreign political thinking of Israeli leaders during last six months. Shift in emphasis during that period from official policy of "neutrality" to "non-identification" to what is now sometimes described as "independent" has prepared ground for shift to more overt ties to [the] West ... Embassy's preliminary appraisal reference proposal is that it is little short of revolutionary in Israeli thinking, that the very fact government leaders have made it is vivid proof of their determination to take whatever steps are necessary to insure their survival as national state, and that it is sufficiently significant to our Near Eastern policy to warrant careful top level attention.[72]

What made such attention even more imperative was the American feeling that Israel was about to cross another "Rubicon." Specifically, she seemed to be on the verge of opening a new chapter in her relations with Britain, the U.S.A.'s major partner in the Middle East region. Principal among the causes for Israel's apparent willingness to let Mandate bygones be bygones was the intimation that the Americans did not themselves intend to defend the region in the event of a world war. As they told Sharett during the course of his visit to the United States in December, "if anything should happen there will anyway only be English in the Middle East."[73] Consequently, they advised that Israel be more explicit about her "willingness to talk with the English" on the subject of regional security.[74] In concrete terms the Americans recommended that Israel agree to the visit of the British general, Robertson, who was to tour the region at the beginning of 1951.[75]

[71] *FRUS*, 5, 1950, p. 1086. In his letter to the Israeli Ambassador in London Kollek wrote late in December 1950 that "changes in the world during the last couple of months and the needs of the state of Israel caused a certain change in our old line of non-identification." See n. 69.
[72] 5.1.1951, *FRUS*, 5, 1951, pp. 561–2.
[73] See Kollek's letter to Ben Gurion referred to in n. 69.    [74] *Ibid.*
[75] See Elath's report on his talk with Herbert Morrison on 19.12.1950, ISA 36/14; Ben Gurion's conversation with Richard Crossman, 4.1.1950, Ben Gurion's diary, BGA; Eytan's despatch to Raphael, 10.1.1951, ISA 2384/21; and an undated memorandum (most probably from early January 1951) on "Anglo–Israeli Rapprochement," ISA 36/3.

As relayed by Kollek, the immediate Israeli response – although positive – was somewhat reserved:

In its desire for collaboration with the U.S. for the defense of the Near East, Israel of course realizes that there is close collaboration between the U.S. and the U.K. in this field. The possibility of Israel collaboration with the U.K. is hindered by a strong psychological barrier, but this barrier is disappearing gradually and can be overcome.[76]

Possibly not even Kollek knew how close he was to the mark. Sharett had in fact considered giving an explicitly positive response on this question while he was in Washington; he also contemplated the possibility of holding meetings with the heads of the British military establishment on his way back to Israel. But his intimate acquaintance with his Premier's personality and opinions gave rise to second thoughts. Ultimately, Sharett decided not to act "without first thoroughly clarifying matters with Ben Gurion."[77] As we shall see, from both a personal and professional viewpoint, that was a wise decision.

Practical Israeli policy over orientation during the final months of 1950 did thus mark a clear break with the previous adherence to non-identification. Nevertheless, there plainly existed three important constraints on Israeli strategy in this period. One was imposed by domestic circumstances; not all Israeli policy-makers agreed to the wisdom or desirability of a change in their country's foreign policy. Several were opposed to any new course.[78] Secondly, there was the sheer immensity of Israel's own needs. Her activity in Washington did express, in the words of an Israeli diplomat, her willingness "to openly join in a common front with all those ready to withstand aggression."[79] But Israel's desire to help came a poor second to her desire to be helped. Finally, whatever changes were taking place they were still embryonic. As a result, the formulation of a prognosis for a

---

[76] *FRUS*, 5, 1950, p. 1083.
[77] Kollek's letter to Elath, 22.12.1950, ISA 2587/7. The British were informed in Washington about Kollek's remarks. Although they seemed to be doubtful whether Israel was indeed ready for a far-reaching turn in its foreign policy orientation the signal was all too clear to ignore and it certainly explains their *démarche* early in 1951 to be discussed below. See correspondence in PRO fo371/91206, e1073/2, 1073/3.
[78] See, for example, correspondence between Sharett and Sasson early in January 1951, ISA 2382/1.
[79] See Keren's despatch to the Foreign Ministry, 29.12.1950, ISA 2475/1. In a discussion on public information held in the Israeli Embassy in Washington it was claimed that the state's global stand was "unclear," 4.1.1951, ISA 337/23.

clear and open strategy of action in military strategic areas was still a long way off. In the words of the same Israeli diplomat:

If for example we are asked how willing we will be to fight in the event of a Soviet attack on Iran, we have no answer to give, if they ask us to provide bases, we shall have to refuse in accordance with our line. If they ask to know our position on the Atlantic Pact or a similar military pact in the Middle East or in the Mediterranean Sea, we have no clear decision.

Altogether, and as will shortly be demonstrated, there existed a sizable and burdensome gap, both domestic and external, between public pronouncements and political actions.

# 11 . SOLIDIFICATION OF A WESTERN ORIENTATION

While Israel's representatives in Washington worked to interest the Americans in various strategic plans at the end of 1950,[1] policymakers in Jerusalem were confronted with a new problem. Acting on the several hints which had been dropped in the United States, the British made a significant move. On 15 January 1951, William Strang (Permanent Under-Secretary at the British Foreign Office) asked Israel's Ambassador in London to obtain his government's authorization for a visit to the country by General Robertson.[2] As presented by Strang, the British plan was to use the visit to explore the idea of a pact with Israel, or as he put it: "Some kind of alliance with [Israel] either on a regional basis [if possible] or also bilateral." Specifically, he had two concrete ideas in mind. One was the establishment of British bases in Gaza which might be connected by a corridor to Jordan; the other was the construction of British bases in Israel itself. The feeling in Israel was that both suggestions had arisen as a result of the difficulties which the British were encountering in negotiations for the continued maintenance of their bases in Egypt.

In Jerusalem, Robertson's visit was authorized. The proposals which Strang submitted before Robertson's arrival, however, became the subject of debate at the very highest level. The full details of the discussions are not known although it is clear that among the participants were Ben Gurion, Sharett, Walter Eytan (Director

[1] See report no. 9 of the Western Europe Section of the Israeli Foreign Ministry, 9.1.1951, ISA 2515/1; Marshall's letter to Sharett, 11.1.1951, ISA 2456/6; internal memorandum, 16.1.1951, ISA 2461/10; and Eban's letter to Ben Gurion, 25.1.1951, ISA 338/15.
[2] The following account is based, unless other indicated, on Elath's memorandum, 15.1.1951, ISA 37/10; Ben Gurion's diary, 27.1.1951, 29.1.1951, BGA; memorandum referred in n. 75 in the previous chapter and PRO fo371/91240, e1205/43. For Anglo–Israeli relations, see I. Pappé, "British Policy Towards the Middle East, 1948–1951" (Unpublished Ph.D. thesis, Oxford University, 1984), pp. 360–430.

General of the Foreign Ministry), Michael Comay (who was the ministry official responsible for the British Commonwealth) and Reuven Shiloah, an influential security and intelligence expert. It is equally certain that Ben Gurion was vehemently opposed to any suggestion that Israel agree to the British initiative. Indeed, he launched a particularly scathing attack on Israel's Ambassador in London. By delivering the message in person, complained Ben Gurion, Elath had unjustifiably raised Britain's expectations. He would have done better "to send [the report] with an envoy." Besides, the British plan was obviously preposterous:

This is not a proposal which can be debated, despite the recent pose [Strang had suggested that the agreement – if signed – be on the basis of "complete equality"] – they wish to get back into Israel, why should we give them a foothold? Their policy in the Near East remains unchanged, despite the change in public opinion and among members of government. It is not Cripps and not Bevan who run foreign policy but Bevin and it is a hostile policy manifested in their support for the [Arab] League whose only activity is war against Israel, [and in] their despatch of arms to Egypt whose purpose at least from the Egyptians' side is not use in a war against Russia but against Israel ... It is probable that this conversation [between Elath and Strang] was conducted with American knowledge and perhaps also upon her advice. With America we are prepared to discuss everything. We receive aid and demand more aid. To date we have not given the Americans anything, and we want the Americans to defend the Near East; in other words to defend us. America has not done us any harm, but only the opposite. This is not the case with England. She now offers us what is in effect an arrangement between her and Egypt at the cost of Israel's independence and well-being. It seems likely that when we have to we will link up with England and America and these two states will obligate themselves to defend us. At the moment no such plan exists. A grant of bases will portray us as an enemy of Russia, is liable to sabotage immigration and will turn us over to the Arabs. We can expel the Arab [Jordanian] Legion when it operates independently of Great Britain ... when the English are in the country we will not be able to [expel them] and they [the British] will control us. This is a humiliating proposal, what are they offering us? Why didn't they ask themselves why Israel should do such a thing?

Quite apart from these considerations, the Prime Minister also harbored an abiding fear of taking Israel into military attachments and obligations whose future direction could not be clearly perceived. As he told his Chief of Staff two days later:

the more I think about these things the more I see that we must not leap in too early and undertake commitments toward a future which is unclear ... an undertaking on war – and who will make undertakings toward us? We can do only one thing – not say how we will act in an uncertain future, but instead, what we shall do from day to day, i.e. become stronger, amass power and be helped by those who are willing to help us, and those who want to help us are Jews, and those Jews are the Jews of the land of freedom. To do this we have to gain trust – not by deception and not by ruses but by what we are.

This uncompromising stand obviously prevented an affirmative response to the British proposal. Formally presenting Israel's reply in London on 9 February, Elath was constrained to mention "the suspicions which still persisted in many circles in Israel with regard to the British."[3] These, he hastened to add (with what must have been evident embarrassment) may have been the prime considerations behind the Israeli attitude, but they were not the only ones. Indeed, he went on to present Strang with a detailed explanation of several additional points:

Turning then to the question of the bases, I explained that in existing circumstances my government would not welcome being presented with fresh proposals of this kind. I elaborated the various reasons for this, stressing our desire to avoid a show-down [with the Soviet Union] so long as there was any possibility of further emigration of Jews from the satellite countries. I explained that our people were convinced that the salvation of Jews was one of the basic principles of Israel's life (and that went for Jews all over the world as well as in Israel); nor should the importance of this aspect be measured in terms of numbers alone: Jewish tradition held the saving of one human being to be in essence as sacred a duty as the saving of multitudes.

Altogether, in fact, the Israeli reply became the occasion of the presentation of as clear a picture as possible of her position *vis-à-vis* the strategic confrontation between the powers. As Elath noted in his preface to the formal response, he was duty bound to stress three elements: first, "under no circumstances is it conceivable that Israel could find herself engaged against the West in an armed conflict"; secondly, only in the event of an inter-bloc war would it be possible to see "all sorts of arrangements" in the strategic area; thirdly, any interim changes in Israel's policy of non-identification had to be "gradual and discreet."[4]

When he did eventually visit Israel (19–21 February), General Robertson did not seem to think it worth while repeating Strang's message.[5] There was hardly any point in his attempting to do so.

---

[3] See Elath's despatch to Comay, 22.2.1951, ISA 37/10 which is the source of the following excerpts.
[4] See Elath's position paper, 2.2.1951, *ibid.*
[5] See Comay's memorandum, 26.2.1951, ISA 36/14.

Israel had already rejected a strategic proposal which was more concrete, and more far-reaching than any other offered to her between her establishment and the eve of the Sinai Campaign. He did, however, relay two other concrete suggestions. He proposed both a possible arrangement with regard to free airspace over Israeli territory and an assurance of the right of passage of British forces through Israel in wartime.[6] Neither idea dispelled Ben Gurion's fears (they perhaps even strengthened them); on intelligence grounds, both incurred the opposition of Israeli military circles. Accordingly, both were rejected.

Israel planned to put Robertson's visit to uses which were far less binding. Her principal aim at that time (and for some time afterwards) was to obtain British arms. To that end, she thought it necessary to illustrate the changes which were taking place in her policy of non-identification. But she was not prepared to tie herself to the wider objectives of Britain's strategic defense plans in the Middle East. And to that end, she had to define the limits of the changes in her policy. In Sharett's words, Israel was quite prepared for "contact and exchange of views and information on defense matters in the region in an informal way." She also wanted to persuade "the West that our strategic aim is the speedy build-up of manpower, productive capacity, military potential, and transport arteries in Israel." But beyond that she was not, at present, prepared to go. That is why he defined Robertson's visit as no more than "a link in a chain or a stage in a process."[7]

So delicate a policy was evidently open to misinterpretation. Indeed, it seems to have been misinterpreted by Michael Bar Zohar, the author of a bulky biography of Ben Gurion. Arguing that the Israeli Prime Minister wanted "to detemine different relations between Israel and England," he takes particular note of the fact that, in his conversation with Robertson, Ben Gurion suggested that Israel might join the British Commonwealth.[8] What Bar Zohar misreads, however, is both the context and motive of Ben Gurion's remarks. They were not designed to bring about a definitive treaty between the two countries (indeed, in the light of what we have already learned about Ben Gurion's position, that notion is clearly incredible). Rather, their purpose was to outline the sort of preconditions which

[6]  See Sharett's despatch to Elath, 28.2.1951, *ibid.*
[7]  *Ibid.*
[8]  M. Bar Zohar, *Ben Gurion* (Tel Aviv, 1978), p. 904 (Hebrew).

had to exist before such a relationship could become possible. That was certainly the understanding of the British Ambassador;[9] and his impression is confirmed by a reading of Michael Comay's protocol of the entire exchange.[10] As the latter recalled:

I was present at all the Robertson talks, and have no doubt in my mind as to what was said. There was not the faintest suggestion of applying for membership of the Commonwealth, either now or in the future. In the course of discussing possible collaboration in the event of a third world war, B.G. [Ben Gurion] wanted to emphasize that political and military commitments were in the last resort less important than the basic relationship. It was in this context that he suggested that the attitude towards us should be what it would have been if we were in the Commonwealth.[11]

Subsequent to the Robertson talks, Israel and Britain did discuss the topic of strategic cooperation, both in 1951 and 1952. But the British made no real attempt to explore the possibility of significant and active Israeli involvement in their defense plans for the Middle East. Far more revealing for our purposes is the parallel absence of will on the Israeli side to become involved.[12] The issue in fact remained dormant until almost the end of 1952, when discussions took place on Israel's possible integration within a Middle East defensive alliance under Anglo-American aegis. By then, however, Israel's leaders were fully occupied with two other major problems affecting their country's strategic and global orientations. One was a domestic information campaign designed to explain the shift in policy which had commenced at the end of 1950; the other was the nurturing of a network of contacts with the power considered to be her most important potential ally – the United States.

---

[9] ISA 2449/1.
[10] See his cable to London, 23.2.1951, PRO FO371/91240, E1201/55.
[11] His despatch to Elath, 24.6.1951, ISA 30/16.
[12] On later contacts, see Ben Gurion's diary, 27.2.1951, BGA; circular despatch to the Israeli embassies in Paris, Rome, Brussels, Stockholm and Hague, 28.2.1951, ISA 2515/1; Comay's despatch to Elath, 28.2.1951, ISA 36/14; PRO FO371/91732, E1196/1; report on Ben Gurion's meeting with the British Ambassador in Tel Aviv on 9.7.1951, ISA 2457/5; Ben Gurion's diary for the same day, BGA; Comay's letter to Elath, 9.7.1951, ISA 37/1; Comay's memorandum, 15.8.1951, ISA 2412/26; Sharett's letter to Ben Gurion, 20.8.1951, ISA 37/1; correspondence from late September 1951 in PRO FO371/91222, F1192/138G; and Ben Gurion's diary, 14.10.1951, BGA. The only tangible result of Robertson's visit was Israel's request to produce war material for the British Army. It was received very coolly in London for obvious political reasons and also because of the prerequisite for such production – the provision of British raw material. It is hardly surprising therefore that the whole episode developed into a historical "might have been." See PRO FO371/91732. On later developments, see Chapter 12.

As early as the second half of 1950, a significant asymmetry in Israel's policy became apparent. In the international arena, the country was increasingly deviating from the strategy of non-identification; but within Israel, domestic public opinion continued to adhere to it rigidly. This gap seemed to widen even further during the first part of 1951. The Washington Embassy staff then cited both newspaper articles and Knesset speeches as evidence that "the population in Israel is not aware" that "our demands on the U.S.A. determine our very existence."[13] The Director of the United States Section in the Israeli Foreign Ministry shared this feeling. He too complained that: "the public has not been prepared for all the changes in (foreign) policy, most people are certain that our government continues to adhere to the same line of identification or independence as it did before."[14]

Sharett appreciated the need for a concerted information campaign, designed to educate Israeli public opinion as to both the scope and limitations of the policy changes. The first forum which he chose for this purpose was the Knesset. An opportunity arose on 31 January when Mapam representatives tabled a fairly ritual catalogue of criticisms against Israel's foreign policy. Sharett's response contained a number of points and comments which had not previously been voiced in the Israeli parliament and, for those who wished to hear it, constituted a clear message of the major political developments in Israel's global policy.[15]

In striving for peace we still watch for signs of the storm, it is not our policy to join a plot and to undertake to enter it. The claim that we promised bases is slanderous but it would be frivolous to ignore the dangers of invasion and conquest and we must therefore prepare and defend ourselves. These preparations mean stockpiles and arms both of which can only be found in the free world. The ingathering of the exiles necessitates substantial aid which it is an honor to ask for and to give.

Two days later he was even more candid and outspoken. Addressing a general meeting of I.D.F. attachés to Israeli legations abroad, he

---

[13] See the protocol of a meeting held at the Embassy, 4.1.1951, ISA 337/23 and Eban's cable dated 29.1.1951, ISA 2308/20.
[14] See Bendor's despatch to Washington, 4.2.1951, ISA 2460/1; Shalit's letter to "Ziama," 5.2.1951, ISA 2398/3; Bendor's despatch to the Israeli Embassy in Washington, 11.2.1951; and Keren's despatch to the Foreign Ministry, 16.2.1951, ISA 2479/9.
[15] See Eytan's report to the Israeli Embassy in Paris, 31.1.1951, ISA 174/2 and Bendor's despatch to the Israeli Embassy in Washington, 4.2.1951, ISA 2460/1, which are the sources for the following excerpts.

delineated several central pillars of Israel's position *vis-à-vis* the inter-bloc confrontation.[16] First:

The state of Israel has a basic interest that Soviet territory in the world not be expanded, not only because any expansion of Soviet territory now means a step closer to war ... [but rather because] it means the loss of contact with Jews, the loss of any possibility of being helped [by them], no freedom of immigration ... Our interest is of course to prevent the conquest of Israel ... by anybody, but in the present situation Israel is not a candidate for conquest by the United States...

On the other hand, Israel had no wish to forge an explicit and total strategic attachment with the West:

We have to make a simple calculation of what is certain and what is possible – it is possible that war will erupt and that it will help us, it is certain that meanwhile we are portraying ourselves as a power which is hostile to the Soviet Union, which causes grave international dangers ... there is no doubt that this could have a malign and fatal effect on immigration. We should be extremely concerned about the fate of Soviet Jewry...

Nevertheless, Israel could not, in advance, proclaim her absolute neutrality. Any declaration of that sort "is liable to strike us a very severe blow and to cause irreparable damage." The United States, it had to be remembered, was in a state of cold war. Aid vital for the maintenance of Israel's existence would continue to come from the West, and in particular from the United States, only "if the impression is created that we are friends." It followed, and this was the essence of the message conveyed by the Foreign Minister, that Israel had to exploit what he considered to be a favorable situation. She had to take advantage of the fact that neither Britain nor the United States had yet determined frameworks for the defense of the Middle East. Her aim was to attain "a maximum of aid with a minimum of undertakings in advance."

The campaign of domestic information reached its peak at a long meeting of the Mapai Knesset faction and the party Central Committee on 3 March.[17] In the most wide-ranging assessment of Israel's global foreign policy hitherto presented to this forum, Sharett repeated his earlier arguments and explanations, to which he now appended a clear recommendation for a new Israeli strategy. "The absence of a formal declaration that we will fight does not prevent aid, while a declaration that we will not help precludes aid immediately."

[16] Protocol of the meeting held on 2.2.1951, ISA 2458/4.    [17] LPA.

On the other hand, he supported "the nurturing of the sort of atmosphere of relations (with the West) which will allow us aid now so that we can become stronger." Besides, he advised, there existed a clear asymmetry in the dangers implicit to Israel were one of the two blocs to emerge victorious from a world war.

We have to think of the future – what will really happen if there is a war, whether we declare ourselves neutral or not? Let us assun e that we make such a declaration and it is to no avail and the war reaches us, endangers us. The options are not equal; the country is in no danger whatsoever of being conquered by Western forces ... intent on imposing a regime which would fundamentally distort the state of Israel ... In the case of Soviet conquest there is a danger of the entire regime of this country being changed.

Another target of the internal information campaign was the staff of the Foreign Ministry in Israel, many of whose members were not acquainted with the finer points of their country's global orientation. A special gathering of all employees was held in the middle of June 1951. There, too, the changes were spelled out and the new terminology freely employed.[18]

Whilst the information campaign was still in full swing, active steps were also taken in a far more significant forum. Israel's leaders attempted to implement their policies by strengthening their direct links with the United States. Two subjects were of particular concern. One (of which mention has already been made) was "Operation Stockpile."[19] Sharett had formally presented the scheme to the American Secretary of Defense during their meeting in December 1950. Over the next few months, Israel's representatives in Washing-

---

[18] See despatch to the Israeli Embassy in Washington from the Foreign Ministry, 26.6.1951, ISA 2460/1.

[19] The following is based on Herzog's despatch to Israel's Chief of Intelligence, 3.1.1951; Bendor's letter to the Director General of the Israeli Foreign Ministry, 3.1.1951, ISA 338/10; a despatch of the Western Europe Section to the Israeli Embassy in Paris, 3.1.1951, ISA 2515/1; a protocol of a meeting at the Israeli Embassy in the U.S.A., 4.1.1951, ISA 337/23; Avner's despatch to the Israeli Embassy in Paris, 9.1.1951, ISA 2515/1; George Marshall's despatch to Sharett, 11.1.1951, ISA 2456/6; Bendor's letter to Sharett, 16.1.1951, ISA 2461/10; Eban's despatch to Ben Gurion, 25.1.1951, ISA 338/15; Eban's memorandum, 31.1.1951, ISA 2403/3; Ben Gurion's letter to the Israeli Chief of Staff, 8.2.1951, ISA 2456/6; Keren's despatch to the Foreign Ministry, 16.2.1951, ISA 2479/9; protocol of a meeting of Mapai Knesset members, 27.2.1951, LPA; Ben Horin's despatch to the Israeli Ambassador in France, 7.3.1951, ISA 2515/1; despatch by the Israeli Deputy Chief of Staff to Shiloah, 29.3.1951, ISA 2479/9; report on Ben Gurion's meeting with Marshall, 21.6.1951, ISA 337/4; Ben Gurion's diary, 3.11.1951, 5.11.1951, BGA; and *FRUS*, 5, 1951, pp. 560–1, 732–5, 820–1.

ton invested considerable effort in attempts to convince officials within the administration that the initiative be pursued. Meetings on the subject were held at various levels; it was also raised by Ben Gurion when he visited the United States in May 1951. The initial American reactions were ambivalent. They did not categorically reject the Israeli suggestions, but they did ask some tricky questions. They raised doubts "concerning our technical possibilities in these fields taking into account the storage problems which exist even now in the country and the difficulties of unloading ships in the ports already available." The Americans also pointed out that the United States was faced with similar requests from many other states and that, "its reserves were . . . insufficient to answer them all." They were even "afraid that if large quantities [of equipment and supplies] are allocated to us [in the framework of 'Operation Stockpile'] some of them will reach the other side of the Iron Curtain." Above all, they warned against excessive Israeli optimism that the scheme, even if acceptable, could be speedily authorized. "After all," as one senior official told Teddy Kollek at the beginning of January, "it took a long time for your government to reach the conclusion that such proposals should be made and it should be clear to you that since the idea is a new one it will of course take time for our government to get used to it and to begin to act."

It is significant that, these warnings notwithstanding, Israeli activities in this field did not cease. On the contrary, they became more intense during the first half of 1951, both in Jerusalem and in Washington. Israel sent the Americans secret memoranda on her economic and industrial capacity to participate in various military efforts; she also initiated several further meetings between the two sides on the subject. Above all, she showed her eagerness to please the Americans by complying with some of their specific requests. In February, for instance, it was decided (at the express behest of the Prime Minister) to reverse previous policy and permit the American Military Attaché in Israel to inspect the facilities of the Israeli military industry. Overriding the concern of the defense establishment at the possible security risks involved was the argument that Israel had to take "every action which is likely to strengthen the other side's trust in us, to oblige it, even if only morally, towards us and to improve its perception of our ability." At the beginning of March, and subsequent to further "strong American pressure," Israeli officials also conceded "that we would henceforth be willing to re-export products which we receive from the United States only to countries outside the Eastern bloc." Once again, the motive was the hope to induce an American responsiveness with regards to "Operation Stockpile." Totally unavailing therefore were counter-arguments, to the effect that: "Re-export facilitates our negotiations with the Eastern bloc on the question of immigration and thus strenghtens our potential." As long as "Stockpile" remained on the drawing boards – and even though it never advanced beyond that stage – it continued to influence the direction of Israel's foreign policy in several areas.

Quite apart from "Operation Stockpile," Israel also attempted to implement "Operation Gift" during the first half of 1951.[20] Here, too, she was forced to examine and define the basics of her global strategic conception. The object of the scheme was to obtain from the United States government a direct grant in aid of $150 million for the 1951/2 financial year, sums which were vitally necessary if Israel were to have any hope of meeting her chronic shortages of various basic products. However, as was discovered by Pinhas Lavon (then Minister of Agriculture) when he undertook an emergency mission to the United States in February 1951, American aid was conditional. Administration officials insisted that all grants were dependent on the extent to which the activities of the nations in need seemed to fall into line with the basic American goal of "the strengthening of the free states."[21] This stipulation demanded far more than an innocuous Israeli assurance that "the receipt of significant financial aid in this year is likely to establish Israel as a staunch stronghold of democracy which is fighting for its life in this region of the world." It required, rather, that an explicit link be made between, on the one hand, Israel's economic stability, political freedom and democracy and, on the other, the *security* of the United States. As Israeli diplomats and politicians realized, this was new – and potentially dangerous – ground. Once she articulated that link – and especially if she did so through the medium of United States legislation – Israel would publicly proclaim her alignment with America's global security efforts, which were mainly anti-Soviet in nature. Hitherto, the Israelis had been wary of crossing that particular "red line" in their foreign policy. "Operation Gift" forced them to reconsider the issue.

---

[20] See report to the Cabinet entitled "Operation Matan," 19.3.1951, CZA s41/419/1.
[21] The following account is based upon and excerpts are taken from material referred to in n. 20, Eban's letter to the American Secretary of State, 21.3.1951, ISA 342/2 and correspondence in ISA 343/4.

Although Israel's leaders were immediately appreciative that a formal request for American aid would jeopardize their policy of non-identification, they were initially able to mask the extent to which that was so. Principally, this was because they managed to avoid including the word "security" in the phrasing used to clarify the goals for which the grant was being requested. That problematic term only appeared in the draft act which was formulated by American congressmen. But the pretense which thus characterized Israel's actions in March 1951 (when her formal request was presented) could not long be maintained. Neither could public debate on the issues which the request raised long be avoided. During the last quarter of that year, two other events forced the matter out into the open and compelled an entirely new assessment of Israel's possible place in Western security arrangements. One was a decision on the part of the American Congress, taken in September, which authorized the President to allocate 10% (i.e. almost $40 million) of all U.S. military aid to the Arab states and Israel, this sum being designated for the defense of the entire region.[22] The second development was a sequence of Western decisions with regards to the establishment of an Allied Command for the defense of the Middle East (S.A.C.M.E. – Supreme Allied Command Middle East); Egypt was to be invited to take part in this framework, Israel was not.

As will be seen, from Israel's viewpoint these two events were interconnected. At the very least, both had clear implications for any future Israeli integration into a Western security arrangement. Of the two, however, the S.A.C.M.E. decision was clearly the more important. Particularly was this so in the context of Israel's regional situation. Were Egypt to accept the invitation to become "a founding member" of the organization, she would attain special political and security rights, and thus become a serious threat to Israel. Ben Gurion conveyed his fears on this matter to the American Ambassador on 15 October. The invitation to Egypt to participate in the Command constituted: "a danger to our security and very existence, Egypt's arms will never be directed against the enemies of freedom and democracy but only against us."

Ben Gurion's apprehensions were in fact ill-founded. Egypt soon declined the invitation. Nevertheless, it was clear that some clarification of Israel's attitude towards the new Western security deployment

---

[22] The following account is based on excerpts are taken from Ben Gurion's diary, 3.10.1951, BGA and from correspondence in ISA 342/37.

was called for. Although she had not been invited to join the Command, she had received hints that she might be able to establish some form of link with it. This was certainly an attractive proposition especially if, as seemed to be the case, Britain seemed to be relinquishing her previous monopoly over the security arrangements of the entire region. Altogether, in fact, it was impossible to adopt anything approximate to an ostrich-like policy. Israel's attitude towards S.A.C.M.E. was likely to exercise a determinant influence on American responses to her requests for economic aid. Furthermore, and perhaps most important of all, who could predict that – notwithstanding Egypt's attitude – S.A.C.M.E. might not eventually come into being and thereby confront Israel with a long list of unprecedented political and security problems? Prior to the end of 1951, Israel had in practice been able to ignore the need for a clear and formal attitude towards Western regional strategic frameworks. She could no longer do so. Indeed, throughout the next half a decade, that became one of her most pressing concerns.

Explicit decisions on these issues were taken at a series of meetings held on 2 and 3 November 1951, which were attended by the Premier, the Foreign Minister, the higher echelons of the Foreign and Defense ministries in Israel and some of Israel's ambassadors overseas.[23] Their opinions on S.A.C.M.E. were finely balanced, with four arguments being advanced in favor of Israel's participation and an equal number against. In favor were: first, Israel's understandable need to safeguard her security in the event of a war which would encompass the Middle East; secondly, her requirement for external aid, or an external guarantee, in order to prevent – or respond to – Arab aggression; thirdly, the question of Israel's economic dependence on the United States whose policy in the region was particularly sensitive to strategic considerations; fourthly, Israel had to preserve her close relations with American Jewry, for which she felt responsible and upon which she to some extent relied. Some of the participants also added a further dimension to the discussion. A positive Israeli attitude towards S.A.C.M.E., especially if contrasted with Egypt's refusal to participate in the organization, might afford an opportunity to improve Israel's general image in the West. Specifically, it might encourage the United States to appreciate the difference between the

[23] The following account is based upon and excerpts are taken from Ben Gurion's diary, 2, 3, 5.11.1951, BGA and correspondence between Comay and Eban in ISA 2457/5.

diplomatic opportunism of the Arabs and Israel's basic and stable attachment to the West and its system of values.

Equally weighty, however, were the arguments advanced against Israeli participation in S.A.C.M.E. For one thing, substantial security risks were involved. A strategic partnership of that sort would require Israel to reveal several of her military secrets, not least to some of the same Arab countries with whom she was still in a state of "slumbering war." More specific were the apprehensions aroused by the lack of clarity surrounding S.A.C.M.E.'s precise aims. Israel's interests would hardly be well served were that framework to allow the Middle East to be used as a stepping-stone for a preventative war aimed at the Soviet Union's "soft underbelly." Furthermore, Israeli participation would endanger the position of the Jews of the Soviet Union and of Eastern Europe and polarize public opinion within Israel itself. To these concrete grounds for rejection was added a more general consideration. The situation in the Middle East was inherently so uncertain that Israel could not undertake any commitments without extreme reservations. Ben Gurion, as always sensitive to this circumstance, summed up the matter thus: "We should always bear in mind that our situation in the Middle East was *sui generis* and could not be fitted into any general pattern."

Ultimately, the rejectionist opinions prevailed, and a primary decision was taken to refrain from actions leading to the creation of a contractual link with a collective Western security alliance in the region. Two prominent features of "non-identification" were thereby confirmed: Israel refused to create a binding, contractual and public link with a collective Western and anti-Soviet security alliance in the region; she also declined to offer foreign powers bases within her territory. In other respects, however, significant shifts had taken place in her policy. Particularly noteworthy, therefore, is a subsidiary cluster of decisions taken at the November meeting whose thrust was to ensure that the lines to the West were definitely to be improved. In order to ensure military, economic and strategic assistance, Israel aimed at the creation of "facts without pacts," by which she meant direct and bilateral arrangements with the Western powers and especially with the United States. To that end, the meeting recommended that Israeli diplomats take every opportunity to stress Israel's clear interest and basic identification with the West (and especially with the United States) and thus counteract whatever negative impressions might be created by her reluctance to participate in a specifically strategic Western framework. It was also decided to take domestic advantage of the opportunities presented by the S.A.C.M.E. issue. Sharett, for one, certainly felt that debates on the matter within Israel could be of some value. At the very least, they might "guide domestic public opinion into realistic channels."

It was with that thought obviously in mind that, on the following day, Sharett himself addressed the Knesset. His speech concluded with an important formulation of Israel's foreign policy. He stressed the fact that Israel had not been asked to join the regional defense organization, and added:

As before, the government will strive to maintain relations of friendship with every peace-loving state, friendly disposed toward Israel. Her vital interests, however, demanded that above all her relations be close with those countries whose Jewish communities are free to further the fulfillment of her historical mission and whose governments render practical assistance to enable her to surmount the trials of today and those which lie in wait for tomorrow.[24]

Sharett was convinced that the implications of his message had been fully understood. By endorsing his statement, he confided in a private letter, the Knesset had confirmed that: "In principle Israel is prepared to cooperate with the West in defense of the Middle East even though she reserves to herself the right to put forward conditions in the event of being invited to participate in a fixed organizational framework for such defense – a program which has not yet actually arisen."[25]

Moreover, as he told the American and British ambassadors: "The Opposition understanding of the speech was correct, and the speeches by Mapam [whose parliamentary representatives had accused the government of significant deviations from its previous diplomatic orientation] rightly determined its actual content."[26]

As Sharett pointed out, Israel's primary decision to reject direct and public contractual links with the West was, of course, considerably facilitated by the fact that she was never formally offered that option. This was a particularly convenient situation from the point of view of Israel's relations with the Soviet Union, and was exploited appropriately. It constituted, in fact, Israel's principal defense against Russian reproaches on the matter. On 21 November, Soviet Deputy Foreign Minister Gromyko handed a long letter to the Israeli

---

[24]  For the English version of the speech, see "News to Israeli Legations Abroad," no. 392, ISA 3063/12.
[25]  See CZA A245/82.          [26]  *Ibid.*

Minister in Moscow on the subject of the Middle East Command; his communication denounced the proposed organization as part of an aggressive imperialist plan against the Soviet Union and warned Israel that her participation was liable to cause severe damage to bilateral relations with the Soviet Union.[27] In a message to Israel's legations throughout the world, the Director General of the Foreign Ministry pointed out that: "The Soviet warning supports one of the main motives behind our pragmatic approach: namely the question of immigration from Eastern Europe." That was true. Nevertheless, Israel was also able to fend off the Russian diplomatic onslaught by noting – blandly, but truthfully – that she had not been invited to join the putative Western Command, and that: "She has not agreed and will not agree to actions or to preparations for aggression directed against the Soviet Union."

Meanwhile, the tone of discussions at the November meeting had been relayed to the British and American representatives in Israel. On 6 November the British Ambassador, Sir Knox Helm, was informed by Sharett that Israel "prefers a practical arrangement over any formal link," and that the government sees no "need for any spectacular step."[28] Four days later, the United States Ambassador was summoned to the Prime Minister, who unfurled the entire scope of official Israeli thinking (and also provided some fascinating insights into his own whimsical fancies).[29] Israel's formal participation in a Western defense pact in the Middle East, the Ambassador was informed, was precluded by several considerations: one was immigration ("we do not want to do anything which will provide a pretext for the cessation of immigration from the Eastern countries or prevent its renewal"); another was the country's security ("we are surrounded by enemies and we are fearful for our security and we do not want information to reach them [the Arabs]").

Nevertheless, argued Ben Gurion, there existed a basic similarity between the Israeli and American strategic conceptions with regard to the region. "The main thing was not the Middle East Command itself but to keep the purpose of the Middle East Command before our

[27] The following account is based on Eytan's circular cable, 23.11.1951, ISA 2289/10; Eliashiv's cable to the Foreign Ministry, 22.11.1951, ISA 2551/8; and correspondence in ISA 341/58, ISA 2512/27 and ISA 39/9. For the American perspective about S.A.C.M.E., see P. Hahan, "Containment and Egyptian Nationalism: The Unsuccessful Effort to Establish the Middle East Command 1950–1953," *Diplomatic History*, 11, 1, 1987, pp. 23–40.    [28] CZA A245/82.
[29] Ben Gurion's diary, 10.11.1951, BGA.

eyes: that is to look to the defense of the Middle East and keep the Russians out."[30] To that end, Israel did desire a direct link with the United States and Britain. Indeed, provided she was given the necessary assistance, she could make four specific contributions. First, she could use her manpower. An increase in the size of the Israeli army, the improvement of its equipment and the standardization of its weapon systems with American arms, would endow the I.D.F. with a capability to contain a Russian attack, in the context of a global war in which the Soviets would be unable to concentrate a large force in the regional area. Secondly, Israel could serve as a workshop: "at a time of need, when there is a large army in the Middle East, English, American or otherwise, and it wishes to repair machines, needs tools and a supply of spare parts and so on. We can do this. Our industry should be developed. We lack raw materials and we perhaps need more machines." Thirdly, Israel could supply important transport services on a large scale – ports, airfields, roads and railway lines. To do this: "Our transport should be helped to develop – Haifa port, the extension of the existing airfields and the building of new ones and a railway from Haifa and Eilat." And finally Israel would be able to help by stockpiling food and oil, "while there is still time."

This basic Israeli approach was conveyed to higher channels a week later when the Israeli Foreign Minister met in Paris with Dean Acheson, the American Secretary of State.[31] In a long, apologetic monologue, Sharett reiterated all the conventional reasons which precluded Israeli participation in the Western defense organization in the Middle East. At the same time, he emphasized two central points. The first was Israel's interest in strengthening her strategic links with the United States; the second was that Israel's relations with the Soviet bloc were determined by the desire, itself directly influenced by the Jewish question, not to give the Russians "an easy excuse for writing us off completely as their enemies but of remaining at least on speaking terms with them." Sharett's principal purpose, however, was to put Acheson's mind at rest. Israel's relations with Russia should not cause the American diplomat "to lose even a wink of sleep. If I were he I would not worry in the slightest." As Sharett shortly thereafter told the British Foreign Secretary: "In the case of a showdown Israel would stand alongside those with whom she belonged."[32]

[30] ISA 2475/5.    [31] 19.11.1951, ISA 2412/27.    [32] 23.11.1951, ISA 2457/1.

In an effort to translate words into deeds, Israel also put forward several concrete proposals. Most of these had already been aired in one form or another. But there was one significant innovation. In October 1951 James Angleton, a member of the C.I.A. and the man who was directly responsible for the Israeli Section in that organization, paid a secret visit to Israel.[33] One tangible result of his journey was Israel's formal agreement to cooperate with the United States in the field of intelligence. Although the projected establishment of S.A.C.M.E. was the immediate motive for Angleton's visit, it seems reasonable to assume that the American interest in his own particular domain extended beyond the Middle East. The United States was also interested in obtaining intelligence from sources inside the Soviet Union and Eastern Europe, a region where Israel possessed some unique contacts and capabilities. Precisely what was decided is not known; but Sharett did give Acheson a clear indication of Israel's readiness to cooperate in their meeting on 19 November: "It might be of help to the U.S. that the Soviet people should continue to feel free to talk to us ... we were happy to have had *recent* evidence that this viewpoint is appreciated in certain governmental quarters in the U.S."[34]

At the beginning of 1952, moreover, several senior members of the Israeli intelligence community left for the U.S.A. in order to take part in a top-secret C.I.A. course in strategic intelligence. These measures certainly helped to create a significant intelligence association between Israel and the United States.[35] As early as July 1953 it was giving rise to serious concern amongst those Israelis who were attempting to improve relations with the Soviet Union. One recommendation explicitly stressed that those efforts would be greatly facilitated by: "The cessation of all information-collecting activities outside the Jewish area; let the Americans deal with this and pay the price for it. In other words the halting of interrogations of immigrants and the cessation of activity in Eastern Europe for the attainment of general information."[36]

From the very outset, the question of Israel's place in S.A.C.M.E. was bound up with her attitude to the possibility that she might

---

[33] The following account is based on private information. On Angleton, see W. Blitzer, *Between Washington and Jerusalem* (Oxford, 1986), pp. 88–9, 91, 94–6. On Israel's intelligence connections with the C.I.A. at that time, see H. Eshed, *One Man Mossad; Reuven Shiloah: Father of Israeli Intelligence* (Tel Aviv, 1988), pp. 160–7 (Hebrew).

[34] ISA 2417/27. Italics added.          [35] See n. 33.

[36] Avner's letter to Levavi, 6.6.1953, ISA 2381/21.

receive American military aid. Under the terms of the Mutual Security Act, it will be remembered, Israel had first become theoretically eligible for direct and free military aid from the United States government at the end of 1951. The Embassy in Washington pressed for a decision to grasp this opportunity. Quite apart from the economic benefits of the framework, an Israeli application would (argued the Embassy) illustrate Israel's identification with the United States.[37]

In Jerusalem, opinions were far less enthusiastic, and direct or systematic discussions of the subject were initially avoided. Any Israeli request, it was appreciated, would necessarily be conditional on an agreement to some form of American supervision over the Israeli military; and that was unacceptable. In the words of one report:

Both our political and our Army leaders shrink from seeing in Israel the kind of blatant interference and control by American Army officers, which exists in certain other countries, and which would undoubtedly produce a backwash of friction and ill-will here, to be gleefully exploited by the Opposition. Not all Americans, as you know, are particularly delicate in their relations with the lesser breeds who enjoy their bounty, and the prospect of having a whole squad of generals throwing their weight around in Israel is not a pleasing one in Israeli Army circles. Furthermore, Yadin [the Chief of Staff] and his colleagues are genuinely concerned about the complete lack of security involved in complete disclosure of information, regardless of any assurances which may be given; such disclosure, they also feel, may indicate that our military strength is not what it is believed to be, and may therefore boomerang.[38]

Whilst these reservations did cause the matter to be shunted aside for a short time, contrary considerations soon demanded a reassessment. Sharett, it was pointed out, could hardly avoid the issue during his visit to the United States at the end of December 1951. An attempt to do so might only confirm a malignant impression that Israel – despite her public protestations to the contrary – was not really interested in forging military links with the Americans and therefore not deserving of any American aid. Silence, in other words, might seriously prejudice the chances of receiving economic help from the United States under other frameworks. It seemed far preferable to

[37] See Eban's letter to Herzog, 1.11.1951, ISA 2461/10; Lurie's despatch to Eban, 5.11.1951, ISA 2457/5; De Shalit's letter to Eban, 15.11.1951; and Eban's despatch to Sharett, 26.11.1951, ISA 341/58.
[38] 18.11.1951, ISA 2600/12.

pursue the path of negotiation and thus reduce the scope of possible American military supervision and the prominence of American delegations. Altogether, Israel ought to aim at a special agreement with the U.S.A. along the lines of the precedent set between the United States and Yugoslavia.[39]

Sharett was prepared fully to implement this approach and to ask for Israel's share of the $40 million included in the Mutual Security Act for the purpose of actual military aid. Ben Gurion, although in general agreement with the policy, was far more reluctant to make so explicit a commitment to the West (or, as he put it, "to place our heads in this noose").[40] He therefore gave instructions for a two-tiered approach. In applying for aid under the terms of the Act, Israel would not request the supply of free arms but financial assistance in construction projects which could be considered as being of defensive value. Actual arms applications were to be treated quite separately. They would be addressed to American government sources on the assumption that they would not demand direct supervision and intervention. Were representatives of the U.S. military establishment nevertheless to be despatched to Israel, it was hoped that they would travel in civilian dress and only remain in the country for as long as it took to complete their *ad hoc* missions.[41]

Before acting on these instructions, Israel's representatives in Washington decided to test the waters and called at the Near East Section of the State Department on 17 January 1952.[42] There, however, an unpleasant surprise awaited them. They were informed that meetings between Truman and Churchill had brought about "a new approach to the subject." All military aid plans to the Middle East would henceforth be dependent upon the development of the S.A.C.M.E organization which was to be advanced and built up. Furthermore, all military aid requests were being deferred until the end of the next financial year; the entire $400 million allocated for 1952 "were needed for Greece and Turkey." Neither was that all. S.A.C.M.E., the Israelis were told, had aroused the positive interest of a number of Arab states (notably Syria); Egypt would again be

---

[39]  See Sharett's letter to Ben Gurion, 4.12.1951, ISA 2455/1 and correspondence in ISA 341/58.
[40]  The following account is based upon and the excerpt taken from Sharett's despatch to Eban, 3.1.1952, ISA 361/8 and Sharett's talk at a meeting of Mapai's Political Committee, 3.1.1952, LPA.
[41]  See Comay's despatch to Goitin, 17.1.1952, ISA 40/19.
[42]  The following account is based upon Comay's despatch to Elath, 28.1.1952, *ibid.*

invited to join the alliance, to which other states in the region might also adhere – even without an explicit invitation. Above all, the United States was not prepared to create "any bilateral military arrangements in [the Middle East] except as S.A.C.M.E. partners."

Admittedly the Americans had not slammed the door in Israel's face. Some consolation could be found in their declaration that Israel would still be entitled to procure military equipment directly from the United States, "subject to availability." All told, however, the pill was a bitter one to swallow. Israel had now to consider the viability of her own plan to request American military aid. She had also to undertake yet another assessment of her possible relationship with S.A.C.M.E.

These questions were discussed during the last week of January 1952 at a meeting attended by Ben Gurion, Sharett and the heads of the defense establishment and the Foreign Ministry. Two important decisions were taken. First, Israel would go ahead with her formal application for aid within the framework of the American Mutual Security Act. Even if the request were rejected, it would still have served the political purpose of demonstrating Israel's interest in an American relationship; it might also improve the chances of obtaining military aid in the next budgetary year. Secondly, it was also decided to attempt to persuade the Americans and the British of the rationality and viability of Israeli thinking with regard to the possibility of a strategic link with the West. Israel, in other words, refused to accept as final the diagnosis which limited the possibilities for strategic links between herself and the West to collective defense plans in the Middle East. Indeed, she hoped that the refusal of the Arab states to join the Western defense organization would bury the entire scheme. Meanwhile, she planned to launch a "campaign of enlightenment" aimed at the American diplomatic and political community.

Acting on the first of these decisions, at the end of January 1952 Israel presented a formal application for direct American military aid (for which she was to pay); on 7 February, she also requested free military aid under the terms of the Mutual Security Act.[43] There followed personal approaches to the American Secretary of State[44] and an information campaign. The latter was designed to convince

[43] See Goitin's despatch to Comay, 7.2.1952, ISA 361/8; protocol of a meeting at the Israeli Embassy in Washington, 23.5.1952, ISA 2460/8; and *FRUS*, 9, 1952–4, pp. 894–6.
[44] See report on the meeting, 6.3.1952, ISA 2460/5.

the Americans of the disadvantages of a policy which made military aid to states in the Middle East conditional upon the establishment of S.A.C.M.E. (an idea which was in any case put into cold storage midway into 1952). More immediate and substantial, it was stressed, were the strategic advantages which would accrue to the United States from the strengthening of Israel.[45]

Thereafter, events proceeded at a sharper pace. On 1 July 1952, the United States recognized Israel's inclusion within the framework of the Mutual Defense Assistance Act, whose conditions and goals Jerusalem formally confirmed three weeks later.[46] In so doing, the Israelis brought to a logical conclusion the policies which they had initiated the previous autumn. Without entirely committing themselves to the West in strategic matters, they had nevertheless significantly departed from the principle of non-identification. Admittedly, their path to that particular destination had been tortuous and troubled; nevertheless, they had ultimately arrived. No wonder therefore that Eliezer Livneh, whose opposition to non-identification had long been a feature of discussions within Mapai, openly rejoiced. "This is my day of victory. We have ceased our stammering about neutrality."[47]

[45] See Eban's report on a meeting with Averell Harriman, 21.4.1952, ISA 2382/22 and memorandum by the Foreign Ministry's Research Section, 1.6.1952, ISA 2445/12.
[46] See a letter from the American Ambassador in Tel Aviv to Ben Gurion, 1.7.1952, ISA 2456/6.
[47] As quoted in Ben Aharon's report to the Secretariat of Hakibbutz Hameuchad on 3.9.1952, AHA.

# 12 . FAILURE OF "FACTS AND PACTS" POLICY

Egypt's refusal to participate in S.A.C.M.E. buried that particular idea. But it was soon replaced by another plan for the defense of the Middle East. In the summer of 1952, the Americans and British suggested the establishment of a Middle East Defense Organization (M.E.D.O.), which was to act as a planning headquarters in peacetime rather than (as the S.A.C.M.E. framework had envisioned) a direct and permanent command.[1] Britain, the United States, France and Turkey were to provide the backbone of M.E.D.O., which was also to encompass military forces from Australia, New Zealand and South Africa. Arab participation was regarded as desirable, but not as immediately essential; Israel's situation was left deliberately vague.

Ultimately, the Arab states refused to participate in M.E.D.O., and by the latter half of 1952 the entire idea had been shelved. Until that outcome became clear, however, Israel was again faced with the need for decision and strategic choice.[2] On the surface, and especially when contrasted with S.A.C.M.E., M.E.D.O. seemed to possess several advantages. It vaguely proposed some planning with Israel, not foreign bases in Israel; it did not offer any single state the sort of special status which S.A.C.M.E. had specified for Egypt; by including New Zealand, South Africa and Australia it widened the arc of Israel's possible supporters. On the other hand, M.E.D.O. still

[1] See M. Avidan, *Principal Aspects of Israel–USA. Relations in the 1950s* (Jerusalem, 1982) and *FRUS*, 9, 1952–4, pp. 195–333.
[2] The following account is based upon and excerpts are taken from a protocol of a meeting at the Israeli Embassy in Washington, 8.8.1952, ISA 2460/5; Sharett's address to Mapai's Political Committee, 24.8.1952, LPA; Sharett's memorandum, 22.10.1952, ISA 2449/1; a memorandum by the Planning Committee of the Israeli Foreign Ministry, 4.11.1952, ISA 2445/12; Sharett's comments on a first draft of that memorandum, 31.8.1952, ISA 2449/1; and protocol of a meeting at the Israeli Embassy in London, 14.11.1952, ISA 2403/18.

retained several of the features which had previously generated Israeli opposition to S.A.C.M.E. These ultimately weighed most heavily with the special planning committee set up to debate the matter within the Foreign Ministry. The decision reached by that body, which Sharett approved, was that Israel react to M.E.D.O. very much as she had in 1951 responded to S.A.C.M.E. She would work towards the creation of some link with Western defense plans, "without us undertaking at the present stage any form of attachment with the final plans of the organization." Realism, the Foreign Minister was later to advise, really left Israel with no other choice:

It is not in our interest to speed up the regional defense pact. If it comes – it comes, and we will have to come up with the right answer for it. I doubt if it is in our interest to hasten its materialization. First of all there could be pressure over peace [terms], secondly it means arms for the Arabs and thirdly in every regional defense organization Egypt will take first place. We are not interested in according this recognition to Egypt.[3]

One operative implication of this perception was that Israel persist in her efforts to forge exclusively bilateral links with the Western powers, and especially with the U.S.A. In doing so, she had constantly to bear in mind her need for the supply of arms and – even more essentially – for economic assistance. On the other hand, however, there was no need for her to go any further towards signaling her basic affinity with Western aims and interests. Public declarations to that effect were simply not called for. Sharett confessed to being totally unmoved:

By the many expressions of opinion I have heard that there is something lacking in our existing policy and that if this is repaired a change will take place in our status. I believe that there is not the slightest doubt in the minds of any of the most important policy-makers in the United States, France and Britain with regard to Israel's complete and unreserved Western position. I say this on the basis of actions and expressions of faith which can only exist with regard to the most trusted allies. I therefore deny the need for general declarations on identification and so forth. [Israel's special concern for Soviet Jewry, and the delicacy which that connection imposed on her relationships with the Soviet Union] has been explained to Acheson, Eden, Churchill, Eisenhower, Schuman . . . and all of them understood it thoroughly. It can be explained here.[4]

Exactly how Israel might obtain the aid which she required was a

---

[3] From a report on a meeting at the Prime Minister's home, 27.3.1953, ISA 2441/1.
[4] See protocol of a meeting at the Israeli Embassy in Washington, 23.5.1952, ISA 2460/8. See also Eban's cable to the Foreign Ministry, 4.1.1953, ISA 42/13.

considerably trickier problem. As before, Israel's most pressing need
was financial; within the United States, however, straightforward
economic aid seemed to be becoming "less and less acceptable."
There the tendency was to talk solely in terms of precisely the sort of
more specific military assistance which Israel was reluctant to
request. This deadlock could not be broken solely by the renewal of
the applications which Israel had (unsuccessfully) tabled in previous
years. They had to be supplemented by other initiatives, designed "to
include as military aid all sorts of [other] projects."[5] To that end, in
July 1952 Israel applied to participate in the United States Off Shore
Procurement Program, whose administrators were authorized to
place massive orders for supplies (military and civilian) on behalf of
American forces overseas.[6] In the event, Israeli plans to profit from
the official American compliance with her application were
frustrated. Faced with stiff European competition, Israel's own
companies failed to meet the challenge, and none of their tenders were
accepted. Nevertheless, the episode was revealing. It provided yet
another indication of the clear direction in which Israel's policy was
moving and of the limits to which (without meeting any domestic
criticism) it was being pushed.

In 1952 Israel's Western orientation took another significant turn.
She then put a stop to further contacts with the British on the creation
of a mutual framework for strategic cooperation, and so closed a
chapter in her foreign policy which was not to be reopened until 1956.
The genesis of this particular development had been far more
auspicious. Indeed, early in 1952 Ben Gurion seems to have harbored
hopes that the new Conservative government might be able to effect a
change in Anglo–Israeli relations. Imbued with a sense of deep
personal admiration for Winston Churchill, he wrote a letter to the
British Premier, proposing that their two countries examine the
possibility of cooperation in strategic areas, on subjects which were of
special interest to Israel.[7] The British agreed to send over a delegation
for preliminary talks, but at that point Ben Gurion's residual mistrust
of their policies again came to the surface. Before talks could commence, he insisted, Britain had formally to agree to the equal status of

[5] Sharett's address to meeting of Mapai's Political Committee, 24.8.1952, LPA.
[6] The following analysis is based on correspondence in MCI 4536/c/32317, ISA 2421/
12, ISA 2456/6 and Ben Gurion's diary, 5, 9.10.1952, BGA.
[7] The following account is based upon Ben Gurion's diary, 30.1.1952; his letter to the
Israeli Chief of Staff, 1.10.1952, BGA; correspondence in ISA 2582/6, ISA 2457/5; and
M. Bar Zohar, *Ben Gurion* (Tel Aviv, 1978), pp. 909–11.

the two states both in the negotiations and in any agreed framework to which they might give rise. This position, together with the British desire to create ties with Israel on a regional rather than a bilateral basis, postponed the talks until October 1952. The delay, however, did not soften Ben Gurion's stand. In the briefing which he then prepared, Ben Gurion instructed the Israeli delegation to discover as much as possible about Western defense plans for the Middle East – the types and quantities of armaments that the Western powers would be willing to supply to Israel and the ways in which they might aid the state through the development of transport projects and oil supply. On the other hand, the Israeli delegation was to divulge only such information as was relevant to Israel's emergency military and economic strength – and even then only in general terms; details regarding the structure and composition of her forces were to remain secret.

Evidence such as this appears to confirm the impression that Ben Gurion (together with most of his colleagues in the Mapai leadership) was still instinctively shackled to the Mandate past. Psychologically, they were ill-equipped to take large strides in the direction of strategic cooperation with Britain. The one exception was Sharett, who was prepared to be far more frank during the military talks and far more ambitious in his proposals (one of his suggestions was that Israel express her willingness to defend "the entire region including areas outside the borders of the country").[8] One year later, Sharett was also to advocate that Britain be offered bases in Israel as alternatives to those which she would soon evacuate in Egypt. Ben Gurion, however, vetoed both proposals[9] and nothing came of either (partly, it should be said, because of the reserve of the British themselves, who did nothing to improve their image in Israel when refusing to provide a modest loan of £5 million sterling).[10] The secret meeting held at the beginning of October 1952 in Ramat Gan between the British and Israeli delegations was inconclusive and talks between the two sides were only resumed – under very different circumstances – on the eve of the Sinai Campaign. Until then, however, Ben Gurion's views on Britain were categorical, disparaging and totally intolerant of any

---

[8] See his letter to Ben Gurion, 3.10.1952, ISA 2457/5.
[9] 8.3.1953, ISA 2408/9; on Sharett's attitude, see his *Personal Diary* (Tel Aviv, 1978), p. 434.
[10] Keren's despatch to Comay, 20.6.1952, ISA 2582/6. On the episode, see also PRO FO371/98805, ER1152/19.

idea that the short-lived prospect of Anglo–Israeli strategic cooperation would be allowed to take root:

England can no longer be a decisive factor in the Middle East neither in time
of peace nor of war. And in this region our power exceeds theirs, and
cooperation between us is possible only on the basis of equality and reci-
procity, as between England and the Dominions. The England of Eden is not
ready and not prepared for this. English policy in the Middle East is
antagonistic toward us, and this should be made known to the English and
the Americans.[11]

Having thus ruled out Britain as a possible strategic partner,
Israel's attention necessarily shifted to the United States. There,
however, matters took a new turn at the end of 1952 with Eisenhower's victory in the Presidential elections. This seemed to be an
ominous sign. The weight and influence of American Jewry were
concentrated within the Democratic Party, which the government of
Israel had become accustomed to regard as an emergency channel for
direct approaches to the President. Eisenhower's election seemed not
only to close that channel but proportionately to increase the
influence of the State Department, where anti-Israel sentiment
seemed to reign supreme.

When, at every meeting [reported one Israeli diplomat in Washington early
in 1953], I see Jernegan [Deputy Assistant to the Secretary of State for Near
Eastern Affairs] playing with his Arab beads like a Moslem in a Jaffa cafe, I
know that for him the Middle East belongs to the Arabs and if Israel exists
there and is entitled to make demands then this is because the ways of Allah
are wondrous and not always within the understanding of the faithful.[12]

Israel's immediate response to this danger was to take steps
designed to refresh the new administration's memory as to Israel's
pro-Western global stance. In January 1953, the Israeli Ambassador
in Washington asked for a letter to be drafted which would reiterate
the arms aid request for the 1953–4 budgetary year: "So that our first
appearance before it [the new administration] be against a background of our joint willingness to defend international security and
the values of freedom and liberty in the world." The fact that the
Soviet Union had recently severed its relations with Israel obviously
added a new and possibly advantageous dimension to such appli-

[11] Meeting of Mapai's Political Committee, 28.3.1953, BGA.
[12] The account is based upon and excerpts are taken from Avidan, *Principal Aspects*, pp.
22–4; Goitin's memorandum from early January 1953, ISA 2460/8; Sharett's letter to
Ben Gurion, 12.4.1953, ISA 2479/11; and Eban's despatch, 8.1.1953, ISA 361/8.

cations. Indeed, that particular circumstance was explicitly adduced as a supplement to Israel's case in February 1953, when Eban, the Ambassador in Washington, made his first formal presentation to the State Department.[13] Badly summarized, his message was one of disappointment with the American attitude towards Israel. The rupture of relations with the Soviet Union had not been followed by a public American announcement of the United States' interest in strengthening the strategic link with Israel. In fact, Israel was still awaiting a reply to the request which she had submitted twelve months previously for American military aid. Surely the Americans did not have to be reminded that that application had "marked the first and so far the only offer by a country of the Middle East to make common cause with the U.S. in defense of the area against possible aggression." Finally, Eban offered the opinion that the United States was acting in a manner both "unjust and inexpedient" when reviving plans for a regional defense organization in the Middle East without Israel ("the only state whose resistance to totalitarian aggression can be relied upon"), but with the participation of the Arab states ("whose willingness to defend freedom is at best highly problematic").

Ben Gurion was particularly convinced of the possible effectiveness of the latter argument. Indeed, he personally made it the pivot of the case presented to John Foster Dulles, who visited Israel in the middle of May 1953.[14] But his confidence seems to have been misplaced. During and after the visit, the American Secretary of State parried Israel's suggestions of a direct strategic link between the two countries; what really interested him was his own conception of a Western-dominated military alliance in the region.[15] This situation was certainly one inducement for the Israelis to restrain their enthusiasm for an explicit American attachment; another was the resumption of their relations with the Soviet Union. Sharett, who replaced Ben Gurion as Prime Minister at the end of January 1954, was sensitive to both circumstances. "Supposing," he was once asked by his own staff, "the Americans say, 'Let's make a pact and Israel will become a base like Greece' what will our answer be?"[16] His

[13] See Eban's memorandum, 11.2.1953, ISA 36/3 and a protocol of a meeting in which Ben Gurion, Sharett and high-ranking Foreign and Defense Ministry officials were present, 8.3.1953, ISA 2408/9.
[14] See correspondence in ISA 2414/29, ISA 2455/1, ISA 3063/13, ISA 2474/4, ISA 2414/29 and *FRUS*, 9, 1952–4, pp. 29–40.
[15] See Avidan, *Principal Aspects*, p. 25.   [16] See correspondence in ISA 2530/10.

answer, composed in the course of a long memorandum, was that
Israel had to tread a wary course:

> It is clear to me that we are not prepared to offer bases to the United States in
> Israel, neither are we interested in doing so. We are also opposed to her
> humiliating military supervision ... it would generate an internal dispute the
> likes of which we have not witnessed since the establishment of the state ... it
> would mean the increase of dependency on the United States and the
> decrease of our independence.

Matters did not, however, have to be presented in altogether negative
terms. There was also a positive aspect to the retention of a free hand.

> With the renewal of relations with the Soviet Union a new factor has appeared
> – or to be more precise an old factor has re-emerged – one which acts against
> an explicit defensive attachment ... our efforts to maintain contact with
> Russian Jewry have been renewed. This contact, in addition to its inherent
> value to us, is an asset to our foreign policy, paradoxically in the area of
> identification with the West. As the only element in the Western world
> capable of attaining fraternal relations with a section of the population of the
> Soviet Union, we are ... not just another geopolitical or strategic location.
> Within the Western network we possess a monopoly which we dare not
> underestimate.

Thus analyzed, Sharett regarded as advantageous the absence of
an American invitation that Israel join a regional defense pact or
enter into any other explicit mutual attachment. ("From a certain
point of view the Lord has been merciful in that the United States is
putting no pressure on us whatsoever. In these circumstances we
should not stir things up, as this will bring no benefit and will
probably do some damage. We shall demand arms for our defense but
we should not anticipate the issue of a military-political attachment.") Shortly thereafter, however, there occurred two developments which seemed to challenge the Foreign Minister's rather
complacent diagnosis. The first took place on 21 April 1954, when the
governments of the United States and Iraq exchanged letters confirming a program of direct American military aid. Unmistakably,
this was a regional turning-point. It contradicted the previous American policy (which Israel had assiduously supported) that no direct
aid be accorded to the Arab states; it also threatened to upset the
entire balance of power between those countries and Israel (who
throughout the 1950s received only very small quantities of American
arms). These were grave considerations for Israel, but nevertheless
not ones which she could easily put to public or diplomatic use.

Altogether, in fact, Israel would find it hard to criticize the American–Iraqi arrangement. How could she object to a program which the American administration portrayed as an indispensable step towards the construction of a viable pro-Western "northern tier" (consisting of Turkey, Iran and Pakistan) against Soviet aggression?

Three months after the conclusion of the American–Iraqi arrangement, Egypt and Britain finally reached agreement over the evacuation of British bases in Egypt. This was undoubtedly a less dramatic development; yet, from Israel's point of view, hardly a less dangerous one.[17] Partly, this was because of the terms ultimately concluded: the agreement contained no mention of Israel's rights to transit through the Suez Canal (a clause which she had pressed the British to include); it left in Egyptian hands the British airfields and bases, and was therefore liable to upset the Israeli–Egyptian balance of power; by transferring to Cairo Britain's radar facilities, it also facilitated Egyptian control over 50% of Israel's airspace. Even more dangerous, however, were the wider implications of the arrangement. It threatened (as Elath had long before warned)[18] to open the way for Egyptian participation in a wider regional defense organization. In fact, according to the information at Israel's disposal, the Americans were about to take the same initiative with regard to Egypt as they had with Iraq. Moreover, their efforts would be based on the same line of reasoning and – undoubtedly – would be crowned with the same degree of success.

In practical terms, there was really very little that Israel could do to meet these challenges. Clearly, the Americans were not going to abandon their plans for a new regional disposition in the Middle East simply because Israel found that particular alignment objectionable. In Eban's words: "If we place them in the position of having to make a choice between satisfying us and relinquishing these plans ... they will decide not to relinquish them and not to satisfy us."[19] The only compensation Israel could request, in fact, was some form of formal and public United States guarantee of Israel's security. Admittedly, that too was an uninviting option. In fact, earlier in 1954 Israel's leaders had adamantly refused even to consider the idea. If rejected,

---

[17] See protocol of a meeting, 19.7.1954, ISA 2384/14 which is the source for the following account.
[18] Elath's cable, 8.3.1954, ISA 417/1. See also Eban's cable, 10.3.1954, ISA 2475/10.
[19] From a protocol of a meeting at the Israeli Embassy in Washington, 6.8.1954, ISA 379/4.

they had argued, an application for an American guarantee could only unmask Israel's isolation; even if accepted, it might lead to nothing more than a catalogue of platitudinous statements which, whilst committing the United States to very little, would constrain Israel's own freedom to act independently when she gauged her own local interests to be threatened.[20] Although both considerations remained relevant in August of that year,[21] they were no longer considered decisive. Instead, in an attempt to assuage the anxieties caused by recent developments in the Middle East, Israel decided to ask the United States to agree to negotiations which would lead to "binding measures" of a concrete nature.[22]

This revolutionary shift in Israel's policy was first formally presented to Dulles by Eban in September 1954. Requesting – almost begging – that the American read between the lines of his statement, the Israeli chose his words with evident care:

I was ... empowered to emphasize that Israel does not possess any contract or agreement with any state requiring that state to give actual military aid to Israel if attacked ... we were observing efforts to integrate nearly every state in the world into some pattern of military security ... and it was a fact that Israel has no such security treaty with anyone. The Secretary could draw any implications he wishes from the fact that I was empowered to emphasize this feature of Israel's security position.[23]

Dulles, however, refused the bait. His response, communicated on 8 October, made it evident that the United States was prepared to go no further than another version of the Tripartite Declaration of 1950. The document of understanding which he proposed would not specify a special American link with Israel; neither would it commit the United States to preserve the arms balance in the region or provide Israel with military aid. In fact, it underscored for the Israelis that the pivot of America's regional policy remained the desire to advance its understanding with the Arab world, and with Egypt in particular. Israel's security was a secondary concern.[24]

---

[20] See Sharett's cable to Eban, 12.6.1954, ISA 42/13; protocol of a meeting at the Israeli Foreign Ministry on the Tripartite Declaration, 5.7.1954, ISA 2449/4; and correspondence in ISA 2480/4. On Israel's military policy, see Z. Schiff and E. Haber, eds., *Israel, Army and Defense: A Dictionary* (Tel Aviv, 1976), p. 430 (Hebrew), and E. Luttwak and D. Horowitz, *The Israeli Army* (London, 1975), pp. 104–38.

[21] See correspondence in ISA 2384/14 and *FRUS*, 9, 1952–4, pp. 1604–6, 1619–20.

[22] Sharett, *Personal Diary*, p. 560. See also his memorandum, 18.8.1954, ISA 2414/28.

[23] The meeting took place on 15.9.1954, see the report in ISA 40/19.

[24] See Eban's despatch to Eytan, 8.10.1954, *ibid.*, and Sharett's despatch to Eban, 11.10.1954, quoted in Raphael's memorandum on 19.4.1955, ISA 2456/4. It should be

It is indicative of Israel's desperation that this rebuff did not deter her leaders from their chosen course. On the contrary, early in 1955 they redoubled their efforts to reach a formal military understanding with Washington. By then, Israel's political isolation seemed to have been further confirmed; in January Iraq allied with Pakistan and Turkey and thus laid the foundations for the framework which, with British participation, was to be known as "the Baghdad Pact." Even though Egypt had balked at the political conditions attached to the American offer of arms, Israel's sense of insecurity now became chronic. Sharett was convinced that the Iraqi move "must increase our isolation in the Middle East and in the global arena since we have no choice here between the two worlds."[25] Israel, therefore, had to act with speed and decision. Specifically, the government decided, she had to strive to "eliminate" and "dismantle" the Tripartite Declaration; to work towards "a separate attachment with each of the Western powers, each in accordance with its own leanings and with our possibilities with regard to it"; above all, Israel had to put forward specific "demands with regard to the U.S.A. – an understanding *vis-à-vis* our defense, guarantee of our existing borders, military aid, an overall balance between ourselves and all the Arabs together in arms-supply policy. The basis for these demands – the United States' responsibility for changes in the region which altered the military and political balance to our disadvantage."[26]

In her attempts thus to place relations with the United States on an entirely new footing, Israel initially had recourse to informal channels. Arthur Dean, Dulles' friend and former business partner, was a particularly valuable connection.[27] In February, Sharett received a letter from Dulles. "Composed after consultation with the President ... every word had been carefully weighed," it "contained an important promise of a guarantee of security for Israel."[28] Dean was asked to convey Sharett's first – informal – reply.[29] Formulated as a statement

noted that the American Embassy in Tel Aviv objected to the idea of an American security guarantee to Israel. Thus, in explaining its attitude, it pointed out that "while Israel would like to have the backing of the U.S. it still has as one of the principal goals the release of as many as possible of 4,000,000 Jews behind the Iron Curtain and therefore cannot be uninhibited in its cooperation with the free world," Russell's despatch to Dulles, 26.8.1954, *FRUS*, 9, 1952–4, p. 1628.
[25] His cable to Elath, 8.2.1955, ISA 2457/2.
[26] Sharett, *Personal Diary*, p. 712; see also his cable to Eban, 9.2.1955, ISA 47/3.
[27] See correspondence in ISA 47/3, 2456/16, 2455/4.
[28] Sharett, *Personal Diary*, p. 854.
[29] See Sharett's cable to Eban, 3.3.1955, ISA 2455/2.

of principles, it asked that the Americans undertake to act in the event
of an attack upon Israel's present borders, and strictly to preserve the
arms balance between Israel and the Arab states. In return Israel
agreed to solve conflicts by peaceful means, to refrain from using arms
against other states, and to declare her readiness to sign non-
aggression pacts with her neighbors. In practice, Israel thereby
specified that she was after an American guarantee of her borders; she
did not seek the kind of mutual defense pact which the United States
had contracted with a number of states outside the Middle East
during this period, and which the Israeli Ambassador in Washington
had previously striven for. Sharett explained the reasons for the
change to Eban:

All of us in the Ministry regard a security agreement as an illusion. The
United States has no such contract with any of the states in the Middle East
and she will not start with us . . . the sensitivities in the Knesset and among the
public during . . . the election campaign against the left oblige us to completely avoid creating the impression that we are groveling before the U.S.A.
to integrate us within the defense of the region, when she herself refuses to do
so. It is one thing to enter into an attachment in order to bolster our power
against our neighbors; it is another when the United States on its own
initiative invites us to take part in regional defense.[30]

Once again, however, Dulles proved to be unreceptive. Instead of
responding favorably to the message communicated through Dean,
he seemed intent on using the bait of a guarantee to exert a restrictive
influence over Israel's policies. This became evident from his reaction
to Israel's large reprisal action against Gaza during the last week of
February 1955. "What has now happened in Gaza," he informed
Sharett, "obliged a reassessment of the previous plans to give [Israel]
a guarantee." What he demanded, in essence, was a solemn undertaking "that we shall not repeat such operations."[31] Clearly, this was
not a matter which could be discussed through informal channels.
Instead, and perhaps in a deliberate attempt to avoid giving any such
undertaking, the Prime Minister decided to apply formally and
openly for a contractual guarantee of Israel's borders. On 11 April an
explicit Israeli request for such an agreement with the United States
was presented for the first time. Appended to it was a renewed
demand for the maintenance of the arms balance between Israel and
the Arab states.[32]

[30] See Sharett's cable to Eban, 24.2.1955, *ibid.*, and Sharett, *Personal Diary*, p. 794.
[31] Sharett, *Personal Diary*, pp. 836, 856.　　　　[32] ISA 2456/4.

From that point onwards, the demand that the United States guarantee the security of her borders became a formal element of Israel's foreign policy. It also became part of her public posture. No longer was the matter restricted to the dark shadows of indirect and secret talks but openly declared in the Knesset. On 2 March, Sharett addressed the Israeli parliament, and issued a statement which – by any standards – was the most stark and explicit declaration of the new Israeli policy. His principal concern, he stressed, was:

the gravity and the urgency of the problem of an efficient guarantee for Israel's existing borders and the integrity of her territory and her defense against any aggression . . .
   And let there be no confusion or misunderstanding among us as to the identity of the side upon whom we are making these demands. We are very interested in good relations with the Soviet Union and we are working toward nurturing them to the limits of our ability and our understanding. But this argument which we are in the midst of today, is between ourselves and the Western world, and it is taking place with *us as a part of it*.[33]

The publicity accorded to the new course of Israel's foreign policy explains the emphasis placed on that issue in the negotiations between Mapai on the one hand and Mapam-Ahdut Ha'Avoda on the other for the formation of a coalition government during 1955. Behind the closed doors of the inter-party meetings a bitter argument ensued over Israel's decision to seek a contractual link with the United States, which the two left-wing parties staunchly opposed.[34] Not until the summer of 1955 did they finally accept a formula whereby Mapai would take note of their position. Both sides seem to have doubted whether an alliance with the United States would in fact ever materialize. Meanwhile, however, a compromise was reached. The left-wing parties undertook not to campaign in public against the idea of an alliance as long as they remained in the government. Should negotiations with the United States ever reach a successful conclusion, however, they would be entitled to vote against the arrangement and to leave the government.
   There existed another – more personalized – domestic influence on Israel's decision to make an American defense agreement the central plank in her foreign policy. In February 1955 Ben Gurion ended the self-imposed "political exile" which, for the previous year, had kept him on Kibbutz Sdeh Boker in the Negev. His return to office, as Minister of Defense of the government headed by Moshe Sharett,

---

[33]  *Ibid*. Emphasis added.        [34]  Bar Zohar, *Ben Gurion*, pp. 1159–60.

significantly augmented the strength of those in power who advocated greater "activism" in Israel's security and foreign policy. In general terms, Ben Gurion agreed with Sharett's conception of the advantages to be gained from an approach to the Americans. Where the two men differed, however, was in their views of the purposes which an American guarantee might serve and of the priority which should be accorded to its attainment. There was more to these differences than a clash of personalities. At issue, too, was a contrasting view of the very essence of Israel's society. Sharett, Ben Gurion complained, to Ze'ev Sharf, the Cabinet Secretary, "is raising a generation of cowards, I won't let him do it. Infiltrators are wandering around here and we are hiding behind fences, I won't let him do it. This will be a generation of fighters."[35] As Ben Gurion saw matters, nothing must be allowed to interfere with Israel's right to react forcefully and immediately to the increasing incidences of Arab terrorist incursions against her civilian population (indeed, it is significant that the decision to launch the Gaza reprisal raid was taken soon after he received the defense portfolio). Consequently, he was totally unmoved by the argument that "our reprisal raids are reducing our chances" of obtaining an American guarantee, "and are liable to sabotage them completely." When Sharett tried to put that case, "B.G. lectured me chapter and verse on his doctrine: an agreement with the U.S.A. is indeed most important, but ongoing security matters are no less important and if there is a contradiction between the two then there is nothing to be done."[36] No less fundamentally did he disagree with Sharett's hope that the Americans might promise to send troops to fight in Israel's defense should the need arise. Ben Gurion was horrified to think that "American soldiers [might] spill their blood in Israel's defense should she be attacked."[37] The true goals of an American agreement, he insisted, were the attainment of an effective deterrent against the Arabs and – above all – the assurance of American arms for Israel's self-defense.

At root, Sharett himself also regarded the supply of American arms to be a far more pressing Israeli need than was a security guarantee. Nevertheless, the constellation of forces which existed in the Israeli Cabinet after Ben Gurion's return, made it politic that he play the latter card for all it was worth. In fact, he made deliberate domestic use of the bait of an American guarantee (and of American arms) in

[35] *Ibid.*, p. 1126.   [36] Sharett, *Personal Diary*, p. 1018.   [37] *Ibid.*, p. 1355.

order to block internal pressure for forceful military action. One outstanding example occurred on 29 March, when he successfully employed this tactic during the Cabinet debate on Ben Gurion's proposal to conquer the Gaza Strip.[38] At the same time, he also used this domestic element of Israeli policy to attain greater external leverage. As he had previously informed the U.S. Ambassador in Tel Aviv, an American rejection of Israel's proposal for a guarantee: "will intensify the feeling [in Israel] that we can rely on nothing except our own limited power, is this really the development which the United States wants?"[39]

Relations with the Russians were much harder to square. For obvious reasons, Israel refused to admit to the Soviet Union the true strategic implications of her approach to the United States. Instead, she repeatedly protested that the idea of an alliance need not be interpreted as an indication of Israel's "estrangement from the Soviet Union and our promise not to participate in any aggression against her stands firm."[40] This was obviously a very weak case. Indeed, it could not possibly provide an answer to Molotov's shrewd assessment that: "In every alliance between America and Israel the American intention and not the Israeli one will be decisive since America is strong and Israel is weak," and that "[the Soviet Union] would perhaps not see another agreement as a source of concern but this is a brick which is being added to others and this whole structure of alliances and agreements is intentionally directed by the Americans against the Soviet Union."[41] By now, however, Israel had made her own clear choice. Her decision publicly to declare her aspirations for a strategic link with the Americans was not significantly affected by the expectation of an unfavorable Soviet reaction. Her attention was concentrated, almost exclusively, on Washington.

There, however, the breakthrough for which the Israelis had cautiously hoped, was not achieved. It took the Americans little more than a week to draft a response to the Israeli request. Formally presented by Dulles to Eban on 16 April 1955, their reply did not altogether close the door on the idea of a defense agreement between the two countries. On the contrary, it deserves to be considered a landmark in their relations because it specifically accepted the idea in

---

[38] *Ibid.*, p. 872.        [39] *Ibid.*, p. 837.
[40] *Ibid.*, pp. 851–2, and Eban's report of his conversation in New York with Molotov in a cable to Sharett, 27.6.1955, ISA 47/3.
[41] *Ibid.*, Eban's report.

principle. On the other hand, however, it also left no doubt that any agreement was conditional. The Senate, Dulles explained, would only consider authorization of an agreement were it to be presented with evidence that the situation in the Middle East was stabilizing and that progress was being made towards an agreement between Israel and the Arabs.[42]

Their cautious satisfaction with the American response notwithstanding, the Israelis wondered whether the price was not too stiff to pay. Sharett still feared that: "this guarantee will serve as a pretext for upsetting the balance [of arms] and for arming the Arabs without giving us anything in return ... The question is how to hold onto the guarantee without letting go of the balance"[43] – and also how to retain Israel's freedom to initiate reprisal actions whenever she thought necessary. "The shift which has taken place," he confided in a political consultation held at the end of April, did possess a positive aspect ("the positive side is the very response to Israeli pressure"); but it also "contains dangers."[44]

Did Israel in fact possess a choice? This was the question which perturbed the Prime Minister, especially at the end of April, when a vociferously anti-Israeli motion was adopted at the Bandung Conference of Third World nations. Here, Sharett felt, was "a new demonstration of Israel's isolation and the crystallization of a large front against us encompassing the overwhelming majority of humanity."[45] Under those circumstances, the attainment of a guarantee from the Americans became even more vital – and the difficulties which had meanwhile arisen in negotiations on that issue had to be ironed out. Specifically, Israel had to show some inclination to accept the American position that the guarantee constitute a supplement to the settlement of the Arab–Israeli dispute and not (as the Israelis had originally insisted) a preliminary to that end.[46] It might also help were Israel – in practice – to avoid reprisals and adopt a flexible stance towards the American plan for solving the conflict over the disposal of the waters of the River Jordan.[47] Underlying these moves was a feeling that – despite the difficulties involved – the American guarantee might still be attained. At a meeting of Israeli ambassadors

---

[42] See Eban's cable to Sharett, 16.4.1955, *ibid.*
[43] Sharett's cable to Eban, 30.1.1955, ISA 2455/2.
[44] 19.4.1955, ISA 2384/14.                          [45] Sharett, *Personal Diary*, p. 954.
[46] See Sharett's despatch to Dulles, 4.5.1955, ISA 47/3.
[47] See Sharett, *Personal Diary*, pp. 726, 1054, and a cable on 8.2.1955 to the Israeli Embassy in London, ISA 47/3.

held in Jerusalem during the last week in May, Sharett reaffirmed that the attempt to attain a guarantee remained "a central aim of our policy,"[48] and ticked off the expected advantages which the agreement might bring to Israel:

a guarantee of security, our strengthening *vis-à-vis* the Arab states, aid for peace, an increase in our international prestige, the encouragement of capital investments, good tidings for world Jewry. To the Soviet bloc and the Asian countries the contract is to be explained as only stemming from our concern for security in view of the hostility of the Arabs and the conclusions of the Bandung Conference ... We are not only demanding a security agreement because we are faced with danger from the Arab states in view of their unrelenting hostility. Our demand stems from the reshuffling of the structure of the Middle East which is taking place as a result of the policy of the Western states ... We are not asking for their charity but that they bear the responsibility for the adverse change in the situation which they initiated.[49]

Once again, however, the American response was disappointing. On 26 August, Dulles publicly clarified that the United States' guarantee was conditional on Jerusalem's acceptance of what the Israelis considered to be radical alterations in the preconditions for negotiations with the Arab states.[50] Particularly painful was his pointed reference to the need for border changes and his specific proposal to lop off parts of the Negev. Sharett's reaction was therefore unavoidable:

The entire issue of the security guarantee is without foundation and has been postponed until the coming of Elijah the Prophet because it is dependent on agreed border changes, which today stand no chance at all ... The only conclusion that can be drawn is that the main intention of the document is ... to tell the Jews of America what they want to hear by giving public and official authorization for the agreement while at the same time in fact removing it from the agenda indefinitely.[51]

In practice, subsequent decisions taken in Jerusalem amounted to a conclusion that this subject could not profitably be pursued. Instead, Israeli diplomatic approaches to the United States would henceforth concentrate on applications for direct military supplies. As has been seen, even at the height of her interest in an American guarantee, arms procurements had always been regarded as Israel's principal goal. With the publication of the Czech–Egyptian arms

[48] A despatch from the Information Section to Avraham Kidron, 24.5.1955, ISA 3068/8.
[49] Sharett, *Personal Diary*, p. 1024.    [50] Avidan, *Principal Aspects*, pp. 57–8.
[51] Sharett's cable to Eban, 29.8.1955, ISA 2455/4.

transaction in October 1955, that issue became a matter of absolute life and death for the Jewish state. Israel now found herself in one of the most difficult periods of her entire troubled history. From a military point of view the Czechoslovakian arms transaction represented a high-level strategic threat, quite different in kind to the low-level tactical dangers which had characterized infiltrations into Israel by Arab irregulars during the previous years. In political terms, it signified a definite Soviet decision to side with Israel's enemies. Both aspects gave cause for serious alarm, particularly in view of the conspicuous failure of Israel's attempts to forge a contractual link with any of the Western powers. They also clarified Israel's own priorities. As Sharett confided to his diary not long after learning of the Czech deal: "The center of gravity is now arms and not a security guarantee. If it is possible to obtain both at one and the same time, so be it, a security guarantee alone is likely to serve now as a fig leaf with which to cover the naked unilateral arming of the Arab states and we should guard ourselves against this danger."[52]

From Sharett's personal perspective, the idea of an American guarantee nevertheless retained at least two of its former attractions. One could be stated in straightforward military terms. "We cannot now [cease] our call for a security contract. Arms alone are not likely to solve the whole problem. Even were the I.D.F. able to absorb, to store, and to activate ample quantities of additional arms there would still remain too great a gap between ourselves and the Arabs."[53] Equally valid (certainly in Sharett's mind), however, was the recurrence of his fear that external developments might remove all constraints in many domestic circles against an adventurous military policy. His fears that pressure for such action would mount were further augmented when it became clear that Ben Gurion would again (in November 1955) assume the premiership, without relinquishing the office of Minister of Defense.[54]

In the wake of the Czech deal, Israel's diplomatic activity focused on Sharett's visit to Europe at the end of October and his meetings there with the foreign ministers of the Great Powers. The main operational goal was to try and annul the deal itself; but Israel also wished to ensure the Middle Eastern arms balance and, at the same time, to demand a written American guarantee of Israel's borders.

[52] Sharett, *Personal Diary*, p. 1180.
[53] Speech to senior echelons of the Foreign Ministry, 14.10.1955, ISA 2456/8.
[54] See Sharett, *Personal Diary*, p. 1206, and Bar Zohar, *Ben Gurion*, p. 1145.

Still in pursuit of the latter, Sharett employed an emotional line of argument at his meeting with Dulles in Paris on 30 October:

> As for the security agreement I repeated that if his heart was not in it and if it was not a viable question, it would be better for us to stop talking about it, and here I moved over to the ... effect of just talking about a security agreement on our relations with the U.S.S.R. and how we lost everything there without gaining a thing from the U.S.A. ... We maintain an Embassy in Moscow mainly in order to encourage the Jews of Russia to hold out – so that they can see before them a mark and a token that the day will come when their link with Israel and the Jewish People will be renewed; but ... the Russians tell us explicitly that they see no point in making any concessions to us on this [issue] as long as we continue to declare our willingness to enter a military alliance with the U.S.A., which to them means subservience, bases and every other abomination.[55]

Dulles' initial answer was evasive. A definitive response was not received until the following week, after consultations between the American Secretary of State and his British counterpart. But the delay did little to mellow the tone of the American document which, in its final form, rejected every one of Israel's initiatives. The United States, it stated, would make every effort to immunize the Arab states against the Soviet danger. Precisely because of that aim, however, "any unilateral action in Israel's favor would be liable to aid Soviet expansion among the Arab states, a security contract with Israel alone would speed up this process." Secondly, the Americans expressed the hope "that there is a remedy for Nasser"; only if "the United States sees after six months" that that was not the case would it "review its policy." But "any party which disturbs her during this period is taking upon itself a heavy responsibility as the abettor of Communist expansion in the region." As for Israel's own security, that (the document ingenuously promised) "will be assured meanwhile by the Tripartite Declaration, on the strengthening of which we are now working. Even without a formal link, which we will reach when the time comes, Israel should trust that the U.S.A. will not abandon her."[56]

Israel made no formal reply to this message. To have done so would have been pointless. Indeed, Sharett did not even bother to raise the question of an American guarantee when he met Dulles in December.[57] Until the middle of the following year it simply disap-

---

55 Sharett, *Personal Diary*, p. 1266.
56 Raphael's cable to the Foreign Ministry, 11.11.1955, ISA 47/3.
57 See Bendor's despatch to the Israeli Ambassador in Paris, 27.2.1956, ISA 192/16.

peared from the agenda of diplomatic contacts between the two states. Admittedly, Sharett and Ben Gurion did in January categorically reject a Foreign Ministry suggestion that Israel formally renounce her interest in an American pact (and thereby, perhaps, improve her standing in Russian eyes); but they knew that – to all intents and purposes – the entire notion had ceased to be practical.[58] By the end of February 1956 it was also pronounced still-born. Addressing the Senate Foreign Affairs and Security Committee, Dulles stated that: "The United States never seriously considered making an alliance [the security agreement] as long as no arrangement had been settled [between Israel and the Arabs]."[59]

Bearing in mind the length of time during which the Americans had agreed actively to negotiate a guarantee to Israel, the Israelis might be excused for labeling Dulles' statement as "base" and "a deceit."[60] But recriminations were no substitute for policy. With the Americans obviously impervious to their requests for arms supplies, the Israelis had to intensify their search for a strategic ally elsewhere. In operational terms, they had to pursue – with far greater urgency than before – the feelers which they had already put out to France. The decision to do so crystallized during the second week of April, when the Americans once again turned down an Israeli request for military supplies.[61] Thereafter, negotiations in Paris proceeded at a speed and intensity which could hardly have been anticipated. By the end of the year, France had granted Israel both arms and military cooperation on the strategic level and had thus supplied her with precisely the requirements which she had previously sought from the United States. It was in that way that Israel's failures in one direction spurred her to seek success in another. Whether at that time Ben Gurion really considered France as a long-term strategic replacement for the U.S.A. is still an open question.[62] However, the debate in Israel on global orientation moved from 1956 to 1967 from the East

---

[58] Sharett, *Personal Diary*, pp. 1121–3.
[59] See memorandum dated 25.2.1956, ISA 2475/5.
[60] *Ibid.*, and Sharett's cable to Eban, 7.3.1956, ISA 2442/8.
[61] See Shiloah's cable to Sharett on 29.3.1956 which informed the Israeli Foreign Minister about the final American refusal to provide arms to Israel, ISA 47/3 and a protocol of a high-ranking meeting on 11.4.1956 which dealt with Israel's strategic connection with the French, ISA 2539/6.
[62] See Bar Zohar, *Ben Gurion*, p. 1178; S. Crosbie, *A Tacit Alliance: France and Israel from Suez to The Six Day War* (Princeton, 1974); M. Bar Zohar, *Bridge Over the Mediterranean* (Tel Aviv, 1964) (Hebrew); and M. Gazit, "Sharett, Ben Gurion and the Arms Deal with France in 1956," *Gesher*, 108, Winter–Spring 1983 (Hebrew).

versus West platform to that of France versus the United States. The Western direction Israel's foreign policy took in 1950–1 was thus clearly reinforced from early 1956. The first quarter of 1956 therefore witnessed the end of an era in Israel's foreign policy, which – in various ways – left a lasting impression on important developments in the succeeding era.

# EPILOGUE: "A PEOPLE THAT DWELLS ALONE"?

In the course of several meetings with Israelis in mid-1954, American officials in both Washington and Jerusalem queried the true extent of Israel's adherence to the Western bloc. Policy-makers in Jerusalem considered this effort "to paint Israel red"[1] a grave danger and, in order to prepare appropriate counter-measures, ordered a thorough analysis of its possible causes. That instruction produced a report which presents a fascinating summary of the broad issues affecting Israel's foreign policy orientation during the first half-decade of the state's existence. The work of a team headed by Isser Halperin (later Harel), the highly influential chief of the Internal Security Service (Shin Beth), the document analyzed with admirable clarity the rationale and manifestations of Israel's efforts to achieve special relationships with both East and West and the limitations of those efforts. Now, an entire generation later, it is possible to review the material again and to attempt an independent retrospective résumé of the various conflicting pressures which affected Israel's actions during the period of the cold war.

As we have seen, the accusations voiced by the Americans in 1954 were without any foundation whatsoever. By then, Israel had clearly formulated a foreign policy which was distinctly pro-Western – even if not formally and explicitly so. Her choice had been determined by both positive and negative considerations. Primary among the latter was the absence of a peace treaty with her Arab neighbors. The fatalistic realization that inveterate Arab hostility to her very existence would long remain a fact of Israeli life was reinforced by the failure to reach a peace treaty with Jordan in the early 1950s; it was confirmed by the behavior of Arab representatives at the U.N. As one

---

[1] The following account is based upon, and the excerpt taken from, material in ISA 2403/13, 2403/2.

276

Israeli diplomat bitterly complained, it was hard to describe the humiliation of having to sit "for months between the delegates of Iraq and Lebanon who talked to each other across him as if he simply did not exist."[2] Under these circumstances, the state clearly had to seek external links beyond the range of the Middle East. Indeed, some Israelis even determined to make a virtue of that necessity. In the words of one prominent Foreign Ministry official early in 1951: "Since we must learn to live without the Arabs or give in, we will jolly well learn to live without them. If they won't trade with us, we'll find other people who will. If we can't get service from the (U.N.) Food and Agriculture Organization regional office in Cairo, we will tie up with the headquarters in Rome. After a period of years all these alternative arrangements will settle down and we [will] become even more integrated with the Western world than we would have been if the Middle East had been open to us from the beginning."[3]

Significant considerations of a material nature also seemed to impel Israel in the same direction. Late in 1952, Sharett expressed what had become conventional wisdom in Jerusalem when stating: "in devoting our attention primarily to the cultivation of relations with Europe and America we are simply obeying an iron law of our national existence, which is unique as a result of the fast growth of our population, our economic build-up, our isolation from the neighboring countries and our special needs for food, oil, raw materials, investments, capital, arms, economic scientific and military instruction and for world-wide political understanding."[4] As has been seen, virtually all of these requirements could then be supplied only from Western sources.

Close relations with the Soviet Union held out no such attractions. In large part, this was because of ideological considerations. This factor certainly influenced official Israeli attitudes towards the Soviet Union itself; it also affected the country's relations with other countries in the Communist orbit. One striking illustration is provided by Israel's reaction to Peking's offer that the two countries establish diplomatic relations. As Brecher has shown,[5] fearful of a punitive American reaction, Israeli diplomats in Washington were careful to keep the United States fully informed of those contacts; indeed, they virtually invited the State Department to demand that

[2] Leo Kohn's words cited in Comay's despatch to Elath, 23.1.1951, ISA 2592/22.
[3] *Ibid.*                    [4] 3.9.1952, ISA 2415/31.
[5] See M. Brecher, *Israel, the Korean War and China* (Jerusalem, 1974).

they be stopped. What has to be noted, however, is the ideological component of Israel's thinking on the entire subject. That was certainly the consideration invoked by Sharett in 1954 when responding to internal and departmental criticism of his official policy:

> Although we claim that China is ... an Asian power, which is the major positive reason for our contacts with her, we should never forget that she is also a Communist power and [that] her penetration into Israel means the solidification of the Communist front in our country with which we are in a state of total war ... It is not simple for us to be the first state in the Middle East to open its gates to the representatives of the same militant Asian Communism which threatens to swallow the entire continent ... we cannot ignore the consequence of such a Chinese appearance, which will plant a deadly Communist dagger in the heart of our state and the Middle East.[6]

A study of Israel's domestic security concerns indicates that Sharett's fears were not necessarily far-fetched. In recent years, the Israeli Shin Beth has attained renown as a result of its handling of the internal security problems posed by the existence of a large Arab minority within the state's borders. During the 1950s, however, that was not its main preoccupation.[7] Israel's security authorities seem to have been more concerned with the problems posed by the extremely intensive – and often equally provocative – intelligence activities initiated by the Soviet Union and its satellites. Ever since the end of the Palestinian Mandate, both the American and the British governments had feared that Russia would exploit the mass emigration from Eastern Europe as a means of infiltrating their spies into the region. Hitherto, this activity has been little publicized and it is unlikely that it will ever be openly discussed; but it does appear to have taken place on a very large scale. When made known to the Israeli authorities (as was often the case), it was bound to substantiate the argument that the short spring in relations between the U.S.S.R. and Israel had been replaced by a cold and bitter winter.

Although thus impelled towards a growing affiliation with the West, Israel was nevertheless reluctant publicly to declare her deviation from her declared policy of "non-identification." Principally, this was because of her deep and utterly sincere sense of responsibility for the fate of the Jewish people beyond the Iron

---

[6] From his despatch to Israel's Chargé d'Affaires in Prague, 10.8.1954. The same motive was expressed in a critical letter Sharett addressed to the Director General of the Foreign Ministry on 4.8.1954. Both documents are in ISA 2414/3.
[7] The following is based on private information. On the subject, see Isser Harel, *Soviet Espionage: Communism in Israel* (Jerusalem, 1987) (Hebrew).

Curtain. The aspiration that Jews in the Communist lands of Eastern Europe might still be permitted to come to Israel on aliyah persisted throughout the early and mid-1950s. Never, in that period, was Israel formally and unequivocally ready therefore to declare herself part of the anti-Communist Western camp. Her absolute opposition to the construction on her territory of Western military bases was a concrete manifestation of the operative influence of that concern.

Several other considerations contributed towards the same result. Although undoubtedly less prominent that the concern for Soviet Jewry, they did sometimes prove weighty. One was the domestic need to maintain internal peace within the country's labor movement. Israel's leaders feared that foreign policy disputes with Mapam might split the Histadrut. To avoid that danger, they deliberately set out (at least in the late 1940s and early 1950s) to formulate a strategy in that sphere to which both sides could agree. In so doing, they had also to remove the entire notion of a strategic alliance with the West from the national agenda.

Military considerations in any case favored that policy. Influential circles within the Israeli defense establishment were altogether opposed to a strategic agreement with Washington. A binding connection of that sort, they feared, would endow the United States with control over the I.D.F. and thereby curtail Israel's freedom of action. Ben Gurion was himself an influential advocate of the thesis that nothing be done to hamper Israel's independence in that sphere; that was a cardinal principle of faith to which a proposed defense pact with the U.S.A. had to take second place. His was the reasoning which explains Jerusalem's hesitations to apply to the American government for free arms and for direct purchases of weapons during the early 1950s.

As has been seen, many of the debates which took place on this and other matters in Israel were ultimately made sterile by decisions taken in Washington. The United States government proved to be consistently and unmistakably reluctant to enter into any exclusive military relationship with Israel, or even to provide her with arms on a large scale and under favorable financial terms. Israel's futile efforts to change this state of affairs necessarily exerted a discouraging effect on her leaders; it also had been forced to come to terms with the negative regional aspects of the strategic concept harbored in both Washington and London. Anglo–American relations with the Arab world always made it somewhat unrealistic to talk of the inclusion of

Israel within an overall Middle Eastern command. Whenever that idea was tentatively broached, Ben Gurion and Sharett had felt compelled to note its drawbacks. Any such political constellation, they predicted, would undoubtedly emphasize Israel's regional inferiority; it would also lead to a local arms race; finally, it would run the grave security risk of unavoidable intelligence leaks. The fact that London was, until very late in our period, at least as responsible as Washington for Middle East defense merely strengthened the force of these arguments. Ben Gurion's almost pathological resistance to any association with the British goes far towards explaining some of his more crucial decisions during the early 1950s.

After 1956, many of these restraints on a declaratory pro-Western foreign policy gradually disappeared. Mapam became a very much weaker influence on Israeli political life; Britain ceased to play a major strategic role in the Middle East; finally, the United States became cognizant of Israel's inherent strategic value to her own interests. At the same time, local parties in the Middle East conflict became polarized. Israel became increasingly dependent on the West (economically and technically, as much as militarily); her Arab enemies received increasing amounts of aid from the Soviet Union – whose position became even more sharply defined when she broke off diplomatic relations with the Jewish state in 1967. The result was the establishment of a *de facto* strategic alliance between Israel and the U.S.A. The Americans supplied the Israelis with increasingly large amounts of sophisticated military hardware; they also became the principal means whereby Israel could exert pressure on the U.S.S.R. for the release of Soviet Jewry. This relationship was unaffected by the global *détente* which characterized relations between the Great Powers after the late 1960s. Although aliyah from the Soviet Union did then begin to materialize, Jerusalem's basic orientation in no way altered. One reason, undoubtedly, was the persistance of Russia's adherence to the Arab cause. Perhaps more insidious, however, was the profound influence of pro-Western views and opinions which had, during the period of this study, become entrenched in Israel itself.

Might events have taken a different course? Could Israel have successfully adopted a different global policy during the early and mid-1950s? Was there really ever an alternative to the strategy which she adopted? The records now open for inspection in the basement of the Prime Minister's office in Jerusalem suggest a negative answer to all three questions: Israel's tilt towards the West was indeed inevitable. Only there could she acquire the assets which she desperately required. A posture of clear or blurred neutrality would have carried no weight whatsoever in Washington during the height of the cold war. Neither could it evoke a significant response in Moscow. Prior to 1950, the Soviets were incapable of affording Israel economic renumeration for her policy of "non-identification"; it is hardly plausible that they might have sanctioned the mass aliyah of their Jewish citizens thereafter, even had Israel not supported the United States over Korea. Admittedly, the Kremlin did not actively side with the Arabs until the Middle Eastern conflict was well under way. In fact, almost half a decade separated Israel's Korean decision from the Czech–Egyptian arms deal. During the intervening period, Israeli policy-makers did undoubtedly commit some basic errors (the most criticized of which was the neglect to establish diplomatic links with Communist China). But the basic lines of their policy were dictated by forces over which they exercised no unilateral control. In deciding on their foreign policy orientation between 1948 and 1956, they really possessed very few alternatives.

# Appendix 1. U.N. VOTING RECORD 40th GENERAL ASSEMBLY (1985)

Percent coincidence with U.S. votes (Yes/No)

| | Africa | Asia and the Pacific | The Americas | Western Europe | Eastern Europe | N.A.T.O. | No affiliation* |
|---|---|---|---|---|---|---|---|
| **Highest** | Ivory Coast 27.3 | Japan 66.3 | Granada 71.7 | United Kingdom 86.6 | Poland 14.8 | United Kingdom 86.6 | Israel 91.5 |
| | Malawi 26.9 | Australia 60.2 | Canada 69.8 | Federal Republic of Germany 84.4 | Rumania 14.6 | Federal Republic of Germany 84.4 | |
| | Liberia 23.7 | New Zealand 55.3 | St. Christopher & Nevis 50.0 | France 82.7 | Hungary 12.3 | France 82.7 | |
| | Zaire 23.1 | Solomons 48.1 | Belize 37.8 | Belgium 82.3 | Ukraine 12.3 | Belgium 82.3 | |
| | Mauritius 22.1 | Samoa 27.4 | Paraguay 35.4 | Italy 81.9 | Bulgaria 12.2 | Italy 81.9 | |
| **Lowest** | Benin 8.8 | Syria 8.1 | Brazil 16.0 | Austria 40.0 | Czechoslovakia 12.2 | Norway 61.2 | |
| | Libya 6.9 | Vietnam 6.5 | Mexico 14.5 | Finland 39.8 | German Democratic Republic 12.2 | Denmark 58.3 | |
| | Mozambique 5.9 | Afghanistan 6.2 | Guyana 13.9 | Turkey 38.1 | U.S.S.R. 12.2 | Spain 55.6 | |
| | Algeria 5.1 | Laos 5.9 | Nicaragua 8.4 | Greece 33.3 | Yugoslavia 11.9 | Turkey 38.1 | |
| | Angola 3.5 | Yemen (P.D.R.) 5.7 | Cuba 6.2 | Malta 16.5 | Albania 6.7 | Greece 33.3 | |
| **Group Average** | 15.1 | 17.0 | 23.7 | 59.1 | 12.4 | 67.9 | |

* Israel is thus classified in the report cited below.

*Source:* U.S. Department of State, *Report to Congress on Voting Practices in the United Nations* (Washington, 6 June 1986).

# Appendix 2 . BIOGRAPHICAL NOTES

Aranne (Aharonovitch), Zalman was born in Russia in 1899 and at an early age became active in the Zionist movement. In 1924–5 he was a member of the Central Committee of the illegal Zionist Socialists in Russia. In 1926 he settled in Palestine where he occupied senior offices in Mapai and in the Histadrut. He was also a member of the Presidium of the Zionist Action Committee. From 1948 to 1951 he was Secretary-General of Mapai. A member of the Knesset from its inception, he was Minister Without Portfolio in 1954–5, subsequently becoming Minister of Education and Culture (1956–60), a post to which he was reappointed in 1963.

Argov (Grabovsky), Meir was born in Russia in 1905 and became active in Zionist organizations there, which resulted in his expulsion to Palestine in 1925. From 1931 he was a member of the Central Committee of Mapai and also worked in the Va'ad Le'umi – "The National Council" – during the British Mandate period. He was an active Mapai member in the Knesset and served as second chairman of its Committee on Foreign Affairs and Security.

Barkat (Burstein), Reuven was born in Lithuania in 1905 and settled in Palestine in 1926. He eventually headed the Political Department of the Histadrut. After 1948 he became a member of the Knesset and also served as Secretary-General of Mapai.

Ben-Aharon, Yitzhak was a prominent leader of Ahdut Ha'Avoda (and of Mapam), and held ministerial positions in the late 1950s and 1960s.

Berger, Herzl was born in Russia and began his political association with Hashomer Haza'ir there. He moved to Poland in 1932 after earning a Ph.D. in law at the University of Vienna. From 1934, when he came to Palestine, he was a member of the editorial committee of *Davar* and contributed to many other publications. He was elected to the first Knesset and later became chairman of the Committee on Foreign Affairs and Security.

Dayan, Shmuel was born in Russia in 1891. He came to Palestine in 1908 and was a founding member of Degania, the first kibbutz in Palestine, and later of the Nahalal settlement. He was active in Hapo'el Haza'ir and subsequently in Mapai, becoming a member of the first, second and third Knesset. His son Moshe Dayan was a prominent Israeli soldier and statesman.

Galili, Eliezer came to Palestine from Russia in 1925 and was active in the kibbutz movement. After 1948 he was a major contributor to various publications of the Israeli Defense Forces.

Halperin, Yehiel was born in Poland in 1896. He earned his Ph.D. in political science in Vienna. In the inter-war period he was active in the Zionist movement in Poland. From his arrival in Palestine on the eve of the Second World War, he was a member of the editorial committee of *Davar*, the Histadrut's daily newspaper.

Haring, Zeev was born in Poland in 1910 and was active in the Zionist movement in that country until the outbreak of the Second World War. During the war he took an active part in the organization of Jewish volunteers to assist the British war effort. After 1948 he became the secretary of the Organizational Department of the Histadrut.

Lavon (Lubianker), Pinhas was born in 1904 in Poland and emigrated to Palestine in 1921, joining Kibbutz Hulda. He was active in the Histadrut and became its Secretary-General in 1949. Five years later he became Minister of Defense, but was removed from power shortly thereafter in the wake of the infamous "Lavon Affair" in which he fought bitterly against Ben Gurion. He was finally ejected from his post as Secretary-General of the Histadrut in 1961.

Livneh (Libenstein), Eliezer was born in 1902. He emigrated to Palestine in 1920 and became active in the labor movement, especially in organizing European emigration to Palestine. During and shortly after the Second World War he dealt with various educational and literary activities of the Haganah. He was a member of Mapai in the first and second Knesset but resigned from the party in 1957 because of policy disagreements.

Locker, Berl was born in Austria in 1889. Active in Zionist youth and student societies, Locker joined the Jewish Socialist Labor Confederation – Po'alei Zion – in 1905 and became one of the early theorists and organizers of that group. Before settling in Palestine in 1936, he was in charge of the Organizational Department of the World Zionist Organization in London. Before the Second World War he was appointed political advisor to the Zionist Executive in London. After 1948 he served as the chairman of the Jerusalem Zionist Executive for eight years and later became a member of Knesset.

Noy (Neistaat), Melech was born in 1895 in Austria. He came to Palestine in 1926 and eventually became a high-ranking official of the Histadrut and an active Mapai delegate to the Zionist Executive.

Offir, Arieh came to Palestine in 1926 and settled in Kibbutz Afikim. He took an active role in the central bodies of Mapai, representing the kibbutzim, and devoted much of his time to contacts with Jewish youth outside Palestine.

Shiloah, Zvi came to Palestine in 1931 and became secretary to the Herzeliya Labor Council. After serving in the Jewish Brigade during the Second World War he became secretary and acting editor of *Hador* from 1949 to 1954.

Soroka, Moshe was born in Poland in 1903. He came to Palestine in 1920 and later became director of "Kupat Holim" (the health organization of the Histadrut).

Yavnieli, Shmuel was born in Russia in 1884. He emigrated to Palestine in
1905 and became active in the aliyah movement, particularly in organizing
the emigration of Jews from Yemen. He later became the secretary of the
Cultural Department of the Histadrut.

## Appendix 3 . ISRAEL'S VOTES AT THE U.N. BETWEEN EAST AND WEST 1948–1956

| Year | Contrary to U.S. and U.S.S.R.* | With U.S. and U.S.S.R. | With U.S. | With U.S.S.R. | With the U.S.S.R. and in conflict with U.S.† | With the U.S. and in conflict with U.S.S.R.† | Total |
|------|------|------|------|------|------|------|------|
| 1948–9 | 2 | 5 | 14 | 3 | 0 | 11 | 24 |
| 1950–1 | 11 | 4 | 15 | 6 | 6 | 11 | 36 |
| 1952–3 | 9 | 6 | 14 | 10 | 1 | 7 | 39 |
| 1954–6 | 11 | 16 | 25 | 13 | 2 | 21 | 55 |

\* Including all the votes in which Israel's stand differed from the two superpowers'.
† Including only the votes in which the superpowers' stand was diametrically opposed to each other.

*Source:* D. Djonovich, *UN Resolutions, Series I – General Assembly* (New York, 1973), Vols. 2–5.

# INDEX

# LSE MONOGRAPHS IN INTERNATIONAL STUDIES

Titles out of print

**KIN WAH CHIN**
The defence of Malaysia and Singapore
*The transformation of a security system 1957–1971*

**RICHARD TAYLOR**
The politics of the Soviet cinema 1917–1929

**ANN TROTTER**
Britain and East Asia 1933–1937

**J. H. KALICKI**
The pattern of Sino-American crisis
*Political military interactions in the 1950s*

**ARYEH L. UNGER**
The totalitarian party
*Party and people in Nazi Germany*

**ALABA OGUNSANWO**
China's policy in Africa 1958–1971

**MARTIN L. VAN CREVELD**
Hitler's strategy 1940–1941
*The Balkan clue*

**EUGEN STEINER**
The Slovak dilemma

**LUCJAN BLIT**
The origisn of Polish socialism
*The history and ideas of the first Polish socialist party 1878–1886*